THE MOTORCYCLE YEARBOOK
2007

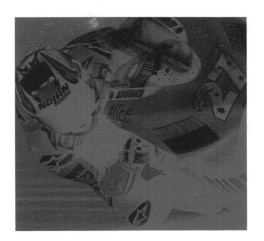

CHRONOSPORTS
EDITEUR

ISBN 978-84707-141-2
Also available in french **ISBN 978-2-84707-134-4**

© **NOVEMBER 2007, CHRONOSPORTS S.A** - Vergnolet Parc, CH-1070 Puidoux, Switzerland.
Phn: +41 (0) 21 694 24 44 - Fax: +41 (0) 21 694 24 46 - Email: info@chronosports.com - www.chronosports.com

COORDINATION & PAGE LAYOUT - Loraine Lequint   **CONCEPTION** - Patricia Soler

PRINTED BY IMPRIMERIE CLERC - 18206 St-Amand Montrond, France.

BOUND BY RELIURES BRUN - 45331 Malesherbes Cedex, France.

THE MOTORCYCLE YEARBOOK
2007

PHOTOS Stan Perec Lukasz Swiderek
THANKS TO Nello Zoppe (Nikon France) for his valued and to Jaime Olivares,
who have provided some of the photos in this book.
TEXTS Jean-Claude Schertenleib

CONTENTS

CALENDAR 2008

9th March	Qatar	Losail-Doha	**20th July**	United States (*)	Laguna Seca
30th March	Spain	Jerez de la Frontera	**17th August**	République tchèque	Brno
13th April	Portugal	Estoril	**31st August**	San Marino & Riviera di Rimini	Misano
4th May	China	Shanghai	**14th September**	Indianapolis	Indianapolis
18th May	France	Le Mans	**28th September**	Japan	Motegi
1st June	Italia	Mugello	**5th October**	Australia	Phillip Island
8th June	Catalunya	Catalunya	**19th October**	Malaysia	Sepang
22nd June	Great Britain	Donington Park	**26th October**	Valencia	Cheste-Valencia
28th June	Netherlands	Assen			
13th July	Germany	Sachsenring	(*): MotoGP only.		

CONTINENTAL CIRCUS

".....And they left their island with dogs, wives and children with a caravan hitched to an old van. Over there, in the south, down near Antibes and Senigallia, spring had already arrived and brought a smile to young men's faces and reddened the cheeks of the girls. Spring was the time of the first races, the first steps that would take them east, west, north and south looking for glory and a bit of money. In October, with the arrival of the first frosts, not everyone returned to the island. The others? They had stopped off on route. There was a sprig of dried flowers left at the foot of a tree in the forest of Masaryk, near Brno; a copper plate on a rock on the road from Hohenstein to Ernsthal in the German Democratic Republic. It was the Continental Circus."

Continental Circus? The formula has changed somewhat as the current motorcycle world championship has become a giant business. These days dollars are more important than acts of chivalry and lawyers and businessmen have replaced the good mates or the half-brother who would give their all to help "their" champion. "Continental Circus" is also the title of a legendary film, the work of Frenchman Jerome Laperrousaz, who followed the entire 1967 season and its fascinating tussle featuring a golden boy and a simple man in the shape of the unevenly matched duel between Giacomo Agostini on his magnificent MV Agusta on the one hand and privateer Jack Findlay and his outdated Matchless on the other.

That was exactly forty years ago and it made a star out of the Australian who had made the decision to leave home and head for Europe, the home of motorised sport. He was an Australian who would become more French than the French, a man with a big heart and an unforgettable accent. This legendary figure in the sport bid his final farewell a few hours before the start of the 2007 French Grand Prix on 20 May.

On that day, two of Findlay's compatriots had stood on the podium at Le Mans. One was Casey Stoner, who finished third in the rain. Casey Stoner became 2007 world champion because, one day, his father Colin and mother Bronwyn bought one way tickets for Europe, the birthplace of motor sport, so that their little lad should become a big lad, so that he could become champion.

No doubt Jack Findlay would have really liked to have still been with us on the day his very worthy successor took the world title, competing in today's version of the "Continental Circus."

JEAN-CLAUDE SCHERTENLEIB

TEAMS | MOTO GP

THE NEW TECHNICAL REGULATION, REDUCING ENGINE CAPACITY FROM 1000 TO 800 CC, MADE ITSELF FELT, AS A NEW COMPETITOR HAS ARRIVED IN THE SHAPE OF ILMOR, EXCEPT THAT IT WILL PACK UP AFTER ONLY ONE GP. DUCATI HAS DOUBLED ITS NUMBERS AND THE FOUR JAPANESE CONSTRUCTORS ALL HAVE AN OFFICIAL PRESENCE WHILE, FOR ANOTHER YEAR, KENNY ROBERTS HAS A SUPPLY OF HONDA ENGINES FOR HIS KR.

Yamaha had gone through enough difficulties the previous year, so that despite the regulation changes, they did not attempt a major revolution. Therefore, the M1 800 maintained the elegant lines of the 990 and pretty much the same architecture. The engine was kept in its "big bang" configuration and the pneumatic valves were ditched. Of course, electronics were a major feature and special emphasis had been placed on the cycle parts, which would be evident right from the first GP in Qatar, when Rossi seemed so comfortable under braking. If there was nothing revolutionary in the entrails of the beast, the big novelty was clear for all to see as, five days before the opening round, the factory team finally unveiled what had been whispered about for months, the fact that its new title sponsor was the giant of the Italian car industry, Fiat. Valentino Rossi, who back in January had already extended his contract to the end of 2008 and Colin Edwards were still the works riders. The marque's second team, running in Dunlop colours was run by Herve Poncharal, who picked up Makoto Tamada and gave a chance to Sylvain Guintoli.

FIAT YAMAHA TEAM

Via Tinelli 67/69, 20050 Gerno di Lesmo (Italy).
www.yamahamotogp.com

ORGANISATION CHART
Team manager: Davide Brivio.
Technical Director: Masahiko Nakajima.
Crew chiefs: Daniele Romagnoli (Colin Edwards) and Jeremy Burgess (Valentino Rossi).

5 COLIN EDWARDS   **46** VALENTINO ROSSI

RIDERS
Colin Edwards
Date of birth: 27th February 1974.
Place of birth: Conroe/Texas (United-States).
First race: 1990.
First GP: Japan, 2003 (MotoGP).
Number of GP victories: -
- United-States 250cc Champion (1992).
- Superbike World Champion (2000).
- Superbike World Champion (2002).

Valentino Rossi
Date of birth: 16th February 1979.
Place of birth: Urbino/Pesaro (Italy).
First race: 1992.
First GP: (125cc) Malaysia, 1996.
Number of GP victories: 43 (12/125cc; 14/250cc; 13/500cc; 45/MotoGP).
First GP victory: (125cc) Czech Republic, 1996.
- Italian Minibike Endurance Champion (1992).
- Italian 125cc Sport-Production Champion (1994).
- 125cc World Champion (1995).
- 125cc World Champion (1997).
- 250cc World Champion (1999).
- 500cc World Champion (2001).
- MotoGP World Champion (2002).
- MotoGP World Champion (2003).
- MotoGP World Champion (2004).
- MotoGP World Champion (2005).

DUNLOP YAMAHA TECH 3

635, chemin du Niel, 83230 Bormes-les-Mimosas (France).
www.yamaha-racing.com

ORGANISATION CHART
Team manager: Hervé Poncharal.
Coordinator: Gérard Vallée.
Chiefs mechanics: Peter Wikberg (Makoto Tamada) and Gary Reynders (Sylvain Guintoli).

6 MAKOTO TAMADA   **50** SYLVAIN GUINTOLI

RIDERS
Makoto Tamada
Date of birth: 4th November 1976.
Place of birth: Ehime (Japan).
First race: 1993.
First GP: Japan, 1998 (250cc).
Number of GP victories: 2 (MotoGP).
First GP victory: Rio, 2004 (MotoGP).
- Japanese Champion 250cc (1994).

Sylvain Guintoli
Date of birth: 24th June 1982.
Place of birth: Montélimar (France).
First race: 1995.
First GP: France, 2000 (250cc).
Number of GP victories: -
- French Scooter Champion (1995).
- French 250cc Champion (2000).

FIAT YAMAHA TEAM

DUNLOP YAMAHA TECH 3

Ducati won the final race of the 990 cc era and the Italian marque would go on to win the first of the 800 cc MotoGP. Therefore, it's fair to say the Borgo Panigale crew had taken up the challenge in remarkable fashion by offering up a smaller and more compact engine. During the winter months there was still a doubt as to whether or not it might be too thirsty. But the engine concept was developed further, as the chassis became shorter and the saddle support was anchored directly to the engine block. As in 2006, the Luis D'Antin team also used Ducatis and, good news, this "B" team had picked up the experienced Alexandre Barros and it had switched to Bridgestone, so as to speed up the tyre-bike development. In the Marlboro camp, alongside Loris Capirossi, who would become a father to little Ricardo during the summer, they played the youth card, with Australia's Casey Stoner, a rough diamond who would not take long to pick up some polish.

DUCATI MARLBORO TEAM

Via Cavalieri Ducati 3, 40132 Bologne (Italy).
www.ducati.com

ORGANISATION CHART
Managing Director Ducati Corse: Claudio Domenicali.
Moto GP Projet Director: Livio Suppo.
Technical manager: Filippo Preziosi.
Crew Chiefs: Cristian Gabarrini (Casey Stoner)
and Cristhian Pupulin (Loris Capirossi).

27
CASEY STONER

65
LORIS CAPIROSSI

RIDERS
Casey Stoner
Date of birth: 16th October 1985.
Place of birth: Kurri-Kurri/Gold Coast (Australia).
First race: 1989.
First GP: Great Britain, 2001 (125).
Number of GP victories: 16 (2/125; 4/250; 10/MotoGP).
First GP victory: Valencia, 2003 (125).
- Australian Champion Aprilia Challenge 125 RS (2000).
- MotoGP World Champion (2007).

Loris Capirossi
Date of birth: 4th April 1973
Place of birth: Bologna (Italy).
First race: 1987.
First GP: (125cc) Japan, 1990.
Number of GP victories: 29 (8/125; 12/250; 2/500; 7/MotoGP).
First GP victory: (125cc) Great Britain, 1990.
- 125cc World Champion (1990).
- 125cc World Champion (1991).
- 250cc World Champion (1998).

PRAMAC D'ANTIN

Poligono Industrial Gitesa, c/Ramon y Cajal 25, 28814 Algete, Madrid (Spain).
www.pramacdantin.com

ORGANISATION CHART
Owner: Luis D'Antin.
Coordinator: Alberto Carrero.
Mechanical Chiefs: Marco Baleiron (Alexandre Barros) and
Martin Zabala (Alexander Hofmann).

4
ALEXANDRE BARROS

66
ALEXANDER HOFMANN

RIDERS
Alexandre Barros
Date of birth: 18th October 1970 in São Paulo (Brasil).
First race: 1978.
First GP: Spain, 1986 (80).
Number of GP victories: 7 (4/500; 3/MotoGP).
First GP victory: FIM (Jarama), 1993 (500).
- Cyclo Brasilian Champion (1978, 1979 and 1980).
- 50cc Brasilian Champion (1981).
- 250cc Brasilian Champion (1985).

Alexander Hofmann
Date of birth: 25th May 1980.
Place of birth: Mindelheim (Germany).
First race: 1984.
First GP: (125cc) Germany, 1997.
Number of GP victories: -
- 80 Motocross German Champion (1992and 93) and 125cc Junior (1994).
- 250cc European Champion (1998).
- 250cc German Champion (1998).

DUCATI MARLBORO TEAM

PRAMAC D'ANTIN

" I don't know if Honda designed the RC212V for Daniel Pedrosa, but looking at it closely, it's certainly designed for a little bloke." Right from the start of winter testing, Valentino Rossi believed that Pedrosa would be his main rival this season. The new HRC 800 seemed tailor-made for the strange measurements of the little Spaniard, which did not go down too well with reigning champion Nicky Hayden. Apart from the two works riders in the Repsol team, Honda still had the services of the Melandri-Elias pairing in the Fausto Gresini team which switched to Bridgestone. Carlos Checa, riding for Lucio Cecchinello and Shinya Nakano with Minolta-Konica were the two transfers from the marque.

REPSOL HONDA TEAM

European Office, Industriezone Noord V, Wijngaardveld 1c, 9300 Aalst (Belgium).
www.hondaproimages.com

ORGANISATION CHART
Team manager: Makoto Tanaka.
Coordinator: Roger Van der Borght.
Chiefs mechanics: Pete Benson (Nicky Hayden) and Mike Leitner (Daniel Pedrosa).

RIDERS
Nicky Hayden
Date of birth: 30th July 1981.
Place of birth: Owensboro/Kentucky (United-States).
First race: 1986.
First GP: (MotoGP) Japan, 2003.
Number of GP victories: 3 (MotoGP).
First GP victory: (MotoGP) United-States, 2005.
- United-States Supersport Champion 600cc (1999).
- United-States Superbike Champion (2002).
- Moto GP World Champion (2006).

Daniel Pedrosa
Date of birth: 29th September 1985.
Place of birth: Castellar del Vallés (Spain).
First race: 1993.
First GP: 125cc Japan, 2001.
Number of GP victories: 27 (8/125cc; 15/250cc; 4/MotoGP).
First GP victory: 125cc Netherlands, 2002.
- Minibike Spanish Champion (1998).
- 125cc World Champion (2003).
- 250cc World Champion (2004).
- 250cc World Champion (2005).

1 NICKY HAYDEN

26 DANIEL PEDROSA

HONDA GRESINI

Gresini Racing S.R.L., via Mengolina 18, 48018 Faenza (Italy).
www.gresiniracing.com

ORGANISATION CHART
Team manager: Fausto Gresini.
Chiefs mechanics: Fabrizio Cecchini (Toni Elias) and
Antonio Jimenez (Marco Melandri).

RIDERS
Antonio «Toni» Elias
Date of birth: 26th March 1983 in Manresa (Spain).
First race:1997.
First GP: (125cc) Spain, 1999.
Number of GP victories: 10 (2/125cc; 7/250cc; 1/MotoGP).
First GP victory: (125cc) Netherlands, 2001.

Marco Melandri
Date of birth: 7th August 1982 in Ravenna (Italy).
First race: 1989.
First GP: (125cc) Czech Republic, 1997.
Number of GP victories: 22 (7/125; 10/250; 5/MotoGP).
First GP victory: (125cc) Netherlands, 1998.
- BMW Italian Champion (1988).
- Minibike Junior A Italian Champion (1992).
- Minibike Junior B Italian Champion (1994).
- 125cc Italian Champion (1997).
- Honda Trophy Italian Champion (1997).
- 250cc World Champion (2002).

24 TONI ELIAS

33 MARCO MELANDRI

REPSOL HONDA TEAM

HONDA GRESINI

KONICA MINOLTA HONDA

JIR, place des Moulins, Le Continental B, 98000 Monaco.
www.konicaminolta.com

ORGANISATION CHART
Team manager: Luca Montiron.
Technical Director: Giulio Bernardelle.

56
SHINYA NAKANO

RIDER
Shinya Nakano
Date of birth: 10th October 1977.
Place of birth: Chiba Prefecture (Japan).
First race: 1982.
First GP: Japan, 1998 (250).
Number of GP victories: 6 (250).
First GP victory: Japon, 1999 (250).
- 250cc Japanese Champion (1998).

HONDA LCR

LCR-X Racing, S.A. M., Gildo Pastor Center, 7 rue du Gabian, 98000 Monaco.
www.lcr.mc

ORGANISATION CHART
Team manager: Lucio Cecchinello
Technical chief: Ramon Forcada.

7
CARLOS CHECA

RIDER
Carlos Checa
Date of birth: 15th October 1972.
Place of birth: Sant Fruitos de Bages/Barcelona (Spain).
First race: 1989.
First GP: Europe, 1993 (125).
Number of GP victories: 2 (500).
First GP victory: Catalunya, 1996 (500).
- 80cc Spanish Champion (1991).
- 250cc European Champion (1995).

KONICA MINOLTA HONDA

HONDA LCR

KAWASAKI RACING TEAM

It was definitely the major tour de force of the winter break as Kawasaki had not only emulated its competitors in developing an all-new bike, it had also and especially reorganised its race department after the divorce with Germany's Harald Eckl, whose company had run the MotoGP programme since it started. The key word in the green camp was "family" as the development programme was still run out of Japan with the technical base set up in the Netherlands, under the watchful eye of new hard man, Ichiro Yoda. In the past he had been head of the project that built the 2000 world championship winning Yamaha 250 and, loyal to his friends, he called up as a team-mate to Randy De Puniet, none other than Olivier Jacque, who had been pretty much retired for the past two years. After two serious injuries, (China and then practice in Catalunya,) on the eve of the British GP, "OJ" announced he was retiring. He returned to be a development rider and his seat was taken by the Australian Anthony West.

Sourethweg 10, 6422 PC Heerlen (Netherlands).
www.kawasaki-motogp.com

ORGANISATION CHART
General Director: Yoshio Kanamura.
Racing Director: Ichiro Yoda.
Team manager: Michael Bartholemy
Chiefs mechanics: Christophe Bourguignon (Randy De Puniet)
and Fiorenzo Fanali (Olivier Jacque then Anthony West).

13 ANTHONY WEST | **14** RANDY DE PUNIET | **19** OLIVIER JACQUE

RIDERS
Anthony West
Birth: 17th July 1981, Mayborough (Australia).
First race: 1997.
First GP: Australia, 1998 /125).
Number of GP victories: 1 (250).
First GP victory: Netherlands, 2003 (250).
- 125cc Australian Champion (1998).
- 250 Production Australian Champion (1998).

Randy De Puniet
Date of birth: 14th February 1982 in Andrésy (France).
First race: 1987.
First GP: (125cc) France, 1998 .
Number of GP victories: 5 (250cc).
First GP victory: (250cc) Catalunya, 2003 .
- French Typhoon Cup Winner (1995).
- French 125cc Promosport Champion (1997).
- French 125cc Champion (1998).

Olivier Jacque
Birth: 29th August 1973, Villerupt (F).
First race: 1990.
First GP: Australia, 1995 (250).
Number of GP victories: 7 (250).
First GP victory: Brasil, 1996 (250).
- 250cc World Champion (2000).

RIZLA SUZUKI MOTOGP

A year earlier, Suzuki caused a sensation with the presentation of a very new GSVR. In fact there was already a lot of the "800" in the design, notably the pneumatic distribution. Therefore, logically enough, the GSV-R800 (XRGO) had a lot in common with the its big sister and right from its first tests in November, the two team riders, John Hopkins and Chris Vermeulen were very much at the front end. In fact, the boss Paul Denning said: "It's definitely the best GP bike the company has ever built." Suzuki remained faithful to Bridgestone, thus further reinforcing the philosophy behind the project, namely, "evolution not revolution."

Crescent Suzuki Performance Centre, 23 Black Moor Road, Ebblake Ind. Est.,
BH31 6AX Verwood (Great Britain).
www.suzuki-motogp.com

ORGANISATION CHART
Team manager: Paul Denning.
Technical Director: Shinichi Sahara,
Track engineers: Stuart Shenton (John Hopkins) and Tom O'Kane (Chris Vermeulen).

21 JOHN HOPKINS | **71** CHRIS VERMEULEN

RIDERS
John Hopkins
Date of birth: 22nd May1983.
Place of birth: Ramona/California (United States).
First race: 1987.
First GP: (MotoGP) Japan, 2002 .
- United States Challenge Aprilia RS 250 Champion (1999).
- United States Supersport 750 Champion (2000).
- United States Formula Xtreme Champion (2001).

Geoffrey «Chris» Vermeulen
Date of birth: 19th June 1982.
Place of birth: Brisbane (Australia).
First race: 1994.
First GP: (MotoGP) Australia, 2005.
- Supersport World Champion (2003).
Number GP of victories: 1.
First GP victory: France, 2007 (Montréal).

KAWASAKI RACING TEAM

RIZLA SUZUKI MOTOGP

TEAM ROBERTS

More often than he should have done, Kenny Roberts had to dip into his own piggy bank to fund his adventure and the change of rules changed nothing in that respect. As was the case the previous year, he had a Honda 212V engine and a home-built chassis, although this year there had been a great deal of cooperation with Honda on this element of the package. Kenny Junior really struggled to get used to this bike. "It's too slow and the rider's too old," was the good natured quip from Dad just before the British GP and it was the youngest member of the clan, Kurtis, who ended up finishing off the season.

Unit 3 MXL Centre, Lombard Way, Banbury, Oxon OX16 4TJ (Great Britain).
www.teamkr.com

ORGANISATION CHART
Team manager: Kenny Roberts Senior.
General Manager: Chuck Aksland.
Technical director: Warren Willing.
Track engineer: Tom Jojhic (Kenny Roberts Junior then Kurtis Roberts).

10 KENNY ROBERTS JUNIOR
80 KURTIS ROBERTS

RIDERS
Kenny Roberts «Junior»
Date of birth: 25th July 1973.
Place of birth: Mountain View/California (United States).
First race: 1988.
First GP: (250cc) United States, 1993.
Number of GP victories: 8 (500).
First GP victory: (500cc) Malaysia, 1999 .
- World Champion 500cc (2000).

Kurtis Roberts
Date of birth: 17th November 1978.
Place of birth: Hickman/California (United States).
First race: 1991.
First GP: Malaysia, 1997 (250).
Number of GP victories: -.
- United States Formula Xtreme Champion (1999).
- United States Supersort 600 Champion (2000).
- United States Formula Xtreme Champion (2000).

ILMOR GP

On paper, admittedly a blank sheet of paper, it was the big news story as the series went from 990 to 800 cc. The team had all the right connections with innumerable wins in Formula Indy and Formula 1 under the Mercedes banner. The Swiss engineer, Mario Illien certainly knows how to build powerful engines and his compatriot, Eskil Suter understands all there is to know about building a chassis. However, taking the next step, building and running a bike, was a whole world always and Ilien and his crew had underestimated what was involved. First and foremost, the project, that first came to light in the autumn of 2006 at the Portuguese GP, had failed to attract backers. Maybe the price was too greedy? Maybe the MotoGP arena was not ideal as a communications tool? During the winter, Mario Ilien would ask himself more and more questions and after a first catastrophic GP (Qatar) the project was officially "suspended." No one was fooled and the only prize won by the X3 was an award for the "most impressive machine" at the traditional Goodwood Festival in England.

Quarry Road, Brixworth, Northampton, NN6 9UB (Great Britain).

ORGANISATION CHART
Project Manager: Mario Illien.
Director: Steve Miller.
Team manager: Mike Janes.
Chiefs mechanics: Duncan Dunbar (Andrew Pitt) and
Mark Woodage (Jeremy McWilliams).

88 ANDREW PITT
99 JEREMY MCWILLIAMS

RIDERS
Andrew Pitt
Date of birth: 19th February 1976.
Place of birth: Kempsey (Australia).
First race: 1994.
First GP: Malaysia, 2002 (MotoGP).
Number of GP victories: -
- Australia Supersport Champion (1999).
- Supersport World Champion (2001).

Jeremy McWilliams
Date of birth: 4th April 1964.
Place of birth: Carmoney (Northern Ireland).
First race: 1988.
First GP: Australia, 1993 (500).
Number of GP victories: 1 (250).
First GP victory: Netherlands, 2001 (250).
- 350 Production Irish Champion (1988).
- 350 Irish Champion (1989).
- 250 Irish Champion (1991).

TEAM ROBERTS

ILMOR GP

TEAMS | 250cc

THAT'S QUALITY! THE FIRST THREE MEN IN THE CLASS, LORENZO, DOVIZIOSO AND DE ANGELIS, HAVE NOT YET MADE THE LEAP UP TO MOTOGP AND YET THE CATEGORY WELCOMES THREE ROOKIES OF THE HIGHEST QUALITY, THE LAST TWO 125 WORLD CHAMPIONS, THOMAS LUTHI AND ALVARO BAUTISTA, AT APRILIA AND THE MAN WHO WAS RUNNER-UP TO THEM THESE PAST FEW YEARS, MIKA KALLIO WITH KTM.

Totally dominant in 2006, the Italian marque strengthened its ranks still further. Its world champion, Jorge Lorenzo decided to stay one more year in the class before trying his luck in MotoGP. Alex de Angelis, who finally tasted victory in the last race of 2006 in Valencia, did the same and at the same time became a test rider for the factory. Hector Barbera, whom Lorenzo no longer wanted as a team mate, found salvation in Hungary with the Toth team. Finally, two newcomers from the lower class were entrusted with the works RSWs and we are not talking about just anyone as the riders concerned were the last two 125 world champions, Switzerland's Thomas Luthi and the Spaniard, Alvaro Bautista.

FORTUNA APRILIA

Bronce 28, Poligon. Industrial Les Guixeres, 08915 Barcelona (Spain).
www.fortunaracing.com

ORGANISATION CHART
Team manager: Dani Amatriain.
Coordinator: Jordi Perres.
Technical Director: Gigi Dall'Igna.
Chief mechanic: Giovanni Sandi (Jorge Lorenzo).

RIDER
Jorge Lorenzo
Date of birth: 4th May 1987.
Place of birth: Palma de Mallorca (Spain).
First race: 1990.
First GP: (125cc) Spain, 2002.
Number of GP victories: 21 (4/125; 17/250).
First GP victory: Rio, 2003 (125).
- 250cc World Champion (2006).
- 250cc World Champion (2007).

1
JORGE LORENZO

MASTER-MAPFRE ASPAR

Plaza Sociedad Musical no 8, 46600 Alzira (Valencia), Spain.
www.teamaspar.com

ORGANISATION CHART
Team manager: Jorge «Aspar» Martinez.
Sporting Director: Gino Borsoi.
Chiefs mechanics: Pietro Caprara (Alex de Angelis) and Andrea Orlandi (Alvaro Bautistá).

RIDERS
Alex De Angelis
Date of birth: 26th February 1984.
Place of birth: Rimini (Italy).
First race: 1995.
First GP: (125cc) Imola, 1999.
Number of GP victories: 1 (250)
First GP victory: (250cc) Valencia, 2006

Alvaro Bautistá
Date of birth: 21st November 1984 in Travera de la Reina (Spain).
First race: 1993.
First GP: Spain, 2002 (125).
Number of GP victories: 10 (8/125; 2/250).
First GP victory: Spain, 2006 (125)
- Minimotos Champion of Madrid (1995).
- Minimotos Champion of Madrid (1996).
- Minimotos Champion of Madrid (1997).
- 125cc Spanish Champion (2003).
- 125cc World Champion (2006).

3
ALEX DE ANGELIS

19
ALVARO BAUTISTÁ

FORTUNA APRILIA

MASTER-MAPFRE ASPAR

TEAM TOTH

Foti ùt 055 Hrsz, 2120 Dunakeszi (Hungary).
www.tothimi.com

ORGANISATION CHART
Team manager: Judit Polinák.
Technical director: Rossano Brazzi.
Chiefs mechanics: Giuseppe Galante (Imre Toth) and
Rossano Brazzi (Hector Barberá).

10
IMRE TOTH

80
HECTOR BARBERÁ

RIDERS
Imre Toth
Date of birth: 6th September 1985.
Place of birth: Budapest (Hungary).
First race: 2000.
First GP: Japan, 2002 (125).
Numbers of GP victories: -

Hector Barberá
Date of birth: 2nd November 1986.
Place of birth: Dos Aguas/Valencia (Spain).
First race: 1995.
First GP: Japan, 2002 (125).
Numbers of GP victories: 7 (6/125; 1/250).
First GP victory: Great Britain, 2003 (125).
- Aprilia 125cc Cup Spanish Champion (2001).
- 125cc Spanish Champion (2002).

EMMI CAFFÈ LATTE APRILIA RACING TEAM

Paddock s.r.o., Jeremiasova 18/1283, 155 00 Praha 5, Czech Republic.
www.emmi-caffe-latte-racingteam.com

ORGANISATION CHART
Owner: Daniel M. Epp.
Team manager: Peter Kern.
Technical Director: Mauro Noccioli.
Telemetry: Gianpaolo Sossai.
Chief mechanic: Markus Egloff.

12
THOMAS LÜTHI

RIDER
Thomas Lüthi
Date of birth: 6th September 1986.
Place of birth: Linden (Suisse).
First race: 1997.
First GP: Germany, 2002 (125).
Numbers of GP victories: 5 (125).
First GP victory: France, 2005 (125).
- Pocket-Bike Junior A Swiss Champion (1999).
- Pocket-Bike Junior B Swiss Champion (2000).
- 125cc World Champion (2005).

TEAM TOTH

EMMI CAFFÈ LATTE RACING TEAM

TEAM SICILIA

Moto Racing Team Matteoni, Via Bandi 5, 47814 Bellaria (Italy).
www.matteoniracing.net

ORGANISATION CHART
Team manager: Massimo Matteoni.

RIDERS
Anthony West
Date of birth: 17th July 1981.
Place of birth: Mayborough (Australia).
First race: 1997.
First GP: Australia, 1998 (125).
Number of GP victories: 1 (250).
First GP victory: Netherlands, 2003 (250).
- 125cc Australian Champion (1998).
- 250cc Production Australian Champion (1998).

Dan Linfoot
Date of birth: 8th July 1988.
Place of birth: Horragate (Great Britain).
First race: 2002.
First GP: Great Britain, 2005 (125).
Number of GP victories: -

14 ANTHONY WEST   **45** DAN LINFOOT

ANGAIA RACING

Andy Racing s.r.l., Corso Milano 41, Novara (Italy).
www.teamangaiaracing.com

ORGANISATION CHART
Owners: Antonietta D'Angella and Paolo Tajana.
Technical Director: Olivier Liégeois.

RIDER
Jules Cluzel
Date of birth: 12th October 1988.
Place of birth: Montluçon (France).
First race: 2001.
First GP: France, 2005 (125).
Number of GP victories: -

16 JULES CLUZEL

CARDION AB MOTORACING

Joukalova 13, Brno GB5 00 (Cezch Republic).
www.abmotoracing.com

ORGANISATION CHART
Owners: Karel Abraham Senior.
Team manager: Zuzana Ulmanova.
Chief mechanic: Didier Langouët.

RIDER
Karel Abraham
Date of birth: 2nd January 1990.
Place of birth: Brno (Czech Republic).
First race: 2001.
First GP: Spain, 2005 (125).
Number of GP victories: -

17 KAREL ABRAHAM

TEAM SICILIA

ANGAIA RACING

CARDION AB MOTORACING

KIEFER-BOS-SOTIN RACING

Kiefer-Bos Racing Team, Zur Rothheck 12, 55743 Idar-Oberstein.
www.kiefer-mot.de

ORGANISATION CHART
Team managers: Stefan and Jochen Kiefer.
Technical Director: Jürgen Lingg.
Chiefs mechanics: Jürgen Lingg (Alex Baldolini) and
Jochen Kiefer (Dirk Heidolf).

25 ALEX BALDOLINI
28 DIRK HEIDOLF

RIDERS
Alex Baldolini
Date of birth: 24th January 1985.
Place of birth: Cesena (Italy).
First race: 1994.
First GP: Italy, 2000 (125).
Number of GP victories: -

Dirk Heidolf
Date of birth: 14th September 1976.
Place of birth: Hohenstein-Ernstthal (Germany).
First race: 1994.
First GP: Germany, 1997 (125).
Number of GP victories: -
- ADAC Minibike Cup winner.

CAMPETELLA RACING

Via De Gasperi 74, 62010 Montecassiano (Italy).
www.campetella.it

ORGANISATION CHART
Team manager: Eros Braconi.
Technical Director: Eros Braconi.
Chiefs mechanics: Fabio Braconi (Fabrizio Lai) and
Gianluca Montanari (Taro Sekiguchi).

32 FABRIZIO LAI
44 TARO SEKIGUCHI

RIDERS
Fabrizio Lai
Date of birth: 14th December 1978.
Place of birth: Rho (Italy).
First race: 1994.
First GP: Valencia, 2001 (125).
Number of GP victories: -
- Minibike European Champion (1996).
- Minibike European Champion (1997).
- Honda Trophy Italian Champion (1999).
- 125cc Italian Champion (2002).

Taro Sekiguchi
Date of birth: 5th December 1975.
Place of birth: Tokyo (Japan).
First race: 1989.
First GP: Japan, 1999 (250).
Number of GP victories: -

BLUSENS APRILIA

Mestre Nicolau, 6 nave 3, Pol. Ind. Sud, 0440 Cardedeu-Barcelona (Spain).
www.teambqr.com

ORGANISATION CHART
Owners: Raúl Romero and Josep Vila.
Team manager: Kino Contreras.
Technical Director: Toni Alfosea.
Chiefs mechanics: Andreu Viudes-Sanchez.

7 EFRÉN VAZQUEZ
9 ARTURO TIZÓN
41 ALEIX ESPARGARO

RIDERS
Efrén Vazquez
Date of birth: 2nd September 1986.
Place of birth: Bilbao (Spain).
First race: 1994.
First GP: Great Britain, 1997 (250).
Number of GP victories: -.

Arturo Tizón
Date of birth: 25th May 1984.
Place of birth: Vall de Uxó (Spain).
First race: 2000.
First GP: Australia, 2005 (250).
Number of GP victories: -
- Supersport Spanish Champion (2005).

Aleix Espargaró
Date of birth: 30th July 1989.
Place of birth: Barcelona (Spain).
First race: 2001.
First GP: Valencia, 2004 (125).
Number of GP victories: -
- 125cc Catalunyian Champion (2003).
- 125cc Spanish Champion (2004).

KIEFER-BOS-SOTIN RACING

CAMPETELLA RACING

BLUSENS APRILIA

HRC had let it be known immediately after the 2006 August break that there would be no spectacular development on their two strokes, with the result that some went looking elsewhere. Luthi, the last man to win a two stroke world title with Honda switched to Aprilia, but Andrea Dovizioso kept the faith and was the only man this season who was able to put up a fight. Takahashi was again alongside him, while in the Repsol camp, Julian Simon joined Shuhei Aoyama. Two teams ran kit versions: Thai Honda PTT-SAG and LCR, with Lucio Cecchinello once again spreading his wings.

KOPRON TEAM SCOT

Via Ponte Mellini 98, 47899 Serravalle (San Marino).
www.kopronteamscot.com

ORGANISATION CHART
Team manager: Cirano Mularoni.
Technical Director: Gianni Berti.
Chiefs mechanics: Tommaso Raponi (Andrea Dovizioso) and Trevor Morris (Yuki Takahashi).

34 ANDREA DOVIZIOSO | **55** YUKI TAKAHASHI

RIDERS
Andrea Dovizioso
Date of birth: 23rd March 1986.
Place of birth: Forlimpopoli (Italy).
First race: 1994.
First GP: (125cc) Italy, 2001.
Number of GP victories: 9 (5/125; 4/250).
First GP victory: (125cc) South Africa, 2004.
- Italian Pocketbike JB Champion (1997).
- Italian Pocketbike JB Champion (1998).
- Italian Challenge Aprilia «under 16» Champion (2000).
- 125cc European Champion (2001).
- 125cc World Champion (2004).

Yuki Takahashi
Date of birth: 12th July 1984.
Place of birth: Saitama (Japan).
First race: 2000.
First GP: (125cc) Pacific, 2001.
Number of GP victories: 2 (250cc).
First GP victory: (250cc) France, 2006.
- 250cc Japanese Champion (2004).

REPSOL HONDA

Calle Progrés no 1, Nave no 12, Poligono Industrial Pedregar, Montmeló, 08.160 Barcelona (Spain).
www.repsolhondateam.com

ORGANISATION CHART
Team manager: Alberto Puig.
Technical Director: Hirokazu Abe.
Chiefs mechanics: Gilles Bigot (Julian Simón) and Guido Cechini (Shuhei Aoyama).

60 JULIAN SIMÓN | **73** SHUHEI AOYAMA

RIDERS
Julian Simón
Date of birth: 3rd April 1987.
Place of birth: Villacañas (Spain).
First race: 1993.
First GP: Spain, 2002 (125).
Number of GP victories: 1 (125).
First GP victory: Great Britain, 2005 (125).
- Motocross 50cc Spanish Champion (1997).

Shuhei Aoyama
Date of birth: 5th December 1984.
Place of birth: Chiba (Japan).
First race: 1998.
First GP: (125cc) Pacific, 2001.
Number of GP victories: -
- 125cc Japanese Champion (2003).
- 250cc Japanese Champion (2005).

KOPRON TEAM SCOT

REPSOL HONDA

THAI HONDA PTT-SAG

Calle Cadi 6, 08272 Sant Fruitos de Bages, Barcelona (Spain).
www.thaihondapttsag.com

ORGANISATION CHART
Owner: Eduardo Perales.
Coordinator: Père Flores.
Chief mechanic: Arnau Vidal.

RIDER
Ratthapark Wilairot
Date of birth: 14th April 1988.
Place of birth: Chonburi (Thailand).
First race: 2003.
First GP: Japan, 2006 (250).
Number GP victories: -

8
RATTHAPARK WILAIROT

HONDA LCR

LCR-X Racing, S.A. M., Gildo Pastor Center, 7 rue du Gabian, 98000 Monaco.
www.hondalcr.com

ORGANIGRAMME
Team manager: Lucio Cecchinello
Technical manager: Ramon Forcada.

RIDER
Eugene Laverty
Date of birth: 3rd June 1986.
Place of birth: Ballymena (Northern Ireland).
First race: 2001.
First GP: Great Britain, 2004 (125).
Number GP victories: -

50
EUGENE LAVERTY

THAI HONDA PTT-SAG

HONDA LCR

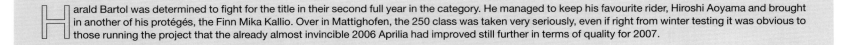

arald Bartol was determined to fight for the title in their second full year in the category. He managed to keep his favourite rider, Hiroshi Aoyama and brought in another of his protégés, the Finn Mika Kallio. Over in Mattighofen, the 250 class was taken very seriously, even if right from winter testing it was obvious to those running the project that the already almost invincible 2006 Aprilia had improved still further in terms of quality for 2007.

RED BULL KTM GP 250

Stallhofnerstrasse 3, 5230 Mattighofen (Austria).
www.ktm.at

ORGANISATION CHART
Technical Director: Harald Bartol.
Coordinator: Francesco Guidotti.
Technical Manager: Mario Galeotti.

4 HIROSHI AOYAMA   **36** MIKA KALLIO

RIDERS
Hiroshi Aoyama
Date of birth: 25th October 1981.
Place of birth: Chiba (Japan).
First race: 1999.
First GP: (250cc) Pacific, 2000.
Number of GP victories: 5 (250).
First GP victory: Japan, 2005 (250)

Mika Kallio
Date of birth: 8th November 1982.
Place of birth: Valkeakoski (Finland).
First race: 1997.
First GP: Germany, 2001 (125).
Number of GP victories: 9 (7/125; 2/250).
First GP victory: Portugal, 2005 (125).

METIS GILERA

s happened a year earlier, an Aprilia RSW was entered under the Gilera banner and this time it was entrusted to Roberto Locatelli. Marco Simoncelli who had this ride in 2006 was alongside the former 125 world champion, but riding an "LE" version, with the promise of a switch to a works bike during the year if he had a good start to the season.

Squadra Corse Metis Gilera
Corso Sempione 43, 20145 Milano (Italy).

ORGANISATION CHART
Sporting Director: Giampiero Sacchi.
Technical Director: Luigi Dall'Igna.
Team manager: Luca Boscoscuro.
Technical Chief: Aligi Deganello.

15 ROBERTO LOCATELLI   **58** MARCO SIMONCELLI

RIDERS
Roberto Locatelli
Date of birth: 5th July 1974 in Bergamo (Italy).
First race: 1989.
First GP: Italy, 1994 (125).
Number of GP victories: 9 (125).
First GP victory: France, 1999 (125).
- Italian Enduro Novice 50 Champion (1990).
- Italian Enduro Novice 80 Champion (1991).
- Italian 125 Sport-Production Champion (1993).
- 125cc World Champion (2000).

Marco Simoncelli
Date of birth: 20th January 1987 in Cattolica (Italy).
First race: 1996.
First GP: (125cc) Czech Republic, 2002 .
Number of GP victories: 2 (125cc).
First GP victory: (125cc) Spain, 2004.
- Italian Minimotos Champion (1999).
- European 125cc Champion (2002).

RED BULL KTM GP 250

METIS GILERA

TEAMS 125cc

THE NUMBER OF RIDERS WHO ARE CONTRACTED FOR THE WHOLE SEASON HAS GONE FROM 38 TO 32. THE MOVE TO THE 250 CLASS BY REIGNING CHAMPION BAUTISTA AND HIS PREDECESSOR LUTHI, ALONG WITH KALLIO, PROVES YET AGAIN THAT THE PYRAMID OF TALENT IS NOW WORKING VERY WELL. SO WE ARE SEEING A YOUNGER PACK, BUT IT IS THE EXPERIENCED RIDERS, TALMACSI, FAUBEL, PESEK AND KOYAMA, WHO ARE THE MOST CONSISTENT PERFORMERS

Totally dominant in the 2006 championship, the Noale marque was yet again the odds-on favourite this year. Two different bikes were available to those riders deemed "official:" the RSA had a superior rotary disc system developed by Dutch engineer, Jan Thiel. Bautista had used this engine, with success in Portugal, for the last two races of the previous season. Mattia Pasini, in a new team, financed by Spanish holiday resort, Polaris, as well as Sergio Gadea and Hector Faubel chose this option. Gabor Talmacsi, who had moved to Aspar Martinez and Sandro Cortese in the Caffe Latte squad, as well as Raffaele De Rosa (Multimedia) and the others, preferred the RSW version.

BANCAJA ASPAR

Plaza Sociedad Musical no 8, 46600 Alzira (Valencia), Spain.
www.teamaspar.com

ORGANISATION CHART
Team manager: Jorge «Aspar» Martinez.
Sporting Director: Gino Borsoi.
Technical Directors: Mauricio Soli (Gabor Talmacsi), Enrique Peris (Sergio Gadea and Hector Faubel).

14 GABOR TALMACSI **33** SERGIO GADEA **55** HECTOR FAUBEL

RIDERS

Gabor Talmacsi
Date of birth: 28th May 1981.
Place of birth: Budapest (Hungary).
First race: 1995.
First GP: Czech Republic, 1997 (125).
Number of GP victories: 6 (125).
First GP victory: Italy, 2005 (125).
- 125cc Hungarian Champion (1999).
- 125cc World Champion (2007).

Sergio Gadea
Birth: 30th December 1984.
Place of birth: Puzol (Spain).
First race: 2001.
First GP: Spain, 2003 (125).
Number of GP victories: 1
First GP victory:
France, 2007(125).

Hector Faubel
Date of birth: 10th August 1983.
Place of birth: Lliria (Spain).
First race: 1993.
First GP: Spain, 2000 (125).
Number of GP victories: 7 (125).
First GP victory: Turkey, 2006 (125).
- Spanish 125 Aprilia Cup Champion (1998).
- Spanish 250 Champion (2002).

POLARIS WORLD

SSM Racing, Spanish Sports Marketing S.L., c/eraso, 36. entreplanta, 28028 Madrid (Spain).
www.ssmracing.com

ORGANISATION CHART
Propriétaires: Augusto April et Rafael Nunef.
Team manager: Roger Marcaccini.
Chiefs mechanics: Enrique Guijal (Joan Olivé) and Mario Martini (Mattia Pasini).

6 JOAN OLIVÉ **75** MATTIA PASINI

RIDERS

Joan Olivé
Date of birth: 22 November 1984.
Place of birth: Tarragona (Spain).
First race: 1992.
First GP: Japan, 2001 (125).
Number of GP victories: -
- Spanish 50 Champion (1998).
- Spanish Joven Cup 125 Champion (1999).
- Spanish 125 Champion (2000).

Mattia Pasini
Date of birth: 13 August 1985.
Place of birth: Rimini (Italy).
First race: 1994.
First GP: South Africa, 2004 (125).
Number of GP victories: 8 (125).
First GP victory: China, 2005 (125).

TEAM SICILIA

Moto Racing Team Matteoni, Via Bandi 5, 47814 Bellaria (Italy).
www.matteoniracing.net

ORGANISATION CHART
Team manager: Massimo Matteoni.

8 LORENZO ZANETTI **20** ROBERTO TAMBURINI

RIDERS

Lorenzo Zanetti
Date of birth: 10th August 1987.
Place of birth: Lumezzane/Brescia (Italy).
First race: 1996.
First GP: Italy, 2004 (125).
Number of GP victories: -

Roberto Tamburini
Date of birth: 15th January 1991.
Place of birth: Rivazzurra (Italy).
First race: 2004.
First GP: Spain, 2006 (125).
Number of GP victories: -

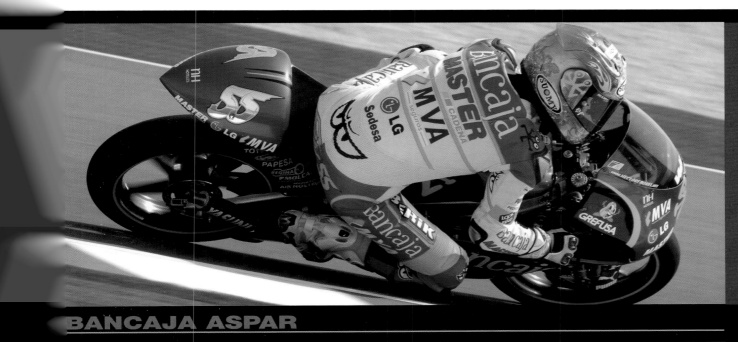

BANCAJA ASPAR

POLARIS WORLD

TEAM SICILIA

EMMI CAFFÈ LATTE APRILIA RACING TEAM

Paddock s.r.o., Jeremiasova 18/1283, 155 00 Praha 5, Czech Republic.
www.emmi-caffe-latte-racingteam.com

ORGANISATION CHART
Owner: Daniel M. Epp
Team manager: Peter Kern.
Technical Director: Lucas Schmidt.
Telemetry: Peter Koch.
Chief mechanic: Jens Stegmeier (Sandro Cortese).

RIDER
Sandro Cortese
Date of birth: 6th January 1990.
Place of birth: Ochsenhausen (Germany).
First race: 1997.
First GP: Spain, 2005 (125).
Number of GP victories: -
- Pocket-Bike Junior A European Champion (1999).
- German Minibike Champion (2002).

11 SANDRO CORTESE

SKILLED RACING TEAM

Fontana Racing s.r.l., Via Cavour 33, 46043 Castiglione delle Stiviere (Italy).
www.fontanaracing.com

ORGANISATION CHART
Team manager: Italo Fontana.
Organisation: Laura Fontana.

RIDERS
Federico Sandi
Date of birth: 12th August 1989.
Place of birth: Voghera (Italy).
First race: 1998.
First GP: Spain, 2005 (125).
Number of GP victories: -

Simone Corsi
Date of birth: 24th April 1987.
Place of birth: Roma (Italy).
First race: 1994.
First GP: Italy, 2002 (125).
Number of GP victories: 1 (125).
First GP victory: Turkey, 2007 (125).

15 FEDERICO SANDI **24** SIMONE CORSI

BLUSENS APRILIA

Mestre Nicolau, 6 nave 3, Pol. Ind. Sud, 0440 Cardedeu-Barcelona (Spain).
www.teambqr.com

ORGANISATION CHART
Owners: Raúl Romero et Josep Vila.
Team manager: Kino Contreras.
Technical Director: Fausto Martinez.
Chief mechanic: Toni Alfosea.

RIDERS
Pablo Nieto
Date of birth: 4th June 1980.
Place of birth: Madrid (Spain).
First race: 1995.
First GP: Catalunya, 1998 (125).
Number of GP victories: 1 (125).
First GP victory: Portugal, 2003 (125).

Hugo Van Den Berg
Date of birth: 23rd May 1990.
Place of birth: Hulshort (Netherlands).
First race: 2000.
First GP: Catalunya, 2005 (125).
Number of GP victories: -

22 PABLO NIETO **56** HUGO VAN DEN BERG

EMMI CAFFÈ LATTE APRILIA RACING TEAM

SKILLED RACING TEAM

BLUSENS APRILIA

WTR TEAM

Plazza E. Enriquez 12, 47891 Dogana (San Marino).
www.wtr-team.com

ORGANISATION CHART
Owner: Loris Castellucci.
Team manager: Matteo Napolitano.

27 STEFANO BIANCO

29 ANDREA IANNONE

RIDERS
Stefano Bianco
Date of birth: 27th October 1985.
Place of birth: Chivasso (Italy).
First race: 2000.
First GP: Australia, 2000 (125).
Numbers of GP victories: -

Andrea Iannone
Date of birth: 9th August 1989.
Place of birth: Vasto (Italy).
First race: 2004.
First GP: Spain, 2005 (125).
Numbers of GP victories: -

MULTIMEDIA RACING

Worldwide Communication sàrl, 43 route d'Arlon, 8009 Strassen (Luxemburg).
www.worldwidegroup.net

ORGANISATION CHART
General Director: Fiorenzo Caponera.
Technical Director: Alessandro Tognelli.
Chiefs mechanics: Simone Falcini (Raffaele de Rosa), Roberto Materasi (Simone Grotzkyj) and Guglielmo Pieretto (Dominique Aegerter).

35 RAFFAELE DE ROSA

53 SIMONE GROTZKYJ

77 DOMINIQUE AEGERTER

RIDERS
Raffaele De Rosa
Date of birth: 25th March 1987 in Napoli (Italy).
First race: 2003.
First GP: Spain, 2005 (125) / Numbers of GP victories: -

Simone Grotzkyj
Date of birth: 28th September 1988 in Pesaro (Italy).
First race: 2001.
First GP: Italy, 2005 (125).
Numbers of GP victories: -
- 125cc Italian Champion (2005).

Dominique Aegerter
Date of birth: 30th September 1990 in Rohrbach (Switzerland).
First race: 1995.
First GP: Portugal, 2006 (125).
Numbers of GP victories: -
- Motocross Kid 60 Swiss Champion (1999).

BELSON CAMPETELLA

Via De Gaspari 74, 62010 Montecassiano (Italy).
www.campetella.it

ORGANISATION CHART
Team manager: Eros Braconi.
Chief mechanic: Massimo Capanna.

44 POL ESPARGARO

RIDERS
Pol Espargaro
Date of birth: 10th June 1991.
Place of birth: Granollers (Spain).
First race: 2000.
First GP: Catalunya, 2006 (125).
Numbers of GP victories: -
- 125cc Catalunyan Champion (2004).
- 125cc Spanish Champion (2006).

WTR TEAM

MULTIMEDIA RACING

BELSON CAMPETELLA

Julian Simon moved up to the 250s with Honda. Mika Kallio, a favourite of team boss Harald Bartol, also went to the bigger category, still with KTM. So there were new faces on the little orange machines: a Japanese rider known to be brilliant, Tomoyoshi Koyama, along with two young hopefuls, Switzerland's Randy Krummenacher, who had made a few appearances already in 2006 and the Californian, Steve Bonsey who had been discovered on the American dirt tracks.

RED BULL KTM 125

Stallhofnerstrasse 3, 5230 Mattighofen (Austria).
www.ktm.at

ORGANISATION CHART
Technical Director: Harald Bartol.
Coordinator: Francesco Guidotti.
Team manager 125: Konrad Haefele.

34 RANDY KRUMMENACHER
51 STEVE BONSEY
71 TOMOYOSHI KOYAMA

RIDERS
Randy Krummenacher
Date of birth: 24th February 1990.
Place of birth: Wetzikon (Switzerland).
First race: 1995.
First GP: Great Britain, 2006 (125).
Numbers of GP victories: -
- Pocket-Bike Junior A Swiss Champion (2001).
- Pro Junior Cup Germany Champion (2003).

Steve Bonsey
Birth: 18th January 1990, in Salinas/Californie (USA).
First race: 1994.
First GP: Qatar, 2007 (125).
Numbers of GP victories: -

Tomoyoshi Koyama
Date of birth: 19th March 1983.
Place of birth: Kanagawa (Japan).
First race: 1999.
First GP: Pacific, 2000 (125).
Numbers of GP victories: 1 (125).
First GP victory: Catalunya, 2007 (125).
- 125cc Japanese Champion (2000).

The Spanish marque, who naturally run the same RSWs as the Aprilia camp, now supplied two teams, including the one financed by Dutch footballer Clarence Seedorf. The second crew was the Finnish Ajo team, which had previously entered Malagutis. Lukas Pesek and Nicolas Terol preferred the RSW to the RSA.

VALSIR SEEDORF DERBI

Racing World, Via Quattro Giugno 39, Serravalle (San Marino).
www.valsirseedorfracing.com

ORGANISATION CHART
Team manager: Stefano Bedon.
Technical Director: Stefano Riminucci.

18 NICOLAS TEROL
52 LUKAS PESEK

RIDERS
Nicolás Terol
Date of birth: 27th September 1988.
Place of birth: Alcoy (Spain).
First race: 2000.
First GP: Valencia, 2004 (125).
Numbers of GP victories: -

Lukas Pesek
Date of birth: 22nd November 1985.
Place of birth: Praha (Czech Republic).
First race: 2002.
Premier GP: Czech Republic, 2002 (125).
Numbers of GP victories: 2 (125).
First GP victory: China, 2007 (125).

AJO MOTORSPORT

Hämeentie 20, 37800 Toijala (Finland).
www.ajo.fi

ORGANISATION CHART
Team manager: Aki Ajo.

60 MICHAEL RANSEDER
95 ROBERT MURESAN

RIDERS
Michael Ranseder
Date of birth: 7th April 1986.
Place of birth: Schärding (Austria).
First race: 1993.
First GP: Czech Republic, 2004 (125).
Numbers of GP victories: -
- 125cc German Champion (2004).

Robert Muresan
Date of birth: 22nd March 1991.
Place of birth: Arad (Romania).
First race: 1998.
First GP: Turkey, 2006 (125).
Numbers of GP victories: -
- 125cc Romanian Champion (2003).
- 125cc Baltic Champion (2004).

RED BULL KTM 125

VALSIR SEEDORF DERBI

AJO MOTORSPORT

The Elit team, that had offered the marque its last two stroke title back in 2005, courtesy of Thomas Luthi, had quit the world's number one motorcycle manufacturer to rejoin Aprilia. The legendary technical chief, Sepp Schlogl, who had worked with the Swiss for the past few years, was integrated into the Repsol team, which was supposed to run Stefan Bradl, but the father of the young German preferred to try another route. Therefore, alongside Bradley Smith, one found Esteve Rabat. There was nothing revolutionary about the 2007 125 Honda, which was totally expected! Frenchman Mike Di Meglio found work in the Scot camp, his place in the France team going to his mate, Alexis Masbou.

REPSOL HONDA 125

Calle Progrés no 1, Nave no 12, Poligono Industrial Pedregar, Montmeló, 08.160 Barcelona (Spain). www.repsolmedia.com

ORGANISATION CHART

Team manager: Alberto Puig.
Technical adviser: Joseph « Sepp » Schlögl.

Team leader: Raúl Jara
Chiefs mechanics: Carlos Pérez (Esteve Rabat) and Santiago Fernandez (Bradley Smith).

12 ESTEVE RABAT
38 BRADLEY SMITH

RIDERS

Esteve Rabat
Date of birth: 25th May 1989.
Place of birth: Barcelona (Spain).
First race: 2002.
First GP: Valencia, 2005 (125).
Number of GP victories: -

Bradley Smith
Date of birth: 28th November 1990.
Place of birth: Garsington (Great Britain).
First race: 1997.
First GP: Spain, 2006 (125).
Number of GP victories: -

KOPRON TEAM SCOT

Via Ponte Mellini 98, 47899 Serravalle (San Marino). www.kopronteamscot.com

ORGANISATION CHART

Team manager: Cirano Mularoni.
Chiefs mechanics: Giancarlo Cecchini (Dino Lombardi) and Mirko Cecchini (Mike Di Meglio).

13 DINO LOMBARDI
63 MIKE DI MEGLIO

RIDERS

Dino Lombardi
Date of birth: 10th May 1990 in Benevento (Italy).
First race: 2002.
First GP: Turquie, 2006 (125).
Number of GP victories: -

Mike Di Meglio
Date of birth: 17th January 1988 in Toulouse (France).
First race: 2001.
First GP: Japan, 2003 (125).
Number of GP victories: 1 (125).
Première victoire en GP: Turkey, 2005 (125).
- 50cc French Champion (2000).
- Contu Cup 50 French Champion (2001).

FFM HONDA GP 125

Fédération française de motocyclisme, 74 Avenue Parmentier, 75011 Paris (France). www.teamffmgp125.com

ORGANISATION CHART

Team manager: Daniel Barthelemy.
Sportings Directors: Alain Bronec et Nicolas Dussauge.
Technical Director: Tiziano Altabella.
Chief mechanic: Franck Gallou.

7 ALEXIS MASBOU

RIDER

Alexis Masbou
Date of birth: 2 juin 1987.
Place of birth: Nîmes (France).
First race: 2001.
First GP: France, 2003 (125).
Number of GP victories: -
- 125cc French Champion (2004).

DE GRAAF GRAND PRIX

Panoven 20, 3401 RA Ijsselstein (Netherlands). www.molenaarracing.com

ORGANISATION CHART

Team manager: Arie Molenaar.
Technical Director: Hans Spaan.

37 JOEY LITJENS
99 DANIEL WEBB

RIDERS

Joey Litjens
Date of birth: 8th February 1990.
Place of birth: Venray (Netherlands).
First race: 2000.
First GP: Netherlands, 2005 (125).
Number of GP victories: -
- Aprilia Cup 125 Dutch Champion (2002).

Daniel Webb
Date of birth: 22 mars 1991.
Place of birth: Pembury (Great Britain).
First race: 1997.
First GP: Catalunya, 2006 (125).
Number of GP victories: -

REPSOL HONDA 125

KOPRON TEAM SCOT

FFM HONDA GP 125

DE GRAAF GRAND PRIX

2007 MotoGP World

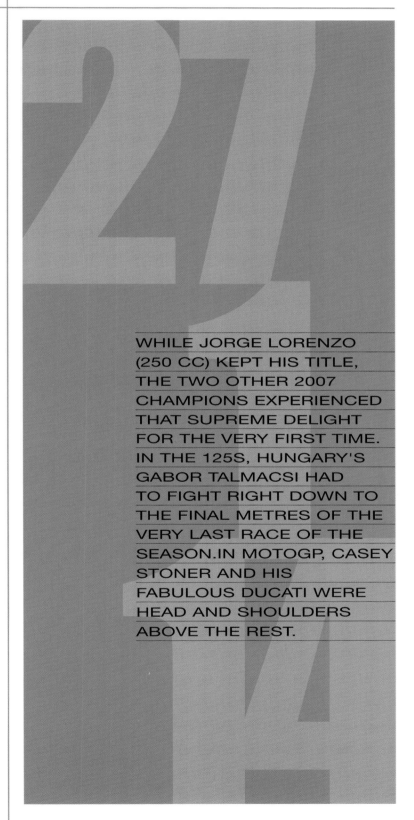

WHILE JORGE LORENZO (250 CC) KEPT HIS TITLE, THE TWO OTHER 2007 CHAMPIONS EXPERIENCED THAT SUPREME DELIGHT FOR THE VERY FIRST TIME. IN THE 125S, HUNGARY'S GABOR TALMACSI HAD TO FIGHT RIGHT DOWN TO THE FINAL METRES OF THE VERY LAST RACE OF THE SEASON.IN MOTOGP, CASEY STONER AND HIS FABULOUS DUCATI WERE HEAD AND SHOULDERS ABOVE THE REST.

ampions

CASEY:
MISSION… POSSIBLE!

I n 2000, Colin, Bronwyn, Kelly and Casey Stoner left Australia heading for England, with one mission, to win! The plan was for Casey, the baby of the family, to become the best rider in the world.

Colin Stoner, with a face that has been chiselled, comes from the back of beyond in a country, Australia, that specialises in backs of beyond. "It's not worth me telling you the name of the place, as it doesn't appear on any maps," says the 2007 world champion with a grin. "Let's say it's about five and half hours drive north of Sydney." It's a place where you don't do much unless it's on a motorbike.

Then there is Bronwyn, the mother, who shares that worried look that all mothers have when their "little ones" take to the track. Kelly is his sister, elder by six years and apparently the one to blame for "Baby" Stoner's desire to get on board a motorbike. He was just three years old when his sister was competing in a few dirt track races on a mini-moto. Casey wanted to have a go and a marvellous raw talent had just come to life. Now it just needed to be honed to perfection.

They sold everything for the sake of the mission

In ten years of dirt track racing, Casey would win no less than 41 races. He was now ready to move on to more serious matters but one major problem reared its head. In Australia one cannot take part in any form of road racing below the age of fourteen. But the Stoners were on a mission and so they decided to head for England, the birthplace of motor sports. They sold their possessions to fund the purchase of some one-way airline tickets, destination London.

They then got to grips with the British 125 cc championship and the far more competitive Spanish one. It was not long before Casey was taking part in his first Grand Prix. Then, in his first complete season in the world championship, he became known as the man who crashed in impressive style. At the time, he was riding in the 250 class as the Stoners had been unable to find him a decent ride in the 125s. The 250 gambit was too soon and too fast for Casey who crashed more often than he should, so that he ended up sulking and isolated in the paddock, where he had few real friends. But the talent was there, as Lucio Cecchinello, his first employer in GPs recalls: "On 22 June 2002, at Jerez, for his first run on the Aprilia 250, we immediately realised on looking at the telemetry that there was something special about him."

From Monaco….to nowhere

And then it happened that he started winning, winning races and a bit of money. Mum and Kelly headed for home, while Colin and Casey were about to move to Monaco, "because there are a lot of Australians in the Principality."

In his second ever MotoGP race, in Qatar in 2006, he stupefied onlookers by taking pole position, even though he had just spent around forty hours in a plane or waiting around in airports as his visa was not in order! The reason for these lengthy journeys is that, whenever possible, he would head home to find some calm, the animals on the family farm and of course, his first love, the eighteen year old Adriana, who on 6 January 2007 became Mrs. Stoner. Eight months and seventeen days later, she also became the wife of a world champion.

Mission….Possible!

INTERVIEW

"I GIVE THIS AS A PRESENT TO ALL THOSE WHO BELIEVED IN ME"

Casey, its 23 September 2007, nearly four in the afternoon...

- And I don't know what to say. I did not expect to pick up the title here in Japan. It's an absolute dream. Can you imagine, having such a big lead with three races to go.

Who are you thinking of at the moment?

- My parents of course. I have just given a present to those who believed in me.

And the others?

- To those who didn't believe, I proved them wrong.

For a long time, it was said you were a bit "strange." We hardly ever saw you in the paddock?

- Living in this environment was very complicated for me. My only mate was Chaz Davies, but he had to leave the GP scene. Now, with Adriana with me, it's different and I am much happier and therefore calmer.

What does it feel like, crossing the finish line in this situation?

- There can be no better moment than crossing the line knowing you are world champion! It's almost unreal

On your world champion T shirt, you have listed your idols: Doohan, Gardner, Rossi, Schwantz, Rainey...

- Yeah and Doohan was there to see me take the title. I spoke to him again the day before the Japanese GP and I can tell you it feels strange to achieve something like this in front of him. You know, I grew up watching him race on the TV.

Casey, were there ever times in the past when you imagined a moment like this one here at Motegi?

- When I was young, I thought about it every day, as I wanted to be 500 World Champion. And I still held onto that dream when I was actually riding in GPs in 125 and 250 cc. Of course, it would have been nice to win already at that level, but it was not my goal.

Does the reality of today match up to that dream?

- I don't know as it is such a long time since I first had this dream. When I started racing, it seemed to me that everything was just getting more difficult. The reality of racing soon gave me a wake-up call and it seemed that all the time, my dream was getting a bit further away.

What does it mean to be the best rider in the world?

- I am not! I have just been, this year, the quickest over the eighteen races on the calendar

If you had to put the following in order: Casey, Adriana (his wife,) Ducati and Bridgestone?

- She's not the reason I am quick, but the most important element for me is definitely Adriana.

For part of the season, your personal performance took a back seat as there was a lot of talk about the super Ducati engine, with some suggestions that it might even be illegal, then there was the superiority of the Bridgestone tyres...

- The situation improved in time, even if I still occasionally hear this sort of remark. You know, I won so many races this year that I think I have proved that I also have the talent, that I was capable of dominating the race despite my youth and my lack of experience, a bit like Hamilton in F1.

Let's continue for a moment with your detractors. Some say you are like a robot, who does not think but who benefits from the Ducati electronics that make the difference?

- First the power, then the tyres, now the electronics... I'll make a suggestion. Let's go back to the days of the savage 500s and let's see who will entertain you the most! You know, I come from dirt track, where you spend your time sliding, so I know how to control the back wheel. But it's true that with modern electronics, it is easier to control the way the power comes in.

Soyons encore un peu méchants. Parlez-nous de ceux qui vous surnommaient «Rolling Stoner», ou alors «Crashey» quand vous tombiez beaucoup au début de votre carrière?

- I never liked those names.

Do you believe in destiny?

- I believe in work and a higher power.

But if we were to rewrite history, you could thank Valentino Rossi who did not want you alongside him in the Yamaha team last year?

- I don't know if I owe him anything. Like today, they say I win because of my bike, but I am very happy to have gone to Ducati. The Italians had faith in me when no other team wanted me, and that deserved a reward didn't it?

Thanks also to Gibernau, who refused to extend his contract...

- If things happened that way, there must have been a reason for it. So yes, maybe I would have ridden for another team this year, but one day I would have ended up at Ducati. End of discussion, I came here and I won and there's no point in wasting your breath wondering what might have happened if...

Coming back to Casey Stoner the man, have you changed this season as a person and also as a rider?

- In the races, I have stayed the same. There are so many people who said nasty things about me...Now that I am at Ducati, they have realised they were wrong. Away from the track, I am more relaxed, calmer, because in a big team, everything is better organised.

What is Casey Stoner like in private?

- In Australia, I like being back on the farm, working with the cattle, the horses, going fishing and riding around on a motocross bike. In Europe, apart from training, it's a quieter life, as there's not much to do in Monaco

When you first came to Europe at the age of 14, what did you think of it?

- At first, it was difficult and it's still not that easy even today. The first two years we lived in England, which was the sacrifice we made to chase my dreams. I thank my parents for following me and for always believing in my talent, even during the difficult times, when we had no more money

Are you religious?

- Yes, I'm Christian and I go to church when I can.

Are you rich now?

- Not that rich. You know, compared to others, us Australians sometimes have to ride for not very much in order to get ourselves known.

And when you will have money?

- I will invest in land and in real estate.

You are 21, your wife is 18; are you already thinking about having a family?

Yes, we think about it, but it's still a bit too early.

Note: interviews in "The Motorcycle Yearbook" are "highlights" of comments recorded during the season.

VISITING CARD		TITLES			
Name Stoner		1989-99	Dirt-track in Australia, 41 victories	2004	5th in the World Championship 125 (KTM)
First name Casey		2000	Australian Champion Aprilia Challenge	2005	2nd in the World Championship 250 (Aprilia)
Date of birth 16 octobre 1985			125 RS, 23rd in the Spanish	2006	8th in the World Championship MotoGP (Honda)
Place of birth Kurri-Kurri (Australia)			125cc Championship (Honda)	2007	Moto GP World Champion (Ducati)
Marital status married with Adriana		2001	29th in the 125cc World Championnship ,		
First race 1989			Spanish and British Vice Champion 125		
First GP Grande-Bretagne, 2001 (125)			(Honda)		
Number of GP victories 16		2002	12th in the World Championship 250		
(2/125; 4/250; 10/MotoGP)			(Aprilia)		
First GP victory Valencia, 2003 (125)		2003	8th in the World Championship 125 (Aprilia)		

Casey's story in six blinks of an eye: the super-talented kid from the Aussie dirt tracks has become world champion in the same year that he married the beautiful Adriana. The title also went to Ducati (below.)

LORENZO:
MOTORCYCLING'S "PEPE"

1

D o you remember, "Pepe" the son of the chief in the cartoon story "Asterix in Hispania?" He was as proud as a peacock and would hold his breath until he got what he wanted. Tennis has its "Pepe" in Rafael Nadal, while Formula 1 has Fernando Alonso and now motorcycle racing has one too in the form of Jorge Lorenzo, now a double world champion in the 250 cc category

There's a look about him, a real look of someone who is scared of nothing, who knows what he wants and also what he does not want anymore. Sometimes it was a dirty look, back in the early days, when he behaved as though he was the only one out on track, the only one in the world. That's the way he is, he knows it and laughs while admitting that he has changed over the years. That might be true, but he refuses to wipe out completely this character trait, born out of his upbringing. This pride, which comes naturally to him is very much a Hispanic strong point. It is this fear of nothing that means one either loves him or hates him but no one can ever be indifferent to him. Lorenzo is the complete opposite to that other Spaniard who is in the news, namely the sad clone of Alberto Puig who is Daniel Pedrosa.

He was too young for his first GP

Lorenzo's story, just like Pedrosa's except with one key difference, is that of a young kid who was pushed into a grown-up world. Worse than that, thrown into a world where no one is handing out presents as one cannot be nice when one wants to take the place of another, pass them on the track and in the hearts of others, so that those who make the big decisions favour you and therefore not the other.

When he arrived in Jerez de la Frontera, in early May of 2002, he was too young to take part in the first practice session. It was only on the Saturday, 4 May, the day of his fifteenth birthday, that he was allowed on track in the saddle of his red Derbi. Spain thought it had found a new hero, while the rest of the world smiled at this extremely precocious youngster. His father was there around the clock and the lad, like all kids the world over only wanted to copy him, to follow his example, to listen and try and understand his advice, because that is the way that Jorge was brought up.

At Palma de Mallorca, a long way away from the beaches infested with tourists chasing the sun, a 15 year old boy only knows one rule: daddy is right. What he says is true. Of course, the father wants to do all he can for the boy because, of course, like all sons, this one is the best. There is no one else like him of course. So the lad listens, believes and does not understand when the facts do not add up. So, he becomes a bad lad, sulky and introverted who only comes out of his own personal bubble to throw a fit at the edge of reason. It will soon be the end of the first part of his career.

Severed ties lead to success

However, one day Jorge would say no. He had understood, along with Dani Amatriain, who now manages his affairs, that the time had come to sever the ties with dad. From somewhere on paradise island, the father cried out about kidnap, about money filtered away, Lorenzo's intrinsic value, as well as what he was beginning to earn.

Jorge did not listen. He had made his decision and would take a new path. Four years later, he had already won two world titles. And next, year, he joins the class of kings, the world of MotoGP.

INTERVIEW

"MY MUCH LOVED APRILIA IS A GREAT LADY OF THE ITALIAN COURT."

So Jorge, we saw you as a boxer at the end of the decisive Malaysian GP: that's something new?
- Yes, it's a little something I wanted to do. When I was feeling low, when things were not going too well for me, I would stick on a DVD of "Rocky 3, the eye of the Tiger," and it would perk me up.

The championship that has just ended was particularly intense, don't you think?
- Absolutely. With the arrival of two world champions (Bautista and Luthi) and a double runner-up (Kallio) the general level has seriously gone up compared to last year. In fact, you only have to look at the fastest times from this season, either in qualifying or in the race.

And you have been head and shoulders above the rest. Perfect for a lad with, shall we say, a well developed ego?
- I have always said this to my real friends: if one day when I woke up I sensed I wasn't the same Lorenzo, then I would feel very bad. In this world, people don't like those who seem to have too much self confidence, but what can I do about that? I was brought up this way and I like the way I am.

Have you not changed over the years and with more experience?
- The years have taught me to moderate my comments a bit, but I will always keep this somewhat proud side that I like so much.

Your Aprilia has been a faithful girlfriend to you, hasn't she?
- My much loved Aprilia is a great lady of the Italian Court. She has always been a family favourite. Right from her birth she has been looked after and educated to become a queen. And maybe in the past, she had simply not met the right prince charming capable of dominating her in the right way for a queen with so much potential.

You seem to rather like the role of a pirate. Why's that, does it stem from a propensity for questioning the established way of things?
- Maybe. I have always liked to be different. If we were

all the same, there would be no charm in it, don't you think?

At your first GP, at Jerez de la Frontera in 2002, you were not yet 15 on the first day of practice and so your weekend could not start until the Saturday. That was a bit unusual wasn't it?
- I remember it as though it was yesterday. I was fifteen years old and I did not feel at all comfortable in what seemed to my young eyes to be the most professional environment. I was always serious, I always wore the same clothes, because that's the way my father was. I did not have much of an idea of what was right and what was wrong, either on the track or off it. I began to change about two years ago: I distanced myself from my father and chose the people I wanted to have around me and basically I became independent. Today, racing is a job, so of course I try to be a bit nicer, but sometimes it's hard to hide one's true character.

Back then did you have an idol?
- The first rider I saw in action was Max Biaggi. I was impressed by his will to win and when I came to Jerez for that famous first GP, he invited me into his motorhome and we talked. From that moment on, he was my idol. I know he's not the best loved rider, but his fans are real supporters, as are mine.

One of your nicknames is "Porfuera." What is the story behind that?
- They started to call me that after a Brazilian GP, where I had gone round the outside, "por fuera" of Pedrosa and Stoner. But the story is older than that. I remember a race in the European championship in Portugal where I also went round another rider, the Italian Angeloni, in the same way.

Let's talk about the future: how do you think things will work out for you in MotoGP?
- Without any pressure, as no one can expect anything of me in 2008. My initial aim is to have a look, learn and try to improve with each race. In 2008, unlike 2009, I will be under no obligation in terms of results.

OK, but you will be in close company with Rossi?
- The way everything will work has not been finalised yet. But obviously we will form a very high quality

team and in this context I am bound to learn a lot and quickly too.

Your confrontations with Pedrosa, both on and off the track, fuelled by some acerbic comments have always been vigorous. You are going to find yourselves together again now.
- As far as I'm concerned it makes no difference to be up against him. I have a lot of respect for him, because he is currently the best Spanish rider, so there will be even more incentive to beat him! But…

But what Jorge?
- It won't be enough. My personal motivation is to be the best of all and that is what I will be working on from the very first day of winter testing.

A modern day rider is a complex person. What is your take on it?
- I train a lot, but I also try every time to find some time to relax. I have learned English and I have taken courses in behaviour and diction in a specialist school. I've also learned how to act in front of a camera. Times have changed and today, it's not enough just to be the quickest on the track.

Now, the best riders in MotoGP have all come through the 250s. A good sign for your future?
- The best is definitely Stoner, who is more talented than Pedrosa. However, Dani is more methodical, a characteristic created by his mentor, Alberto Puig. Casey doesn't seem to follow strict rules and he has been criticised for training less than the others, but he's the one who has won everything this year, so…

The best of all?
- Valentino Rossi, but he's not from another planet. He's had his good days and some less good. So he is beatable, but it's true he has a little something more than the others.

Note: interviews in "Motorcycle Grand Prix Yearbook" are "highlights" of comments recorded during the season.

VISITING CARD	TITLES		
Name Lorenzo Guerrero	**2000** 17th in the 125 Spanish Championship (Honda)	**2004** 4th in the 125 World Championship (Derbi)	
First name Giorgio "Jorge"	**2001** 6th in the125 European Championship	**2005** 5th in the 250 World Championship (Honda)	
Date of birth 4th Mai 1987	4th in the125 European Championship (Honda)	**2006** 250 World Champion (Aprilia)	
Place of birth Palma de Mallorca (Spain)	**2002** 21st in the 125 World Championship (Derbi)	**2007** 250 World Champion (Aprilia)	
Marital status single	**2003** 12th in the 125 World Championship		
First race 1990	15th in the 125 Spanish Championship (Derbi)		
First GP Spain, 2002 (125)			
Number of GP victories 21 (4/125; 17/250)			
First GP victory Rio, 2003 (125)			

Whether he transforms himself into a boxer, a knight or a pirate, Jorge Lorenzo never forgets he was once a little boy, almost like any other. Almost, because from a very early age, he was already watching his racing lines.

Pole position, victories and honour lap: the season of Gabor Talmacsi ended on a big emotion, in Valencia.

14

TALMACSI:
A BOXER WHO NEVER DROPS HIS GUARD

Budapest, Hungary has a rich and complex history, the city and the country both for a long time now divided into two worlds. It has a well developed tradition of culture and the city shone brightly during the "Belle Epoque" before the curtain, the iron curtain came down on Pest and on Buda. Events are well documented: the invasion of Soviet troops, the resistance, the repression…

But Hungary is a passionate country and that extends to motorcycle racing which is personified by a hero by the name of Janos Drapal, the winner of four GPs in the middle of the Seventies. Those exploits are just memories now, but come 2007 and a certain Gabor Talmacsi came along to finally give his countrymen a world championship title to cheer about.

Gabor? First off, there's real presence here, a real rough hewn physique that one could imagine in an old fashioned boxer who hides a heart of gold behind the looks of a thug. Gabor is a sensitive chap too. The early steps in his career were not easy, despite the passionate support of a father who built him his first motor bike and despite the fact that after years in the wilderness, Budapest and Hungary were keen to show that they too deserved a world champion rider.

He was discovered on "his" track

After competing in the national championship, Gabor burst on the international scene at a round of the European championship at "his" Hungaroring circuit. Soon the time came for him to travel further afield, to nearby Germany, to the Czech Republic and Brno, where he took part in his first GP in 1997, before moving up to take on the world.

However it is not easy to find a ride with a good organisation when you come from a country that seems to be a bit too exotic for some team bosses, who are mainly Italian and Spanish. So, every year, or almost, Gabor changes teams, even if one can see signs of real character and real courage. In 2004, he therefore pulls off some impressive performances with the primitive Malaguti and, in 2005, he switches to KTM where he finally gets his hands on a bike worthy of his ambition. He wins his first GP at Mugello, but the season spent in the service of the Austrian manufacturer is particularly noteworthy for his refusal to give best to his team-mate Mika Kallio in Qatar, even though the Finn was fighting for the title up against the Swiss rider Thomas Luthi. That incident ended up with a torn up contract at the end of the year

Aspar" the saviour

Would he recover from this latest contretemps? In 2006, he rides a Honda which is no longer on the pace, but he never gives up the fight. Because a boxer with self respect never drops his guard, leaving his opponent not even the slightest opening. What will become of him? He will find sanctuary in Spain with Jorge "Aspar" Martinez, the man who already saved Alvaro Bautista. A trap or the lottery win? That's all very well, goes the line of thought in the paddock, but how will this Hungarian manage to gain the respect of his two Spanish team-mates, Faubel and Gadea? Talmacsi is a boxer and therefore a puncher and this rugged looking man wastes no time in reminding everyone of that fact, right from the first race of the season. But he can be clever too and when asked what three things he would take to a desert island, without hesitation he replies, "three pretty girls!"

A nice winter programme for a world champion!

INTERVIEW

"BY CHRISTMAS, I HOPE I WILL HAVE FINISHED ACKNOWLEDGING EVERYONE'S CONGRATULATIONS!"

Gabor, what does this world championship title mean to you?
- It's fantastic, but to be honest, it's difficult to talk about it just now. In fact it was a very difficult race because Hector (Faubel) had a quicker bike than me and he passed me down the straight before blocking me afterwards. It was not always very correct and we touched a few times. I could feel him right behind me all the time, ready to do crazy things, especially as he could catch me easily. It was hard to stay calm, but I still tried to stay concentrated on my pace, even though I couldn't read my pit board as there was too much information on it! So I tried to manage everything on my own, occasionally looking behind me. I know that's not the best thing to do to keep concentration, but in the end, finishing second was good enough to take the title.

What was the key factor this year?
- First of all, I have to thank Aprilia, because they gave me fantastic support all season long. I really enjoyed myself with this bike, even if it was not always the quickest when up against the RSA. Season after season, I learned how to go quicker, how to win races and finally I have got this title. I hope this experience will help coming generations.

What made you choose the 2006 factory Aprilia, rather than the new RSA?
- Last year, I had a Honda and when Aprilia got me to try the factory 2006 bike at the start of the year, I immediately felt very comfortable on it, as I set a new record for the Jerez track. We began working on this bike, because we felt it could bring us success. It seems it was the right decision (laughs.) Just before Australia, I had the offer to switch to the RSA, but I had so much feeling and data for the older bike that I preferred not to risk making the change. Of course, the RSA is a better bike and now I can't wait to start working with it.

You are the first Hungarian motorcycle world champion...
- Yes, I reckon it will be mad when I get back home. I think I'll probably have to reply to a thousand SMS messages. If all goes well, I should have finished by Christmas and finally celebrate! (even more laughter)

You had a ten point lead coming into the final race. Did you have a particular strategy?
- Yes, my strategy was to win the championship! In fact, it was not so easy, because I had a small lead, but I was not yet champion. I mainly tried to stay calm and focussed all weekend long. My experience taught me to concentrate on the corners one at a time and ride always at the maximum, without thinking about winning. If, mid-race, I had thought I had an advantage and that I could win the race, the second group might have caught us earlier and then everything could have become much more complicated.

After a difficult season last year with Honda (just one podium, at Brno,) how did you end up on a Jorge Martinez team Aprilia?
- It was down to my manager Stefano Favaro, who did a great job for me. He got in touch with Gino Borsoi (the sporting director of the Aspar team) and Jorge Martinez and the negotiations started in the middle of last season. I was very happy when the contract was signed.

You will be repeating the process next year with the same team and naturally enough the aim is to go for another crown. Will it be easier?
- This is a world championship so nothing is ever easy (smiles.) It is difficult to say now if I can win again in 2008. There will be new riders and team changes. I hope I will find a rival as strong as Faubel was this year and that we will have some good scraps.

After the RSW, the RSA?
- Yes, last year I signed a contract for two years with the Aspar team, to ride an Aprilia RSA and it's fantastic. It is even the first time in my career that I get to stay in the same team with the same mechanics. These last six years, each winter, I had to adapt to a new team and a new bike. That's difficult and it puts you under a lot of pressure. Here, we have started something big and we can now continue together.

It is said that in this fantastic team, there is complete equality between the riders. Is that really the case?
- Yes really. It was difficult to believe that at first, but I always got the same support as my Spanish team-mates. I had the same opportunities as Hector (Faubel) and Sergio (Gadea,) even though I am Hungarian and this a Spanish team with Spanish sponsors. I don't know how Jorge Martinez does it. He's a great bloke!

The championship featured quite a few failures...
- Faubel broke, I broke, but the champion is still the champion.

What was the key moment of the season?
- The Malaysian GP. It was my last win so far. We found some really good settings on the bike and when we arrived here in Valencia, they also worked well. There were a lot of other good moments this year, such as the Sachsenring for example.

What was the atmosphere like in the garage on the morning of this fantastic finale?
- Normal, the same as usual. I was calm, because I had prepared well during practice. I knew I would have a good race pace. Even after the start, I was reasonably relaxed, until Hector turned up at half distance (smiles.)

Have you spoken to him?
- We don't chat much, because he does not speak any English. I have more contact with Sergio Gadea.

You are superstitious: will you have the number 1 on your bike next year?
- Good question...I don't know. I will have to think about that. It would be nice and I would be proud to use the number 1. But so far, I had luck on my side and maybe I will use a combination of the two numbers.

VISITING CARD	TITLES		
Name Talmacsi	**1995** 2nd in the 125 Hungarian Championship (Honda)	**2001**	18th in the 125 World Championship (Honda)
First name Gabor	**1996** 3rd in the Hungarian Championship	**2002**	22nd in the World Championship
Date of birth 28th May 1981	5th in the 125 Czech Rep. Championship		15th in the 125 Spanish Championship (Honda)
Place of birth Budapest (Hungary)	(Honda)		39th in the Supersport European Championship
Marital status single	**1997** 18th in the 125 European Championship (Honda)		(Suzuki)
First race 1995	**1998** 28th in the 125 European Championship (Honda)	**2003**	14th in the 125 World Championship (Aprilia)
First GP Czech Republic, 1997 (125)	15th in the 125 Spanish Championship (Derbi)		7th in the 125 Spanish Championship (Malaguti)
Number of GP victories 6 (125)	**1999** 40th in the 125 European Championship	**2004**	17th in the 125 World Championship (Malaguti)
First GP victory Italia, 2005 (125)	125 Hungarian Champion (Honda)	**2005**	3rd in the 125 World Championship (KTM)
	2000 5th in the 125 European Championship	**2006**	7th in the 125 World Championship (Honda)
	14th in the German Championship (Honda)	**2007**	125 World Champion (Aprilia)

Casey Stoner majestic ahead of Valentino Rossi who can only follow and wonder.

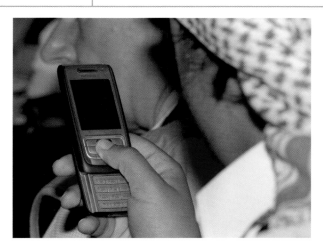

STONER'S
FIRST STRIKE

THE AUSTRALIAN HAD A FERRARI, BEHIND HIM, ROSSI ONLY HAD A FIAT: RIGHT FROM THE FIRST GP OF THE SEASON THE TREND FOR 2007 WAS SET. EUROPEAN TECHNOLOGY HAD BEATEN THE JAPANESE GIANTS IN THE BATTLE OF THE 800S.

THE RACE

HOW TO BEAT A FERRARI….WITH A FIAT?

Stoner's thoroughbred kicks out as Rossi catches his breath: the image of this first GP.

"We should at least remember one thing, that I was the last one to wave the white flag." Valentino Rossi would not be Valentino Rossi if he suddenly became unable to turn a defeat into a bon mot. Up against the power of the new Ducati GP7 and the talent of its new young rider, Australian Casey Stoner, Valentino was powerless. "The Ducati runs as though it hasn't changed its engine since last year when the capacity was 990 cc instead of the current 800 cc," he said. The MotoGP king had tried his all to disconcert his main rival on the day. He was the only man to have tried some otherworldly late braking to make up for what his bike lacked on the straights of the Losail circuit. "There were two or three points where I was better than Stoner and I got ahead once as we headed for the line, but Casey was already back in front by the time we crossed it. From then on it was hopeless.

And fair play to Stoner, he didn't make the slightest mistake, so I had to settle for second place."

A difference of 12 km/h. The figures are hard to swallow for the Japanese constructors. Over the whole weekend, the four Ducatis on track were credited with the four highest top speeds. During qualifying, when the engines are all kicking out maximum power, (324.7 km/h for Stoner, 323.5 for Capirossi, 322.6 for Hofmann and 322.6 for Barros) came up at the same time, but it was not enough to stop Rossi taking pole, after he was flashed at 309.9! In the race, while many teams were concerned about going the distance on just the 21 litres of fuel permitted this year, Stoner (314.1) was still regularly beating Rossi (302.4) by 12 km/h. That had never been seen at this level of the sport.

A great coup for Stoner. The little Australian claimed the win with his first ride in the saddle of the Ducati, but he did not just make the difference

down the main straight at the Losail track. In fact, he had been perfect from start to finish, as had his bike and his tyres. "I set my fastest lap on the last lap, which proves we had done our job perfectly," confided Stoner having wiped the tears away from his still boyish face. Alongside him, Rossi could only applaud, maybe not that unhappy to have discovered another real rival on the race track.

Facing a real challenge. The outcome of this first race of the new era, with four constructors in the top four places confirmed one thing: the Japanese engineers would have to do their homework again, because Valentino Rossi was insistent as only a rider can be, realizing that it is simply impossible for a Fiat to beat a Ferrari in a straight fight and the little red beauties Ducati build in Borgo Panigale are often referred to as two-wheeled Ferraris.

Olivier Jacque (above) scores Kawasaki's first points of the season. Stoner picks up his first trophy, while McWilliams (below) is unaware that this will be the Ilmor's only appearance this season

STONER MASTERCLASS, ROSSI IN AWE… AND PEDROSA GRIMACES

RUNNERS AND RIDERS

So this was the dawn of a new era in the MotoGP class, with a drop in engine capacity from 990 to 800 cc, a reduction in the fuel capacity from 22 to 21 litres and the number of slick tyres to be used by a rider per weekend reduced to 31. However, Dunlop who have yet to win in MotoGP do not have to comply with this rule. All 21 entries are present, including Hopkins despite doing serious damage to his right wrist three weeks earlier here at Doha for the test.

QUALIFYING

The two works Yamaha riders - pardon me, Fiat-Yamaha riders, since the name of the title sponsor had been officially announced on the Monday prior to the race - had enjoyed a splendid winter, so Rossi and Edwards were looking good, even if in the end, "Vale" only pipped Stoner by 5 thousandths of a second. As they had done at the championship dress rehearsal in Jerez, the Ducatis are comfortably quickest in terms of top speed. Hayden does not seem that happy with his new bike and the reigning world champion is only on the third row.

START

Rossi shoots into the lead ahead of Stoner, Elias, Pedrosa, Edwards and Hopkins. On the straight, Stoner makes the most of the Ducati's formidable power to go to the front. Pedrosa is third. Hampered by his injuries, McWilliams (Ilmor) was unable to start.

LAP 2

Same penalty, a difference in top speeds, for Rossi, but this time up against Pedrosa. But it did not go the same way, as "Vale" immediately regains the upper hand.

LAP 4

Hopkins has just set the fastest lap and is fifth, less than 8 tenths off the leader, Stoner.

LAP 6

Capirossi has rejoined the lead group, so that six of them are covered by 1.5 seconds.

LAP 7

Capirossi is a faller.

LAP 8

Randy de Puniet is a faller.

LAP 9

Checa falls. You can throw a handkerchief over the top four: Stoner, Rossi, Pedrosa and Hopkins.

HALF DISTANCE (11 LAPS)

Stoner, Rossi, Hopkins and Pedrosa: the leading quartet are all in the same precise 974 thousandths. Then there's a chasm to Edwards who is over 5 seconds behind.

LAP 13

Carried along by a lap record from Stoner, the Ducati rider and Rossi have made the break from the Pedrosa-Hopkins duo, who now trail by 2 seconds.

LAP 17

Elias plays in the sand. Pitt retires.

FINISH (22 LAPS)

A lead of 622 thousandths going into the final lap and so there is nothing Rossi could do, even though he is a past master of last minute attacks, but the speed differential between the Ducati and the Yamaha is too great.

GP QATAR | 10th March 2007 | Losail | 5.380 m

STARTING GRID				
1	46	V. Rossi	Yamaha	1'55.002
2	27	C. Stoner	Ducati	1'55.007
3	5	C. Edwards	Yamaha	1'55.233
4	24	T. Elias	Honda	1'55.358
5	26	D. Pedrosa	Honda	1'55.361
6	21	J. Hopkins	Suzuki	1'55.833
7	65	L. Capirossi	Ducati	1'55.851
8	14	R. De Puniet	Kawasaki	1'55.933
9	69	N. Hayden	Honda	1'56.041
10	33	M. Melandri	Honda	1'56.222
11	56	S. Nakano	Honda	1'56.306
12	7	C. Checa	Honda	1'56.609
13	71	C. Vermeulen	Suzuki	1'56.639
14	19	O. Jacque	Kawasaki	1'56.754
15	4	A. Barros	Ducati	1'56.814
16	50	S. Guintoli	Yamaha	1'57.257
17	66	A. Hofmann	Ducati	1'57.274
18	10	K. Roberts	KR211V	1'57.495
19	6	M. Tamada	Yamaha	1'58.024
20	99	J. McWilliams	Ilmor	1'59.606
21	88	A. Pitt	Ilmor	1'59.725

RACE: 22 laps = 118.360 km		
1	Casey Stoner	43'02.758 (164.975 km/h)
2	Valentino Rossi	+ 2''838
3	Dani Pedrosa	+ 8''530
4	John Hopkins	+ 9''071
5	Marco Melandri	+ 17''433
6	Colin Edwards	+ 18''647
7	Chris Vermeulen	+ 22''916
8	Nicky Hayden	+ 23''057
9	Alex Barros	+ 25''961
10	Shinya Nakano	+ 28''456
11	Alex Hofmann	+ 35''029
12	Olivier Jacque	+ 42''948
13	Kenny Roberts Jnr	+ 42''977
14	Toni Elias	+ 42''989
15	Sylvain Guintoli	+ 51''639
16	Makoto Tamada	+ 57''853

Fastest lap
Stoner, in 1'56.528 (166.208 km/h). New record.
Previous: Rossi, in 1'57.305 (165.108 km/h/2006)

Outright fastest lap
Rossi, in 1'55.002 (168.414 km/h/2007).

CHAMPIONSHIP		
1	C. Stoner	25 (1 win)
2	V. Rossi	20
3	D. Pedrosa	16
4	J. Hopkins	13
5	M. Melandri	11
6	C. Edwards	10
7	C. Vermeulen	9
8	N. Hayden	8
9	A. Barros	7
10	S. Nakano	6

IT'S LORENZO IMMEDIATELY, BUT THE ROOKIES ARE RIGHT THERE

RUNNERS AND RIDERS

With five world champions on the entry list - Lorenzo, Bautista, Luthi, Dovizioso and Locatelli - all riding works bikes, it has been clear since winter testing that the category has moved up a notch in terms of quality. It will not disappoint: five Aprilia RSWs, one Gilera (Locatelli and Simoncelli have an "LE,") and two KTMs and four Hondas all give a bit of class to the field. Everyone is on parade for this first GP, even if Simon (Honda) is still feeling the effects of his fall at Jerez, when he dislocated his left shoulder.

QUALIFYING

Coming under pressure from his fellow countrymen Barbera and Bautista and also from De Angelis and Luthi, world champion Lorenzo has to pull out all the stops to make sure of pole. In so doing, he improves on his lap time from the previous year by....2.3 seconds, something never seen before. The five Aprilias are covered by less than 9 tenths, with the opposition trailing 1.2 seconds down.

START

A super start from Luthi off the second row as he charges into the lead ahead of Lorenzo, Kallio and Dovizioso. The world champion takes the lead a bit further on and after one lap, Lorenzo has a 193 thousandths lead over the rookie. Dovizioso is third ahead of Kallio and Barbera.

LAP 3

Dovizioso catches Luthi napping, Barbera is back in touch and the four of them are covered by just 574 thousandths. Hiroshi Aoyama is a faller

LAP 4

Bautista is a faller and Barbera is now third and about to catch out Dovizioso before setting off in pursuit of his enemy Lorenzo.

LAP 6

In fifth place, De Angelis has just beaten the lap record: he is precisely 2 seconds off Luthi.

HALF-DISTANCE (10 LAPS)

The pace has seriously hotted up as, on the previous lap, the record is beaten by three riders (Lorenzo, Barbera and De Angelis; the latter having now caught up.) Lorenzo leads Barbera by 939 thousandths. Dovizioso, Luthi and De Angelis are wheel to wheel.

LAP 12

Lorenzo now leads Barbera by 1"224. De Angelis will swoop past Luthi for 3rd place.

LAP 15

Lorenzo has broken clear and there are now three of them fighting for second place: De Angelis, Barbera and Luthi.

LAP 19

Kallio retires.

FINISH (20 LAPS)

The reigning champion wanted to stamp his authority on it right from the start, showing he was not about to be caught out. He wins in superb style. Also superb was rookie Thomas Luthi, who tried everything to beat Hector Barbera in the final corner.

CHAMPIONSHIP

Four Aprilias in the top four places sets the tone. And it is already clear that it will all depend on which rider makes the least mistakes.

Sensation at the first corner: the three rookies (Luthi/12, Kallio/36 and Bautista/19) are in the lead. But Jorge Lorenzo (below) will soon take charge.

GP QATAR | 10th March 2007 | Losail | 5.380 m

STARTING GRID

1	1	J. Lorenzo	Aprilia	1'59.432
2	80	H. Barberá	Aprilia	1'59.782
3	3	A. De Angelis	Aprilia	1'59.871
4	19	A. Bautista	Aprilia	2'00.127
5	12	T. Lüthi	Aprilia	2'00.316
6	4	H. Aoyama	KTM	2'00.700
7	34	A. Dovizioso	Honda	2'00.702
8	36	M. Kallio	KTM	2'00.721
9	55	Y. Takahashi	Honda	2'00.801
10	60	J. Simón	Honda	2'01.087
11	15	R. Locatelli	Gilera	2'01.216
12	58	M. Simoncelli	Gilera	2'01.368
13	73	S. Aoyama	Honda	2'01.554
14	32	F. Lai	Aprilia	2'01.614
15	9	A. Tizón	Aprilia	2'02.504
16	41	A. Espargaro	Aprilia	2'02.525
17	14	A. West	Aprilia	2'02.733
18	28	D. Heidolf	Aprilia	2'02.954
19	10	I. Toth	Aprilia	2'02.962
20	25	A. Baldolini	Aprilia	2'02.968
21	17	K. Abraham	Aprilia	2'03.228
22	8	R. Wilairot	Honda	2'03.326
23	16	J. Cluzel	Aprilia	2'03.911
24	50	E. Laverty	Honda	2'04.411
25	44	T. Sekiguchi	Aprilia	2'04.878

RACE: 20 laps = 107.600 km

1	Jorge Lorenzo	40'23.753 (159.181 km/h)
2	Alex De Angelis	+ 1"224
3	Hector Barberá	+ 2"911
4	Thomas Lüthi	+ 3"234
5	Andrea Dovizioso	+ 12"698
6	Roberto Locatelli	+ 21"568
7	Yuki Takahashi	+ 31"540
8	Julian Simón	+ 40"467
9	Marco Simoncelli	+ 46"192
10	Shuhei Aoyama	+ 58"678
11	Aleix Espargaro	+ 1'02.762
12	Fabrizio Lai	+ 1'07.715
13	Anthony West	+ 1'10.622
14	Ratthapark Wilairot	+ 1'11.594
15	Dirk Heidolf	+ 1'12.499
16	Jules Cluzel	+ 1'23.751
17	Alex Baldolini	+ 1'33.143
18	Eugene Laverty	+ 1'38.458
19	Imre Toth	+ 1'38.548

Fastest lap
De Angelis, in 2'00.121 (161.237 km/h). New record.
Previous: De Angelis, in 2'03.015 (157.444 km/h/2004).

Outright fastest lap
Lorenzo, in 1'59.432 (162.167 km/h/2007).

CHAMPIONSHIP

1	J. Lorenzo	25 (1 win)
2	A. De Angelis	20
3	H. Barberá	16
4	T. Lüthi	13
5	A. Dovizioso	11
6	R. Locatelli	10
7	Y. Takahashi	9
8.	J. Simón	8
9	M. Simoncelli	7
10	S. Aoyama	6

73 THOUSANDTHS BETWEEN FAUBEL AND TALMACSI: WHAT YOU CALL TEAM WORK?

RUNNERS AND RIDERS
There are now only 32 riders entered for the entire championship and there are no more reigning champions, as the last two, Luthi and Bautista, have taken the plunge in the 250s. One rider missing, injured for this first GP, Italy's Stefano Musco

QUALIFYING
The question was whether or not the Aprilias and their Spanish clones, entered under the Derbi name, would still be the dominant force. The answer was yes. The bikes from Noale swamp the top six places on the grid, ahead of Koyama's KTM and the first Honda, in the hands of Rabat. In the heart of the current champion team, the one managed by Jorge "Aspar" Martinez, Talmacsi and his RSW has beaten his team-mate Faubel on the RSA.

START
It's a romp for the "Aspar" boys, with Gadea, Faubel and Talmacsi shooting into the lead ahead of De Rosa and Pasini. Crossing the line for the first time, Faubel has managed himself a 7 tenths advantage over the first bunch of pursuers; Gadea, Pasini and Talmacsi.

LAP 2
Worries for Pasini whose engine is cutting out down the straight. Faubel now leads by 1.633.

LAP 4
Pasini is only sixteenth, while Faubel maintains a lead of almost 2 seconds over Talmacsi with De Rosa a brilliant third.

LAP 6
Pesek has passed De Rosa for third place. Pasini pits only to rejoin for a few more laps.

HALF-DISTANCE (9 LAPS)
The positions seemed fixed: 1"508 between Faubel and Talmacsi. Fighting for third, Pesek and De Rosa are wheel to wheel, but over 9 seconds behind. In seventh place, Rabat is the best Honda rider in a pack where it is nice to see the Frenchman Masbou.

LAP 12
Talmacsi has closed to within 9 tenths of his team-mate and leader. Gadea is also having big problems down the straight and is only 18th.

LAP 14
Talmacsi has just taken the lead. Is it a tactical move or the start of problems for the third and last of the Aprilia riders still on the pace with the RSA version and its superior rotary disc? Gadea pits.

LAP 16
Faubel retakes the lead.

FINISH (18 LAPS)
71 thousandths going into the final lap; Talmacsi gets by shortly afterwards, but Faubel has the last word thanks to the power of his RSA when slipstreaming. It is his third GP win, but above all it is the continuing dominance in this category of the Jorge Martinez squad.

CHAMPIONSHIP
Of course, the result of this first GP also provides the championship order where one can already pick out two favourites - Pasini and Gadea - and they have already played a joker.

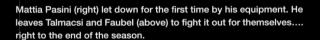

Mattia Pasini (right) let down for the first time by his equipment. He leaves Talmacsi and Faubel (above) to fight it out for themselves.... right to the end of the season.

GP QATAR | 10th March 2007 | Losail | 5.380 m

STARTING GRID

1	14	G. Talmacsi	Aprilia	2'06.011
2	55	H. Faubel	Aprilia	2'06.091
3	75	M. Pasini	Aprilia	2'06.135
4	52	L. Pesek	Derbi	2'06.767
5	35	R. De Rosa	Aprilia	2'07.130
6	33	S. Gadea	Aprilia	2'07.139
7	71	T. Koyama	KTM	2'07.207
8	12	E. Rabat	Honda	2'07.275
9	38	B. Smith	Honda	2'07.348
10	24	S. Corsi	Aprilia	2'07.525
11	22	P. Nieto	Aprilia	2'07.865
12	44	P. Espargaro	Aprilia	2'07.987
13	60	M. Ranseder	Derbi	2'07.992
14	29	A. Iannone	Aprilia	2'08.048
15	7	A. Masbou	Honda	2'08.081
16	27	S. Bianco	Aprilia	2'08.236
17	34	R. Krummenacher	KTM	2'08.294
18	63	M. Di Meglio	Honda	2'08.360
19	18	N. Terol	Derbi	2'08.419
20	6	J. Olive	Aprilia	2'08.552
21	11	S. Cortese	Aprilia	2'08.662
22	15	F. Sandi	Aprilia	2'08.753
23	53	S. Grotzkyj	Aprilia	2'08.873
24	95	R. Muresan	Derbi	2'09.903
25	37	J. Litjens	Honda	2'10.112
26	99	D. Webb	Honda	2'10.238
27	77	D. Aegerter	Aprilia	2'10.324
28	8	L. Zanetti	Aprilia	2'10.388
29	51	S. Bonsey	KTM	2'10.614
30	20	R. Tamburini	Aprilia	2'12.387
31	56	H. Van Den Berg	Aprilia	2'14.125

RACE: 20 laps = 96.840 km

1	Hector Faubel	38'12.029 (152.102 km/h)
2	Gabor Talmacsi	+ 0''073
3	Lukas Pesek	+ 17''499
4	Raffaele De Rosa	+ 17''754
5	Simone Corsi	+ 25''642
6	Tomoyoshi Koyama	+ 25''877
7	Pol Espargaro	+ 28''437
8	Esteve Rabat	+ 28''527
9	Pablo Nieto	+ 28''708
10	Alexis Masbou	+ 33''669
11	Joan Olivé	+ 40''665
12	Bradley Smith	+ 40''679
13	Michael Ranseder	+ 40''915
14	Mike Di Meglio	+ 41''671
15	Andrea Iannone	+ 41''764
16	Nicolas Terol	+ 48''643
17	Sandro Cortese	+ 48''656
18	Lorenzo Zanetti	+ 48''858
19	Randy Krummenacher	+ 1'03.160
20	Dominique Aegerter	+ 1'23.074
21	Joey Litjens	+ 1'23.147
22	Steve Bonsey	+ 1'31.521
23	Roberto Tamburini	+ 1'59.152
24	Hugo Van Den Berg	+ 2'00.040

Fastest lap
Talmacsi, in 2'06.267 (153.389 km/h). New record.
Previous: Bautistá, in 2'08.591 (150.617 km/h/2006).

Outright fastest lap
Talmacsi, in 2'06.011 (153.700 km/h/2007).

CHAMPIONSHIP

1	H. Faubel	25 (1 win)
2	G. Talmacsi	20
3	L. Pesek	16
4	R. De Rosa	13
5	S. Corsi	11
6	T. Koyama	10
7	P. Espargaro	9
8	E. Rabat	8
9	P. Nieto	7
10	A. Masbou	6

A Yamaha charges through the Andalusian countryside: Rossi is back.

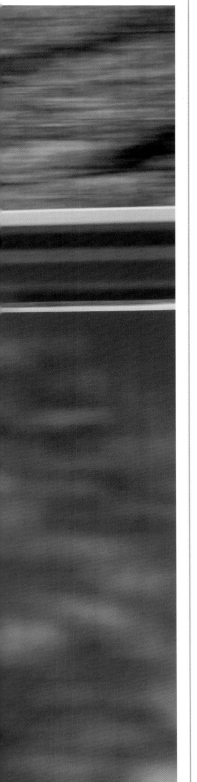

ROSSI IMMEDIATELY
TAKES CHARGE AGAIN

BEATEN IN TERMS OF TOP SPEED IN
QATAR, VALENTINO ROSSI KNEW THAT
THE JEREZ TRACK WOULD SUIT HIM
BETTER. HE HELPED HIMSELF TO THE
LEAD IN THE CHAMPIONSHIP FOR THE
ONLY TIME THIS SEASON.

THE RACE

WHEN ROSSI SCORE A "STRIKE"

Before tasting the champagne, Rossi pulls off the perfect strike, unaware that Stoner will be back on his feet very soon.

Emilio Perez de Rozas is a little man with a piercing voice, a well groomed beard and an acerbic wit. This Spanish journalist from the "Periodico de Catalunya" has a speciality which is to spend his Sundays teasing his Italian colleagues each time one of his fellow countrymen wins, shouting and waving his arms around.

It has to be said that for several years now, Italy and Spain have been the dominant force in GP racing, as is the case on this first weekend of the European season, with 41 of the 83 riders taking part coming from one of these two countries. Sure enough, there was a Spanish victory courtesy of Lorenzo in 250, an Italian win for Rossi in MotoGP and it is also worth adding that Hungary's Talmacsi won the 125 race on an Italian machine run by a Spanish team!

All this serves as a preamble to the fact that the ebullient Emilio, convinced that "his" Dani Pedrosa was going to teach Valentino Rossi a lesion, is looking a bit down in the dumps on this sunny Sunday evening. "There'll be no world title this year," he says while Rossi goes mad at the side of the track, as Pedrosa comes back to his pits his head hung low. Back on the circuit, at the foot of one of the overheated grandstands, Valentino lined up some members of his fan club, dressed up as skittles. He took up a pose and threw an imaginary bowling ball to record the perfect strike. "When you have the right tools, it's much easier!" he says, before admitting that it was while watching a game of American Football

that, along with his friends, he came up with this scenario for his first win of the season.

On track, Rossi ran the race from the front and when he picked up the pace it seemed as though Pedrosa was left stuck to the spot. Master Valentino, beaten in Qatar two weeks earlier, was keen to remind everyone as soon as possible that he intended remaining the master of the game. He did the necessary so that those who felt the Rossi-Yamaha combo was not necessarily unbeatable this season, should calm their ardour.

That's the way he is, this lad who will make his mark for all time on the sport of motorcycling: for him, every defeat is transformed into a new challenge. Last year, it was ever so slightly his own fault (Valencia) but mainly through the fact that in the early part of the season his Yamaha M1 was not up to the level of the opposition that Rossi had to hand over his title. And, as he abhors defeat, he set off even more motivated than ever, determined to take back what was rightfully his.

But there it was, in the season opener, on the straight at the Doha circuit, he was powerless against the speed and incredible power of the new Ducati. Beaten again, but beaten once again without his immense talent coming under scrutiny, "Vale" knew that on a track like Jerez de la Frontera, he could reset the clocks. Pedrosa believed he would have the legs of him, but he was wrong. Much to the chagrin of Emilio Perez de Rozas, no, the title would not come his way this year!

ROSSI FENDS OFF PEDROSA. IN FIFTH, STONER SOON REALISED IT SOMETIMES PAYS TO STAY COOL.

RUNNERS AND RIDERS

It had been on the cards for several months now: the Ilmor adventure is already over, due to lack of sponsorship. "In Formula 1, with Mercedes, when I needed an extra 4 or 5 million, all I had to do was ask, but here, I found nothing," admitted Mario Illien a few days after the Qatar GP. However, it is common knowledge that the Swiss engine man had embarked on this project with a view to convincing someone - Kawasaki - to come on board, except that this dream partner has managed to get by on its own. A third Suzuki is on track, in the hands of test rider Kousuke Akiyoshi.

QUALIFYING

One month earlier, Valentino Rossi had left Jerez de la Frontera the richer by one BMW M5 Coupe, and the outright fastest lap in the history of the Andalusian circuit. Beaten in the dress rehearsal for the championship, here, Dani Pedrosa takes a superb revenge by 51 thousandths of a second. Looking very comfortable since the start of the season, Carlos Checa completes the front row.

START

A perfect start from Pedrosa, ahead of Rossi, Edwards, Checa, Hayden and Stoner. Rossi takes charge a bit further on and rattles off the opening lap with a lead of 195 thousandths over Pedrosa. Hofmann pits and gets going again a bit later.

LAP 4

Rossi, Pedrosa and Edwards are covered by less than 4 tenths. Hayden and Hopkins are not far off, while there's a scrap for sixth spot involving Checa, Melandri, Stoner and Elias.

LAP 5

Alex Hofmann is shown the black flag.

LAP 6

Rossi has upped the pace: he now leads Pedrosa by 682 thousandths.

LAP 11

Elias catches Stoner. At the front, the gap between Rossi and Pedrosa remains unchanged.

HALF-DISTANCE (13 LAPS)

One second separates the two top men in the category. Edwards is third, 3 seconds down. Hayden still controls Hopkins and will soon have to deal with Elias who is coming back fast.

LAP 17

Hopkins passes Hayden and falls a bit further on. Rossi's lead is now 2"512 and so it seems the game is over. Elias has just scalped the world champion to go fourth.

LAP 20

For the past three laps, Stoner has been the fastest man on track. He passes Hayden to go fifth.

LAP 22

The reigning champion drops another place as Checa has just passed Hayden.

FINISH (27 LAPS)

Rossi has rediscovered the sweet smell of success, which had eluded him since 10th September 2006, in Sepang, Malaysia.

CHAMPIONSHIP

45 points out of a possible 50, the moto king has a 9 point lead over Stoner and Pedrosa and 19 over Edwards.

The old Rossi is back, Hopkins hits the deck and De Puniet still holding off Capirossi: the race in three images.

GP SPAIN | 24th March 2007 | Jerez | 4.423 m

STARTING GRID

1	26	D. Pedrosa	Honda	1'39.402
2	46	V. Rossi	Yamaha	1'39.453
3	7	C. Checa	Honda	1'39.460
4	5	C. Edwards	Yamaha	1'39.486
5	27	C. Stoner	Ducati	1'39.524
6	21	J. Hopkins	Suzuki	1'39.625
7	56	S. Nakano	Honda	1'39.632
8	24	T. Elias	Honda	1'39.660
9	33	M. Melandri	Honda	1'39.722
10	10	K. Roberts	KR211V	1'39.727
11	69	N. Hayden	Honda	1'39.834
12	14	R. De Puniet	Kawasaki	1'39.883
13	4	A. Barros	Ducati	1'40.196
14	71	C. Vermeulen	Suzuki	1'40.328
15	65	L. Capirossi	Ducati	1'40.391
16	19	O. Jacque	Kawasaki	1'40.405
17	6	M. Tamada	Yamaha	1'40.617
18	66	A. Hofmann	Ducati	1'40.710
19	64	K. Akiyoshi	Suzuki	1'41.202
20	50	S. Guintoli	Yamaha	1'41.219

RACE: 27 laps = 119.421 km

1	Valentino Rossi	45'53.340 (156.143 km/h)
2	Dani Pedrosa	+ 1''246
3	Colin Edwards	+ 2''701
4	Toni Elias	+ 4''351
5	Casey Stoner	+ 4''993
6	Carlos Checa	+ 10''000
7	Nicky Hayden	+ 14''146
8	Marco Melandri	+ 19''969
9	Chris Vermeulen	+ 24''786
10	Shinya Nakano	+ 24''955
11	Alex Barros	+ 25''008
12	Loris Capirossi	+ 25''852
13	Randy De Puniet	+ 26''445
14	Makoto Tamada	+ 36''653
15	Sylvain Guintoli	+ 36''744
16	Kenny Roberts Jnr	+ 48''911
17	Kousuke Akiyoshi	+ 50''784
18	Olivier Jacque	+ 1'00.901
19	John Hopkins	+ 1'03.371

Fastest lap

Rossi, in 1'40.905 (157.799 km/h).
Record: Rossi, in 1'40.596 (158.284 km/h/2005).

Outright fastest lap

Capirossi, in 1'39.064 (160.732 km/h/2006).

CHAMPIONSHIP

1	V. Rossi	45 (1 win)
2	C. Stoner	36 (1 win)
3	D. Pedrosa	36
4	C. Edwards	26
5	M. Melandri	19
6	N. Hayden	17
7	C. Vermeulen	16
8	T. Elias	15
9	J. Hopkins	13
10	A. Barros	12

STILL LORENZO, BUT BAUTISTA FOUGHT TO THE VERY END.

RUNNERS AND RIDERS

Hiroshi Aoyama, who broke the little finger on his right hand when he fell at Losail, is first announced as a no-show, but he turns up as usual. There are three wild cards, including one for Alex Debon, Aprilia's development rider.

QUALIFYING

Lorenzo still rules the roost and to prove it, on Friday, Simoncelli, his closest pursuer is almost a second down. On Saturday, Barbera closes to three tenths, by hanging onto the champion's back wheel. But the major news is all about Locatelli's terrible crash at the end of Saturday morning's free practice. The former world champion's Gilera 125 piled into a wall and Locatelli is picked up with his left ankle in a pitiful state, a broken left collar bone, but most importantly, injuries to the skull, face and vertebrae.

START

Lorenzo, Dovizioso and Barbera swerve off into the lead. Simoncelli does not go far as he falls, while Dovizioso pulls offa great move down the inside of Lorenzo. Crossing the line for the first time, the Honda rider has a lead of 260 thousandths over Barbera and 443 over Lorenzo. A gap has already grown as Bautista is 1.2 seconds off the world champion.

LAP 6

Bautista has closed on the leaders, so there are now four of them (Dovizioso, Lorenza, Barbera and Bautista) within 1"318. De Angelis is not far behind and Luthi leads the group that is

Gran Premio bwin.com de España
Jerez 2007

Lorenzo (above) jumps for joy, but Alvaro Bautista, the reigning 125 champion, was the man of the weekend, going the distance with Lorenzo and Dovizioso. And yet, in terms of concentration, he had been spared nothing on the grid.

scrapping over sixth place.

LAP 7

Luthi stops in the gravel trap, with a seized engine.

LAP 9

Bautista ambushes Lorenzo.

LAP 10

An on form Bautista is second!

HALF-DISTANCE (13 LAPS)

Bautista has taken the lead one lap earlier and has 182 thousandths in hand over Dovizioso, who is followed by Barbera, Lorenzo and De Angelis. Simon has just fallen.

LAP 15

Dovizioso takes back the lead. Lorenzo is third, going at it hammer and tongs with Barbera.

LAP 16

Barbera falls.

LAP 17

Lorenzo retakes what he assumes is his rightful place, namely first place.

LAP 18

It's getting crazy out there. Lorenzo, Dovizioso and Bautista all hit the braking area together and it's the reigning 125 champion who retakes the lead.

LAP 20

Retirement for Kallio.

LAP 23

Lorenzo has taken control again and manages to step up the pace. As a result, Bautista and Dovizioso are now 8 tenths behind.

FINISH (26 LAPS)

Grandiose is the only word to describe the three way scrap between Bautista's panache, Dovizioso's courage and Lorenzo's intelligence.

CHAMPIONSHIP

Two races, two wins, 50 points add up to an ideal start for Lorenzo. De Angelis is already trailing by 17 points and Dovizioso is 23 down.

GP SPAIN | 24th March 2007 | Jerez | 4.423 m

STARTING GRID

1	1	J. Lorenzo	Aprilia	1'43.099
2	80	H. Barberá	Aprilia	1'43.383
3	60	J. Simón	Honda	1'43.707
4	34	A. Dovizioso	Honda	1'43.764
5	19	A. Bautistá	Aprilia	1'43.955
6	58	M. Simoncelli	Gilera	1'44.096
7	15	R. Locatelli	Gilera	1'44.116 (*)
8	73	S. Aoyama	Honda	1'44.174
9	6	A. Debón	Aprilia	1'44.185
10	12	T. Lüthi	Aprilia	1'44.200
11	36	M. Kallio	KTM	1'44.221
12	32	F. Lai	Aprilia	1'44.329
13	3	A. De Angelis	Aprilia	1'44.358
14	4	H. Aoyama	KTM	1'44.469
15	55	Y. Takahashi	Honda	1'44.994
16	14	A. West	Aprilia	1'45.307
17	41	A. Espargaro	Aprilia	1'45.589
18	28	D. Heidolf	Aprilia	1'45.621
19	8	R. Wilairot	Honda	1'45.876
20	31	A. Molina	Aprilia	1'45.934
21	10	I. Toth	Aprilia	1'46.268
22	17	K. Abraham	Aprilia	1'46.542
23	25	A. Baldolini	Aprilia	1'47.030
24	44	T. Sekiguchi	Aprilia	1'47.239
25	50	E. Laverty	Honda	1'47.280
26	16	J. Cluzel	Aprilia	1'47.362
27	9	A. Tizón	Aprilia	1'47.545
28	53	S. Barragan	Honda	1'48.683

(*): Seriously injured on Saturday during the very last qualifying lap, the 125cc former world champion had to withdraw.

RACE: 26 laps = 114.998 km

1	Jorge Lorenzo	45'35.846 (151.321 km/h)	
2	Alvaro Bautistá	+ 0''218	
3	Andrea Dovizioso	+ 0''478	
4	Alex De Angelis	+ 8''156	
5	Alex Debón	+ 14''747	
6	Hiroshi Aoyama	+ 15''045	
7	Shuhei Aoyama	+ 17''918	
8	Yuki Takahashi	+ 28''438	
9	Anthony West	+ 39''435	
10	Dirk Heidolf	+ 1'02.689	
11	Fabrizio Lai	+ 1'06.813	
12	Ratthapark Wilairot	+ 1'07.166	
13	Alex Baldolini	+ 1'07.371	
14	Eugene Laverty	+ 1'11.793	
15	Karel Abraham	+ 1'13.896	
16	Jules Cluzel	+ 1'32.684	
17	Taro Sekiguchi	+ 1'33.041	
18	Imre Toth	+ 1 lap	

Fastest lap

De Angelis, in 1'44.295 (152.670 km/h). New record.
Previous: Kato, in 1'44.444 (152.452 km/h/2001)

Outright fastest lap

Pedrosa, in 1'42.868 (154.788 km/h/2005).

CHAMPIONSHIP

1	J. Lorenzo	50 (2 wins)
2	A. De Angelis	33
3	A. Dovizioso	27
4	A. Bautistá	20
5	Y. Takahashi	17
6	H. Barberá	16
7	S. Aoyama	15
8	T. Lüthi	13
9	A. Debón	11
10	H. Aoyama	10

TALMACSI WINS AT HIS MAIN RIVAL'S HOME TRACK

RUNNERS AND RIDERS
There have been changes, at least in terms of the name of some teams. That in turn means that there has been a change to the way they are financed. Thus it's a case of exit Humangest and the Scot team goes back to its original name. Stefano Musco is absent and Dino Lombardi has yet to replace him officially as he is the recipient of a wild card, along with three Spanish riders. As for Arie Molenaar, he has renamed his team "De Graff Grand Prix" in honour of his main sponsor.

QUALIFYING
Mattia Pasini (Aprilia RSA) confirms he is the quickest man in the category at this early point in the season, as indeed he was during winter testing. He sets the fastest time on both Friday and Saturday and takes another pole. The Hondas are still struggling, with Smith eleventh, while Di Meglio has a heavy fall and gets up with a broken left collar bone.

START
Pasini breaks down on the warm-up lap and starts on his second bike, but from the last slot on the grid. Talmacsi gets the hole shot ahead of Espargaro, Koyama and Pesek. Rabat fails to complete the opening lap, which Talmacsi completes it with a 902 thousandth lead over Espargaro. Pasini is already tenth.

LAP 2
Smith and Pasini are fallers, the latter getting back in the saddle but getting no further than pit lane.

LAP 3
Corsi falls.

HALF DISTANCE (12 LAPS)
Pesek has closed to within 8 tenths of Talmacsi who has led the race since the first corner. Faubel is around 5 seconds further back, all alone in third spot. Alexis Masbou falls while in thirteenth place.

LAP 14
Pesek has got even closer to Talmacsi (254 thousandths.)

LAP 20
Koyama is a faller, having been fourth on the KTM.

FINISH (23 LAPS)
Pesek has closed to 205 thousandths going into the last lap and the Czech passes the Hungarian with a stunning move in the braking area, but Talmacsi gets better drive out of the final corner and wins by 14 thousandths. Once again it is a total triumph for Piaggio technology, as the Aprilia and Derbi riders camp out in the top twelve places! The best of the rest is a nice surprise in the shape of the very young American, Steve Bonsey (KTM,) who thus scores his first world championship points.

CHAMPIONSHIP
Talmacsi kills two birds with one stone, as he takes the lead in the world championship, with a four point lead over his team-mate Faubel and Qatar GP winner Pesek who is third, nine lengths back, in a points table which still does not feature the name of Mattia Pasini.

Talmacsi takes his first win of the season by 14 thousandths (left, the finish between Pesek and the Hungarian.) Krummenacher (right) got a fright in qualifying.

GP SPAIN | 24th March 2007| Jerez | 4.423 m

STARTING GRID

1	75	M. Pasini	Aprilia	1'47.245
2	14	G. Talmacsi	Aprilia	1'47.483
3	52	L. Pesek	Derbi	1'47.485
4	33	S. Gadea	Aprilia	1'47.670
5	55	H. Faubel	Aprilia	1'47.727
6	71	T. Koyama	KTM	1'47.791
7	44	P. Espargaro	Aprilia	1'48.030
8	24	S. Corsi	Aprilia	1'48.115
9	22	P. Nieto	Aprilia	1'48.153
10	11	S. Cortese	Aprilia	1'48.435
11	38	B. Smith	Honda	1'48.499
12	35	R. De Rosa	Aprilia	1'48.642
13	60	M. Ranseder	Derbi	1'48.831
14	6	J. Olivé	Aprilia	1'48.943
15	29	A. Iannone	Aprilia	1'49.007
16	7	A. Masbou	Honda	1'49.056
17	8	L. Zanetti	Aprilia	1'49.316
18	30	P. Tutusaus	Aprilia	1'49.375
19	12	E. Rabat	Honda	1'49.460
20	63	M. Di Meglio	Honda	1'49.607
21	15	F. Sandi	Aprilia	1'49.793
22	27	S. Bianco	Aprilia	1'49.914
23	18	N. Terol	Derbi	1'50.026
24	34	R. Krummenacher	KTM	1'50.269
25	53	S. Grotzkyj	Aprilia	1'50.367
26	51	S. Bonsey	KTM	1'50.396
27	56	H. Van Den Berg	Aprilia	1'50.724
28	76	I. Maestro	Honda	1'50.894
29	95	R. Muresan	Derbi	1'50.905
30	99	D. Webb	Honda	1'51.046
31	37	J. Litjens	Honda	1'51.220
32	13	D. Lombardi	Honda	1'51.230
33	77	D. Aegerter	Aprilia	1'51.349
34	78	D. Saez	Aprilia	1'51.871
35	20	R. Tamburini	Aprilia	1'52.243

RACE: 23 laps = 101.729 km

1	Gabor Talmacsi		41'52.149 (145.781 km/h)
2	Lukas Pesek		+ 0''014
3	Hector Faubel		+ 5''720
4	Pol Espargaro		+ 6''489
5	Sergio Gadea		+ 6''867
6	Pablo Nieto		+ 9''219
7	Sandro Cortese		+ 19''078
8	Joan Olivé		+ 19''133
9	Michael Ranseder		+ 19''664
10	Lorenzo Zanetti		+ 28''434
11	Stefano Bianco		+ 28''815
12	Andrea Iannone		+ 28''816
13	Steve Bonsey		+ 43''699
14	Nicolas Terol		+ 46''436
15	Simone Grotzkyj		+ 48''081
16	Peré Tususaus		+ 48''579
17	Randy Krummenacher		+ 51''253
18	Robert Muresan		+ 52''160
19	Dominique Aegerter		+ 1'11.825
20	Hugo Van Den Berg		+ 1'13.134
21	Joey Litjens		+ 1'20.289
22	Ivan Maestro		+ 1'23.752
23	Dino Lombardi		+ 1'28.888
24	Daniel Saez		+ 1'31.676
25	Roberto Tamburini		+ 1'45.176
26	Bradley Smith		+ 1'45.208

Fastest lap
Talmacsi, in 1'47.976 (147.466 km/h).
Record: Pesek, in 1'47.404 (148.251 km/h/2006).

Outright fastest lap
Pasini, in 1'46.937 (148.898 km/h/2006).

CHAMPIONSHIP

1	G. Talmacsi	45 (1 win)
2	H. Faubel	41 (1 win)
3	L. Pesek	36
4	P. Espargaro	22
5	P. Nieto	17
6	R. De Rosa	13
7	J. Olivé	13
8	S. Gadea	11
9	S. Corsi	11
10	T. Koyama	10

Perfect on the brakes, in an equally perfect race: the Stoner-Bridgestone combo confirmed its form in Istanbul.

TIRED,
OF TYRES...

IT HAD BEEN ON THE CARDS AND
NOW IT'S CONFIRMED: THE 2007
CHAMPIONSHIP WOULD BE ALL
ABOUT TYRES

THE RACE

ROSSI: A RUBBERY TALE.

The sun was a perfect red sphere but it did not hang around before going to bed, hiding behind the hills that border the Bosphorus. The roads that run through Istanbul are hellish and particularly so on this Sunday night. Valentino Rossi has neither the time still less the inclination to admire the scenery, to experience the daily routine of millions of Turks. It is a Sunday that "Vale" would like to forget as soon as possible. Why? Because the seven times world champion is angry. He is angrier than ever, feeling a bit like a soldier who has been betrayed by his superiors. Was it betrayal? No, but it was a tough and painful new blow in the 2007 tyre war. Because the tyres are the real story of this championship that is playing itself out so differently to its predecessors. Tyre wars in

Istanbul? You bet! The Bridgestone riders began by dominating Friday practice with "race" tyres, when only Rossi managed to get his Yamaha M1 amongst the opposition. But then on Saturday, the Michelin men regained the upper ground with the qualifying tyres. What would the scenario be come the race? Certainly no one could have guessed that it would have turned into a veritable massacre for Rossi and his fellow riders shod by the French tyre manufacturer.

What is going on? As in all important tales, quite a lot actually.

The proof…

Olivier Jacque's mistake. Episode one: at the end of the first lap in the braking zone at the end of the straight. Olivier Jacque, possibly nudged by Pedrosa,

tries a suicidal move. As he falls, he takes Rossi's shotgun man Edwards with him, as well as Pedrosa and Vermeulen.

The Ducati carnival. Out in front, Stoner and his red Ducati could not ask for more. The little Australian shot off into the distance, while Rossi briefly tried to fight back, but he was ever more hesitant with every passing lap. Something was not quite right on the lovely number 46 bike and "Vale" was to gradually slip down the order, swallowed by the others, who under normal circumstances hardly dare look him in the eye.

A Bridgestone triumph. Bridgestone gets a royal flush as Stoner finds himself leading the championship for a second time this season and it seems that something very important has just taken place.

Faulty construction. What is going on? The rear tyre in question has immediately been taken back by the Michelin engineers for analysis at Clermont-Ferrand. Immediately after the race on Sunday night at the Turkish GP, a faulty construction was the number one suspect. "I am very angry, because all the work we did over the past two days has been for nothing. Right from the start, I had a strange feeling and in the final laps, I quite simply didn't dare try anything," said Rossi. He was the dejected victim of a problem that was not of his own making.

The lesson? With the change of rules relating to tyres, limiting the number of slicks, the tyre manufacturers' work would be even more important than usual this season. In fact it could well be decisive.

Livio Suppo, the Marlboro-Ducati team manager had good reason to smile, with both his riders on the podium. Rossi (below) can only scowl. Elias and Capirossi are catching him and his descent into hell is not yet over.

SIX BRIDGESTONE RIDERS IN THE TOP SIX.

RUNNER AND RIDERS

No changes, apart from on the family front, as Loris Capirossi has become a dad, after wife Ingrid gave birth to little Ricardo in early April.

QUALIFYING

Tyres are playing an ever more important role. On the first day of practice, seven of the top eight are Bridgestone runners, with Rossi the only man capable of mixing it with the opposition. But on Saturday, with qualifying rubber, Michelin does the triple with the two Yamahas of Rossi and Edwards ahead of Pedrosa.

START

Rossi, Edwards, Stoner and Capirossi lead away, but the Texan cannot fend off the two red rockets for long, nor Hopkins shortly afterwards. Rossi goes off on the grass but stays upright. Braking at the end of the main straight, Jacque provokes a multiple pile-up that claims Edwards, Pedrosa, Vermeulen (who would start again) and OJ himself. Out in front, the Bridgestone riders didn't bother hanging around as Stoner leads Capirossi, Hopkins, Elias and Rossi.

LAP 5

Rossi has just ambushed Elias for fourth place. One lap later, he squeezes past Hopkins in a gap not big enough for a mouse. In the lead, Stoner heads Capirossi by 1"291.

LAP 9

Rossi finds a chink in Capirossi's armour. He is 1"946 behind Stoner.

HALF-DISTANCE (11 LAPS)

Stoner has just set the fastest race lap. He has a 2"369 lead over Elias, who in turn now heads Rossi by 1"160. Just behind, Capirossi is tussling with Hopkins and Melandri.

LAP 13

One after the other, Capirossi has to give best to Hopkins and then Melandri. Stoner keeps going quicker and now leads by over three seconds.

LAP 15

Long faces in the Michelin camp: Rossi, with a failing rear tyre is passed by Hopkins, Melandri and Capirossi and he will soon give best to Barros. There are now six Bridgestone riders in the top six places.

LAP 16

Hayden passes Rossi.

LAP 18

Capirossi has pulled away from the group of riders fighting for third place. Hayden is now sixth.

LAP 20

De Puniet passes Rossi, who is now no better than ninth

LAP 21

Hofmann has passed Rossi!

FINISH (22 LAPS)

Stoner has ridden faultlessly, as indeed has a great Elias. When you learn that the Capirossi-Barros duel lit up the final lap in style, then it is clear that Bridgestone (and Ducati, with three Borgo Panigale bikes in the top four!) have been the big winners on the day.

CHAMPIONSHIP

Stoner moves back into the series lead. He is ten points ahead of Rossi and 25 in front of Pedrosa, which is the equivalent of one race win.

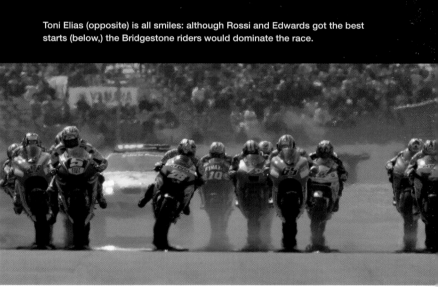

Toni Elias (opposite) is all smiles: although Rossi and Edwards got the best starts (below,) the Bridgestone riders would dominate the race.

GP TURKEY | 22nd April 2007 | Istanbul | 5.340 m

STARTING GRID

1	46	V. Rossi	Yamaha	1'52.795
2	5	C. Edwards	Yamaha	1'52.944
3	26	D. Pedrosa	Honda	1'52.971
4	27	C. Stoner	Ducati	1'53.375
5	65	L. Capirossi	Ducati	1'53.559
6	69	N. Hayden	Honda	1'53.613
7	21	J. Hopkins	Suzuki	1'53.637
8	14	R. De Puniet	Kawasaki	1'53.706
9	71	C. Vermeulen	Suzuki	1'53.771
10	24	T. Elias	Honda	1'53.835
11	19	O. Jacque	Kawasaki	1'53.847
12	56	S. Nakano	Honda	1'53.988
13	4	A. Barros	Ducati	1'54.082
14	33	M. Melandri	Honda	1'54.143
15	6	M. Tamada	Yamaha	1'54.206
16	7	C. Checa	Honda	1'54.221
17	66	A. Hofmann	Ducati	1'54.421
18	10	K. Roberts	KR211V	1'54.527
19	50	S. Guintoli	Yamaha	1'54.845

RACE: 22 laps = 117.480 km

1	Casey Stoner	42'02''850 (167.638 km/h)	
2	Toni Elias	+ 6''207	
3	Loris Capirossi	+ 8''102	
4	Alex Barros	+ 8''135	
5	Marco Melandri	+ 8''289	
6	John Hopkins	+ 10''186	
7	Nicky Hayden	+ 10''239	
8	Randy De Puniet	+ 14''734	
9	Alex Hofmann	+ 16''042	
10	Valentino Rossi	+ 18''999	
11	Chris Vermeulen	+ 26''249	
12	Carlos Checa	+ 29''546	
13	Shinya Nakano	+ 36''922	
14	Makoto Tamada	+ 38''540	
15	Sylvain Guintoli	+ 39''337	
16	Kenny Roberts Jnr	+ 1'09.336	

Fastest lap

Vermeulen, in 1'54.026 (168.593 km/h).
Record: Elias, in 1'52.877 (170.309 km/h/2006).

Outright fastest lap

Gibernau, in 1'52.334 (171.132 km/h/2005).

CHAMPIONSHIP

1	C. Stoner	61 (2 wins)
2	V. Rossi	55 (1 win)
3	D. Pedrosa	36
4	T. Elias	35
5	M. Melandri	30
6	C. Edwards	26
7	N. Hayden	26
8	A. Barros	25
9	J. Hopkins	23
10	C. Vermeulen	21

Dovizioso (right) has no reason to sulk as he has just won a superb duel with Lorenzo. The rookies make their mark, with Bautista third, while Luthi had the temerity to dive underneath the reigning champion early in the race.

ALWAYS AMAZING, ANDREA DOVIZIOSO BEATS JORGE LORENZO.

RUNNERS AND RIDERS

One notable absentee, namely Roberto Locatelli. The Italian was seriously injured in Jerez and has been repatriated to Italy where he has undergone reconstructive surgery on his face. He left the hospital over the Easter weekend and dreams of being back in time for the Italian GP. He is not replaced

QUALIFYING

Andrea Dovizioso is on fine form and is the only man who dares give Jorge Lorenzo a fight. On his Honda, the Italian takes pole at the end of a perfect lap, having made the most of last minute traffic problems for his main rival. The two men are 9 tenths quicker than the pack who are all bunched together: 2 tenths between third placed Bautista and eighth man, Simon.

START

A great getaway from Dovizioso, ahead of Bautista and Luthi. Hiroshi Aoyama is a faller, having already hit the dirt in the warm-up. Crossing the line for the first time, Dovizioso has a 1"107 lead over the chasing pack now made up of Bautista, Lorenzo, Luthi and De Angelis.

LAP 4

Out in front, the pack has pushed itself up to Dovizioso and Bautista goes into the lead. Five of them are within 1"050: Bautista, Dovizioso, Lorenzo, Luthi and De Angelis. In sixth place, Kallio is already over 4 seconds behind.

LAP 7

Bautista and Dovizioso are separated by 290 thousandths. In third, Lorenzo has just set the fastest race lap and he is taking De Angelis and Luthi along as they try and hang onto him.

LAP 8

Simoncelli is a faller from eighth place.

HALF-DISTANCE (10 LAPS)

Dovizioso has just retaken the lead and now heads Bautista by 213 thousandths. But Lorenzo has closed to within nine tenths, with De Angelis on his back wheel. Luthi has been dropped - rear tyre problems - but he still has a substantial lead of 7"827 over his closest pursuer, Mika Kallio.

LAP 12

Another fastest lap for Lorenzo who is now just half a second off new leader Bautista.

LAP 13

Lorenzo passes his two rivals in just one move. Dovizioso hits him but no harm done.

LAP 16

Dovizioso is back in the lead again, while De Angelis is right on Bautista's wheel for third place.

FINISH (20 LAPS)

Lorenzo, Dovizioso and Bautista embark on the final lap covered by a tiny 381 thousandths. A super Dovizioso and his Honda has the last word in the confrontation with the two Aprilia-mounted Spaniards after an extraordinary final skirmish in the double uphill chicane before the chequered flag.

CHAMPIONSHIP

Lorenzo still has a solid 18 point lead over Dovizioso and is 24 ahead of De Angelis. Bautista is fourth, ahead of Barbera and Luthi, who are equal fifth.

GP TURKEY | 22nd April 2007 | Istanbul | 5.340 m

STARTING GRID

1	34	A. Dovizioso	Honda	1'57.473
2	1	J. Lorenzo	Aprilia	1'57.550
3	19	A. Bautistá	Aprilia	1'58.405
4	3	A. De Angelis	Aprilia	1'58.481
5	58	M. Simoncelli	Gilera	1'58.572
6	12	T. Lüthi	Aprilia	1'58.581
7	36	M. Kallio	KTM	1'58.588
8	60	J. Simón	Honda	1'58.649
9	4	H. Aoyama	KTM	1'58.676
10	80	H. Barberá	Aprilia	1'58.817
11	55	Y. Takahashi	Honda	1'58.906
12	73	S. Aoyama	Honda	1'59.125
13	14	A. West	Aprilia	1'59.494
14	32	F. Lai	Aprilia	1'59.798
15	41	A. Espargaro	Aprilia	1'59.889
16	16	J. Cluzel	Aprilia	2'00.572
17	8	R. Wilairot	Honda	2'01.073
18	25	A. Baldolini	Aprilia	2'01.214
19	28	D. Heidolf	Aprilia	2'01.302
20	9	A. Tizón	Aprilia	2'01.328
21	50	E. Laverty	Honda	2'01.388
22	10	I. Toth	Aprilia	2'01.455
23	44	T. Sekiguchi	Aprilia	2'01.506
24	17	K. Abraham	Aprilia	2'02.083

RACE: 20 laps = 106.800 km

1	Andrea Dovizioso	39'31.153 (162.148 km/h)
2	Jorge Lorenzo	+ 0''103
3	Alvaro Bautistá	+ 0''318
4	Alex De Angelis	+ 4''894
5	Thomas Lüthi	+ 19''755
6	Mika Kallio	+ 22''946
7	Julian Simón	+ 23''283
8	Hector Barberá	+ 47''678
9	Marco Simoncelli	+ 58''482
10	Fabrizio Lai	+ 58''734
11	Aleix Espargaro	+ 1'08.588
12	Karel Abraham	+ 1'09.032
13	Dirk Heidolf	+ 1'10.005
14	Alex Baldolini	+ 1'17.732
15	Ratthapark Wilairot	+ 1'17.732
16	Shuhei Aoyama	+ 1'28.469
17	Eugene Laverty	+ 1'49.828

Fastest lap
Dovizioso, in 1'57.815 (163.171 km/h).
Record: Pedrosa, in 1'57.595 (163.476 km/h/2005).

Outright fastest lap
De Angelis, in 1'56.930 (164.406 km/h/2005).

CHAMPIONSHIP

1	J. Lorenzo	70 (2 wins)
2	A. Dovizioso	52 (1 win)
3	A. De Angelis	46
4	A. Bautistá	36
5	H. Barberá	24
6	T. Lüthi	24
7	J. Simón	17
8	Y. Takahashi	17
9	S. Aoyama	15
10	F. Lai	15

The final battle (left) between Corsi and Olive ends in victory for the Italian. Above, the young Swiss, Dominique Aegerter (77) and opposite, the pretty Hungarian, Nikolett Kovacs, failed to qualify.

THIRD RACE
THIRD WINNER

RUNNERS AND RIDERS

Injured in Jerez (collarbone,) Frenchman Mike Di Meglio is replaced by Englishman Kevin Coghlan. Hungary can be proud because not only does its most brilliant performer, Gabor Talmacsi, arrive in Turkey as championship leader, but furthermore, two of his countryman, the charming Nikolett Kovacs and Alen Gyorfi have been given wild card entries.

QUALIFYING

His points meter still points at zero, but Mattia Pasini is definitely the quickest man in the category in this early part of the season and the Italian helped himself to another pole. A nice surprise from Simone Corsi (third,) worries for Gadea (only fifteenth) and a failure to make the time cut for Nikolett Kovacs, by a substantial 4 seconds.

START

Corsi, Faubel and Pasini are quickest away. Pasini quickly takes control of the situation and completes the opening lap with a lead of 356 thousandths over Faubel, Talmacsi, Corsi and Pesek.

LAP 2

Faubel has gone to the front, but not for long as Pasini will soon get the lead back. Bonsey is a faller but picks his bike up.

LAP 4

Pasini's run of bad luck continues as he stops at the side of the track, before rejoining thirtieth. Faubel and Talmacsi are glued together at the front.

LAP 7

Corsi is in the lead, by 449 thousandths from a group made up of Faubel, Talmacsi, Koyama and De Rosa. Pasini has moved up to 25th place.

HALF-DISTANCE (10 LAPS)

Seven riders in one second or 1"077 to be precise proves there is nothing boring about the 125s. Corsi now leads from Olive, Koyama, Faubel, De Rosa, Talmacsi and Pesek. Pasini is the fastest man on track and is back up to 19th.

LAP 12

Masbou, who had been fighting for the final point is a faller.

LAP 15

Olive has managed to craft himself a lead of 684 thousandths. There are still a group of six battling behind him.

LAP 16

De Rosa forces Faubel off onto the grass. Corsi has closed back up to the leader.

LAP 17

Olive and Corse have made the break, while Smith and Zanetti have rejoined the chasing group.

FINISH (19 LAPS)

Going into the final lap, Olive and Corse are wheel to wheel (121 thousandths.) But Corsi has the last word by 98 thousandths, to take his maiden win at the top level. Koyama is third (Faubel goes off the track,) ahead of De Rosa and Talmacsi. Pasini retires in the final moments.

CHAMPIONSHIP

With Faubel only tenth, Talmacsi finishes fifth and thus extends his lead in the championship; 9 points ahead of his team-mate and ten over Pesek. Corsi is fourth.

GP TURKEY | 22nd April 2007 | Istanbul Park | 5.340 m

STARTING GRID

1	75	M. Pasini	Aprilia	2'04.722
2	55	H. Faubel	Aprilia	2'04.951
3	24	S. Corsi	Aprilia	2'05.299
4	14	G. Talmacsi	Aprilia	2'05.372
5	52	L. Pesek	Derbi	2'05.386
6	71	T. Koyama	KTM	2'05.434
7	6	J. Olivé	Aprilia	2'05.748
8	60	M. Ranseder	Derbi	2'06.051
9	18	N. Terol	Derbi	2'06.189
10	11	S. Cortese	Aprilia	2'06.209
11	35	R. De Rosa	Aprilia	2'06.267
12	22	P. Nieto	Aprilia	2'06.400
13	38	B. Smith	Honda	2'06.408
14	8	L. Zanetti	Aprilia	2'06.464
15	33	S. Gadea	Aprilia	2'06.726
16	34	R. Krummenacher	KTM	2'06.732
17	29	A. Iannone	Aprilia	2'06.885
18	44	P. Espargaro	Aprilia	2'06.974
19	7	A. Masbou	Honda	2'07.238
20	20	R. Tamburini	Aprilia	2'07.382
21	12	E. Rabat	Honda	2'07.464
22	27	S. Bianco	Aprilia	2'07.553
23	15	F. Sandi	Aprilia	2'07.703
24	37	J. Litjens	Honda	2'07.754
25	51	S. Bonsey	KTM	2'07.838
26	53	S. Grotzkyj	Aprilia	2'08.002
27	54	K. Coghlan	Honda	2'08.311
28	95	R. Muresan	Derbi	2'08.836
29	77	D. Aegerter	Aprilia	2'08.954
30	99	D. Webb	Honda	2'09.131
31	56	H. Van Den Berg	Aprilia	2'09.632
32	13	D. Lombardi	Honda	2'09.647
33	40	A. Gyorfi	Aprilia	2'11.384
34	41	T. Siegert	Aprilia	2'12.956
Not qualified:				
	39	N. Kovacs	Honda	2'17.221

RACE: 19 laps = 101.460 km

1	Simone Corsi	40'03.557 (151.964 km/h)
2	Joan Olivé	+ 0''098
3	Tomoyoshi Koyama	+ 1''943
4	Raffaele De Rosa	+ 2''191
5	Gabor Talmacsi	+ 2''646
6	Lukas Pesek	+ 2''939
7	Lorenzo Zanetti	+ 3''119
8	Bradley Smith	+ 3''120
9	Andrea Iannone	+ 10''353
10	Hector Faubel	+ 10''842
11	Pol Espargaro	+ 14''446
12	Michael Ranseder	+ 15''421
13	Pablo Nieto	+ 15''665
14	Esteve Rabat	+ 15''870
15	Randy Krummenacher	+ 16''136
16	Nicolas Terol	+ 15''136
17	Stefano Bianco	+ 24''203
18	Roberto Tamburini	+ 33''668
19	Federico Sandi	+ 34''531
20	Joey Litjens	+ 45''615
21	Kevin Coghlan	+ 45''630
22	Robert Muresan	+ 46''162
23	Daniel Webb	+ 49''852
24	Dominique Aegerter	+ 51''982
25	Steve Bonsey	+ 1'11.252
26	Hugo Van Den Berg	+ 1'55.696
27	Tobias Siegert	+ 1 lap

Fastest lap
De Rosa, in 2'05.217 (153.525 km/h).
Record: Olivé, in 2'03.825 (155.251 km/h/2006).

Outright fastest lap
Lüthi, in 2'03.585 (155.552 km/h/2005).

CHAMPIONSHIP

1	G. Talmacsi	56 (1 win)
2	H. Faubel	47 (1 win)
3	L. Pesek	46
4	S. Corsi	36 (1 win)
5	J. Olivé	33
6	P. Espargaro	27
7	T. Koyama	26
8	R. De Rosa	26
9	P. Nieto	20
10	L. Zanetti	15

Chinese lantern show? No, but a sparky European demonstration from an Australian rider.

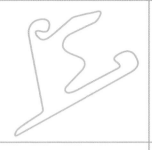

CASEY IS THE BOSS,
NO ONE ELSE, JUST CASEY

THIRD WIN IN FOUR GPS FOR THE
DUCATI RIDER: ONCE AGAIN ROSSI
TRIED EVERYTHING BUT IN VAIN.

THE RACE

ALL YOU CAN DO IS LAUGH ABOUT IT, DON'T YOU AGREE "VALE?"

Rossi is beaten, but Rossi is laughing and that is a rare enough occurrence for questions to be asked. For the second time this season, the first being the Qatar GP, the motorbike king claims he is happy to finish second. "Yes, because we knew that we would have a really tough job at these two circuits," explained the Italian. There were two simple reasons for this. Not only had the young Australian, Casey Stoner committed no mistakes whatsoever, but also his Ducati is so quick down the interminably long straights that, even for his bravest rivals, the task of beating him is on the lines of being a mission impossible.

China provided the perfect rerun of the season opener. It was an engrossing duel between Stoner and Rossi "the master" putting total pressure on his young and very straightforward rival. Little Casey lives up to his role, dishing up surprisingly pure slides as he dominates his Ducati, even through the most complex sections of the track, while getting every last drop of power out of the GP7 down the very long 1002 metre straight at the Shanghai circuit.

In those circumstances, what could Valentino Rossi try to do? "There was no way I was going to let Casey have an easy time. And as my bike was very good under braking - yes, he said the bike, but in actual fact he is the one who is good under braking! - I tried as best I could," he recalled, with a big smile on his face. He pushed it all the way to the limit and beyond and his mistake came with six laps to go. Stoner did

Stoner on a charge, Rossi (below) is not yet a pedestrian, but he's already a spectator!

not need to ask for more. "The way he has matured is amazing, when you consider how many crashes he used to have when he raced in 125s and 250s. Now, there seem to be no weak points in his repertoire and he has fought off Rossi for two whole races. It's mega," marvels a knowledgeable spectator in the shape of former 125 world champion, Switzerland's Thomas Luthi.

There is no doubt that Casey is the man of the moment, Casey the reckless lad who flew through the air in his early GP days. Stoner's parents sold everything so that they could follow him to England so that he could learn the job of being a rider. Already, back in Australia, he is compared to the all time greats. "If you want to buy tickets for Phillip Island, there's no time to lose because it's nearly sold out," said some Australian lads on Sunday night, having come to cheer on their hero and see the phenomenon in action.

Two hand to hand battles won against Rossi, a solo demonstration in Turkey and a slightly more considered race in Spain: at 21 years of age, the little blonde lad from the Antipodes was definitely a worthy leader of the world championship. And Ducati had become the marvellous new dominant force, as every time in the four events held to date, the four GP7 machines were quickest in terms of top speed in practice and the race. Faced with this superiority it had taken the sparkling talent of "Vale" Rossi and steady progress from the Hopkins-Suzuki-Bridgestone trio to ensure the racing does not become boring.

STONER PERFECT, ROSSI A GOOD LOSER AND JACQUE K.O.

RUNNERS AND RIDERS
The big news story of the week comes from the Ilmor team. As had been rumoured after the Qatar GP, Mario Ilien's project has definitely been suspended, with the staff made redundant.

QUALIFYING
Olivier Jacque is already out come Friday, after he falls and traps his forearm between the road and his Kawasaki. There are no broken bones, but a very nasty cut. Helicoptered to a hospital in Shanghai, "OJ" is already repatriated to France on Friday night. On track, it is Rossi who is the star, beating everyone by almost 9 tenths, and going 0.5 seconds quicker on his 800 than the 2006 record set on the 1000!

START
Hopkins and Rossi charge into the lead. It all goes wrong at the first corner for Elias and Barros, while Hayden has to take avoiding action in the grass. Rossi goes into the lead a bit further on, but Stoner goes with him and passes on the straight.

LAP 2
Melandri passes Rossi. At the front, Stoner has built up a lead of 461 thousandths.

LAP 4
Nakano and Tamada hit the deck. Stoner's lead is now 859 thousandths.

LAP 5
Fastest lap for Rossi who goes

Rossi, Stoner and Hopkins: three different marques on the podium. Above, the first corner was "difficult" for Elias and Barros. Opposite, O.J. pits after falling in practice, his right arm bleeding.

second again, 5 tenths behind Casey Stoner.

LAP 8
Rossi gets the upper hand, but not for long as Stoner goes by down the straight with another attack that "Vale" can do nothing about. Hopkins has shaken off Melandri and Pedrosa and is not far back.

HALF-DISTANCE (11 LAPS)
Stoner, Rossi (who is momentarily back in the lead) and Hopkins are covered by just 1"005. Pedrosa is fourth, but over 3 seconds behind the Suzuki rider.

LAP 15
The pace steps up again, as Stoner has just set the fastest race lap. Rossi trails by 360 thousandths, with Hopkins still in touch.

LAP 16
Rossi brakes late yet again, but this time he goes too far and escapes through the gravel trap. This means Stoner now has a 1"274 lead over Hopkins. Valentino is third.

LAP 18
Rossi has recaptured second place, but is up against a deficit of 2"2795 to Stoner.

LAP 19
Capirossi and Vermeulen are back in touch with Randy De Puniet for sixth place and will pass him.

FINISH (22 LAPS)
Casey Stoner has the luxury of looking over his shoulder 200 metres from the line and can see that Rossi is beaten yet again, while Hopkins is third.

CHAMPIONSHIP
A fifteen point lead for Stoner after four races and the Australian seems to be immune to making mistakes. His Bridgestone-shod Ducati is, at this point of the season, the absolute weapon of choice.

GP CHINA | 6th May 2007 | Shanghai | 5.281 m

STARTING GRID

1	46	V. Rossi	Yamaha	1'58.424
2	21	J. Hopkins	Suzuki	1'59.315
3	5	C. Edwards	Yamaha	1'59.406
4	27	C. Stoner	Ducati	1'59.516
5	26	D. Pedrosa	Honda	1'59.602
6	33	M. Melandri	Honda	1'59.863
7	14	R. De Puniet	Kawasaki	1'59.985
8	4	A. Barros	Ducati	2'00.052
9	69	N. Hayden	Honda	2'00.087
10	56	S. Nakano	Honda	2'00.157
11	66	A. Hofmann	Ducati	2'00.175
12	24	T. Elias	Honda	2'00.205
13	7	C. Checa	Honda	2'00.319
14	65	L. Capirossi	Ducati	2'00.369
15	71	C. Vermeulen	Suzuki	2'00.680
16	10	K. Roberts	KR211V	2'00.763
17	50	S. Guintoli	Yamaha	2'01.157
18	6	M. Tamada	Yamaha	2'01.178

RACE: 22 laps = 116.182 km

1	Casey Stoner	44'12''891 (157.660 km/h)
2	Valentino Rossi	+ 3''036
3	John Hopkins	+ 6''663
4	Daniel Pedrosa	+ 14''090
5	Marco Melandri	+ 17''276
6	Loris Capirossi	+ 26''256
7	Chris Vermeulen	+ 26''501
8	Randy De Puniet	+ 27''025
9	Alex Hofmann	+ 28''108
10	Carlos Checa	+ 32''957
11	Colin Edwards	+ 35''053
12	Nicky Hayden	+ 37''327
13	Sylvain Guintoli	+ 50''705
14	Alex Barros	+ 55''264
15	Kenny Roberts Jnr	+ 57''746

Fastest lap
Stoner, in 1'59.857 (158.1619 km/h).
Record : Pedrosa, in 1'59.318 (159.335 km/h/2006).

Outright fastest lap
Rossi, en 1'58.424 (160.538 km/h/2007).

CHAMPIONSHIP

1	C. Stoner	86 (3 wins)
2	V. Rossi	71 (1 win)
3	D. Pedrosa	49
4	M. Melandri	41
5	J. Hopkins	39
6	T. Elias	35
7	C. Edwards	31
8	L. Capirossi	30
9	N. Hayden	30
10	C. Vermeulen	30

LORENZO COPIES STONER: THREE OUT OF FOUR!

RUNNERS AND RIDERS
There is still only one Gilera on track, as Locatelli has not been replaced. There are two new Yamaha riders, the Chinese Shi Zhao Huang and Jin Xiao with wild cards. World Champion Jorge Lorenzo celebrates his 20th birthday on the first day of practice.

QUALIFYING
In terms of speed, it's a case of Lorenzo and then the others. Not content with dominating every session, the reigning champion hammers the point home, taking pole by no less than 742 thousandths ahead of his nearest pursuer and fellow countryman, Hector Barbera. The second placed man, along with Kallio (3rd) set his time by getting a tow off Dovizioso, who is thus dumped off the front row. Yuki Takahashi is a faller, breaking his left arm, while China's Huang has a terrifying cartwheel, after colliding with De Angelis, ending up in the wall and escaping with bruising.

START
Kallio swerves into the lead ahead of Dovizioso, Lorenzo and Barbera. Lorenzo then snatches the lead but gets it wrong braking for the hairpin. Crossing the line for the first time, Kallio heads Dovizioso by 290 thousandths.

LAP 3
Dovizioso now leads. In sixth place, Lorenzo is the quickest man on track.

LAP 6
"Dovi" is still fighting off the Aprilias of De Angelis and Lorenzo. Bautista has passed Luthi for seventh place.

LAP 7
Lorenzo heads the field with the three leaders having pulled out a gap of 1"417.

LAP 8
A fall for Shuhei Aoyama.

HALF-DISTANCE (10 LAPS)
Lorenzo ups the pressure and now leads Dovizioso by 1"637 with De Angelis hanging on. Further back, a great tussle for fourth spot between Barbera, Kallio, Simon and Bautista. Luthi has lost touch caused by problems with the automatic gear shifter.

LAP 13
Bautista is back up to fourth and is closing on team-mate Alex De Angelis

LAP 14
Simoncelli falls from ninth place.

LAP 16
An on-form Bautista has just caught the experienced De Angelis.

LAP 18
Bautista continues the carnival, closing to 8 tenths of Dovizioso and the fight for second place.

LAP 20
Job done: Bautista is second!

FINISH (20 LAPS)
With almost five seconds in hand going into the final lap, it's no worries for Lorenzo. Behind, it's Dovizioso who is back in control but not for long, as the 125 champion blocks him at the end of the straight, like an old pro.

CHAMPIONSHIP
95 points from a possible 100: Lorenzo is the master of the category. Dovizioso is already 30 points behind while Alvaro Bautista closes on the provisional podium, showing all the signs of being an immense talent!

Lorenzo celebrates another perfect weekend: pole, the win and a new race lap record, while Bautista remembers that this weekend is also Mothers' Day (opposite.) The reigning 125 champion (left) was intransigent towards Dovisioso.

GP CHINA | 6th May 2007 | Shanghai | 5.281 m

STARTING GRID

Pos	No	Rider	Bike	Time
1	1	J. Lorenzo	Aprilia	2'04.543
2	80	H. Barberá	Aprilia	2'05.285
3	36	M. Kallio	KTM	2'05.416
4	60	J. Simón	Honda	2'05.587
5	34	A. Dovizioso	Honda	2'05.595
6	19	A. Bautistá	Aprilia	2'05.650
7	12	T. Lüthi	Aprilia	2'05.718
8	3	A. De Angelis	Aprilia	2'05.938
9	73	S. Aoyama	Honda	2'06.489
10	58	M. Simoncelli	Gilera	2'06.778
11	4	H. Aoyama	KTM	2'06.914
12	32	F. Lai	Aprilia	2'07.037
13	14	A. West	Aprilia	2'07.711
14	28	D. Heidolf	Aprilia	2'07.772
15	41	A. Espargaro	Aprilia	2'07.792
16	55	Y. Takahashi	Honda	2'07.815 (*)
17	8	R. Wilairot	Honda	2'07.892
18	25	A. Baldolini	Aprilia	2'08.527
19	10	I. Toth	Aprilia	2'08.575
20	16	J. Cluzel	Aprilia	2'08.589
21	17	K. Abraham	Aprilia	2'08.637
22	50	E. Laverty	Honda	2'08.713
23	44	T. Sekiguchi	Aprilia	2'09.106
24	9	A. Tizón	Aprilia	2'09.274
25	62	S. Huang	Yamaha	2'10.939 (*)
26	63	J. Xiao	Yamaha	2'12.202

(*): Victim of a terrifying fall on Saturday, S. Huang (CHI, Yamaha) withdraws. As Y. Takahashi (J, Honda), who broked his left arm.

RACE: 21 laps = 110.901 km

Pos	Rider	Time/Gap
1	Jorge Lorenzo	44'17.095 (150.255 km/h)
2	Alvaro Bautistá	+ 3''904
3	Andrea Dovizioso	+ 5''031
4	Alex De Angelis	+ 6''560
5	Mika Kallio	+ 10''248
6	Hector Barberá	+ 10''502
7	Julian Simón	+ 10''832
8	Thomas Lüthi	+ 30''484
9	Hiroshi Aoyama	+ 32''895
10	Fabrizio Lai	+ 50''977
11	Aleix Espargaro	+ 51''699
12	Ratthapark Wilairot	+ 53''036
13	Anthony West	+ 1'01.663
14	Taro Sekiguchi	+ 1'14.603
15	Arturo Tizón	+ 1'14.754
16	Jules Cluzel	+ 1'39.890
17	Eugene Laverty	+ 1'47.005
18	Imre Toth	+ 1'50.516
19	Jin Xiao	+ 1 lap

Fastest lap

Lorenzo, in 2'05.738 (151.200 km/h). New record. Previous: Dovizioso, in 2'06.865 (149.856 km/h/2006).

Outright fastest lap

Lorenzo, in 2'04.543 (152.650 km/h/2007).

CHAMPIONSHIP

Pos	Rider	Points
1	J. Lorenzo	95 (3 wins)
2	A. Dovizioso	68 (1 win)
3	A. De Angelis	59
4	A. Bautistá	56
5	H. Barberá	34
6	T. Lüthi	32
7	J. Simón	26
8	M. Kallio	21
9	F. Lai	21
10	H. Aoyama	17

Pesek rejoices (above,) Masbou watches (opposite) as the Chinese GP also revealed the talents of Esteve Rabat (right) tussling with the winner on the day.

A FIRST FOR PESEK, THE FOURTH WINNER OF THE SEASON.

RUNNERS AND RIDERS
France's Mike di Meglio is back, having had an operation on his left collar bone (a fall at Jerez.) "It all went well, although there's a risk that I might still be in a bit of pain this weekend," he rejoiced. As for the rest, no change as the promoters found no riders worth entering under a wild card.

QUALIFYING
The quickest time is set by…Mattia Pasini of course, who has stuck a black cat in his garage in the hope of fending off any bad luck! He is the only one to slip under the 2'12 bracket right from the first day of qualifying, in a performance that will not be beaten on Saturday. Faubel, Pesek, the latter the victim of a fall with Zanetti that could have had serious consequences in the key moments and Talmacsi complete the front row. Hats off to Bradley Smith who puts his Honda on row 2 in fifth place.

START
Pasini pulls off the perfect start ahead of Corsi, Talmacsi and Pesek. Crossing the line for the first time, the Italian already has a lead of 1"242 over next man up, Simone Corsi. Behind, Sandi and Switzerland's Krummenacher come together, the latter pitting for repairs to bent handlebars before going back on track.

LAP 2
Terol and the American youngser Bonsey are fallers.

LAP 3
Talmacsi, Faubel, Pesek and the pack have closed up behind Pasini.

LAP 6
Pasini, Talmacsi, Pesek, Faubel, Corsi and De Rosa: all six in 1"331.

LAP 8
Koyama has caught the leaders.

HALF-DISTANCE (10 LAPS)
Talmacsi, who had taken the lead one lap earlier, has an advantage of 162 thousandths over team-mate Faubel, who heads Pasini, Pesek, Corsi, Koyama and De Rosa. The top seven are all in a gnat's whisker of 1.442 seconds

LAP 12
Gadea, Rabat and Ranseder have joined the train, which means ten of them are now wheel to wheel.

LAP 13
Those betting on long odds can afford to smile as a Honda leads a 125 GP thanks to Rabat, a newcomer to the world of GP.

17° TOUR
It is now Gadea's turn to drive the train.

FINISH (19 LAPS)
Pesek is in front as they head into the final lap and he makes no mistakes to take his first GP win. Top marks to Rabat, who is third in the end. Pasini finally scores his first points, taking six for tenth place.

CHAMPIONSHIP
Pesek gets it all, as he now leads the championship by two points from Talmacsi and four from Faubel. Among the youngsters who are growing up fast, Pol Esparagaro (9th on the day) is fifth in the classification.

GP CHINA | 6th May 2007 | Shanghai | 5.281 m

STARTING GRID

1	75	M. Pasini	Aprilia	2'11.946
2	55	H. Faubel	Aprilia	2'12.284
3	52	L. Pesek	Derbi	2'12.384
4	14	G. Talmacsi	Aprilia	2'12.433
5	38	B. Smith	Honda	2'12.547
6	33	S. Gadea	Aprilia	2'12.774
7	24	S. Corsi	Aprilia	2'12.841
8	71	T. Koyama	KTM	2'12.987
9	60	M. Ranseder	Derbi	2'13.093
10	11	S. Cortese	Aprilia	2'13.526
11	35	R. De Rosa	Aprilia	2'13.581
12	12	E. Rabat	Honda	2'13.599
13	22	P. Nieto	Aprilia	2'13.686
14	6	J. Olivé	Aprilia	2'13.817
15	29	A. Iannone	Aprilia	2'13.866
16	18	N. Terol	Derbi	2'13.868
17	20	R. Tamburini	Aprilia	2'13.872
18	44	P. Espargaro	Aprilia	2'13.880
19	15	F. Sandi	Aprilia	2'13.923
20	27	S. Bianco	Aprilia	2'13.977
21	8	L. Zanetti	Aprilia	2'14.006
22	7	A. Masbou	Honda	2'14.130
23	63	M. Di Meglio	Honda	2'14.226
24	34	R. Krummenacher	KTM	2'14.498
25	53	S. Grotzkyj	Aprilia	2'14.522
26	95	R. Muresan	Derbi	2'15.008
27	51	S. Bonsey	KTM	2'15.060
28	77	D. Aegerter	Aprilia	2'15.512
29	37	J. Litjens	Honda	2'14.685
30	99	D. Webb	Honda	2'15.908
31	13	D. Lombardi	Honda	2'15.974
32	56	H. Van Den Berg	Aprilia	2'17.111

RACE: 19 laps = 100.339 km

1	Lukas Pesek	42'25.923 (141.881 km/h)	
2	Hector Faubel	+ 0''187	
3	Esteve Rabat	+ 0''481	
4	Gabor Talmacsi	+ 0''782	
5	Simone Corsi	+ 1''140	
6	Sergio Gadea	+ 1''191	
7	Michael Ranseder	+ 2''375	
8	Bradley Smith	+ 2''400	
9	Pol Espargaro	+ 2''717	
10	Mattia Pasini	+ 3''423	
11	Andrea Iannone	+ 8''360	
12	Raffaele De Rosa	+ 8''640	
13	Alexis Masbou	+ 12''680	
14	Mike Di Meglio	+ 16''671	
15	Lorenzo Zanetti	+ 16''777	
16	Pablo Nieto	+ 24''444	
17	Simone Grotzkyj	+ 27''337	
18	Sandro Cortese	+ 32''924	
19	Joan Olivé	+ 35''029	
20	Roberto Tamburini	+ 36''883	
21	Dominique Aegerter	+ 46''084	
22	Joey Litjens	+ 46''456	
23	Daniel Webb	+ 48''131	
24	Dino Lombardi	+ 1'08.983	
25	Hugo Van Den Berg	+ 1'09.714	
26	Robert Muresan	+ 1 lap	
27	Randy Krummenacher	+ 1 lap	

Fastest lap
Pesek, in 2'12.420 (143.570 km/h).
Record: Bautistá, in 2'12.131 (143.884 km/h/2006).

Outright fastest lap
Kallio, in 2'11.572 (144.495 km/h/2006).

CHAMPIONSHIP

1	L. Pesek	71 (1 win)
2	G. Talmacsi	69 (1 win)
3	H. Faubel	67 (1 win)
4	S. Corsi	47 (1 win)
5	P. Espargaro	34
6	J. Olivé	33
7	R. De Rosa	30
8	T. Koyama	26
9	E. Rabat	26
10	M. Ranseder	23

Sylvain Guintoli charges on, Randy De Puniet glances behind him as two Frenchmen lead "their" GP.

IT WAS GREAT:
TWO FRENCHMEN LEADING THEIR GP

THE RACE WAS FINALLY WON BY AN
AUSTRALIAN - CHRIS VERMEULEN - BUT THE
HIGHLIGHT OF THE FRENCH GP WAS THE
SURPRISING LEADING DUO OF GUINTOLI
AND DE PUNIET.

THE RACE

FRANCE DARES AND…..

De Puniet charging through La Sarthe: he ends up making one mistake too many. The winner? Chris Vermeulen (71.)

I n the campaign for the presidential elections, which had ended two weeks earlier, much had been made of a France that "dares" and in contrast naturally enough, the France that does not dare.

Among the French who "dare," is Claude Michy, the promoter of the French GP, the man who brought the crowds back to Le Mans, who saved an event which, despite being a classic on the calendar, had been falling asleep for several years now, suffering a bad case of lethargy.

Also among those who are prepared to dare against the wind and sometimes the tide of media indifference leading to a lack of interest from potential sponsors is Herve Poncharal. Not the president of IRTA, the GP teams association, but the actual boss of the team that took the 250 world title with Olivier Jacque and which lines up two Yamahas here in MotoGP. Because, on this Sunday with everyone expecting the downpour predicted at the start of the race, Herve has with him a rider who also decided to dare in the shape of Sylvain Guintoli. "On the start

line, he said to me, don't worry, in three laps I'll be in the lead. At that precise moment, I understood something was about to happen. And god was it good, despite the unfortunate end to it all, as Guintoli fell while battling for the lead with his compatriot Randy De Puniet.

Because Randy was another one who had opted to go for the dare on this Sunday of his home GP. And when Randy is in that sort of mood, people notice. There was no way he was going to do anything else in this strange race, as the Kawasaki rider, who had made a break for it going for the lead, got it wrong just a few hundred metres before reaching the pits to change onto his second bike, fitted with rain tyres.

End of scene one and time to move onto scene two which featured Frenchmen who for their part, had not dared. "I think that at Michelin, they must have seen there were three Bridgestone riders on the podium for "their" GP!" This sentiment, which must still be ringing in the ears of some people at Clermont-Ferrand, came from the mouth of Valentino Rossi. Not

happy, really not happy at all with having to ride on the defensive, not happy with yet again losing precious points to his new major rival, Casey Stoner. What happened in the Bibendum camp? "Guilty, we plead guilty," explains Jean-Philippe Weber, the man in charge of the motorcycle programme in the Michelin Competition department. "With Valentino Rossi's bike we were too conservative in the choice of rain tyres, too hard. If we had dared to go a bit further, as was the case with Hayden and even more so with Pedrosa - the little Spaniard suddenly discovered an unknown love of riding in the rain - it would have worked."

But there you have it, it did not work. Therefore, Chris Vermeulen helped himself to a first GP win. Casey Stoner was faultless once again, despite these difficult conditions and extended his lead over Rossi even further. And that on a circuit where his Ducati could have, should have even been put in serious bother by the number 46 Yamaha.

A first turning point?

Le Mans 2007

Melandri, Vermeulen, Stoner is a great result for the Japanese manufacturer, less so for the French one. Above, Elias falls and opposite, a lesson in cheek from Sylvain Guintoli.

A BRIDGESTONE TRIPLE IN THE LAND OF BIBENDUM

RUNNERS AND RIDERS
Olivier Jacque is being looked after in Barcelona, by Professor Mir who has given up on applying skin grafts to his right arm. Unfortunately, the wounds have not yet healed up and "OJ" has to give up on his home grand prix. He is replaced by Alfonso "Fonsi" Gonzales-Nieto.

QUALIFYING
A nice surprise in the shape of Edwards, who takes his maiden GP pole, ahead of Stoner and Checa.

START
It is not actually raining dead on 14h00, but the start is declared "wet," even though everyone starts on slicks. Stoner gets a good one, but Rossi does even better and shoots into the lead just after the Dunlop bridge to end the opening lap 701 thousandths ahead of the Ducati rider.

LAP 2
Guintoli is on an amazing charge and is fourth.

LAP 3
Rossi now has a lead of 1.802 over Barros. Stoner is third ahead of De Puniet and Guintoli. Edwards pits to change bikes.

LAP 4
The crowd, over 70,000 of them, go wild as De Puniet is second.

LAP 6
De Puniet and Guintoli pass Rossi, with the Dunlop rider catching out his fellow countryman a bit further on

LAP 7
De Puniet has got the place back. Hopkins bumps into Rossi who finds himself fifth. Checa is a faller.

LAP 8
Guintoli falls, followed by Elias. De Puniet has a lead of 1.669 seconds over Hopkins and is 2.095 ahead of Pedrosa. Guintoli and then Hofmann change bikes.

LAP 9
It is definitely raining and De Puniet falls as the entire field pits to swap bikes.

LAP 11
A new race is underway. Vermeulen leads Hopkins by 45 thousandths. Melandri is third ahead of Pedrosa and Rossi.

HALF-DISTANCE (14 LAPS)
Hopkins who had been fourth, goes for a trip through the gravel. Vermeulen's lead over Melandri is now 1.117 seconds. Rossi is third at 4.147 with Stoner fourth.

LAP 16
Vermeulen and Melandri are lapping 2 seconds quicker than the Rossi-Stoner duo.

LAP 17
Melandri is 2 seconds off Vermeulen and Stoner has just passed Rossi.

LAP 21
Nakano falls.

LAP 25
Rossi is riding on egg shells as he passed first by Pedrosa and then by Hofmann. Out in front, Vermeulen has dropped Melandri.

LAP 27
Hayden falls and his Honda is destroyed.

FINISH (28 LAPS)
Barros is a faller on the final lap. Vermeulen had ridden perfectly to take his first GP win. Hats off to Stoner and also to Pedrosa, who had never performed so well in the wet.

CHAMPIONSHIP
Stoner increases his advantage over Rossi by a further six points, to build a lead of 21 points, or around one race win.

GP FRANCE | 20th May 2007 | Le Mans | 4.180 m

STARTING GRID

1	5	C. Edwards	Yamaha	1'33.616
2	27	C. Stoner	Ducati	1'33.710
3	7	C. Checa	Honda	1'33.859
4	46	V. Rossi	Yamaha	1'33.875
5	21	J. Hopkins	Suzuki	1'34.102
6	24	T. Elias	Honda	1'34.125
7	69	N. Hayden	Honda	1'34.247
8	14	R. De Puniet	Kawasaki	1'34.318
9	33	M. Melandri	Honda	1'34.360
10	26	D. Pedrosa	Honda	1'34.412
11	50	S. Guintoli	Yamaha	1'34.507
12	71	C. Vermeulen	Suzuki	1'34.574
13	4	A. Barros	Ducati	1'34.817
14	56	S. Nakano	Honda	1'34.834
15	65	L. Capirossi	Ducati	1'34.903
16	6	M. Tamada	Yamaha	1'35.346
17	66	A. Hofmann	Ducati	1'35.578
18	10	K. Roberts	KR211V	1'35.681
19	11	A. Gonzales-Nieto	Kawasaki	1'36.312

RACE: 28 laps = 117.040 km

1	Chris Vermeulen	50'58.713 (137.752 km/h)
2	Marco Melandri	+ 12''599
3	Casey Stoner	+ 27''347
4	Daniel Pedrosa	+ 37''328
5	Alex Hofmann	+ 49''166
6	Valentino Rossi	+ 53''563
7	John Hopkins	+ 1'01.073
8	Loris Capirossi	+ 1'21.241
9	Makoto Tamada	+ 1 lap
10	Sylvain Guintoli	+ 1 lap
11	«Fonsi» Gonzales-Nieto	+ 1 lap
12	Colin Edwards	+ 3 laps

Fastest lap
Hopkins, in 1'38.678 (152.495 km/h).
Record: Rossi, in 1'35.087 (158.255 km/h/2006).

Outright fastest lap
Edwards, in 1'33.616 (160.741 km/h/2007).

CHAMPIONSHIP

1. C. Stoner	102 (3 wins)
2. V. Rossi	81 (1 win)
3. D. Pedrosa	62
4. M. Melandri	61
5. C. Vermeulen	55 (1 win)
6. J. Hopkins	48
7. L. Capirossi	38
8. T. Elias	35
9. C. Edwards	35
10. A. Hofmann	30

LORENZO, STILL AND ALWAYS.

RUNNERS AND RIDERS

A sensation, as Locatelli, who was seriously injured in Jerez is already back in action! Injured in China - a fractured left arm - Takahashi is absent and is not replaced. The former 125 champion, Thomas Luthi, made it into a major Swiss tabloid paper a week before the GP, by going public about his love for the third placed contestant from the 2006 Miss Switzerland contest.

QUALIFYING

It would not be an all-Iberian front row as Thomas Luthi spoilt the party, setting the fourth fastest time at the circuit where he had won for the past two years in the 125 class. Lorenzo is on pole. Managing no better than 24th time, Locatelli decides not to start the race.

START

Lorenzo is majestic and it's Bautista, off the second row, who tucks into second place ahead of Luthi. Espargaro is a faller. First time round and Lorenzo already has a lead of 803 thousandths.

LAP 2

Barbera and Dovizioso pass Luthi, who a bit further on retires with a broken engine.

LAP 4

Bautista is now in Lorenzo's wheel tracks and Dovizioso catches out Barbera.

LAP 5

Bautista gets it wrong and goes straight on at a corner.

LAP 6

In super form, Dovizioso is second.

LAP 7

De Angelis sets the fastest race lap and he is now third, 278 thousandths off Lorenzo.

LAP 8

Dovizioso has taken charge and crosses the line with a four tenths lead over the reigning champion.

LAP 10

Lorenzo is ambushed by De Angelis.

HALF-DISTANCE (13 LAPS)

Hiroshi Aoyama has retired. Out in front, Dovizioso has a lead of precisely 308 thousandths over De Angelis, who heads Lorenzo by 5 tenths. Barbera and Simon are fighting for fourth place, just over 2 seconds behind the podium places.

LAP 15

De Angelis moves into the lead: the three at the front are all within a mere 369 thousandths. Behind them, Barbera has closed to within 1.379 seconds.

LAP 16

Lorenzo and Dovizioso collide and De Angelis does not hang around waiting for them.

LAP 21

De Angelis has a moment, so Lorenzo does not need to be asked twice and retakes the lead.

LAP 23

Lap record for Dovizioso, who passes De Angelis and finds himself 477 thousandths off the leader.

FINISH (26 LAPS)

Lorenzo had retaken the lap record on the penultimate lap, but Dovizioso is even quicker on the final one so the Italian is finally beaten by just 156 thousandths. On the lap of honour, the world champion is handed a victory flag by a clone, squeezed into an identical set of leathers.

CHAMPIONSHIP

120 points from a possible total of 125: Lorenzo now has a 32 point lead over Dovizioso.

Lorenzo and Dovizioso are inseparable: the two stars of the championship dominated the race. Meanwhile, Espargaro (opposite) maintains a low profile and Locatelli (below) surprises everyone by turning up for qualifying.

GP FRANCE | 20th May 2007 | Le Mans | 4.180 m

STARTING GRID

1	1	J. Lorenzo	Aprilia	1'37.934
2	60	J. Simón	Honda	1'38.463
3	80	H. Barberá	Aprilia	1'38.610
4	12	T. Lüthi	Aprilia	1'38.772
5	19	A. Bautistá	Aprilia	1'38.820
6	3	A. De Angelis	Aprilia	1'38.826
7	58	M. Simoncelli	Gilera	1'38.888
8	34	A. Dovizioso	Honda	1'38.890
9	36	M. Kallio	KTM	1'38.982
10	4	H. Aoyama	KTM	1'39.200
11	14	A. West	Aprilia	1'39.217
12	73	S. Aoyama	Honda	1'39.256
13	32	F. Lai	Aprilia	1'39.741
14	41	A. Espargaro	Aprilia	1'39.884
15	16	J. Cluzel	Aprilia	1'40.359
16	28	D. Heidolf	Aprilia	1'40.488
17	17	K. Abraham	Aprilia	1'40.515
18	44	T. Sekiguchi	Aprilia	1'40.591
19	50	E. Laverty	Honda	1'40.630
20	8	R. Wilairot	Honda	1'40.716
21	10	I. Toth	Aprilia	1'41.338
22	25	A. Baldolini	Aprilia	1'41.422
23	9	A. Tizón	Aprilia	1'41.432
24	15	R. Locatelli	Gilera	1'41.719

RACE: 26 laps = 108.680 km

1	Jorge Lorenzo	43'12.237 (150.930 km/h)
2	Andrea Dovizioso	+ 0''156
3	Alex De Angelis	+ 2''733
4	Hector Barberá	+ 5''971
5	Julian Simón	+ 6''111
6	Marco Simoncelli	+ 22''753
7	Mika Kallio	+ 23''139
8	Alvaro Bautistá	+ 27''416
9	Shuhei Aoyama	+ 28''915
10	Anthony West	+ 33''950
11	Ratthapark Wilairot	+ 57''900
12	Fabrizio Lai	+ 58''011
13	Alex Baldolini	+ 1'06.251
14	Taro Sekiguchi	+ 1'06.720
15	Eugene Laverty	+ 1'07.649
16	Dirk Heidolf	+ 1'14.837
17	Arturo Tizón	+ 1'31.455
18	Aleix Espargaro	+ 1'39.701

Fastest lap

Dovizioso, en 1'38.566 (152.669 km/h). Nouveau record. Ancien: A. Aoyama, en 1'39.964 (150.534 km/h/2006).

Outright fastest lap

Lorenzo, in 1'37.934 (153.654 km/h/2007).

CHAMPIONSHIP

1	J. Lorenzo	120 (4 wins)
2	A. Dovizioso	88 (1 win)
3	A. De Angelis	75
4	A. Bautistá	64
5	H. Barberá	47
6	J. Simón	37
7	T. Lüthi	32
8	M. Kallio	30
9	F. Lai	25
10	M. Simoncelli	24

SERGIO GADEA
BECOMES
THE FIFTH
MAN.

RUNNERS AND RIDERS
The gang's all here. And in addition, five young riders from the French championship have wild cards. One of them, Debise, injures himself on the first day of practice, while another, Gwen Le Badezet, will fail to make the cut in qualifying.

QUALIFYING
Once again, we are treated to a festival from Pasini, who beats his nearest pursuer (Smith) by almost half a second. Hero of the Chinese GP, Esteve Rabat is knocked out of the game on Friday with a broken foot and multiple bruising.

START
Koyama is the promptest off the mark, but Pasini gets by before the Dunlop chicane. Zanetti falls, but gets going again. Crossing the line for the first time, Pasini is already ahead of Koyama by 1.184 seconds. Gadea is third ahead of Smith and Pesek.

LAP 4
Gadea has helped himself to second place on the previous lap and is 922 thousandths off Pasini.

LAP 7
Pasini has just set the fastest race lap to lead Gadea by 746 thousandths. Smith and Pesek are duelling for third spot.

HALF-DISTANCE (12 LAPS)
Pasini still leads, but Gadea is now under two tenths behind. Smith and Pesek, the latter having just broken the lap record, are also in touch. Talmacsi is fifth, but already 4 seconds adrift.

LAP 13
Raffaele De Rosa is a faller, having been in the group that was battling for sixth.

LAP 15
Iannone falls. Out in front, Pasini, Gadea, Smith and Pesek are all glued together within 865 thousandths.

LAP 17
Gadea takes the lead, but will lose it next time round.

LAP 19
A superb battle between Gadea and Pasini. Smith and Pesek are very close.

LAP 20
Bad luck sticks to Pasini like chewing gum to a shoe and he stops, once again beaten by his equipment. As he returns to the pits, he is the one who has to console his technical team! Gadea has a 9 tenths lead over the Smith-Pesek duo.

FINISH (24 LAPS)
Pesek has closed to within 524 thousandths on the run into the final lap, but Gadea will have none of it and takes his first GP win. Another first, a podium for Bradley Smith who finishes third. Talmacsi comes off best in the superb fight for fourth place. Pablo Nieto, having cut the chicane, is saddled with a 20 second penalty and is dropped back to fifteenth.

CHAMPIONSHIP
Although beaten, Pesek does not do too badly, as he increases his lead over Talmacsi to 9 points. Faubel is 14 points down on the leader. The first three, plus Espargaro and Ranseder have now scored points in every GP.

...nother winner - Sergio Gadea (above.) As for Pasini, it's yet another retirement, while Zanetti ...a style all of his own through the first chicane.

GP FRANCE | 20th May 2007 | Le Mans | 4.180 m

STARTING GRID

1	75	M. Pasini	Aprilia	1'43.111
2	38	B. Smith	Honda	1'43.569
3	71	T. Koyama	KTM	1'43.664
4	55	H. Faubel	Aprilia	1'43.745
5	52	L. Pesek	Derbi	1'43.773
6	33	S. Gadea	Aprilia	1'43.774
7	29	A. Iannone	Aprilia	1'43.999
8	14	G. Talmacsi	Aprilia	1'44.191
9	60	M. Ranseder	Derbi	1'44.191
10	63	M. Di Meglio	Honda	1'44.192
11	7	A. Masbou	Honda	1'44.267
12	35	R. De Rosa	Aprilia	1'44.305
13	24	S. Corsi	Aprilia	1'44.518
14	11	S. Cortese	Aprilia	1'44.558
15	34	R. Krummenacher	KTM	1'44.668
16	8	L. Zanetti	Aprilia	1'44.680
17	22	P. Nieto	Aprilia	1'44.958
18	6	J. Olivé	Aprilia	1'44.968
19	44	P. Espargaro	Aprilia	1'45.193
20	27	S. Bianco	Aprilia	1'45.280
21	53	S. Grotzkyj	Aprilia	1'45.310
22	18	N. Terol	Derbi	1'45.729
23	13	D. Lombardi	Honda	1'45.909
24	95	R. Muresan	Derbi	1'46.095
25	77	D. Aegerter	Aprilia	1'46.139
26	12	E. Rabat	Honda	1'46.144 (*)
27	20	R. Tamburini	Aprilia	1'46.272
28	51	S. Bonsey	KTM	1'46.520
29	56	H. Van Den Berg	Aprilia	1'46.676
30	37	J. Litjens	Honda	1'46.724
31	15	F. Sandi	Aprilia	1'46.984
32	99	D. Webb	Honda	1'47.001
33	45	V. Debise	Honda	1'48.872
34	46	R. Maitre	Honda	1'49.031
35	48	J. Cartron	Honda	1'49.354
36	47	S. Le Coquen	Honda	1'50.116

Not qualified:

49		G. Le Badezet	Honda	1'50.616

(*): Injured on Friday afternoon, E. Rabat (E, Honda) had to withdraw.

RACE: 24 laps = 100.320 km

1	Sergio Gadea	41'50.112 (143.878 km/h)
2	Lukas Pesek	+ 0''478
3	Bradley Smith	+ 2''963
4	Gabor Talmacsi	+ 13''516
5	Joan Olivé	+ 13''845
6	Hector Faubel	+ 15''098
7	Sandro Cortese	+ 15''603
8	Simone Corsi	+ 15''664
9	Mike Di Meglio	+ 15''777
10	Tomoyoshi Koyama	+ 19''108
11	Pol Espargaro	+ 23''920
12	Alexis Masbou	+ 24''210
13	Randy Krummenacher	+ 29''517
14	Michael Ranseder	+ 29''701
15	Pablo Nieto	+ 34''936
16	Lorenzo Zanetti	+ 45''124
17	Stefano Bianco	+ 45''308
18	Simone Grotzkyj	+ 46''142
19	Nicolas Terol	+ 46''350
20	Dominique Aegerter	+ 1'00.825
21	Dino Lombardi	+ 1'00.948
22	Roberto Tamburini	+ 1'09.701
23	Robert Muresan	+ 1'10.101
24	Hugo Van Den Berg	+ 1'10.295
25	Joey Litjens	+ 1'10.471
26	Federico Sandi	+ 1'16.496
27	Daniel Webb	+ 1'21.822
28	Romain Maitre	+ 1 lap
29	Steve Le Coquen	+ 1 lap

Fastest lap
Pesek, in 1'43.859 (144.888 km/h). New record.
Previous: Gadea, in 1'44.637 (143.811 km/h/2006).

Outright fastest lap
Pasini, in 1'43.111 (145.939 km/h/2007).

CHAMPIONSHIP

1	L. Pesek	91 (1 win)
2	G. Talmacsi	82 (1 win)
3	H. Faubel	77 (1 win)
4	S. Corsi	55 (1 win)
5	S. Gadea	46 (1 win)
6	J. Olivé	44
7	P. Espargaro	39
8	B. Smith	36
9	T. Koyama	32
10	R. De Rosa	30

Rossi parades in front of his subjects: the king did not want to give anything away in his kingdom.

06

WELCOME TO THE KINGDOM
OF HIS MAJESTY VALENTINO

SOME THINGS ARE JUST NOT DONE,
SUCH AS DARING TO CHALLENGE
ROSSI'S DOMINANCE ON HIS HOME
TURF AT MUGELLO. GOD! WHAT A
GREAT EVENT…

THE RACE

THE KING IN HIS COURT.

Pedrosa (here in the lead) tried to hold him off, but it was Rossi who ended up conducting the choir when it was time for the national anthem.

To say that Valentino Rossi is not that keen on being beaten is a masterpiece of understatement in the paddock. Therefore, when His Majesty is holding an audience at home at the Mugello circuit, where he has won five times in succession in the blue riband category, one can expect the odd firework to fly. And so it proved

But the magisterial Master still needs a few weapons of his own, even if they are not up to the standard of those used by the opposition. Because on this track, that winds, climbs and drops through the Tuscan hills, with its long and slightly downhill straight, one could expect the Demosedici to use every last ounce of their incredible power. All the more so on this weekend as, for valuable service given to the Ducati cause since the company came into MotoGP, the Borgo Panigale engineers have prepared a special bike for the struggling Loris Capirossi, which should suit him better. Despite all this, the Master is

confident, as Yamaha and Michelin have been busy since the French GP.

Rossi against Ducati? Actually he's got a bigger fight on his hands as one has to include Honda in the list of those who want to knock out the king on his home turf. And the Japanese constructor has given up any pretence and it is now clear that Dani Pedrosa can rely totally on the services of HRC, the racing department of the biggest name in the world of bikes. They are no longer hiding the fact that it's all for Dani, but would it be enough?

Even if you don't know the answer you can feel it: it would turn out to be no! No, because Valentino Rossi, after a difficult opening lap - "I struggled a bit to find the right rhythm" - produced yet another perfect performance. He dealt with his rivals with precise yet painful blows. Stoner was first, finally settling for some big points, not even fighting off a great comeback from veteran Alexandre Barros on a "private" Ducati.

In the end, Pedrosa was the last to surrender, powerless to resist.

Valentino Rossi had won again and made up valuable points on his closest rival in the championship, even if Stoner looked as carefree as ever. But Rossi knows he is still the king and that Mugello is his court. At the moment when the track invasion began he had to head for the pit lane down an escape road and climb once again onto his favourite spot, the highest step on the podium, from which he would address his subjects thus: "This win is for you!" The crowd had only needed this as a signal to burst into the National Anthem, under the conductor's baton of their "Vale." He led from the heart and finally, his special helmet, the one decorated with those giant red hearts was tossed into the waiting crowd.

The King, the Master, knows how to look after his own at home in Tuscany, even if he shows less good manners towards his rivals.

ROSSI DOMINATES, BARROS THE TROUBLE MAKER

RUNNERS AND RIDERS

Olivier Jacque is back in the saddle of the second Kawasaki. There is a second KR212V on track for Kenny Roberts' young brother, Kurtis. For the Italian GP, Ducati has prepared a special bike for Loris Capirossi, with a modified electronic management system.

QUALIFYING

Daniel Pedrosa is quickest on the dry track, which means on Friday and Saturday morning, as well as the Sunday morning warm-up. Saturday afternoon's qualifying takes place in mixed conditions and it is

championship leader Casey Stoner, who makes the best of it, ahead of Vermeulen and Rossi. Jacque does well to take fourth, while Edwards is struggling in sixteenth place.

START

Casey Stone is perfect, as are Vermeulen, Capirossi and Barros, while Rossi is only eighth at the first split. Stoner completes the opening lap 802 thousandths ahead of team-mate Capirossi and Rossi is seventh.

LAP 2

Randy De Puniet is a faller, again. Melandri is third behind the two works Ducatis. Behind them come Vermeulen, Pedrosa, Hopkins, Barros and Rossi.

LAP 4

On superb form, Capirossi takes the lead! Seven of them are now all within 1.356 seconds: Capirossi, Stoner, Melandri, Pedrosa, Hopkins, Rossi and Vermeulen.

LAP 6

Capirossi makes a mistake at the end of the straight and amazingly, Pedrosa takes the lead ahead of Stoner, Rossi, Melandri and Hopkins.

LAP 7

Rossi is second!

LAP 9

They are going mad on the Tuscan hills as Rossi takes the lead.

LAP 10

Checa is a faller.

HALF-DISTANCE (12 LAPS)

Rossi wants to remain master of Mugello, a circuit where he has won five times in a row in the blue riband category. He now heads Pedrosa by 298 thousandths and Stoner by 1.551. Further back, Hopkins and Barros are still in touch with the series leader. Capirossi is only sixth, 3"319 off the Brazilian.

LAP 16

Pedrosa has tried a few moves, but all in vain. Rossi now has seven tenths in hand over the Spaniard. In 3rd, Stoner is managing the Hopkins, Barros situation.

LAP 17

Barros passes Hopkins.

LAP 21

An on-form Barros has caught out Stoner, so that the Brazilian is now third on the D'Antin team Ducati.

FINISH (23 LAPS)

1.941 seconds in favour of Rossi going into the final lap and victory is in the bag. However, the scrap between Barros and Stoner is fierce for the final spot on the podium and it's Barros who has the last word.

CHAMPIONSHIP

With Stoner "only" fourth, Rossi closes to within 9 points of the top slot. Pedrosa is still third, but 33 points down.

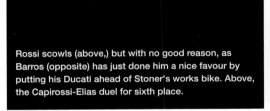

Rossi scowls (above,) but with no good reason, as Barros (opposite) has just done him a nice favour by putting his Ducati ahead of Stoner's works bike. Above, the Capirossi-Elias duel for sixth place.

GP ITALIA | 3rd June 2007 | Mugello | 5.245 m

STARTING GRID

1	27	C. Stoner	Ducati	2'00.359
2	71	C. Vermeulen	Suzuki	2'01.381
3	46	V. Rossi	Yamaha	2'01.695
4	19	O. Jacque	Kawasaki	2'01.709
5	65	L. Capirossi	Ducati	2'01.797
6	33	M. Melandri	Honda	2'02.001
7	14	R. De Puniet	Kawasaki	2'02.443
8	26	D. Pedrosa	Honda	2'02.776
9	21	J. Hopkins	Suzuki	2'02.932
10	4	A. Barros	Ducati	2'03.025
11	66	A. Hofmann	Ducati	2'03.920
12	56	S. Nakano	Honda	2'04.185
13	69	N. Hayden	Honda	2'04.353
14	7	C. Checa	Honda	2'04.971
15	24	T. Elias	Honda	2'05.592
16	5	C. Edwards	Yamaha	2'06.254
17	50	S. Guintoli	Yamaha	2'06.426
18	10	K. Roberts	KR211V	2'06.660
19	80	Ku. Roberts	KR212V	2'07.571

DNQ (Did Not Qualified), but allowed to race:

6	M. Tamada	Yamaha	2'09.080

RACE: 23 laps = 120.635 km

1	Valentino Rossi	42'42.385 (169.485 km/h)
2	Daniel Pedrosa	+ 3"074
3	Alexandre Barros	+ 5"956
4	Casey Stoner	+ 6"012
5	John Hopkins	+ 13"244
6	Toni Elias	+ 19"255
7	Loris Capirossi	+ 19"646
8	Chris Vermeulen	+ 22"810
9	Marco Melandri	+ 22"837
10	Nicky Hayden	+ 24"413
11	Alex Hofmann	+ 24"781
12	Colin Edwards	+ 28"001
13	Shinya Nakano	+ 36"733
14	Sylvain Guintoli	+ 45"098
15	Makoto Tamada	+ 45"145
16	Olivier Jacque	+ 45"217
17	Kenny Roberts Jnr	+ 1'27.222

Fastest lap

Pedrosa, in 1'50.357 (171.099 km/h).
Record: Biaggi, in 1'50.117 (171.472 km/h/2005).

Outright fastest lap

Gibernau, in 1'48.969 (173.278 km/h/2006).

CHAMPIONSHIP

1	C. Stoner	115 (3 wins)
2	V. Rossi	106 (2 wins)
3	D. Pedrosa	82
4	M. Melandri	68
5	C. Vermeulen	63 (1 win)
6	J. Hopkins	59
7	L. Capirossi	47
8	T. Elias	45
9	A. Barros	43
10	C. Edwards	39

THE FIRST ONE FOR ROOKIE BAUTISTA

RUNNERS AND RIDERS
Yuki Takahashi is back, even if his arm still hurts. Locatelli, who had taken part in practice in France, but did not start the race, is trying again here.

QUALIFYING
Rain on the first day and best time for De Angelis. On Saturday, the riders take to the track on intermediates, but soon stop to fit slicks. They will get two laps on a track that has dried out quickly, as it is quite warm and there is some wind, before another strong shower. Sensationally in what is something of a poker game, the reigning world champion and current leader, Jorge Lorenzo, stays in his garage during this fine spell and fails

to make the qualifying cut, but he will be admitted onto the grid like all the others.

START
A super getaway from Luthi, who charges off into the lead ahead of Bautista and Dovizioso. The Spaniard moves to the front as they cross the line. Lorenzo is already eighth.

LAP 2
Lorenzo rips off Kallio's exhaust at full speed, so the Finn has to retire. At the front, Bautista leads from Dovizioso, Luthi and De Angelis.

LAP 3
Bautista and Dovizioso manage to build themselves a lead of a second over De Angelis, while Luthi suffers with road holding problems.

LAP 5
De Angelis has joined the lead duo. Barbera, Lorenzo and Simon have broken away from Luthi, who now

finds himself seventh

LAP 8
Bautista and Barbera are wheel to wheel within just 26 thousandths. De Angelis is third at 911 thousandths, with Dovizioso and Lorenzo next up.

HALF-DISTANCE (10 LAPS)
28 thousandths between the two Spaniards who are out in front. De Angelis is third, with Lorenzo and Dovizioso in close attendance. Lorenzo is sixth, followed by Simon and the Aoyama brothers.

LAP 12
He had started from twentieth on the grid. He is about to take the lead before handing back again to Barbera, who will then go off the track. Lorenzo is without a doubt just a bit special.

LAP 13
Time to pause to draw breath and

see that Lorenzo has a 3 tenths lead over De Angelis, followed by Bautista and Dovizioso.

LAP 17
Bautista and De Angelis have passed Lorenzo. Dovizioso cannot keep up and is 1.3 seconds down.

FINISH (21 LAPS)
Lorenzo, De Angelis and Bautista are separated by 422 thousandths. Bautista catches out Lorenzo, who hits the deck, but will somehow come home in eighth place. At the line, the 125 champion beats his elder, De Angelis by 87 thousandth, with Barbera making it a 100% Aprilia podium.

CHAMPIONSHIP
As Dovizioso finished "only" fourth, Lorenzo maintains a lead of 27 points. De Angelis is third, but Bautista is getting closer.

Alvaro Bautista (left) triumphs at his sixth attempt in 250 cc, on a weekend marked by Lorenzo's mistake (opposite) during qualifying and the oh so Italian colours on Dovizioso's Honda.

GP ITALIA | 3rd June 2007 | Mugello | 5.245 m

STARTING GRID

Pos	No	Rider	Bike	Time
1	19	A. Bautistá	Aprilia	1'57.435
2	34	A. Dovizioso	Honda	1'57.923
3	73	S. Aoyama	Honda	1'58.874
4	12	T. Lüthi	Aprilia	1'58.971
5	3	A. De Angelis	Aprilia	1'59.107
6	80	H. Barberá	Aprilia	1'59.449
7	4	H. Aoyama	KTM	1'59.455
8	36	M. Kallio	KTM	1'59.792
9	14	A. West	Aprilia	2'00.022
10	60	J. Simón	Honda	2'00.237
11	10	I. Toth	Aprilia	2'00.417
12	25	A. Baldolini	Aprilia	2'00.813
13	58	M. Simoncelli	Gilera	2'00.876
14	17	K. Abraham	Aprilia	2'01.529
15	15	R. Locatelli	Gilera	2'01.985
16	28	D. Heidolf	Aprilia	2'02.175
17	64	O. Menghi	Aprilia	2'04.693
18	16	J. Cluzel	Aprilia	2'05.061
19	8	R. Wilairot	Honda	2'05.511

DNQ, but allowed to race:

	No	Rider	Bike	Time
	1	J. Lorenzo	Aprilia	2'07.987
	50	E. Laverty	Honda	2'09.297
	41	A. Espargaro	Aprilia	2'10.810
	9	A. Tizón	Aprilia	2'11.127
	32	F. Lai	Aprilia	2'11.161

	No	Rider	Bike	Time
65		T. Tallevi	Yamaha	2'12.495
44		T. Sekiguchi	Aprilia	2'14.749
55		Y. Takahashi	Honda	2'24.976

RACE: 21 laps = 110.145 km

Pos	Rider	Time
1	Alvaro Bautistá	40'18.605 (163.946 km/h)
2	Alex De Angelis	+ 0''087
3	Hector Barberá	+ 7''665
4	Andrea Dovizioso	+ 7''751
5	Thomas Lüthi	+ 27''267
6	Shuhei Aoyama	+ 27''522
7	Julian Simón	+ 27''774
8	Jorge Lorenzo	+ 32''238
9	Marco Simoncelli	+ 51''455
10	Anthony West	+ 1'04.308
11	Yuki Takahashi	+ 1'04.318
12	Aleix Espargaro	+ 1'04.462
13	Fabrizio Lai	+ 1'04.556
14	Alex Baldolini	+ 1'04.570
15	Taro Sekiguchi	+ 1'05.162
16	Karel Abraham	+ 1'10.583
17	Dirk Heidolf	+ 1'10.587
18	Roberto Locatelli	+ 1'20.650
19	Jules Cluzel	+ 1'20.921
20	Eugene Laverty	+ 1'21.282
21	Hirosho Aoyama	+ 1'46.776
22	Imre Toth	+ 1'54.965
23	Arturo Tizón	+ 1 lap
24	Thomas Tallevi	+ 1 lap

Fastest lap
Barberá, in 1'54.061 (165.542 km/h). New record.
Previous: De Angelis, in 1'54.332 (165.150 km/h/2005).

Outright fastest lap
Lorenzo, in 1'53.457 (166.424 km/h/2005).

CHAMPIONSHIP

Pos	Rider	Points
1	J. Lorenzo	128 (4 wins)
2	A. Dovizioso	101 (1 win)
3	A. De Angelis	95
4	A. Bautistá	89 (1 win)
5	H. Barberá	63
6	J. Simón	46
7	T. Lüthi	43
8	S. Aoyama	32
9	M. Simoncelli	31
10	M. Kallio	30

FAUBEL BECOMES THE FIRST DOUBLE WINNER OF THE SEASON

RUNNERS AND RIDERS
Injured at le Mans, the Spaniard Esteve Rabat has still not recovered, but he is not replaced at Repsol-Honda. Three riders have wild cards: Lacalendola, Sancioni and the German Siegert.

QUALIFYING
Right from the first day, the 125 riders have to deal with tricky conditions, as the Friday session began on a track that was not yet completely wet. The result of this was that by the end of the session, only ten riders were qualified! It rains more seriously on Saturday and the two best times from the previous day (Faubel and De Meglio) are unattainable by around 3 seconds. However, a further sixteen meet the 107% of fastest time qualifying rule, but the eight who fail to make the cut are then allowed in anyway

START
A super start from Tomoyoshi Koyama (KTM) off the second row. Talmacsi and Faubel soon take charge of matters. Lombardi falls at the end of the opening lap which Talmacsi completes with a lead of 149 thousandths over Faubel. Next up come Pasini, De Rosa, Corsi and Smith.

LAP 2
Pasini slips into the lead.

LAP 4
Mike Di Meglio is a faller from ninth place. Joan Olive retires.

LAP 5
Seven of them are covered by 9 tenths: Pasini, Talmacsi, De Rosa, Faubel, Corsi, Pesek and Iannone.

LAP 6
Gadea and Koyama have caught back up to the group and so there are now nine of them in less than a second.

LAP 8
Masbou is a faller while fighting for fifteenth place.

HALF-DISTANCE (10 LAPS)
Faubel, Pasini, De Rosa, Corsi, Talmacsi, Iannone, Pesek, Koyama, Gadea and Cortese: ten of them wheel to wheel, with the gap from front to back being 1.489 seconds. Behind this group, Smith is out on his own, over 2 seconds off the quick pack, but he is about to close up.

LAP 13
Talmacsi has moved to the front with a lead of 322 thousandths over Faubel and Pasini, who immediately mount a counter attack.

LAP 15
They are down to seven in the lead group, covered by just 533", as Cortese, Iannone, Smith, who had caught the pack and especially Pesek, have now all lost touch.

LAP 17
Iannone is a faller. Cortese has rejoined the pack.

FINISH (20 LAPS)
Nine of them are covered by a mere 835 thousandths going into the final lap. It's too tight and De Rosa and Pesek both fall, although the Italian will cross the finish line, pushing his bike. But it's Faubel who surprises everyone, with Gadea beaten by 20 thousandths, Corsi by 66.

CHAMPIONSHIP
Pesek is the big loser on the day, as Faubel moves into the lead with 102 points, ahead of team-mate Talmacsi (95) and the previous leader (91.)

Gadea (33) is beaten by 20 thousandths by team-mate Faubel (55.) Third is a hidden Corsi and it's clear that fourth placed Gabor Talmacsi is not far behind. On the right, Di Meglio hits the deck as Koyama (number 71) is the first non-Aprilia.

GP ITALIA | 3rd June 2007 | Mugello | 5.245 m

STARTING GRID

1	55	H. Faubel	Aprilia	2'15.309
2	63	M. Di Meglio	Honda	2'16.053
3	14	G. Talmacsi	Aprilia	2'18.750
4	13	D. Lombardi	Honda	2'18.829
5	71	T. Koyama	KTM	2'19.118
6	35	R. De Rosa	Aprilia	2'19.132
7	29	A. Iannone	Aprilia	2'19.136
8	52	L. Pesek	Derbi	2'19.780
9	75	M. Pasini	Aprilia	2'19.810
10	6	J. Olivé	Aprilia	2'20.090
11	38	B. Smith	Honda	2'20.352
12	7	A. Masbou	Honda	2'20.504
13	95	R. Muresan	Derbi	2'20.897
14	24	S. Corsi	Aprilia	2'21.008
15	11	S. Cortese	Aprilia	2'21.143
16	60	M. Ranseder	Derbi	2'21.833
17	8	L. Zanetti	Aprilia	2'22.268
18	37	J. Litjens	Honda	2'22.421
19	34	R. Krummenacher	KTM	2'22.469
20	33	S. Gadea	Aprilia	2'22.529
21	18	N. Terol	Derbi	2'22.699
22	44	P. Espargaro	Aprilia	2'23.354
23	87	R. Lacalendola	Aprilia	2'23.809
24	77	D. Aegerter	Aprilia	2'23.962
25	22	P. Nieto	Aprilia	2'24.187
26	42	S. Sancioni	Aprilia	2'24.391

DNQ, but allowed to race:

	15	F. Sandi	Aprilia	2'25.253
	53	S. Grotzkyj	Aprilia	2'25.461

99	D. Webb	Honda	2'25.674
27	S. Bianco	Aprilia	2'26.154
20	R. Tamburini	Aprilia	2'26.175
51	S. Bonsey	KTM	2'26.582
41	T. Siegert	Aprilia	2'29.687
56	H. Van Den Berg	Aprilia	2'33.106

RACE: 20 laps = 104.900 km

1	Hector Faubel	40'14.164 (156.426 km/h)
2	Sergio Gadea	+ 0''020
3	Simone Corsi	+ 0''066
4	Gabor Talmacsi	+ 0''134
5	Tomoyoshi Koyama	+ 1''662
6	Mattia Pasini	+ 1''691
7	Sandro Cortese	+ 1''813
8	Bradley Smith	+ 2''959
9	Pol Espargaro	+ 17''495
10	Lorenzo Zanetti	+ 18''277
11	Michael Ranseder	+ 23''855
12	Nicolas Terol	+ 32''919
13	Randy Krummenacher	+ 36''260
14	Raffaele De Rosa	+ 38''199
15	Dominique Aegerter	+ 1'05.054
16	Joey Litjens	+ 1'05.106
17	Simone Sancioni	+ 1'05.395
18	Federico Sandi	+ 1'05.548
19	Robert Muresan	+ 1'05.700
20	Steve Bonsey	+ 1'25.417
21	Daniel Webb	+ 1'25.595
22	Simone Grotzkyj	+ 1'45.299

23	Hugo Van Den Berg	+ 1'46.907
24	Roberto Tamburini	+ 1 lap

Fastest lap
Gadea, in 1'58.636 (159.159 km/h). New record.
Previous: Pasini, in 1'58.677 (159.104 km/h/2006).

Outright fastest lap
Pesek, in 1'58.202 (159.743 km/h/2006).

CHAMPIONSHIP

1	H. Faubel	102 (2 wins)
2	G. Talmacsi	95 (1 win)
3	L. Pesek	91 (1 win)
4	S. Corsi	71 (1 win)
5	S. Gadea	66 (1 win)
6	P. Espargaro	46
7	J. Olivé	44
8	B. Smith	44
9	T. Koyama	43
10	R. De Rosa	32

Rossi and De Puniet get the best starts, but yet again it is Stoner who will win.

STONER WINS "ROSSI STYLE!"

« TODAY, I'M TELLING YOU CASEY WON
ROSSI STYLE. » WHO SAID THAT?
VALENTINO HIMSELF, WHO SEEMS TO
HAVE MET HIS MATCH IN THE FORM OF
THE YOUNG AUSTRALIAN.

THE RACE

FABLES, FOXES AND CROWS.

There's an old French fable about a crow sitting comfortably in a tree, holding a valuable piece of cheese in his mouth, while a wily old fox tries to get the crow to open his beak to speak and drop it. In MotoGP terms, Stoner is that well placed crow and Rossi is the cunning fox who believes he has what it takes to be there once the pressure and praise get too much for the young Aussie so that he can get that prized world championship lead away from him.

But this time, the fable is not going to plan in this high-tech environment, in this world of courage and psychological games. Valentino has tried everything but Casey has not done as much as even smile, or at least not until he was safely back on his podium perch, from where he could safely see all those trying to knock him off it. His Catalunya race was apparently "won in Rossi style" and this was no mere sound-bite as the comment came from Valentino himself.

Rossi was beaten fair and square by a lad who did not settle for simply making the most of the great bike that Ducati had handed him, but who also gave as good as he got in every attacking move from Rossi, copying the maestro in braking just a little bit later with every passing lap.

Casey the crow and Rossi the fox brought with them Dani the ferret, not quite up to the level of his two prestigious rivals, but always there "just in case." But there was no just in case in Catalunya and Pedrosa had now lost more than a race, as his points difference to Stoner was now up to 42, or the equivalent of almost two race wins. Indeed, the classification looks bad for everyone except Valentino Rossi, the only one still hanging on in there. However, one can well ask since the start of the season, since the switch to these new rules that have produced some enchanting action with five different marques in the top five places, if the Stoner-Ducati duo

really needs races in hand, given that the little Australian no longer seems to make the slightest mistake.

While it is clear to the engineers that the Ducati has taken a major step forward on the electronics side, everyone is also in awe of Casey Stoner, who had come in for all sorts of criticism in past years and who this year has quite simply become, Mr. Perfect. He deserves that title for putting the man who developed the Desmosedici, Loris Capirossi in the shade and for now succeeding in going toe to toe with Valentino Rossi, something that requires a totally calm approach at all times.

So, like that fabled crow that never opens its mouth wide enough to drop that all important piece of cheese, Casey never laughs out loud, but allows himself the slightest of grins, delighted to be holding this superb cheese that tastes of the world championship crown.

Red and white: the colours of another triumph for Casey Stoner. At the finish, Rossi could do no more than congratulate his new rival, having spent the whole race with him and Dani Pedrosa (number 26, above.)

Champagne for Rossi, even though he is only second. Opposite: a moment of concentration for Sylvain Guintoli. Above: Elias, De Puniet, Melandri and Edwards have already lost touch with the lead group

STONER STOOD UP TO ROSSI. PEDROSA WAS POWERLESS

RUNNERS AND RIDERS
Take the same pack from the Italian GP, shuffle them around and let's start again. Having injured a knee in Tuscany, Randy De Puniet undergoes intensive treatment during the week, but keeps his ride.

QUALIFYING
Randy De Puniet would have deserved pole position for courage alone, as his knee looked like a watermelon, as a result of internal hemorrhaging, but in the end he was pipped by just 61 thousandths by Valentino Rossi. Olivier Jacque had a serious fall on Saturday morning, he was stretchered to the medical centre with a neck brace on and was then taken to a Barcelona hospital, suffering with a twisted neck.

START
Pedrosa, Stoner, Hopkins and Rossi are the first quartet to lead, followed closely by De Puniet and Elias. Pedrosa comes across the line for the first time with a lead of 132 thousandths over Stoner, who passes him at the end of the straight.

LAP 3
Rossi has finally found a way past Hopkins and is third, but 1.081 behind Casey Stoner, who has Pedrosa almost sitting on his seat with him.

LAP 5
Elias and De Puniet have a coming together, but both men stay upright.

LAP 6
Rossi has just set the fastest race lap and closed to 539 thousandths off Stoner.

LAP 11
Rossi scalps Pedrosa with a great move under braking. He is now 196 thousandths behind Stoner.

HALF-DISTANCE (12 LAPS)
Stoner, Rossi, Pedrosa and Hopkins: four within less than a second. De Puniet is fifth, holding off Elias. Capirossi has just got the better of Melandri for seventh spot.

LAP 16
Elias' engine blows. Rossi is now 206 thousandths behind Stoner.

LAP 17
There are now only 384 thousandths between Stoner, Rossi and Pedrosa and the big scrap is underway.

LAP 18
Rossi goes into the lead.

LAP 19
Stoner has gone back to the front and it is a crazy three way fight as Pedrosa is still involved.

LAP 22
Rossi in the lead again.

FINISH (25 LAPS)
Stoner has taken command again with 115 thousandths in hand charging into the final lap. At the flag, that gap has gone down to 69. Once again, it has been a spectacular afternoon and in an impressive side story, the badge of courage goes to Randy De Puniet, who finishes fifth, his best result at this level.

CHAMPIONSHIP
Valentino Rossi had closed the gap to Stoner a week earlier but now Casey eases the gap out again, leading Valentino by 14 points. Pedrosa is third, but already trailing the fantastic Ducati rider by 42.

GP CATALUNYA | 10th June 2007 | Catalunya | 4.727 m

STARTING GRID

1	46	V. Rossi	Yamaha	1'41.840
2	14	R. De Puniet	Kawasaki	1'41.901
3	26	D. Pedrosa	Honda	1'42.002
4	27	C. Stoner	Ducati	1'42.117
5	21	J. Hopkins	Suzuki	1'42.233
6	5	C. Edwards	Yamaha	1'42.283
7	1	N. Hayden	Honda	1'42.522
8	24	T. Elias	Honda	1'42.607
9	33	M. Melandri	Honda	1'42.623
10	66	A. Hofmann	Ducati	1'42.860
11	71	C. Vermeulen	Suzuki	1'42.967
12	56	S. Nakano	Honda	1'43.334
13	50	S. Guintoli	Yamaha	1'43.557
14	4	A. Barros	Ducati	1'43.722
15	7	C. Checa	Honda	1'43.729
16	6	M. Tamada	Yamaha	1'43.947
17	65	L. Capirossi	Ducati	1'43.948
18	10	K. Roberts	KR211V	1'44.263
19	80	Ku. Roberts	KR212V	1'45.223

RACE: 25 laps = 118.175 km

1	Casey Stoner	43'16.907 (163.821 km/h)
2	Valentino Rossi	+ 0''069
3	Daniel Pedrosa	+ 0''390
4	John Hopkins	+ 7''814
5	Randy De Puniet	+ 17''853
6	Loris Capirossi	+ 19''409
7	Chris Vermeulen	+ 19''495
8	Alexandre Barros	+ 24''862
9	Marco Melandri	+ 24''963
10	Colin Edwards	+ 35''348
11	Nicky Hayden	+ 36''301
12	Makoto Tamada	+ 38''720
13	Alex Hofmann	+ 40''934
14	Sylvain Guintoli	+ 44''399
15	Shinya Nakano	+ 54''103
16	Kenny Roberts Jnr	+ 59''655
17	Carlos Checa	+ 1'02.315
18	Kurtis Roberts	+ 1'03.322

Fastest lap
Hopkins, in 1'43.252 (164.812 km/h).
Record: Hayden, in 1'43.048 (165.138 km/h/2006).

Outright fastest lap
Rossi, in 1'41.840 (167.097 km/h/2007).

CHAMPIONSHIP

1	C. Stoner	140 (4 wins)
2	V. Rossi	126 (2 wins)
3	D. Pedrosa	98
4	M. Melandri	75
5	C. Vermeulen	72 (1 win)
6	J. Hopkins	72
7	L. Capirossi	57
8	A. Barros	51
9	T. Elias	45
10	C. Edwards	45

LORENZO AGAIN, DE ANGELIS SQUEEZES BETWEEN THE SPANIARD AND ANDREA DOVIZIOSO

RUNNERS AND RIDERS

No absentees, but as is usual in Spain, three wild cards: Debon, Aprilia's development rider; Molina, the European champion and Barragan, who would fail to qualify.

QUALIFYING

Jorge Lorenzo has no real rivals in terms of pure speed. "But you know, I am still human and can make mistakes sometimes." Nevertheless he has little else to do except go for unattainable records. And he succeeds in attaining them, as is the case on Saturday 9 June 2007, when he becomes the quickest ever two stroke rider in history. He has in fact beaten Valentino Rossi's last 500 class pole, set in 2001, by almost 5 seconds!

START

Once again, Luthi makes the perfect getaway, but Lorenzo soon takes control, with Dovizioso immediately moving into second place. Crossing the line at the end of the opening lap, the world champion has a lead of 446 thousandths over Dovizioso and 865 over Luthi, who is followed by Kallio. Bautista and Barbera are only 13th and 14th.

LAP 4

Still Lorenzo, with Dovizioso trailing by 253 thousandths. Luthi is third at half a second ahead of Kallio, who is about to be swallowed up by De Angelis.

LAP 7

De Angelis has caught the lead

Dovizioso (above) was powerless up against the speed of the Aprilias. Below: Alex Debon hits the deck just as he was catching Luthi in their fight for fourth place.

For the fifth time this season, Jorge Lorenzo has cause to jump for joy.

group: Lorenzo, Dovizioso, Luthi and the San Marino rider are in a tiny pocket of 852 thousandths. Kallio is 1.355 behind, with Debon a bit further back on his own. Bautista and Barbera have moved up to 7th and 8th.

GP CATALUNYA | 10th June 2007 | Catalunya | 4.727 m

STARTING GRID

Pos	No	Rider	Bike	Time
1	1	J. Lorenzo	Aprilia	1'45.098
2	80	H. Barberá	Aprilia	1'46.013
3	34	A. Dovizioso	Honda	1'46.201
4	6	A. Debón	Aprilia	1'46.333
5	12	T. Lüthi	Aprilia	1'46.382
6	3	A. De Angelis	Aprilia	1'46.422
7	19	A. Bautistá	Aprilia	1'46.436
8	36	M. Kallio	KTM	1'46.629
9	4	H. Aoyama	KTM	1'46.664
10	58	M. Simoncelli	Gilera	1'46.666
11	55	Y. Takahashi	Honda	1'46.667
12	60	J. Simón	Honda	1'46.836
13	73	S. Aoyama	Honda	1'47.037
14	41	A. Espargaro	Aprilia	1'47.100
15	15	R. Locatelli	Gilera	1'47.820
16	14	A. West	Aprilia	1'47.894
17	28	D. Heidolf	Aprilia	1'47.903
18	44	T. Sekiguchi	Aprilia	1'47.932
19	25	A. Baldolini	Aprilia	1'48.180
20	17	K. Abraham	Aprilia	1'48.383
21	32	F. Lai	Aprilia	1'48.452
22	8	R. Wilairot	Honda	1'49.139
23	50	E. Laverty	Honda	1'49.310
24	16	J. Cluzel	Aprilia	1'49.347
25	31	A. Molina	Aprilia	1'49.416
26	10	I. Toth	Aprilia	1'49.729
27	9	A. Tizón	Aprilia	1'49.928

Not qualified:

	53	S. Barragan	Honda	1'54.203

RACE: 23 laps = 108.721 km

Pos	Rider	Time/Gap
1	Jorge Lorenzo	40'51.620 (159.647 km/h)
2	Alex De Angelis	+ 3''194
3	Andrea Dovizioso	+ 10''596
4	Thomas Lüthi	+ 17''100
5	Alvaro Bautistá	+ 20''298
6	Mika Kallio	+ 20''566
7	Hiroshi Aoyama	+ 20''615
8	Hector Barberá	+ 23''584
9	Marco Simoncelli	+ 36''703
10	Julian Simón	+ 36''767
11	Shuhei Aoyama	+ 39''592
12	Roberto Locatelli	+ 48''028
13	Jules Cluzel	+ 1'07.085
14	Karel Abraham	+ 1'11.868
15	Taro Sekiguchi	+ 1'17.387
16	Alex Debón	+ 1'19.654
17	Ratthapark Wilairot	+ 1'19.822
18	Alex Baldolini	+ 1'23.243
19	Eugene Laverty	+ 1'35.553
20	Aleix Espargaro	+ 1'42.529
21	Anthony West	+ 1'55.832
22	Imre Toth	+ 1 lap
23	Alvaro Molina	+ 1 lap

Fastest lap

De Angelis, in 1'45.925 (160.653 km/h). New record.
Previous: Pedrosa, in 1'47.302 (158.591 km/h/2004).

Outright fastest lap

Lorenzo, in 1'45.098 (161.917 km/h/2007).

CHAMPIONSHIP

Pos	Rider	Points
1	J. Lorenzo	153 (5 wins)
2	A. Dovizioso	117 (1 win)
3	A. De Angelis	115
4	A. Bautistá	100 (1 win)
5	H. Barberá	71
6	T. Lüthi	56
7	J. Simón	52
8	M. Kallio	40
9	M. Simoncelli	28
10	S. Aoyama	37

KOYAMA AND KTM TRIUMPH. KRUMMENACHER DOES ALMOST AS WELL AS LUTHI FOUR YEARS EARLIER.

RUNNERS AND RIDERS
Stefano Bianco was injured at Mugello, suffering a minor fracture to the sternum. He is not replaced. Esteve Rabat (Honda) is back.
Sign of the times, or rather a desire to internationalise the Spanish championship, there are two "foreigners" among the wild card riders, including Germany's Stefan Bradl, who won here at the Catalunya circuit two weeks earlier in the Open.

QUALIFYING
With Pasini weakened after getting up from a Friday fall with bruising to his right hand, the Aspar team get a nice triple, in the order Talmacsi, Faubel and Gadea. A pleasant surprise in fourth spot for Bradley Smith and his Honda.

START
Faubel, Gadea and Talmacsi lead away from the line. Dutchman Litjens is a faller. First time across the line, the three Aspar boys lead the dance, with Faubel now ahead of Talmacsi and Gadea. Next up come Pesek, Koyama, Smith and Pasini.

LAP 3
Pasini's bike seizes and he falls before giving his Aprilia bodywork a really good kicking. One really has to beleive that he is the victim of some sort of evil spell.

A Swiss rider leads a 125 GP: four years after a first podium for Thomas Luthi, Randy Krummenacher (no 34 and on the podium) was the hero of the Catalunya GP, as was the young Pol Espargaro, who takes a bow as he crosses the line.

LAP 4
Koyama is now third and coming up to eighth is the young Swiss rider, Randy Krummenacher, who has just set two consecutive fastest laps.

LAP 5
Eight of them are covered by exactly 1.5000 seconds: Gadea, Talmacsi, Pesek, Faubel, P. Esparagaro, Smith, Koyama and Krummenacher.

HALF-DISTANCE (11 LAPS)
Gadea has just stepped up the pace. He crosses the line at the mid-point of the race with 619 thousandths over the rest of the lead pack which comprises Faubel, Pesek, Talmacsi, Esparagaro, Krummenacher, Koyama and Smith.

LAP 13
Pesek now leads the dance. The first group are separated by a mere 1.134 seconds.

LAP 16
Place a bet on these long odds: Gadea leads Krummenacher and Espargaro!

LAP 17
The Gadea-Krummenacher duo have pulled out a gap of 6 tenths.

LAP 19
Faubel falls but gets going again and Pesek also hits the deck. Krummenacher leads Gadea.

FINISH (22 LAPS)
Koyama, Krummenacher, Gadea and Talmacsi: all four in 551 thousandths. Koyama has the final word, 49 thousandths ahead of Talmacsi, with Krummenacher taking his first podium at the same track where, back in 2003 the GP world discovered another Swiss rider by the name of Thomas Luthi.

CHAMPIONSHIP
Talmacsi is of course the big winner on the day, as he goes back to the lead in the championship, with a 13 point advantage over Faubel and 21 on Pesek. Corsi is fourth, ahead of Gadea and the winner on the day, Tomoyoshi Koyama.

GP CATALUNYA | 10th June 2007 | Catalunya | 4.727 m

STARTING GRID

1	14	G. Talmacsi	Aprilia	1'50.012
2	55	H. Faubel	Aprilia	1'50.336
3	33	S. Gadea	Aprilia	1'50.529
4	38	B. Smith	Honda	1'50.806
5	52	L. Pesek	Derbi	1'50.933
6	35	R. De Rosa	Aprilia	1'50.945
7	71	T. Koyama	KTM	1'51.072
8	75	M. Pasini	Aprilia	1'51.170
9	24	S. Corsi	Aprilia	1'51.170
10	29	A. Iannone	Aprilia	1'51.295
11	11	S. Cortese	Aprilia	1'51.744
12	12	E. Rabat	Honda	1'51.799
13	17	S. Bradl	Aprilia	1'51.801
14	6	J. Olivé	Aprilia	1'51.925
15	34	R. Krummenacher	KTM	1'51.930
16	63	M. Di Meglio	Honda	1'51.985
17	60	M. Ranseder	Derbi	1'51.995
18	44	P. Espargaro	Aprilia	1'52.050
19	18	N. Terol	Derbi	1'52.069
20	22	P. Nieto	Aprilia	1'52.113
21	8	L. Zanetti	Aprilia	1'52.273
22	7	A. Masbou	Honda	1'52.383
23	95	R. Muresan	Derbi	1'52.386
24	56	H. Van Den Berg	Aprilia	1'52.676
25	30	P. Tutusaus	Aprilia	1'52.677
26	15	F. Sandi	Aprilia	1'52.699
27	77	D. Aegerter	Aprilia	1'52.819
28	53	S. Grotzkyj	Aprilia	1'53.072
29	20	R. Tamburini	Aprilia	1'53.195
30	85	P. Eitzinger	Honda	1'53.619
31	37	J. Litjens	Honda	1'53.648
32	51	S. Bonsey	KTM	1'53.662
33	13	D. Lombardi	Honda	1'53.688
34	76	I. Maestro	Aprilia	1'53.859
35	99	D. Webb	Honda	1'54.939

RACE: 22 laps = 103.994 km

1	Tomoyoshi Koyama	41'06.339 (151.795 km/h)	
2	Gabor Talmacsi	+ 0''049	
3	Randy Krummenacher	+ 0''131	
4	Sergio Gadea	+ 0''500	
5	Pol Espargaro	+ 2''081	
6	Bradley Smith	+ 4''792	
7	Simone Corsi	+ 16''840	
8	Joan Olivé	+ 16''910	
9	Stefan Bradl	+ 16''919	
10	Michael Ranseder	+ 16''922	
11	Sandro Cortese	+ 17''112	
12	Esteve Rabat	+ 17''255	
13	Lukas Pesek	+ 17''263	
14	Lorenzo Zanetti	+ 23''707	
15	Dominique Aegerter	+ 28''366	
16	Alexis Masbou	+ 28''637	
17	Andrea Iannone	+ 28''658	
18	Pere Tutusaus	+ 29''026	
19	Mike Di Meglio	+ 29''619	
20	Pablo Nieto	+ 31''800	
21	Federico Sandi	+ 46''773	
22	Roberto Tamburini	+ 47''361	

23	Nicolas Terol	+ 53''881
24	Robert Muresan	+ 54''045
25	Hugo Van Den Berg	+ 54''103
26	Daniel Webb	+ 1'20.170
27	Ivan Maestro	+ 1'36.934

Fastest lap
Krummenacher, in 1'50.732 (153.679 km/h). New record. Previous: Faubel, in 1'50.773 (153.622 km/h/2006).

Outright fastest lap
Talmacsi, in 1'50.012 (154.684 km/h/2007).

CHAMPIONSHIP

1	G. Talmacsi	115 (1 win)
2	H. Faubel	102 (2 wins)
3	L. Pesek	94 (1 win)
4	S. Corsi	80 (1 win)
5	S. Gadea	79 (1 win)
6	T. Koyama	68 (1 win)
7	P. Espargaro	57
8	B. Smith	54
9	J. Olivé	52
10	M. Ranseder	36

A background from olden times for a modern champion. Stoner wins once again.

CASEY STONER,
THE QUIET FORCE

ANOTHER DEMONSTRATION FROM THE
AUSTRALIAN IN DIFFICULT WEATHER.
ROSSI, THE ROBIN HOOD OF THE GPS
DID NOT FARE SO WELL.

THE RACE

HARD TIMES FOR ROBIN HOOD.

At first we knew him disguised as Robin Hood, a cool man of justice who loved stealing from the rich and giving to the poor. After his days in 125s and 250 cc, he had joined the upper echelons of the works Honda team, first in the 500 class and then in MotoGP. Then, he became the Sheriff of Nottingham, who handed out a vast range of penalties to his rivals.

At the same time, as he was earning more and more money, he had, officially and administratively, left the country of his birth to live a life of exile in the English capital. Rich beyond his dreams, the Sheriff still had something of Robin Hood in him and he went and joined the "poor folk" (it's a case of poetic license) at Yamaha, to try and defeat the "rich" Honda empire and we all know how well that went.

But here's the thing, the years have passed and Robin Valentino has joined the nobility, with every word and deed now recorded in the media. But he still loves his work. Therefore, while the doors of another kingdom - Formula 1 - had been opened wide for him, he said no, preferring to stay in his own kingdom.

Last year, still as the lawmaker, he lost his crown, because in the early part of the season, his bike let him down too often. And also because he found Nicky Hayden in his way and the Kentucky Kid made fewer mistakes than him.

Were the days of Robin Valentino over? Everyone would have a good laugh this year, not far from

Rossi Robin Hood flat out, his nose buried in the fairing of his Yamaha, but once again super Stoner wins.

Sherwood Forest, at the new adventures of the sheriff who now had another very surprising trio in his sights, made up of a very young Australian, Casey Stoner, a legendary Italian constructor, Ducati and a Japanese manufacturer, Bridgestone.

Since the start of the year, Rossi, well aware of the worth of his rival, has not gone for his usual strategy of using the media to destabilise Stoner. Probably, because he sees something of himself in the Australian: a straightforward youngster, who having learnt his trade, sometimes painfully in the blue riband category the year before, is this time round operating on another planet. Without making the slightest mistake.

The Ducati's phenomenal power made the difference in Doha from the very start of these new adventures. How would they evolve? We soon found out. Rain or shine, on twisty or sweeping tracks, Stoner is always there, the calm Olympian with a hint of panache and total mastery of his art.

He did this to such an extent that on this very rainy Sunday spent near Sherwood Forest, he was the one to resort to fire words like arrows: "What we have just achieved shows everyone that the Ducati Desmosedici is not just more powerful than the opposition."

As for Robin Hood, or Valentino Rossi, he could do nothing but put his arrows back in his quiver. At least for one more week.

AND SUDDENLY STONER UPS THE PACE. ROSSI HAD BEEN BEATEN FOR A WHILE BY THEN

RUNNERS AND RIDERS

"The day comes when your body tells you to stop and that day came in Barcelona." After a serious fall in practice in Catalunya, Olivier Jacque has decided to hang up his helmet and, with immediate effect, he becomes Kawasaki's development rider. He is replaced by Anthony West, who until now had been riding a customer 250 Aprilia and he has just won the last two rounds of the world supersport series with Yamaha. Kenny Roberts Junior is absent and in the words of his dad: "the bike's too slow and the rider's too old."

QUALIFYING

Qualifying is dominated by the two Yamahas with Edwards ahead of Rossi! Next up, the two works Hondas, but in the rain things are very different. This means that, come the warm-up, West turns up to top the time sheet!

START

Super fast reflexes from Edwards who shoots into the lead at Redgate corner, ahead of Pedrosa, Hayden and Rossi. Stoner gets it wrong and is only twelfth first time across the line. Pedrosa takes the lead before the end of the opening lap, ahead of Edwards and Rossi.

LAP 3

Rossi is only sixth, as Hayden and Hopkins have just swept past.

LAP 5

Hayden is a faller. Seven of them are covered by 3.766 seconds: Edwards, Stoner, Hopkins, Vermeulen, Pedrosa, Rossi and West.

LAP 8

West goes off the track when lying fourth and puts on a superb dirt track demonstration. Further ahead, Stoner is 6 tenths off Edwards.

LAP 11

Rossi, who has opted for a harder rear tyre than the others, passes Hopkins, but goes off a bit further on.

LAP 12

Rossi re-passes Hopkins for 3rd place.

HALF-DISTANCE (15 LAPS)

Edwards still leads, but Stoner has closed up to within 781 thousandths. In third, Rossi is 9.023 off the leader. Hopkins and Vermeulen are scrapping over fourth place. Pedrosa has just been ambushed by Capirossi and Barros.

LAP 16

Stoner makes the most of a moment's hesitation from Edwards to take the lead.

LAP 20

Capirossi surprises De Puniet for sixth spot. Out in front, Stoner now leads Edwards by 3.821 seconds.

LAP 25

Capirossi's impressive comeback is over as he hits the deck.

LAP 26

Vermeulen has closed to within a half second of Rossi.

LAP 27

Vermeulen is third.

FINISH (30 LAPS)

Stoner is impressive, having not made the slightest mistake. Edwards is second, ahead of Vermeulen and Rossi.

CHAMPIONSHIP

Of course, this has been a very good day's work for Stoner as he now has a lead of 26 points, which equates to a race in hand.

Shinya Nakano (on left) suffered in the rain, but not as much as Nicky Hayden (opposite.) The British weekend was also the moment for Olivier Jacque, seen here with Kawasaki boss Ichiro Yoda, to say goodbye.

GP GREAT BRITAIN | 24th June 2007 | Donington | 4.023 m

STARTING GRID

1	5	C. Edwards	Yamaha	1'28.531
2	46	V. Rossi	Yamaha	1'28.677
3	26	D. Pedrosa	Honda	1'28.863
4	1	N. Hayden	Honda	1'29.025
5	27	C. Stoner	Ducati	1'29.061
6	21	J. Hopkins	Suzuki	1'29.073
7	7	C. Checa	Honda	1'29.281
8	14	R. De Puniet	Kawasaki	1'29.415
9	33	M. Melandri	Honda	1'29.498
10	24	T. Elias	Honda	1'29.711
11	56	S. Nakano	Honda	1'29.718
12	71	C. Vermeulen	Suzuki	1'29.793
13	65	L. Capirossi	Ducati	1'29.900
14	66	A. Hofmann	Ducati	1'29.911
15	4	A. Barros	Ducati	1'30.071
16	50	S. Guintoli	Yamaha	1'30.271
17	13	A. West	Kawasaki	1'30.718
18	6	M. Tamada	Yamaha	1'30.800
19	80	Ku. Roberts	KR212V	1'31.543

RACE: 30 laps = 120.690 km

1	Casey Stoner	51'40.739 (140.122 km/h)
2	Colin Edwards	+ 11''768
3	Chris Vermeulen	+ 15''678
4	Valentino Rossi	+ 21''827
5	John Hopkins	+ 35''518
6	Randy De Puniet	+ 36''474
7	Alexandre Barros	+ 38''094
8	Daniel Pedrosa	+ 38''992
9	Alex Hofmann	+ 39''239
10	Marco Melandri	+ 1'01.526
11	Anthony West	+ 1'06.486
12	Toni Elias	+ 1'34.074
13	Kurtis Roberts	+ 1 lap
14	Shinya Nakano	+ 1 lap
15	Makoto Tamada	+ 2 laps
16	Sylvain Guintoli	+ 2 laps
17	Nicky Hayden	+ 4 laps

Fastest lap
Elias, in 1'41.428 (142.788 km/h).
Record: Pedrosa, in 1'28.714 (163.252 km/h/2006).

Outright fastest lap
Pedrosa, in 1'27.676 (165.185 km/h/2006).

CHAMPIONSHIP

1	C. Stoner	165 (5 wins)
2	V. Rossi	139 (2 wins)
3	D. Pedrosa	106
4	C. Vermeulen	88 (1 win)
5	J. Hopkins	83
6	M. Melandri	81
7	C. Edwards	65
8	A. Barros	60
9	L. Capirossi	57
10	T. Elias	49

Lorenzo tenses up, Dovizioso escapes and the Italian reopens the championship battle. Above, a spectacular fall for Luthi on the stroke of midday on Saturday. Opposite, Hiroshi Aoyama has rediscovered the route to the podium.

© Christian Cueille

LORENZO DOES NOT LIKE THE RAIN, DOVIZIOSO MAKES THE MOST OF IT

RUNNERS AND RIDERS

The former 125 world champion, Switzerland's Thomas Luthi has undergone surgery on both arms to prevent "pump up" syndrome on the Friday after the Catalunya GP. With Anthony West "promoted" to MotoGP, the Sicilia team Aprilia is entrusted to Englishman Dan Linfoot. In the Blusens Aprilia Germany camp, one finds the Spaniard, Efren Vazquez as the nominated rider, Arturo Tizon has some personal problems.

QUALIFYING

De Angelis is untouchable, be it in the rain on Friday or in the dry on Saturday.

He takes pole, four tenths quicker than Lorenzo. In Saturday morning's free practice, Luthi has a heavy fall, experiencing his first 250 highside, but he gets up with bruising on his left side.

START

In the rain, De Angelis and Dovizioso make the best starts, ahead of Lorenzo, Simon and Simoncelli. Crossing the line for the first time, De Angelis and Dovizioso are separated by 374 thousandths. Barbera falls no less than three times on this opening lap!

LAP 2

Simoncelli is a faller. De Angelis, Lorenzo and Dovizioso are crammed into a space of 1"220.

LAP 7

De Angelis now has a lead of 1.717 over the two who made the break with him. Further back, Bautista is having a solitary race in fourth place.

LAP 9

Bautista is a faller.

LAP 10

Simoncelli falls for a second time.

LAP 11

A thunderbolt, as the championship leader Lorenzo falls, as does Thomas Luthi, who had been fighting with Takahashi for fifth place.

HALF-DISTANCE (13 LAPS)

De Angelis still leads, but Dovizioso, who has just set the fastest race lap in the downpour, is 1.211 behind. There is another duel for third place, this one between Hiroshi Aoyama and Simon. Takahashi is under 2 seconds off a potential podium finish.

LAP 15

Locatelli falls.

LAP 19

Simon falls, just as Takahashi catches the duo battling for third place. The

Spaniard rejoins in seventh place.

LAP 23

De Angelis has lost time lapping Espargaro, who falls a bit further down the road. Dovizioso closes to within 386 thousandths.

LAP 26

Alex de Angelis is a faller, but he gets going again in second place.

FINISH: (27 LAPS)

With a massive cushion of 26.438 over his unfortunate rival, Dovizioso can afford to settle for a safe finish. Hiroshi Aoyama is third ahead of Takahashi. Mika Kallio falls in the last few metres, but hangs onto sixth place.

CHAMPIONSHIP

Of course, this relaunches Dovizioso's challenge as he has now closed to 11 points off Lorenzo, while De Angelis is 18 behind.

GP GREAT BRITAIN | 24th June 2007 | Donington | 4.023 m

STARTING GRID

1	3	A. De Angelis	Aprilia	1'32.391
2	1	J. Lorenzo	Aprilia	1'32.801
3	60	J. Simón	Honda	1'33.043
4	19	A. Bautistá	Aprilia	1'33.096
5	36	M. Kallio	KTM	1'33.130
6	34	A. Dovizioso	Honda	1'33.170
7	58	M. Simoncelli	Gilera	1'33.179
8	80	H. Barberá	Aprilia	1'33.209
9	12	T. Lüthi	Aprilia	1'33.211
10	4	H. Aoyama	KTM	1'33.390
11	55	Y. Takahashi	Honda	1'33.555
12	73	S. Aoyama	Honda	1'34.026
13	15	R. Locatelli	Gilera	1'34.046
14	32	F. Lai	Aprilia	1'34.065
15	50	E. Laverty	Honda	1'34.489
16	41	A. Espargaro	Aprilia	1'34.634
17	8	R. Wilairot	Honda	1'34.857
18	25	A. Baldolini	Aprilia	1'35.033
19	28	D. Heidolf	Aprilia	1'35.237
20	16	J. Cluzel	Aprilia	1'35.398
21	45	D. Linfoot	Aprilia	1'35.448
22	44	T. Sekiguchi	Aprilia	1'35.705
23	10	I. Toth	Aprilia	1'35.812
24	17	K. Abraham	Aprilia	1'35.815
25	7	E. Vazquez	Aprilia	1'35.819
26	81	T. Markham	Yamaha	1'38.733

Not qualified:

82	A. Sawford	Yamaha		1'39.602
83	A. Kenchington	Yamaha		1'40.695
84	L. Lawrence	Honda		2'03.189

RACE: 27 laps = 108.621 km

1	Andrea Dovizioso	48'40.173 (133.908 km/h)
2	Alex De Angelis	+ 22''102
3	Hiroshi Aoyama	+ 1'03.137
4	Yuki Takahashi	+ 1'03.370
5	Shuhei Aoyama	+ 1'25.269
6	Mika Kallio	+ 2'07.333
7	Julian Simón	+ 1 lap
8	Ratthapark Wilairot	+ 1 lap
9	Dan Linfoot	+ 1 lap
10	Karel Abraham	+ 1 lap
11	Fabrizio Lai	+ 1 lap
12	Dirk Heidolf	+ 1 lap
13	Taro Sekiguchi	+ 1 lap
14	Alex Baldolini	+ 1 lap
15	Imre Toth	+ 1 lap
16	Efren Vazquez	+ 2 laps
17	Toby Markham	+ 2 laps

Fastest lap

De Angelis, in 1'45.461 (160.653 km/h).
Record: Dovizioso, in 1'33.029 (155.680 km/h/2006).

Outright fastest lap

Lorenzo, in 1'31.659 (158.007 km/h/2006).

CHAMPIONSHIP

1	J. Lorenzo	153 (5 wins)
2	A. Dovizioso	142 (2 wins)
3	A. De Angelis	135
4	A. Bautistá	100 (1 win)
5	H. Barberá	71
6	J. Simón	61
7	T. Lüthi	56
8	M. Kallio	50
9.	S. Aoyama	48
10	H. Aoyama	42

Fifth pole position and finally, the first win of the season for Pasini. Opposite, Mike Di Meglio reminds us he quite likes the rain…. which does not appear to be the case for Corsi, Krummenacher and Rabat (above.)

PASINI VOULAIT ENFIN SA REVANCHE ET L'A OBTENUE: VICTOIRE!

RUNNERS AND RIDERS
Stefano Bianco is back. Injured in Catalunya, Dino Lombardi is replaced in the Scot team by Spain's Enrique Jerez. Five British riders have wild cards.

QUALIFYING
Eighth race and fifth pole position for Mattia Pasini, the unluckiest man so far this season. The Italian deals with it all with a smile: "If I don't find a ride for next season, it's easy, I'll just open a watch shop, selling off all the ones I've already won this season!" (Tissot presents the pole man with a watch.) The grid was decided on just one day,

the second, as it was raining on Friday. Losing out big time is Lukas Pesek who falls and is only 21st.

START
The track had gradually dried out over the past hours - the 125 race is the last of the day. Pasini (on slicks,) Corsi (handcut tyres) and Koyama charge off in the lead. Crossing the line for the first time, Pasini has a 381 thousandths lead over Koyama who is followed by Faubel, Corsi, Nieto and Masbou.

LAP 2
Masbou is a faller but gets going again. Corsi takes the lead.

LAP 5
No less than thirteen of them are covered by a mere 3 seconds.

LAP 7
There's a break. From Corsi to Talmacsi, there are nine of them

fighting for second, covered by 1.559. The second group is made up of Pol Espargaro, Smith, Rabat, Krummenacher and Olive.

LAP 9
Espargaro is a faller.

LAP 10
Dragged along by Olive, who has just set the fastest race lap, the pursuers have regrouped with 13 of them within 3.145 seconds.

HALF-DISTANCE (12 LAPS)
Pasini has stepped up the pace and now has a lead of 655 thousandths over Faubel, who precedes Koyama, Corsi, Talmacsi and De Rosa.

LAP 14
De Rosa and Corsi collide but both stay upright. A bit later, things get worse as Corsi falls in the hairpin leading onto the straight, as do Rabat and Krummenacher.

LAP 16
Pasini now leads Faubel by 2.240 seconds, with Koyama glued to the second placed man.

LAP 19
Talmacsi retires.

FINISH (25 LAPS)
Going into the final lap, Pasini has a lead over 4.316 seconds over Koyama. This time, there would be no unpleasant surprises and the Italian finally wins, ahead of Koyama and Faubel. Having kicked it to bits in Catalunya, this time Mattia spends the lap of honour lovingly caressing his bike.

CHAMPIONSHIP
With Talmacsi and Pesek failing to score points, it is thrown wide open again, as Faubel takes the lead by three points from Talmacsi and 24 ahead of Pesek.

GP GREAT BRITAIN | 24th June 2007 | Donington | 4.023 m

STARTING GRID

1	75	M. Pasini	Aprilia	1'37.399
2	24	S. Corsi	Aprilia	1'37.846
3	71	T. Koyama	KTM	1'38.073
4	14	G. Talmacsi	Aprilia	1'38.153
5	33	S. Gadea	Aprilia	1'38.217
6	55	H. Faubel	Aprilia	1'38.238
7	22	P. Nieto	Aprilia	1'38.365
8	7	A. Masbou	Honda	1'38.386
9	38	B. Smith	Honda	1'38.394
10	6	J. Olivé	Aprilia	1'38.427
11	34	R. Krummenacher	KTM	1'38.441
12	35	R. De Rosa	Aprilia	1'38.504
13	44	P. Espargaro	Aprilia	1'38.519
14	29	A. Iannone	Aprilia	1'38.813
15	63	M. Di Meglio	Honda	1'38.990
16	11	S. Cortese	Aprilia	1'39.006
17	8	L. Zanetti	Aprilia	1'39.007
18	60	M. Ranseder	Derbi	1'39.012
19	20	R. Tamburini	Aprilia	1'39.095
20	27	S. Bianco	Aprilia	1'39.229
21	52	L. Pesek	Derbi	1'39.267
22	18	N. Terol	Derbi	1'39.510
23	15	F. Sandi	Aprilia	1'39.640
24	31	E. Jerez	Honda	1'39.678
25	77	D. Aegerter	Aprilia	1'39.708
26	95	R. Muresan	Derbi	1'40.065
27	56	H. Van Den Berg	Aprilia	1'40.126
28	12	E. Rabat	Honda	1'40.169
29	37	J. Litjens	Honda	1'40.184
30	51	S. Bonsey	KTM	1'40.566
31	53	S. Grotzkyj	Aprilia	1'40.771
32	99	D. Webb	Honda	1'41.131
33	84	R. Stewart	Honda	1'41.417
34	82	L. Jones	Honda	1'42.090
35	83	N. Coates	Honda	1'42.347
36	54	K. Coghlan	Honda	1'42.804

RACE: 25 laps = 100.575 km

1	Mattia Pasini	41'49.049 (144.305 km/h)
2	Tomoyoshi Koyama	+ 3''253
3	Hector Faubel	+ 5''094
4	Sergio Gadea	+ 6''781
5	Joan Olivé	+ 7''212
6	Mike Di Meglio	+ 7''335
7	Bradley Smith	+ 13''505
8	Raffaele De Rosa	+ 13''885
9	Pablo Nieto	+ 14''367
10	Simone Corsi	+ 26''672
11	Lorenzo Zanetti	+ 27''060
12	Sandro Cortese	+ 27''403
13	Randy Krummenacher	+ 38''212
14	Enrique Jerez	+ 41''905
15	Andrea Iannone	+ 48''782
16	Robert Muresan	+ 1'05.000
17	Simone Grotzkyj	+ 1'05.720
18	Lukas Pesek	+ 1'05.847
19	Alexis Masbou	+ 1'18.100
20	Michael Ranseder	+ 1'18.438
21	Joey Litjens	+ 1'23.222
22	Luke Jones	+ 1'24.001
23	Steve Bonsey	+ 1'24.309
24	Nicolas Terol	+ 1'27.391

25	Daniel Webb	+ 1'33.592
26	Hugo Van Den Berg	+ 1'38.942
27	Nikki Coates	+ 1'40.403
28	Robbie Stewart	+ 1'40.553
29	Roberto Tamburini	+ 1 lap
30	Tom Hayward	+ 1 lap

Fastest lap
Pasini, in 1'38.188 (147.500 km/h).
Record: Bautistá, in 1'37.312 (148.828 km/h/2006).

Outright fastest lap
Bautista, in 1'36.203 (150.544 km/h/2006).

CHAMPIONSHIP

1	H. Faubel	118 (2 wins)
2	G. Talmacsi	115 (1 win)
3	L. Pesek	94 (1 win)
4	S. Gadea	92 (1 win)
5	T. Koyama	88 (1 win)
6	S. Corsi	86 (1 win)
7	J. Olivé	63
8	B. Smith	63
9	P. Espargaro	57
10	M. Pasini	41 (1 win)

Special colours to promote the new Fiat Cinquecento....but a classic smile: Valentino Rossi beat Stoner fair and square.

ROSSI LIKES ASSEN

IT'S THE MOTORCYLCING MECCA.
IT IS « THE » MEETING OF THE YEAR,
THE DUTCH GP IS ALL OF THIS AND
MORE, SO IT'S RIGHT THAT THE
GREATEST WINS

THE RACE

HE IS THE KING!

Rossi triumphant once more, the "Doctor" riding with new colours takes the lead from Casey Stoner: the key moment in the most important GP of the year

I t's the story of a young prince, as good looking as young men of his age often are. He is discrete and well behaved and several months ago, took his princess, his first love, for his wife. As the prince himself explained: "I didn't want to lose her." The prince who set out to tackle the world is naturally gifted and he also knows how to play his luck, which is how, as another campaign gets underway, he has joined a major European company where everything is done with passion, but also with precision and efficiency. Making use of the horses, and there are many of them in this new Court, prince Casey Stoner began to fight on a regular basis with the man who had ruled the battlefield for the past seven years as they travelled to seventeen circuits around this Earth. They are all different and in some

ways intransigent. The king of course, beaten more often than he is used to in 2007, is Valentino Rossi.

And as ever, Rossi is still a complex character, a mix of nice guy and a redoubtable old devil. He is a genius, both as a rider and in his ability to handle the media. You only have to look at his recent amorous adventures, which saw the latest one of his fiancées, the beautiful Elisabetta Canalis deny their relationship in public. "The press has invented this," she claims. "I hardly know Valentino, but in any case our relationship is not as serious as some people are making out." A shame for Valentino reckon "some people."

As for the king himself, having completed a tough race, starting from eleventh place on the grid and gone on to win, leaving prince Stoner in his wake on the way to victory, all that remains is to hand him a microphone to try and get some pearls of wisdom.

His first thoughts are for an absent friend. "First of all, I would like to say hi to Toni Elias, who was seriously hurt on Thursday and I hope he will soon be back with us."

His lesson in tactics. "I've just been asked how I could stay so calm at the end of the opening lap, while Stoner already had a lead of almost two seconds over the second placed man, which means he was much further ahead of me as I was only ninth. But I wasn't thinking about that. Right from the first corner, I only had one target, to find a way past Hofmann who was ahead of me and then the next one, so as I crossed the line for the first time, I was already thinking how to catch Capirossi who was ahead of me. And that's how it went until I got to Casey."

His lesson in humility. "I still think that actually this might be one of my five best ever races. You know, it's not the first time I've won from eleventh place, like last year at the Sachsenring. But to be honest, I didn't sleep too well on Friday night, as I didn't know how this was going to work out."

His page in the history book. "I am very happy, here at the legendary Assen circuit, to have recorded Yamaha's 150th victory."

It was the 87th of his career and not his last.

Rossi his arms aloft, Hayden rediscovers the joy of podium and it is clear that there were no prisoners (above) between Melandri and Barros.

ROSSI CAN JUMP FOR JOY AS HE TAKES THE 87TH WIN OF HIS CAREER

RUNNERS AND RIDERS

Still no Kenny Robers Junior. The two Yamahas are turned out with an original livery to mark the launch, on 4 July, of the new Fiat Cinquecento.

QUALIFYING

It rains on Friday afternoon…and Vermeulen helps himself to pole ahead of Stoner and De Puniet. The day before, Tony Elias had been a victim of the curse of Assen. For the third year in a row, the Spaniard had to pull out of the Dutch event, this time with a broken left femur after a completely run of the mill crash, which had dramatic consequences when Elias buried himself in the gravel trap, with his ankle locking up immediately.

START

Stoner gets the perfect hole shot ahead of Vermeulen and Hopkins. Rossi is tenth at the first split as De Puniet got it wrong off the front row. At the end of the opening lap, the world championship leader already has an advantage of 1.256 over the next man, who is now Hopkins. Rossi is ninth.

LAP 4

Rossi has passed Capirossi and Edwards: he is now sixth. At the front, Stoner is 1.365 ahead of Hopkins.

LAP 5

Rossi has surprised Vermeulen and is now 7 tenths off Pedrosa.

LAP 7

Rossi sets the fastest lap of the race for the second time in a row. On the way he has just swallowed up Pedrosa and sets off in pursuit of Hayden.

LAP 8

Rossi is third. Next in his sights is Hopkins, 2.657 ahead of him.

LAP 12

If anyone had any doubts about Rossi's current state of mind, king "Vale" has just replied. He puts in a string of fastest laps and finds himself second, 1.528 off Stoner. At that exact moment, De Puniet and Vermeulen come together as they fight for seventh place: the Frenchman is eliminated while Vermeulen gets back on track.

HALF-DISTANCE (13 LAPS)

The duel is now on between the prince and the king, between Stoner and Rossi. Valentino has closed to 588 thousandths off Casey. Hopkins is third at 1.927, as he fights off the attentions of Hayden and Pedrosa.

LAP 14

The two works Honda pass Hopkins' Suzuki.

LAP 17

Rossi tries, but Stoner still holds him off. Capirossi, who had been touring for several laps, comes to a stop.

LAP 23

Rossi finds a way past at the chicane and the crowd of 91,429 spectators is delighted.

FINISH (26 LAPS)

He can be proud of his work. Having started eleventh, Valentino Rossi wins this grand prix with a master's touch. Well done to Stoner and to Hayden, who has found his form at last.

CHAMPIONSHIP

Stoner had led by 26 points, now the gap is down to 21 coming to the mid-point of the season.

DUTCH GP | 30th June 2007 | Assen | 4.555 m

STARTING GRID

1	71	C. Vermeulen	Suzuki	1'48.555
2	27	C. Stoner	Ducati	1'48.572
3	14	R. De Puniet	Kawasaki	1'49.579
4	33	M. Melandri	Honda	1'49.679
5	21	J. Hopkins	Suzuki	1'49.684
6	5	C. Edwards	Yamaha	1'49.691
7	13	A. West	Kawasaki	1'49.807
8	66	A. Hofmann	Ducati	1'49.927
9	26	D. Pedrosa	Honda	1'50.132
10	65	L. Capirossi	Ducati	1'50.169
11	46	V. Rossi	Yamaha	1'50.392
12	4	A. Barros	Ducati	1'50.402
13	1	N. Hayden	Honda	1'50.581
14	80	Ku. Roberts	KR212V	1'51.259
15	56	S. Nakano	Honda	1'51.827
16	7	C. Checa	Honda	1'53.271
17	50	S. Guintoli	Yamaha	1'54.253

Not qualified:

	6	M. Tamada (*)	Yamaha	1'57.525
	24	T. Elias	Honda	---

(*): M. Tamada is allowed to race

RACE: 26 laps = 118.430 km

1	Valentino Rossi	42'37.149 (166.727 km/h)
2	Casey Stoner	+ 1''909
3	Nicky Hayden	+ 6''077
4	Daniel Pedrosa	+ 10''465
5	John Hopkins	+ 13''138
6	Colin Edwards	+ 15''139
7	Alexandre Barros	+ 36''075
8	Alex Hofmann	+ 41''768
9	Anthony West	+ 43''605
10	Marco Melandri	+ 43''796
11	Carlos Checa	+ 43''826
12	Shinya Nakano	+ 47''896
13	Makoto Tamada	+ 54''068
14	Sylvain Guintoli	+ 57''718
15	Kurtis Roberts	+ 1'28.637
16	Chris Vermeulen	+ 1'34.808

Fastest lap
Rossi, in 1'37.433 (168.300 km/h).
Record: Hayden, in 1'37.106 (168.867 km/h/2006).

Outright fastest lap
Hopkins, in 1'36.411 (170.084 km/h/2006).

CHAMPIONSHIP

1	C. Stoner	185 (5 wins)
2	V. Rossi	164 (3 wins)
3	D. Pedrosa	119
4	J. Hopkins	94
5	C. Vermeulen	88 (1 win)
6	M. Melandri	87
7	C. Edwards	75
8	A. Barros	69
9	L. Capirossi	57
10	N. Hayden	57

Lorenzo celebrates his sixth victory of the season with his double. Above, the traditional Assen chicane shot, with De Angelis leading proceedings

LORENZO IN CHARGE AGAIN AND THE APRILIA STRANGLEHOLD INTENSIFIES

RUNNERS AND RIDERS
Nothing of note among the contracted riders. Four Dutch riders have wild cards (Gevers, Beitler, Velthuijzen and Smees.)

QUALIFYING
Only one dry qualifying session, the Thursday afternoon one. Lorenzo is majestic, as proved by the fact he whips Dovizioso by over 7 tenths. In fact, in the Sunday morning warm-up, he ups the gap to 1.6 seconds! A faller on Friday

morning, Thomas Luthi is again suffering with muscle pain due to inflammation in his right arm. Having set the sixth fastest qualifying time, he rests up in the afternoon.

START
Lorenzo and Dovizioso show the best reflexes, ahead of Barbera and Luthi. First time round, the two main title contenders, split by 380 thousandths, have already pulled out a lead of 1.607 over the chasing group, dragged along by De Angelis, Barbera, Bautista and Luthi.

LAP 4
Luthi has passed Barbera and is fifth. At the front, Lorenzo now has a whole second in hand over Dovizioso.

LAP 6
For the past two laps, De Angelis has been the quickest man on track, to close to within 1.010 of Dovizioso.

LAP 8
De Angelis is going like a train and has just taken second place, 1.625 off the leader. Julian Simon retires.

HALF-DISTANCE (12 LAPS)
Lorenzo still leads with De Angelis now just 1.175 behind. Dovizioso is third at 3.244. Then come Bautista, who has just set a personal best lap, Luthi, who is having a lonely race and a quartet all scrapping for sixth place: Hiroshi Aoyama, Kallio, Simoncelli and Barbera.

LAP 15
It's all happening, as Bautista has closed right up to Dovizioso's rear wheel and the group consisting of Hiroshi Aoyama, Simoncelli, Barbera and Kallio has caught Luthi.

LAP 16
Bautista is third.

LAP 17
H. Aoyama, Simoncelli and Barbera

have passed Luthi.

LAP 19
Luthi stops in the pits.

LAP 21
Lorenzo is controlling the situation and De Angelis knows he is powerless. The most interesting fight concerns fifth place, between H. Aoyama, Simoncelli and Barbera.

FINISH (24 LAPS)
It is more than domination, it is a master class. Jorge Lorenzo does it again for the inevitable Aprilia top three. Dovizioso had been powerless, while Hiroshi Aoyama and Simoncelli were right on the edge of legality in their battle for fifth.

CHAMPIONSHIP
Again, a 23 point lead for Lorenzo and this time, a second Aprilia rider, De Angelis, has climbed up to Dovizioso's level. Bautista is a solid fourth.

DUTCH GP | 30th June 2007 | Assen | 4.555 m

STARTING GRID

1	1	J. Lorenzo	Aprilia	1'39.958
2	34	A. Dovizioso	Honda	1'40.681
3	19	A. Bautistá	Aprilia	1'41.128
4	4	H. Aoyama	KTM	1'41.226
5	80	H. Barberá	Aprilia	1'41.367
6	12	T. Lüthi	Aprilia	1'41.408
7	3	A. De Angelis	Aprilia	1'41.443
8	58	M. Simoncelli	Gilera	1'41.532
9	60	J. Simón	Honda	1'41.574
10	36	M. Kallio	KTM	1'41.892
11	32	F. Lai	Aprilia	1'41.986
12	41	A. Espargaro	Aprilia	1'42.924
13	15	R. Locatelli	Gilera	1'42.938
14	73	S. Aoyama	Honda	1'42.987
15	55	Y. Takahashi	Honda	1'42.996
16	25	A. Baldolini	Aprilia	1'43.079
17	8	R. Wilairot	Honda	1'43.115
18	16	J. Cluzel	Aprilia	1'43.649
19	44	T. Sekiguchi	Aprilia	1'43.781
20	17	K. Abraham	Aprilia	1'43.894
21	50	E. Laverty	Honda	1'44.148
22	28	D. Heidolf	Aprilia	1'44.314
23	45	D. Linfoot	Aprilia	1'44.569
24	72	H. Smees	Aprilia	1'44.652
25	10	I. Toth	Aprilia	1'44.787
26	7	E. Vazquez	Aprilia	1'44.959
27	69	R. Beitler	Honda	1'46.765
28	68	R. Gevers	Aprilia	1'46.887

Not qualified:

	70	M. Velthuijzen	Honda	1'48.800

RACE: 24 laps = 109.320 km

1	Jorge Lorenzo	40'25.904 (162.229 km/h)
2	Alex De Angelis	+ 3''857
3	Alvaro Bautistá	+ 8''683
4	Andrea Dovizioso	+ 17''948
5	Hiroshi Aoyama	+ 30''800
6	Marco Simoncelli	+ 31''135
7	Hector Barberá	+ 33''323
8	Mika Kallio	+ 40''807
9	Roberto Locatelli	+ 1'11.829
10	Yuki Takahashi	+ 1'18.958
11	Fabrizio Lai	+ 1'19.361
12	Taro Sekiguchi	+ 1'26.810
13	Shuhei Aoyama	+ 1'26.850
14	Ratthapark Wilairot	+ 1'28.717
15	Karel Abraham	+ 1'28.949
16	Dirk Heidolf	+ 1'30.407
17	Aleix Espargaro	+ 1'33.812
18	Efren Vazquez	+ 1'37.706
19	Alex Baldolini	+ 1'44.925
20	Jules Cluzel	+ 1'47.373
21	Eugene Laverty	+ 1 lap
22	Imre Toth	+ 1 lap
23	Ronald Beitler	+ 1 lap
24	Randy Gevers	+ 3 laps

Fastest lap
De Angelis, in 1'40.354 (163.401 km/h). New record. Previous: Lorenzo, in 1'40.500 (163.164 km/h/2006).

Outright fastest lap
Lorenzo, in 1'39.958 (164.048 km/h/2007).

CHAMPIONSHIP

1	J. Lorenzo	178 (6 wins)
2	A. Dovizioso	155 (2 wins)
3	A. De Angelis	155
4	A. Bautistá	116 (1 win)
5	H. Barberá	80
6	J. Simón	61
7	M. Kallio	58
8	T. Lüthi	56
9	H. Aoyama	53
10	S. Aoyama	51

PASINI HAS DEVELOPED A TASTE FOR WINNING. BEHIND HIM, THE "ASPAR BOYS" WERE NOT DOING ANYONE ANY FAVOURS

RUNNERS AND RIDERS

Spain's Enrique Jerez is still standing in for Dino Lombardi at Kopron Team Scot. There are five wild cards, three of them Dutch (Stoffer, Iwema and Pouw,) one for Germany's Stefan Bradl, who is racing in the Spanish championship this year and one for the Austrian, Eitzinger.

QUALIFYING

The mood for the start of qualifying is nervous, as right from Thursday morning's free practice, Bradley Smith, who had slowed at the side of the track, was hit hard by Andrea Iannone. The Englishman broke the left fifth metatarsal and metacarpal bones and had to pull out. Iannone broke the little finger on his left hand and tackled the wet track on Friday and therefore failed to qualify but was picked up in the "repechage." The grid is decided by the one session, on Thursday and of course it is Mattia Pasini who takes yet another pole ahead of Pesek, Corsi and Gadea. The first Honda (Di Meglio) is down in sixteenth place!

START

Corsi does it best, ahead of Pasini and Gadea. Crossing the line for the first time, it's Pasini who has a 434 thousandths advantage over Gadea, who is followed by Corsi, Talmacsi, Pesek, Faubel and Koyama, a group that represents the major players in the championship.

LAP 3

Pasini is the fastest man on track and his lead is now 1.362. Five of them are scrapping for second place: Gadea, Corsi, Talmacsi, Faubel and Pesek.

LAP 6

Webb falls and Bonsey and Aegerter only just miss him.

LAP 10

Di Meglio is a faller.

HALF-DISTANCE (11 LAPS)

Pasini is still riding on another planet. He now has a lead of 3.349 over his pursuers led by Talmacsi, Gadea, Corsi, Faubel, Pesek and Koyama. Further back, over six seconds off the Japanese rider come Ranseder, Bradl and Cortese, all

fighting for eighth place.

LAP 18

The battle for second place is thrilling as is the one for eighth. Out in front, Pasini's lead has gone up to over 5 seconds.

FINISH (22 LAPS)

Pasini embarks on the final lap with a 6.158 second cushion over the six lads who certainly don't want to lay their heads on any cushion. Gadea leads the pack, but Faubel is the cleverest in the chicane, finishing second ahead of Talmacsi and the third of the "Aspar boys," Gadea.

CHAMPIONSHIP

Faubel scores four more points than Talmacsi and so he now leads the series by seven points. Gadea is 33 behind, for Pesek it is 35. The unluckiest man in the early stages of the season is Mattia Pasini and he is now seventh on 66 points.

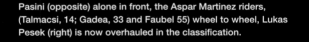
Pasini (opposite) alone in front, the Aspar Martinez riders, (Talmacsi, 14; Gadea, 33 and Faubel 55) wheel to wheel, Lukas Pesek (right) is now overhauled in the classification.

DUTCH GP | 30th June 2007 | Assen | 4.555 m

STARTING GRID

1	75	M. Pasini	Aprilia	1'45.603
2	52	L. Pesek	Derbi	1'45.783
3	24	S. Corsi	Aprilia	1'46.198
4	33	S. Gadea	Aprilia	1'46.204
5	11	S. Cortese	Aprilia	1'46.216
6	14	G. Talmacsi	Aprilia	1'46.416
7	55	H. Faubel	Aprilia	1'46.853
8	35	R. De Rosa	Aprilia	1'46.946
9	17	S. Bradl	Aprilia	1'46.999
10	60	M. Ranseder	Derbi	1'47.021
11	6	J. Olivé	Aprilia	1'47.260
12	18	N. Terol	Derbi	1'47.275
13	71	T. Koyama	KTM	1'47.344
14	8	L. Zanetti	Aprilia	1'47.400
15	22	P. Nieto	Aprilia	1'47.454
16	63	M. Di Meglio	Honda	1'47.568
17	44	P. Espargaro	Aprilia	1'47.665
18	27	S. Bianco	Aprilia	1'47.841
19	12	E. Rabat	Honda	1'47.848
20	7	A. Masbou	Honda	1'47.972
21	95	R. Muresan	Derbi	1'48.028
22	37	J. Litjens	Honda	1'48.248
23	20	R. Tamburini	Aprilia	1'48.303
24	51	S. Bonsey	KTM	1'48.617
25	34	R. Krummenacher	KTM	1'48.703
26	31	E. Jerez	Honda	1'48.719
27	53	S. Grotzkyj	Aprilia	1'49.061
28	77	D. Aegerter	Aprilia	1'49.113
29	15	F. Sandi	Aprilia	1'49.134
30	99	D. Webb	Honda	1'49.322
31	90	R. Pouw	Aprilia	1'50.025
32	56	H. Van Den Berg	Aprilia	1'50.244
33	89	J. Iwena	Honda	1'50.292
34	72	P. Vd Waarsenburg	Honda	1'51.225
35	88	F. Stoffer	Honda	1'52.407
36	85	P. Eitzinger	Honda	1'52.862

Not qualified:

29	A. Iannone		Aprilia	2'08.420 (*)
38	B. Smith		Honda	---

(*): Iannone is allowed to race.

RACE: 22 laps = 100.210 km

1	Mattia Pasini	38'58.171 (154.289 km/h)
2	Hector Faubel	+ 6''115
3	Gabor Talmacsi	+ 6''146
4	Sergio Gadea	+ 6''354
5	Simone Corsi	+ 6''454
6	Tomoyoshi Koyama	+ 6''633
7	Lukas Pesek	+ 6''643
8	Sandro Cortese	+ 17''696
9	Michael Ranseder	+ 17''890
10	Stefan Bradl	+ 21''780
11	Pol Espargaro	+ 22''867
12	Randy Krummenacher	+ 22''938
13	Esteve Rabat	+ 23''095
14	Raffaele De Rosa	+ 34''247
15	Lorenzo Zanetti	+ 36''991
16	Alexis Masbou	+ 37''145
17	Nicolas Terol	+ 37''407
18	Joan Olivé	+ 37''597
19	Stefano Bianco	+ 40''237
20	Andrea Iannone	+ 48''387

21	Hugo Van Den Berg	+ 51''244
22	Roberto Tamburini	+ 51''374
23	Enrique Jerez	+ 51''923
24	Federico Sandi	+ 55''947
25	Simone Grotzkyj	+ 57''183
26	Joey Litjens	+ 59''846
27	Steve Bonsey	+ 1'18.758
28	Dominique Aegerter	+ 1'19.653
29	Philipp Eitzinger	+ 1'29.071
30	Roy Pouw	+ 1 lap
31	Patrick vd Waarsenburg	+ 1 lap
32	Jasper Iwema	+ 1 lap
33	Ferry Stoffer	+ 1 lap

Fastest lap
Faubel, in 1'45.551 (155.356 km/h).
Record: Gadea, in 1'45.098 (156.025 km/h/2006).

Outright fastest lap
Kallio, in 1'44.532 (156.870 km/h/2006).

CHAMPIONSHIP

1	H. Faubel	138 (2 wins)
2	G. Talmacsi	131 (1 win)
3	S. Gadea	105 (1 win)
4	L. Pesek	103 (1 win)
5	T. Koyama	98 (1 win)
6	S. Corsi	97 (1 win)
7	M. Pasini	66 (2 wins)
8	J. Olivé	63
9	B. Smith	63
10	P. Espargaro	62

Rossi has just passed Randy De Puniet, but for once he overestimated his own talent and the championship seemed to slip away.

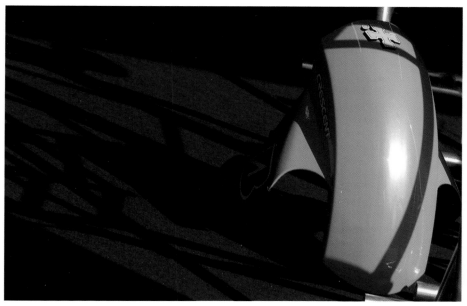

RUDE OFF
FOR VALENTINO!

IT ONLY HAPPENS VERY RARELY, BUT
IN A GERMAN GP WHERE THE
BRIDGESTONE RIDERS WERE IN
TROUBLE, ROSSI MADE A STRANGE
MISTAKE

THE RACE

WHEN GENIUS SLIPS UP

Every five hundred years, Italy gives birth to a genius. After Michaelangelo, we now have Valentino Rossi," joked Australian Jeremy Burgess, the chief engineer to the king of motorcycling and one time mentor to the great Michael Doohan, on the Sunday morning of the German Grand Prix in a major Italian newspaper. He could never have guessed that on this infernally hot Sunday 15th July, in front of over one hundred thousand spectators, "his " genius would make such a mess of things. It would be obvious enough to prompt a wave of catcalling from the packed Sachsenring grandstands that would not have been out of place at a football match when the home team misses an open goal. A mess that would have an immediate effect on Valentino Rossi's hopes of closing the gap to Casey Stoner with the supreme title up for grabs

Randy, the first witness. "We brushed against one another and Valentino's bike was still so cranked over when he opened the throttle again that there was no chance of a miracle. He was going much too quickly at that point," said a privileged witness, Frenchman Randy De Puniet who only just avoided the crash. But he didn't avoid seeing it all as the bike began its slide in a shower of sparks, before the blue and white Yamaha ended up in the gravel trap. Then Rossi tried to lift it up, tried to get going again, but unfortunately the bike was too badly damaged. At that precise moment, he could not be aware that the Bridgestone riders, with the exception of Capirossi who tried a

daring gamble in an attempt to win, were going to be in bother come the closing stages. Valentino Rossi could not have known that he had held in his hands a golden opportunity to close on Casey Stoner, the series leader.

Valentino, the accused. "One mistake a year is not a lot," suggested the genius later that afternoon, trying to diffuse the situation. And then, having indicated the man who had been the privileged witness to this mistake of the year ("at some points, De Puniet was very quick and in others he was much slower. I unfortunately got the impression that he was thinking more about blocking Rossi than of going as quickly as possible,") Valentino asked forgiveness. "I would like to apologise for this mistake to our

partners and to all my fans, to everyone. After the morning warm-up, I knew I would have a strong race pace. It was the perfect opportunity to close the gap to Stoner…until that bloody sixth lap." It was the lap on which Rossi committed his mistake of the year. It's true that one error is not much, but this one was going to be costly. Because in Germany, in intensely hot conditions, Michelin was totally dominant against Bridgestone with a win for Daniel Pedrosa and a third place for Nicky Hayden. And more importantly, Stoner and the others ended the race driving on egg shells. And that was the aspect of the day that irritated Rossi the most, because he knew that chances like this would not come along too often before the end of this championship.

Randy De Puniet had a front row seat and saw it all: Rossi goes round the outside at an impossible angle, leading to sliding and sparks and a trip back to the pits on the pillion of a scooter!

Pedrosa (opposite) wins out on his own, but the biggest smile of the day (below) belongs to Loris Capirossi, standing on the second rung of the podium.

LAP 6
Sensational: Rossi, who had just passed De Puniet for sixth place, hits the deck. Out in front, Pedrosa has a 4 tenths lead over Stoner. In the pits, the pit boards for the two leaders indicate "Rossi KO."

LAP 10
Barros falls.

HALF-DISTANCE (15 LAPS)
Pedrosa is controlling the situation and his lead over Stoner is now 3.484 seconds. Melandri is third ahead of Capirossi and Hopkins. In sixth place, De Puniet is now having to fight off the reigning world champion, Nicky Hayden.

LAP 17
Hayden has found a way past.

LAP 19
Edwards gets the better of De Puniet.

LAP 21
Stoner, who had been losing a lot of time for the past few laps, is passed by Capirossi.

LAP 23
Melandri passes Stoner.

LAP 24
Hayden, Hopkins and Edwards have closed up on Stoner. Hayden is the first to get by.

LAP 27
Stoner gets back ahead of Melandri.

FINISH (30 LAPS)
Pedrosa embarks on the final lap with a lead of 13.433 seconds over Capirossi. He thus hands Honda its first win in the 800 cc era. Stoner has finally managed to fend off the attentions of Melandri and Hopkins for fifth place. De Puniet, the eternal bad luck boy, does not complete the last lap.

CHAMPIONSHIP
Although seriously beaten - Michelin won the heat war - Stoner does rather well out of the day, as his lead over Rossi has now grown to 32 points. Pedrosa is now 20 points behind the weekend's big loser.

THANKS TO PEDROSA, HONDA TOOK ITS FIRST WIN OF THE 800 CC ERA

RUNNERS AND RIDERS
Injured at Assen, Toni Elias is replaced by the Italian, Michel Fabrizio. A thunderbolt in the paddock with the news, declared official the night before the first day of practice, that John Hopkins would be making the switch from Suzuki to Kawasaki.

QUALIFYING
Rossi has the 'flu, Stoner is unbeatable, by 4 thousandths of a second. In the presence of the new boss of HRC, Masumi Hamane, Pedrosa is definitely under pressure. Another rider might have been able to out-qualify everyone: Randy De Puniet was up on Stoner's split time but the Frenchman got it wrong while braking and found himself hitting the gravel trap at 250 km/h, where he showed his displeasure by jumping on his Kawasaki!

START
Pedrosa charges into the lead ahead of Stoner and Melandri. At the end of this opening lap, the Spaniard has a lead of 288 thousandths over the championship leader. Rossi is eighth.

LAP 3
Stoner mounts his first attack and Pedrosa counters. Checa is a faller. The Race Director announces that Vermeulen jumped the start.

LAP 4
Guintoli is a faller - in the Dunlop camp it had been obvious since the start of the weekend that none of their tyres would go the distance.

GERMAN GP | 15th July 2007 | Sachsenring | 3.671 m

STARTING GRID						RACE: 30 laps = 110.130 km				CHAMPIONSHIP		
1	27	C. Stoner	Ducati	1'22.384		1	Daniel Pedrosa	41'53.196 (157.754 km/h)		1	C. Stoner	196 (5 wins)
2	26	D. Pedrosa	Honda	1'22.388		2	Loris Capirossi	+ 13''166		2	V. Rossi	164 (3 wins)
3	33	M. Melandri	Honda	1'22.397		3	Nicky Hayden	+ 16''771		3	D. Pedrosa	144 (1 win)
4	14	R. De Puniet	Kawasaki	1'22.539		4	Colin Edwards	+ 18''299		4	J. Hopkins	103
5	21	J. Hopkins	Suzuki	1'22.561		5	Casey Stoner	+ 31''426		5	M. Melandri	97
6	46	V. Rossi	Yamaha	1'22.605		6	Marco Melandri	+ 31''917		6	C. Vermeulen	93 (1 win)
7	65	L. Capirossi	Ducati	1'22.615		7	John Hopkins	+ 33''395		7	C. Edwards	88
8	4	A. Barros	Ducati	1'22.897		8	Anthony West	+ 41''194		8	L. Capirossi	77
9	50	S. Guintoli	Yamaha	1'22.958		9	Alex Hofmann	+ 43''214		9	N. Hayden	73
10	56	S. Nakano	Honda	1'22.969		10	Michel Fabrizio	+ 44''459		10	A. Barros	69
11	71	C. Vermeulen	Suzuki	1'23.039		11	Chris Vermeulen	+ 1'01.894				
12	13	A. West	Kawasaki	1'23.056		12	Kurtis Roberts	+ 1'10.721				
13	5	C. Edwards	Yamaha	1'23.090		13	Makoto Tamada	+ 2 laps				
14	1	N. Hayden	Honda	1'23.151		14	Carlos Checa	+ 3 laps				
15	7	C. Checa	Honda	1'23.182								
16	66	A. Hofmann	Ducati	1'23.199								
17	84	M. Fabrizio	Honda	1'23.491								
18	6	M. Tamada	Yamaha	1'23.744								
19	80	Ku. Roberts	KR212V	1'24.209								

Fastest lap
Pedrosa, in 1'23.082 (159.066 km/h). New record.
Previous: Pedrosa, in 1'23.355 (158.545 km/h/2006).

Outright fastest lap
Pedrosa, in 1'21.815 (161.530 km/h/2006).

WITH AOYAMA AND KALLIO, KTM TAKES ITS FIRST EVER ONE-TWO IN 250

RUNNERS AND RIDERS

All quite in the pack. Switzerland's Thomas Luthi is the only one of the five works Aprilia riders to have retired this year with mechanical problems, the third time just two weeks earlier at Assen! On behalf of the Italian manufacturer, Mauro Noccioli the technical director of Luthi's team duly apologised to his partners. Three wild cards, including one for multiple European champion in the discipline, Spain's Alvaro Molina.

QUALIFYING

The works Aprilia riders are making heavy weather of setting up their chassis on this track where, ideally, one would have two completely different bikes, for the two very different sections of the track. Those who suffer the most with this problem are the two rookies, Alvaro Bautista (9th) and Luthi (12th.) First pole in the 250 class for another rookie, Mika Kallio. In the Sunday morning warm-up, it is his KTM team-mate Hiroshi Aoyama who sets the quickest time. We will mention the two "oranges" again in the race.

START

Andrea Dovizioso, Kallio and Alex de Angelis spot the lights going out quicker than the rest. Crossing the line for the first time, Dovizioso has a lead of 581 thousandths over De Angelis, who leads Kallio and H. Aoyama.

LAP 3

Bautista is a faller and a bit later so is

Chequered flag for the two "oranges:" KTM has just beaten Aprilia (De Angelis and Lorenzo finish third and fourth.) Above, the strange look of Frenchman Jules Cluzel and, opposite, it's champagne time for Aoyama and Kallio.

Vazquez. At the front, De Angelis is right on Dovizioso's back wheel.

LAP 5

De Angelis takes the lead.

LAP 10

Barbera does a "barbera" to Kallio and indeed, there will be others during the race. De Angelis is still controlling Dovizioso as the two men have 7 tenths over their pursuers, Hiroshi Aoyama, Barbera, Kallio, Simon, Lorenzo and Simoncelli.

HALF-DISTANCE (15 LAPS)

Simon falls. De Angelis now has a 706 thousandths advantage over Dovizioso, who is fending off Barbera, H. Aoyama, Kallio, Lorenzo and Simoncelli.

LAP 22

Simoncelli has been dropped by the lead group. As for Hiroshi Aoyama, he has closed up to Alex De Angelis.

LAP 23

Now it is Barbera's turn to be dropped.

FINISH (29 LAPS)

189 thousandths separate De Angelis and H. Aoyama going into the final lap. Kallio is third, 4 tenths behind. Aoyama moves ahead and, in the final corner, the Finn assures KTM of its first one-two in the 250 class. Lorenzo has done the necessary to stay ahead of Dovizioso and he celebrates as though he has won

CHAMPIONSHIP

Lorenzo now has a 20 point lead over a new pursuer in the shape of Alex De Angelis. Dovizioso is third, 25 points down, or the equivalent of one race win. Bautista is still fourth, but his gauge stays stuck on 116 points.

GERMAN GP | 15th July 2007 | Sachsenring | 3.671 m

STARTING GRID

1	36	M. Kallio	KTM	1'24.413
2	34	A. Dovizioso	Honda	1'24.643
3	3	A. De Angelis	Aprilia	1'24.647
4	1	J. Lorenzo	Aprilia	1'24.735
5	60	J. Simón	Honda	1'24.845
6	4	H. Aoyama	KTM	1'24.870
7	80	H. Barberá	Aprilia	1'24.910
8	58	M. Simoncelli	Gilera	1'24.928
9	19	A. Bautistá	Aprilia	1'25.082
10	55	Y. Takahashi	Honda	1'25.099
11	41	A. Espargaro	Aprilia	1'25.213
12	12	T. Lüthi	Aprilia	1'25.240
13	28	D. Heidolf	Aprilia	1'25.585
14	15	R. Locatelli	Gilera	1'25.599
15	25	A. Baldolini	Aprilia	1'25.616
16	32	F. Lai	Aprilia	1'25.800
17	73	S. Aoyama	Honda	1'25.856
18	44	T. Sekiguchi	Aprilia	1'26.225
19	7	E. Vazquez	Aprilia	1'26.236
20	17	K. Abraham	Aprilia	1'26.685
21	16	J. Cluzel	Aprilia	1'26.890
22	8	R. Wilairot	Honda	1'26.960
23	31	A. Molina	Aprilia	1'27.066
24	10	I. Toth	Aprilia	1'27.644
25	45	D. Linfoot	Aprilia	1'27.886
26	50	E. Laverty	Honda	1'27.984
27	18	J. Sommer	Honda	1'28.840
28	38	T. Walther	Honda	1'28.962

RACE: 29 laps = 106.459 km

1	Hiroshi Aoyama	41'16.191 (154.774 km/h)	
2	Mika Kallio	+ 0''119	
3	Alex De Angelis	+ 0''274	
4	Jorge Lorenzo	+ 0''579	
5	Andrea Dovizioso	+ 1''296	
6	Hector Barberá	+ 11''851	
7	Marco Simoncelli	+ 17''308	
8	Yuki Takahashi	+ 22''309	
9	Thomas Lüthi	+ 28''858	
10	Roberto Locatelli	+ 35''983	
11	Aleix Espargaro	+ 37''377	
12	Shuhei Aoyama	+ 42''211	
13	Dirk Heidolf	+ 51''095	
14	Alex Baldolini	+ 53''416	
15	Jules Cluzel	+ 55''996	
16	Taro Sekiguchi	+ 56''105	
17	Alvaro Bautista	+ 1'07.435	
18	Fabrizio Lai	+ 1'09.728	
19	Ratthapark Wilairot	+ 1'17.640	

Fastest lap

Kallio, in 1'24.762 (155.914 km/h). New record.
Previous: Porto, in 1'25.118 (155.262 km/h/2004).

Outright fastest lap

Kallio, in 1'24.413 (156.558 km/h/2007).

CHAMPIONSHIP

1	J. Lorenzo	191 (6 wins)
2	A. De Angelis	171
3	A. Dovizioso	166 (2 wins)
4	A. Bautistá	116 (1 win)
5	H. Barberá	90
6	H. Aoyama	78 (1 win))
7	M. Kallio	78
8	T. Lüthi	63
9	J. Simón	61
10	M. Simoncelli	57

TALMACSI WINS AND MOVES BACK INTO THE LEAD OF THE CHAMPIONSHIP

RUNNERS AND RIDERS

Smith, who was injured in practice at Assen, is already back, even if he needs crutches to get around. Also back is Lombardi. Five German riders have wild card entries.

QUALIFYING

Mattia Pasini does not take pole position, which is a rare enough occurrence to make it worth mentioning. Hats off therefore to Gabor Talmacsi, who was very much at ease on the contours of the Sachsenring, who beat his nearest pursuer by 4 tenths, a veritable chasm. But the real hero of qualifying is Smith, who forgets the pain to grab a slot on the front row.

START

Talmacsi shoots into the lead. As usual, riders go down at the first corner; this time it's Pasini, Lombardi and Espargaro. Crossing the line for the first time, the Hungarian already has a 1.238 seconds advantage over Faubel, who is followed by Corsi, Pesek, Cortese, Iannone and Krummenacher.

LAP 4

Iannone (9th) is deemed to have jumped the start. At the front, Talmacsi now has 3.208 seconds in hand over a quartet made up of Pesek, Faubel, Corsi and Cortese.

LAP 8

Koyama, Gadea and Krummenacher rejoin the chasing group, so that there are now seven fighting over the last two places on the podium, all within two tenths. De Rosa retires.

Faubel is happy, but it's his team-mate Gabor Talmacsi who is the big winner of the weekend.

As for Pasini (below) he will not have any fond memories of the first corner...

LAP 12

Pasini, who had rejoined after falling on the opening lap, pits for good this time.

HALF-DISTANCE (13 LAPS)

Talmacsi is perfectly in control of the situation. His lead increases now to 4.128 seconds. In second place, Corsi has built himself a small lead of 1.731 over Faubel, Pesek, Gadea, Koyama and Krummenacher. Cortese has been dropped.

LAP 18

Corsi now trails Talmacsi by over 5 seconds. There is a superb scrap for third place between Faubel, Koyama, Gadea, Krummenacher and Pesek.

LAP 20

Koyama has passed Faubel with the Japanese rider third.

LAP 21

Corsi, Koyama and Faubel are wheel to wheel and the Japanese rider is on the verge of taking the lead. Further back, Gadea, Krummenacher and Pesek have lost touch and are a little bit over two seconds off the podium battle.

FINISH (27 LAPS)

4.372 seconds lead for Talmacsi going into the last lap: the Hungarian has ridden a perfect race. He takes the victory ahead of Koyama and Faubel. Gadea, who was trying to fight off Krummenacher and Pesek for fifth place, falls at the foot of the final climb.

CHAMPIONSHIP

They continue (but for how much longer?) to exchange polite remarks within the team run by "Aspar" Martinez. So, Talmacsi retakes the lead by two points from team-mate Hector Faubel.

GERMAN GP | 15th July 2007 | Sachsenring | 3.671 m

STARTING GRID

1	14	G. Talmacsi	Aprilia	1'26.839
2	75	M. Pasini	Aprilia	1'27.255
3	55	H. Faubel	Aprilia	1'27.266
4	38	B. Smith	Honda	1'27.576
5	52	L. Pesek	Derbi	1'27.706
6	11	S. Cortese	Aprilia	1'27.728
7	24	S. Corsi	Aprilia	1'27.798
8	34	R. Krummenacher	KTM	1'27.829
9	33	S. Gadea	Aprilia	1'27.839
10	12	E. Rabat	Honda	1'28.094
11	60	M. Ranseder	Derbi	1'28.108
12	29	A. Iannone	Aprilia	1'28.204
13	44	P. Espargaro	Aprilia	1'28.212
14	6	J. Olivé	Aprilia	1'28.268
15	71	T. Koyama	KTM	1'28.277
16	17	S. Bradl	Aprilia	1'28.318
17	22	P. Nieto	Aprilia	1'28.343
18	20	R. Tamburini	Aprilia	1'28.689
19	63	M. Di Meglio	Honda	1'28.711
20	95	R. Muresan	Derbi	1'28.825
21	64	G. Fröhlich	Honda	1'28.894
22	27	S. Bianco	Aprilia	1'28.905
23	35	R. De Rosa	Aprilia	1'29.038
24	8	L. Zanetti	Aprilia	1'29.076
25	37	J. Litjens	Honda	1'29.136
26	7	A. Masbou	Honda	1'29.431
27	15	F. Sandi	Aprilia	1'29.489
28	18	N. Terol	Derbi	1'29.499
29	53	S. Grotzkyj	Aprilia	1'29.575
30	51	S. Bonsey	KTM	1'29.712
31	56	H. Van Den Berg	Aprilia	1'30.139
32	66	P. Unger	Aprilia	1'30.180
33	77	D. Aegerter	Aprilia	1'30.264
34	99	D. Webb	Honda	1'30.363
35	13	D. Lombardi	Honda	1'30.669
36	65	E. Hübsch	Aprilia	1'30.746
37	67	S. Eckner	Honda	1'32.176

RACE: 27 laps = 99.117 km

1	Gabor Talmacsi		39'30.802 (150.506 km/h)
2	Tomoyoshi Koyama		+ 3''532
3	Hector Faubel		+ 3''610
4	Simone Corsi		+ 4''444
5	Randy Krummenacher		+ 11''851
6	Lukas Pesek		+ 11''920
7	Sandro Cortese		+ 17''271
8	Bradley Smith		+ 19''484
9	Pablo Nieto		+ 20''950
10	Michael Ranseder		+ 22''628
11	Joan Olivé		+ 26''044
12	Esteve Rabat		+ 27''096
13	Stefan Bradl		+ 42''805
14	Georg Fröhlich		+ 43''503
15	Mike Di Meglio		+ 44''402
16	Stefano Bianco		+ 46''386
17	Robert Muresan		+ 53''208
18	Steve Bonsey		+ 53''719
19	Alexis Masbou		+ 53''739
20	Roberto Tamburini		+ 53''887
21	Dominique Aegerter		+ 1'00.165
22	Nicolas Terol		+ 1'00.625
23	Federico Sandi		+ 1'09.928
24	Andrea Iannone		+ 1'16.082
25	Hugo Van Den Berg		+ 1'18.721
26	Eric Hübsch		+ 1'18.836
27	Daniel Webb		+ 1'27.243
28	Lorenzo Zanetti		+ 1 lap
29	Sebastien Eckner		+ 1 lap

Fastest lap

Talmacsi, in 1'26.909 (152.062 km/h). New record.
Previous: Bautistá, in 1'27.519 (151.002 km/h/2006).

Outright fastest lap

Talmacsi, in 1'26.839 (152.185 km/h/2007).

CHAMPIONSHIP

1	G. Talmacsi	156 (2 wins)
2	H. Faubel	154 (2 wins)
3	T. Koyama	118 (1 win)
4	L. Pesek	113 (1 win)
5	S. Corsi	110 (1 win)
6	S. Gadea	105 (1 win)
7	B. Smith	71
8	J. Olivé	68
9	M. Pasini	66 (2 wins)
10	P. Espargaro	62

Stoner has just got himself through the infamous "corkscrew:" the Australian is really living the Californian dream.

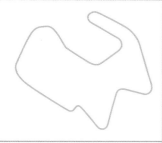

CASEY DISCOVERS
"HIS" AMERICA

POLE POSITION, LAP RECORD,
TOTAL DOMINATION FROM
LIGHTS TO FLAG: STONER
MADE THE U.S. GP HIS OWN

THE RACE

CALIFORNIAN DREAMS AND NIGHTMARES

California captured: Stoner triumphs, Rossi suffers and Melandri can afford to smile: third in the race, he has just signed with Ducati.

"Californian dreams»: there is often a very thin line between dreams and nightmares. The United States GP, set against the backdrop of the arid hills of Laguna Seca, near Monterey California, did not dispel this idea. On a weekend in mid-July, never had dreams and nightmares been so entwined.

Let's start with the dream. That means another perfect weekend for Casey Stoner; fastest in each session, even affording himself the luxury in the warm-up of breaking his outright lap record set the previous day, a win that no one could deny him and a big helping of points by comparison with Valentino Rossi. The Australian definitely deserved a few days holiday. "I'm finally going home. My plans? Rest, rest and more rest….even if I think some of my mates have prepared a nice welcome home party."

Now, on with the nightmare. It started in the very first practice session for Alexander Hofmann,

who was hit by Guintoli at the top of the Corkscrew and came very close indeed to losing part of his left hand, trapped between the ground and his Ducati. There was also a nightmare for Loris Capirossi, to whom it was made clear that, "yes, if you like, we could run a third Ducati for you next year, but you will need to come up with some serious funding of your own." He was only able to show what he could do for a handful of laps in the race, as he fell victim to a mechanical failure. Finally, it was also a nightmare for those running on Michelin tyres, such as Valentino Rossi and Daniel Pedrosa, who soon realised they had been reduced to the role of spectators at the show.

The dream… and the nightmare, to finish. Of course it is possible to experience both a dream and a nightmare at pretty much the same time, as was the case with Marco Melandri at Laguna Seca. Flashback: it is Saturday at a quarter past two and, on a quick lap, Melandri comes across Kurtis

Roberts cruising in the middle of the track, turning round on his KR212V to see… to see that Melandri has not understood what move he is pulling off and that the Italian is about to clip Kurtis' foot rest. Unbalanced, his Honda is propelled at high speed into the gravel trap. Marco does not think about it for long and bales out of the machine which destroys itself in the tyres of the so-called safety barrier, while the Italian, despite his efforts, performs a series of frightening rolls. Having taken a big knock, Melandri gets up with difficulty and is taken to the circuit medical centre, where Dr. Costa takes charge. Twenty minutes later - the session had been stopped so that the officials could put everything back in place - he returns to his pit and goes out again to set the tenth fastest time. For him, the nightmare is over and the next day will be a dream. Melandri finishes third and announces he has signed a two year deal with Ducati!

Wayne Rainey (on left) now has a corner that bears his name at Laguna Seca. Centre, Stoner does it once again, in a GP that featured an appearance from Roger Lee Hayden, the world champion's little brother.

IT'S A MASSACRE FOR THE MICHELIN RIDERS: STONER PERFECT YET AGAIN

RUNNERS AND RIDERS
Here in California, Canadian Miguel Duhamel, who had competed in a full season of the 500 world championship back in the Nineties, is riding Elias' Honda RC212V. A third Kawasaki is on track in the hands of Roger Lee Hayden, the reigning world champion's little brother.

QUALIFYING
Hofmann's GP only lasted five laps, as he is a faller in the famous Corkscrew turn after a collision with Guintoli, which leaves him with a broken left hand. He pulls out and his Ducati ride is picked up by Chas Davies, who is racing in the US championship this year. While Stoner dominates every session, the unluckiest (or maybe luckiest) man in qualifying is called Melandri, caught out by a stupid move from Kurtis Roberts, cruising in the middle of the track, he ends up crashing into the gravel trap at high speed, deciding to bale out of his Honda before the inevitable crash into the barriers. The Italian gets away with a twisted left ankle.

START
Pedrosa, Stoner and Nicky Hayden prove they have the sharpest reflexes, but in the first downhill lefthander, it is Hopkins, who had started from the third row, who falls, clipping the bike of Nicky Hayden, who manages to stay in the saddle.

LAP 4
Stoner has taken the lead before the end of the first lap and now it is Vermeulen in second place. Rossi is fourth, while Capirossi retires with electrical problems.

LAP 9
Melandri passes Rossi to go fourth.

LAP 12
Melandri has closed on Pedrosa. Duhamel retires.

HALF-DISTANCE (16 LAPS)
Stoner's lead over Vermeulen is 3.5 seconds. At the exact halfway point, Melandri passes Pedrosa.

LAP 20
Rossi is true to himself and does all he can, thus becoming the best Michelin runner in the race, as he passes Pedrosa.

LAP 24
Nicky Hayden had been suffering problems ever since his first lap collision with Hopkins and pits.

FINISH (32 LAPS)
A sixth victory for Casey Stoner with once again a more than perfect performance. It is an Australian one-two and a Bridgestone triple. In what is clearly a war between the manufacturers, one notes that on a circuit where it has gained a great deal of experience, Dunlop is on the pace with a good eighth place for Tamada.

CHAMPIONSHIP
With eight races remaining, Stoner has a 44 point lead over Rossi and that is very significant. If Rossi was to win every remaining GP, Stoner would just have to follow him home to be crowned champion. In equal fourth place, Vermeulen and Melandri have not finished their battle for the podium.

GP UNITED STATES | 22nd July 2007 | Laguna Seca | 3.610 m

STARTING GRID

1	27	C. Stoner	Ducati	1'22.292
2	26	D. Pedrosa	Honda	1'22.501
3	71	C. Vermeulen	Suzuki	1'22.590
4	1	N. Hayden	Honda	1'22.624
5	46	V. Rossi	Yamaha	1'22.683
6	65	L. Capirossi	Ducati	1'22.914
7	21	J. Hopkins	Suzuki	1'22.033
8	5	C. Edwards	Yamaha	1'22.943
9	56	S. Nakano	Honda	1'23.006
10	33	M. Melandri	Honda	1'23.018
11	6	M. Tamada	Yamaha	1'23.036
12	13	A. West	Kawasaki	1'23.091
13	14	R. De Puniet	Kawasaki	1'23.113
14	50	S. Guintoli	Yamaha	1'23.207
15	7	C. Checa	Honda	1'23.263
16	95	R.-L. Hayden	Kawasaki	1'23.425
17	4	A. Barros	Ducati	1'23.557
18	80	Ku. Roberts	KR212V	1'23.662
19	17	M. Duhamel	Honda	1'23.923
20	57	C. Davies	Ducati	1'24.098

RACE: 32 laps = 115.520 km

1	Casey Stoner	44'20.325 (156.323 km/h)
2	Chris Vermeulen	+ 9''865
3	Marco Melandri	+ 25''641
4	Valentino Rossi	+ 30''664
5	Daniel Pedrosa	+ 35''622
6	Randy De Puniet	+ 38''306
7	Anthony West	+ 41''422
8	Makoto Tamada	+ 42''355
9	Alex Barros	+ 43''520
10	Roger Lee Hayden	+ 43''720
11	Colin Edwards	+ 47''376
12	Shinya Nakano	+ 52''848
13	Sylvain Guintoli	+ 58''410
14	Carlos Checa	+ 1'15.366
15	John Hopkins	+ 2 laps
16	Chaz Davies	+ 3 laps

Fastest lap
Stoner, in 1'22.542 (157.447 km/h). New record.
Previous: Pedrosa, in 1'23.333 (155.952 km/h/2006).

Outrigth fastest lap
Stoner, in 1'21.975 (158.536 km/h/2007).

CHAMPIONSHIP

1	C. Stoner	221 (6 wins)
2	V. Rossi	177 (3 wins)
3	D. Pedrosa	155 (1 win)
4	C. Vermeulen	113 (1 win)
5	M. Melandri	113
6	J. Hopkins	104
7	C. Edwards	93
8	L. Capirossi	77
9	A. Barros	76
10	N. Hayden	73

Randy De Puniet and his green Kawasaki against a forest background

12

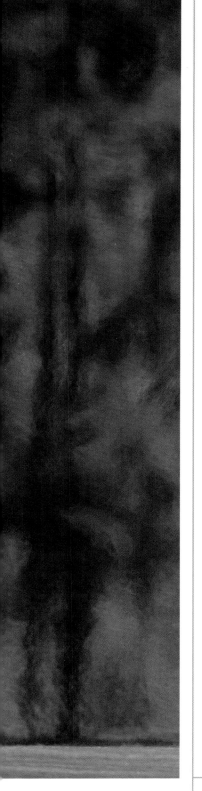

ROSSI, TAXED
WITH TAX WORRIES

BEFORE YET ANOTHER STRIKE FOR
STONER, VALENTINO ROSSI IS
SKITTLED BY IMPLICATIONS
CONCERNING A SULPHUROUS
TAX FIDDLE

THE RACE

ROSSI: A WOUNDED MAN

It's 13h40 on Sunday 19 August. Sunglasses perched on his nose, Valentino Rossi storms into the garage having just pushed a too pushy cameraman out of the way. It is the second time this weekend that that he has shown signs of being on edge. Uccio, his childhood friend, his shadow, his accomplice says something funny to diffuse the situation, Valentino waves a straightforward hello to the official camera before talking to his engineers. The usual Rossi? No. This Rossi is not his usual smiling self. Instead he looks serious and unhappy and he is too preoccupied to play his usual role of band leader, the man who likes to please the fans, the perfectionist in the shape of a bike rider, the millionaire, the global star.

He was being attacked on all side and his throne looked a precarious perch. The first attack was the sort that no rider likes, namely being beaten on the track and that had been going on since the start of the season courtesy of young Australian, Casey Stoner, who was not yet 22 years old. This weekend, he took

his seventh win in the saddle of his Ducati which he described as "the perfect bike whatever the conditions!" Rossi could do no better than seventh.

Then Rossi was attacked by the legal system and his empire looked to be in trouble. While the on-track battles only served to sharpen our super-hero's resolve, now the Italian tax authorities were playing hard ball with accusations of cheating, 60 million Euros hidden away, fines, interest, criminal charges, the risk of going to prison. If it all turned nasty, Rossi might have to cough up 120 million, yes, 120 million which would do him some serious damage.

He is also getting too much attention from the media and his image is tarnished. In this case, the man who was known as a master of communication, adept at mesmerising the public with his stories by using the media, has himself been silenced for once here in Brno, thus missing out on a great opportunity to explain himself.

How did it reach this state of affairs? On 3 August,

right in the middle of the holidays, two Italian tax officials turned up at Rossi's villa in Tavullia to inform him that, according to their records, he had short changed the tax office out of 60 million Euros between 2000 and 2004. Almost immediately, the news went public. Some media went into a frenzy while a larger number claimed to be just doing their job. The moto king's private life was under the microscope with claims that he was spending too much time in his native Italy, when his residence for tax purposes is London. The affair took motorcycle racing off the sports pages and installed it firmly on the front page. Even ministers were getting involved and the mysterious "Gibo" Badioli, Rossi's manager, spoke of a set-up while others claimed it was "a political move prompted by the communists." All of Italy was following this soap story. But Rossi refused to comment. In Brno, his only words came via the Fiat-Yamaha press releases.

Faced with such a scandal even the king of communication was lost for words.

Rossi is now a man alone. He has also become an observer as Casey Stoner wins again in Brno.

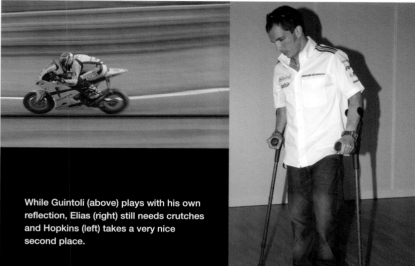

While Guintoli (above) plays with his own reflection, Elias (right) still needs crutches and Hopkins (left) takes a very nice second place.

STONER MAJESTIC, HOPKINS A BRILLIANT SECOND… ROSSI IS SERIOUSLY BEATEN

RUNNERS AND RIDERS

A thunderbolt had hit the "Rossi machine," in the shape of a tax investigation claiming that between 2000 and 2004, the moto king had hidden away more than sixty million Euros! Spain's Ivan Silva replaces Hofmann in the D'Antin camp. On the Thursday before practice, Capirossi reveals he will ride for Suzuki the following year.

QUALIFYING

Marco Melandri's GP is all over by first practice on Friday morning, when he suddenly finds himself incapable of lifting up his left arm. The Italian is suffering from a herniated vertebra which could be the result of his fall in the Catalunya GP,… of 2006 that is! The hero of day one is Guintoli who gets the very most out of his Dunlop qualifiers. On Saturday, Stoner helps himself to pole ahead of the two factory Honda riders. Rossi is "only" sixth, which means he can conveniently avoid meeting the media in the press conference.

START

Stoner catches it perfectly, charging off into the lead ahead of Pedrosa, Hopkins and Hayden. As they cross the line for the first time, the championship leader is already around 8 tenths ahead of his closest pursuer, who is still Hopkins. Rossi is sixth.

LAP 12

Edwards falls.

LAP 3

Capirossi passes Pedrosa and finds himself fourth. At the front, the gap is constant between Stoner and Hopkins.

LAP 5

Pedrosa gets the better of Capirossi once again, as Rossi and De Puniet make the most of the duel to close up.

LAP 7

Stoner still ahead of Hopkins. Hayden is third, four seconds down and leading Pedrosa by 1.7. The fifth place fight is between Capirossi, Rossi, who is about to go past, De Puniet and Vermeulen.

HALF-DISTANCE (11 LAPS)

Stoner is totally dominant with a lead of 1.734 over a revitalised Hopkins. Hayden is a lonely third ahead of Pedrosa. Rossi is now fifth and De Puniet has been caught and passed by Vermeulen.

LAP 12

Vermeulen passes his future team-mate, Loris Capirossi.

LAP 14

Rossi is down to sixth as Vermeulen is back.

LAP 15

"Vale's" descent into hell continues as Capirossi gets him.

FINISH (22 LAPS)

Stoner was never worried. Hopkins celebrates his second place with a mind blowing wheelie on his Suzuki. Hayden is third and happy. Rossi finishes seventh at the end of a nondescript race for a man in turmoil.

CHAMPIONSHIP

Stoner: 246 points; Rossi: 186. With a lead of 60 points the young Australian now has more than two races in hand, with six rounds remaining.

GP CZECH REPUBLIC | 19th August 2007 | Brno | 5.403 m

STARTING GRID

1	27	C. Stoner	Ducati	1'56.884
2	1	N. Hayden	Honda	1'57.164
3	26	D. Pedrosa	Honda	1'57.179
4	21	J. Hopkins	Suzuki	1'57.567
5	14	R. De Puniet	Kawasaki	1'57.599
6	46	V. Rossi	Yamaha	1'57.640
7	65	L. Capirossi	Ducati	1'57.665
8	71	C. Vermeulen	Suzuki	1'57.699
9	5	C. Edwards	Yamaha	1'57.702
10	50	S. Guintoli	Yamaha	1'57.732
11	56	S. Nakano	Honda	1'57.969
12	7	C. Checa	Honda	1'58.143
13	4	A. Barros	Ducati	1'58.204
14	24	T. Elias	Honda	1'58.264
15	6	M. Tamada	Yamaha	1'58.399
16	13	A. West	Kawasaki	1'59.386
17	80	Ku. Roberts	KR212V	1'59.446
18	22	I. Silvá	Ducati	2'59.721

RACE: 22 laps = 118.866 km

1	Casey Stoner	43'45.810 (162.965 km/h)
2	John Hopkins	+ 7''903
3	Nicky Hayden	+ 13''100
4	Daniel Pedrosa	+ 15''800
5	Chris Vermeulen	+ 17''303
6	Loris Capirossi	+ 19''363
7	Valentino Rossi	+ 22''485
8	Randy De Puniet	+ 23''073
9	Alex Barros	+ 32''292
10	Carlos Checa	+ 35''153
11	Toni Elias	+ 37''748
12	Anthony West	+ 38''250
13	Sylvain Guintoli	+ 43''694
14	Shinya Nakano	+ 57''069
15	Kurtis Roberts	+ 1'09.603
16	Ivan Silvá	+ 1'21.410
17	Makoto Tamada	+ 1'25.804

Fastest lap

Stoner, in 1'58.301 (164.417 km/h).
Capirossi, in 1'58.157 (164.618 km/h/2006).

Outright fastest lap

Rossi, in 1'56.191 (167.403 km/h/2006).

CHAMPIONSHIP

1	C. Stoner	246 (7 wins)
2	V. Rossi	186 (3 wins)
3	D. Pedrosa	168 (1 win)
4	C. Vermeulen	124 (1 win)
5	J. Hopkins	124
6	M. Melandri	113
7	C. Edwards	93
8	N. Hayden	89
9	L. Capirossi	87
10	A. Barros	83

LORENZO AGAIN AND ALWAYS AND HE NOW HAS A THIRTY POINT LEAD

RUNNERS AND RIDERS

Jorge Lorenzo has confirmed his switch to MotoGP with Yamaha. De Angelis is here, having visited Laguna Seca as a spectator and Dovizioso maintains that his only valid contract is the one with his current employer in 250 and thant he will race in MotoGP next year! There are four wild cards, including Debon, who will do the whole of the 2008 championship and is riding the new Aprilia RSA.

QUALIFYING

Rain brings Friday qualifying to a premature end, so that it all boils down to just three laps and, sensationally, it is Debon who is quickest. On the Saturday, his world champion team-mate takes matters in hand again and how! He beats the outright best time in the category by 1.2 seconds, a record that had been held by Pedrosa for the past two years. Dovizioso and De Angelis, the latter not qualified on the first day after a fall, complete the front row. Sekiguchi takes a frightening tumble in the warm-up, when he launches himself off Simoncelli's bike, who had fallen just in front of him. The Japanese rider is hurled into a dangerous double forward somersault, but escapes alive with fractures to his pelvis and ribs.

START

Lorenzo's super reflexes see him shoot into the lead ahead of Dovizioso and De Angelis. After one lap, the San Marino rider is pursued by Kallio, H. Aoyama, Barbera, Luthi and Bautista.

LAP 2

Lorenzo and Dovizioso have worked themselves a lead of 655 thousandths over De Angelis.

LAP 3

Simoncelli is a faller.

LAP 4

Takahashi falls, while De Angelis has closed down Dovizioso with Kallio and Barbera not far away.

HALF-DISTANCE (10 LAPS)

Lorenzo, who has just set the fastest race lap and Dovizioso have upped the pace. In third place, De Angelis is 1"264 off the Honda rider and struggling with Kallio. Barbera is a solitary fifth.

LAP 11

Debon, who had been eighth, falls right in front of Luthi.

LAP 14

Lorenzo breaks his record yet again and Dovizioso finds himself 7 tenths adrift.

LAP 15

Kallio has surprised De Angelis, while Bautista has passed Barbera for fifth place. At the head of the field, Lorenzo has a 2 second lead.

LAP 18

Alex de Angelis falls, almost taking Kallio with him.

FINISH (20 LAPS)

As he has a lead of almost 6 seconds going into the final lap, there is nothing to be done about Lorenzo and Dovizioso has understood that. Therefore, all the interest centres on the scrap for fourth between Barbera, Bautista and H. Aoyama and the three riders finish in that order

CHAMPIONSHIP

Lorenzo now leads Dovizioso by 30 points and De Angelis by 40.

Lorenzo is all smiles, Espargaro (right) concentrates and Kallio (below) once again on the podium: that's Brno 2008, 250 cc style.

GP CZECH REPUBLIC | 19th August 2007 | 19 août 2007 | Brno | 5.403 m

STARTING GRID

1	1	J. Lorenzo	Aprilia	2'01.368
2	6	A. Debón	Aprilia	2'02.026
3	34	A. Dovizioso	Honda	2'02.036
4	3	A. De Angelis	Aprilia	2'02.148
5	80	H. Barberá	Aprilia	2'02.568
6	55	Y. Takahashi	Honda	2'02.690
7	60	J. Simón	Honda	2'02.907
8	73	S. Aoyama	Honda	2'02.945
9	36	M. Kallio	KTM	2'02.956
10	4	H. Aoyama	KTM	2'03.009
11	19	A. Bautistá	Aprilia	2'03.026
12	12	T. Lüthi	Aprilia	2'03.372
13	41	A. Espargaro	Aprilia	2'03.788
14	58	M. Simoncelli	Gilera	2'03.890
15	44	T. Sekiguchi	Aprilia	2'04.049 (*)
16	15	R. Locatelli	Gilera	2'04.057
17	28	D. Heidolf	Aprilia	2'04.535
18	32	F. Lai	Aprilia	2'04.797
19	8	R. Wilairot	Honda	2'04.853
20	7	E. Vazquez	Aprilia	2'05.157
21	17	K. Abraham	Aprilia	2'05.258
22	16	J. Cluzel	Aprilia	2'06.005
23	25	A. Baldolini	Aprilia	2'06.210
24	10	I. Toth	Aprilia	2'06.372
25	50	E. Laverty	Honda	2'06.543
26	45	D. Linfoot	Aprilia	2'07.120

Not qualified:

89	H. Chow	Aprilia	2'09.932
87	J. Mayer	Honda	2'12.731
88	Z. Wang	Aprilia	2'13.049

(*): Having fallen during the warm-up, T. Sekiguchi (J, Aprilia), had to withdraw.

RACE: 20 laps = 108.060 km

1	Jorge Lorenzo	41'04.954 (157.818 km/h)
2	Andrea Dovizioso	+ 7''708
3	Mika Kallio	+ 11''107
4	Hector Barberá	+ 13''422
5	Alvaro Bautistá	+ 13''844
6	Hiroshi Aoyama	+ 13''989
7	Thomas Lüthi	+ 22''817
8	Julian Simón	+ 36''339
9	Shuhei Aoyama	+ 36''367
10	Roberto Locatelli	+ 37''552
11	Alex De Angelis	+ 1'02.616
12	Fabrizio Lai	+ 1'13.529
13	Aleix Espargaro	+ 1'14.063
14	Karel Abraham	+ 1'14.575
15	Efren Vazquez	+ 1'14.643
16	Ratthapark Wilairot	+ 1'15.165
17	Dirk Heidolf	+ 1'15.474
18	Jules Cluzel	+ 1'40.064
19	Imre Toth	+ 1'53.798
20	Dan Linfoot	+ 1'57.103

Fastest lap

Lorenzo, in 2'02.299 (159.043 km/h). New record.
Previous: Pedrosa, in 2'02.554 (158.712 km/h/2005).

Outright fastest lap

Lorenzo, in 2'01.368 (160.263 km/h/2007).

CHAMPIONSHIP

1	J. Lorenzo	216 (7 wins)
2	A. Dovizioso	186 (2 wins)
3	A. De Angelis	176
4	A. Bautistá	127 (1 win)
5	H. Barberá	103
6	M. Kallio	94
7	H. Aoyama	88 (1 win)
8	T. Lüthi	72
9	J. Simón	69
10	S. Aoyama	62

FAUBEL TAKES CHARGE AGAIN AND PESEK GETS A PODIUM AT HOME

RUNNERS AND RIDERS
Riders in this category, just like their 250 colleagues, had enjoyed a full five weeks holiday. No change among the regulars. Five hopefuls had wild cards, including Spain's Ricard Cardus, the nephew of Carlos, who had won five 250 GPs with Honda in the Eighties. Among the other invited riders, one notes the names of German Toni Wirsing and Karel Pesek, Lukas' younger brother.

QUALIFYING
There were no presents being handed out, especially not in terms of any team orders in the squad run by "Aspar" Martinez. Beaten by Pesek on the first day, before the Czech is a faller on Saturday, Talmacsi takes pole with a time over 5 tenths quicker than his team-mate, Faubel. Pasini and Koyama complete the front row.

START
Talmacsi, Gadea, who comes through all the way from seventh and Faubel are the first out front, ahead of Pasini, Corsi, from 12th on the grid and Espargaro. At the end of the first lap, Talmacsi has 3 tenths in hand over Faubel, who leads Pasini.

LAP 2
Pasini has taken the lead, with Talmacsi hanging on grimly, while Faubel is in close attendance. The group of Gadea, Pesek and Koyama is a second behind..

LAP 3
There are only two out front, as Faubel has dropped back and is now fighting with Gadea and Pesek.

LAP 4
Talmacsi is in the lead. Pesek has just set the fastest race lap, while lying third, 1.509 behind Pasini.

LAP 7
Pasini has retaken the lead and Gadea has got ahead of Pesek again.

HALF-DISTANCE (10 LAPS)
Pasini still leads Talmacsi by a tiny amount (138 thousandths.) Three of them are wheel to wheel in the fight for third spot: Gadea, Pesek and Faubel. Koyama is a bit further back

LAP 11
The pack has caught up so that the first five are now covered by just 663 thousandths.

LAP 12
Nieto falls, having been seventh

LAP 15
Pasini tries to make the break, but his lead tops out at 6 tenths. There is still all to play for and the crowd is delighted with the spectacle.

LAP 17
Gadea falls while lying second, so it is now just a four way fight and Pasini has made the most of it to pull out an advantage of 7 tenths.

FINISH (19 LAPS)
The first four are covered by a handkerchief of 284 thousandths as the last lap gets underway. Faubel is in the lead and he has the final word, crossing the line ahead of Pasini, Pesek and Talmacsi at the end of the final breathtaking 129 seconds.

CHAMPIONSHIP
Faubel comes off best this weekend, as he goes back into the lead of the championship with 10 points in hand over Talmacsi. Pesek is third, but 50 lengths (two races) off the leader.

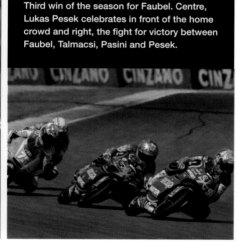

Third win of the season for Faubel. Centre, Lukas Pesek celebrates in front of the home crowd and right, the fight for victory between Faubel, Talmacsi, Pasini and Pesek.

GP CZECH REPUBLIC | 19th August 2007| 19 août 2007 | Brno | 5.403 m

STARTING GRID

1	14	G. Talmacsi	Aprilia	2'06.861
2	55	H. Faubel	Aprilia	2'07.402
3	75	M. Pasini	Aprilia	2'07.429
4	71	T. Koyama	KTM	2'08.155
5	52	L. Pesek	Derbi	2'08.200
6	34	R. Krummenacher	KTM	2'08.421
7	33	S. Gadea	Aprilia	2'08.578
8	11	S. Cortese	Aprilia	2'08.614
9	22	P. Nieto	Aprilia	2'08.694
10	44	P. Espargaro	Aprilia	2'08.712
11	60	M. Ranseder	Derbi	2'08.952
12	24	S. Corsi	Aprilia	2'08.955
13	38	B. Smith	Honda	2'09.375
14	20	R. Tamburini	Aprilia	2'09.392
15	7	A. Masbou	Honda	2'09.463
16	6	J. Olivé	Aprilia	2'09.652
17	29	A. Iannone	Aprilia	2'09.726
18	12	E. Rabat	Honda	2'09.729
19	63	M. Di Meglio	Honda	2'09.734
20	8	L. Zanetti	Aprilia	2'09.845
21	15	F. Sandi	Aprilia	2'09.847
22	35	R. De Rosa	Aprilia	2'10.055
23	95	R. Muresan	Derbi	2'10.328
24	27	S. Bianco	Aprilia	2'10.477
25	18	N. Terol	Derbi	2'10.546
26	56	H. Van Den Berg	Aprilia	2'10.598
27	51	S. Bonsey	KTM	2'10.786
28	37	J. Litjens	Honda	2'10.820
29	77	D. Aegerter	Aprilia	2'11.121
30	86	R. Cardus	Aprilia	2'11.176
31	94	T. Wirsing	Honda	2'11.808
32	99	D. Webb	Honda	2'11.933
33	53	S. Grotzkyj	Aprilia	2'11.942
34	13	D. Lombardi	Honda	2'12.631
35	93	M. Prasek	Honda	2'13.786
36	91	K. Majek	FGR	2'15.108
37	92	K. Pesek	Aprilia	2'15.723

RACE: 19 laps = 102.657 km

1	Hector Faubel	40'57.408 (150.388 km/h)	
2	Mattia Pasini	+ 0''070	
3	Lukas Pesek	+ 0''222	
4	Gabor Talmacsi	+ 0''272	
5	Tomoyoshi Koyama	+ 7''607	
6	Pol Espargaro	+ 12''066	
7	Simone Corsi	+ 12''394	
8	Michael Ranseder	+ 13''003	
9	Randy Krummenacher	+ 19''764	
10	Sandro Cortese	+ 24''043	
11	Esteve Rabat	+ 33''634	
12	Joan Olivé	+ 33''725	
13	Bradley Smith	+ 33''863	
14	Alexis Masbou	+ 34''263	
15	Stefano Bianco	+ 39''034	
16	Steve Bonsey	+ 43''841	
17	Lorenzo Zanetti	+ 44''121	
18	Raffaele De Rosa	+ 44''413	
19	Federico Sandi	+ 44''468	
20	Mike Di Meglio	+ 44''666	
21	Roberto Tamburini	+ 52''028	
22	Nicolas Terol	+ 57''920	
23	Ricard Cardus	+ 58''099	
24	Joey Litjens	+ 58''538	
25	Toni Wirsing	+ 1'10.607	
26	Dino Lombardi	+ 1'12.782	
27	Hugo Van Den Berg	+ 1'16.595	
28	Daniel Webb	+ 1'23.792	
29	Dominique Aegerter	+ 1'23.879	
30	Simone Grotzkyj	+ 1'29.979	
31	Karel Pesek	+ 1 lap	

Fastest lap
Pesek, in 2'08.145 (151.787 km/h).
Record: Cecchinello, in 2'07.836 (152.154 km/h/2003).

Outright fastest lap
Talmacsi, in 2'06.8619 (153.323 km/h/2007).

CHAMPIONSHIP

1	H. Faubel	179 (3 wins)
2	G. Talmacsi	169 (2 wins)
3	L. Pesek	129 (1 win)
4	T. Koyama	129 (1 win)
5	S. Corsi	119 (1 win)
6	S. Gadea	105 (1 win)
7	M. Pasini	86 (2 wins)
8	B. Smith	74
9	J. Olivé	72
10	P. Espargaro	72

Stoner has just turned round and he has understood: Pedrosa is out, Hayden is delayed and De Puniet is miraculous.

BOWLED OVER AT TURN 1

*OFF BALANCE JUST AFTER THE START,
DE PUNIET PLAYS SKITTLES, STONER
WILL WIN AGAIN, WHILE ROSSI, HIS
HEART NOT IN IT, PULLS OUT WITH A
TECHNICAL PROBLEM*

THE RACE

THE KING HAS SPOKEN…BUT NOT FOR LONG

He had played the shadow, the ghost, the fugitive, the chased and the hunted at Brno. But he could not settle for ever for these roles that do not suit him. Therefore, at Misano, Valentino Rossi decided to storm the barricades, to speak at last and not just about the new pneumatic valve system he had tested the day after the Czech Grand Prix.

No, this time, Valentino was back the way we like him, tackling all questions, even those that bothered him. True enough, the setting is a unique one in that Misano is "his" circuit, the one where he saw his first race, where he took part in his first race, the one where he got on a real GP bike, an Aprilia 125, for the first time. And of course, Misano is close to home, or at least to the place of his birth, given that, as everyone knows, Valentino now lives in London. Misano is his "paese," just a dozen kilometers from Tavullia, the town that has been decked out in yellow, where you can get a nice cappuccino with a chocolate 46 floating on its surface and from where, on Saturday morning, a march of 400 people would set out for the circuit, a peace march if you will, a march against all the stories that had dogged the champion this summer. It was a march for a king who would finally, at least everyone was convinced of it, pick up his sceptre once again. But everyone was wrong…

Valentino spoke and he did not stint himself. He admitted he was going through a difficult period:

For the first time since the start of this squalid tax business, Valentino Rossi spoke about it. At the time, he had no way of knowing that he would be let down by his equipment in the race.

"When you ride a race bike, you have to be one hundred percent concentrated on it and I have felt that recently, some people had forgotten we do a dangerous job. I have seen and heard strange things about myself, things that hurt. I say this now in front of you all, everything I did was according to the law. I have done no better nor worse than those who are in a similar situation to myself. I am therefore calm about all the threats and if, after another investigation, it turns out I have done something wrong, I will accept all the responsibility."

Serious matters out of the way, Rossi was once again "Vale," smiling and teasing when asked if over the last few weeks he had spent more time in the lawyers' offices or on the beach. "On the beach of course!" No one pursued the matter, no one asked him if the beaches alongside the Thames in London were sandy or made of pebbles. Rossi was back and that was the main thing and now we would see what might happen. What we would see was an extraordinary duel with Casey Stoner in qualifying with the final word going to the Ducati rider. But then, not much to see in the race from Number 46: three careful opening laps, as Rossi had opted for harder tyres than his rivals and then the shock and the silence that fell on the yellow army as the Yamaha limped back to the pits as Valentino lowered his head. This time he knew the championship was lost. Because, out in front, it was another Stoner spectacle…

STONER AGAIN AND CONFIRMATION THAT THE SUZUKIS ARE ON FINE FORM

RUNNERS AND RIDERS
Finally, Valentino Rossi speaks out on the Thursday before the event and, contrary to what had been expected, he did not restrict his comments to Misano and motorcycling, touching as well on his fiscal problems. "I have done everything according to the law, just like other people in my situation have done. If it turns out we have made a mistake, I will accept all the responsibility." Still on the Thursday, Kawasaki confirms Anthony West for 2008, with the Australian teaming up with John Hopkins. Melandri and Hofmann are back.

QUALIFYING
The Stoner-Rossi duel reaches amazing heights: the two men forget all other rivals, but once again it is Stoner, or more accurately, "the SDB combo; Stoner-Ducati-Bridgestone," as Valentino has amusingly called it, having the last word as usual. Hayden just squeezes onto the front row, as he beats De Puniet, who has shone throughout the session, by a mere 37 thousandths.

START
Casey pulls off the perfect start, but there's some rough stuff in the opening rush between Randy De Puniet, Hayden (who gets going again) and Pedrosa. First time across the line and Stoner already leads Hopkins, the first of his pursuers by 886 thousandths. Vermeulen is in close attendance and Rossi is fourth, 1.907 off the leader

LAP 5
The crowd is hushed, as Rossi is cruising along the side of the track. In front, Stoner now has a lead of 1.188 over the Hopkins-Vermeulen duo, as the two Suzuki riders take no prisoners. Melandri is now fourth, ahead of Capirossi.

LAP 6
Vermeulen has managed to break away from Hopkins.

HALF-DISTANCE (14 LAPS)
Clearly, one had expected too much of this race, as it slumps into monotony. A shame for Stoner, who is still doing a perfect job, with a lead of 1.888 over Vermeulen, who has definitively shaken off Hopkins (now 5.622 behind his team-mate.) Melandri is fourth, ahead of Capirossi and a strong Checa.

LAP 17
Barros retires from seventh place.

FINISH (28 LAPS)
Stoner must have found this a long race, as he begins his final lap 5.377 before Vermeulen. It is his eighth win of the year and there is nothing else to be said.

CHAMPIONSHIP
It's the time for mathematical possibilities in the title race. With a lead of 85 points, Stoner could be crowned as of the Portuguese GP. If he wins in Estoril and Rossi does no better than sixth, it will all be in the bag with a good four races in hand before the curtain comes down

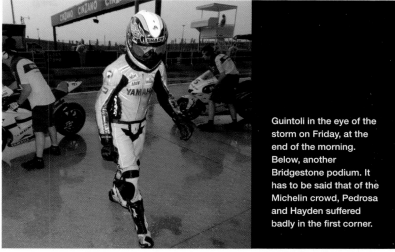

Guintoli in the eye of the storm on Friday, at the end of the morning. Below, another Bridgestone podium. It has to be said that of the Michelin crowd, Pedrosa and Hayden suffered badly in the first corner.

GP SAN MARINO | 2nd September 2007 | Misano | 4.180 m

STARTING GRID

1	27	C. Stoner	Ducati	1'33.918
2	46	V. Rossi	Yamaha	1'34.094
3	1	N. Hayden	Honda	1'34.469
4	14	R. De Puniet	Kawasaki	1'34.506
5	21	J. Hopkins	Suzuki	1'34.536
6	26	D. Pedrosa	Honda	1'34.580
7	7	C. Checa	Honda	1'34.628
8	71	C. Vermeulen	Suzuki	1'34.717
9	5	C. Edwards	Yamaha	1'34.768
10	13	A. West	Kawasaki	1'34.939
11	50	S. Guintoli	Yamaha	1'35.202
12	33	M. Melandri	Honda	1'35.236
13	65	L. Capirossi	Ducati	1'35.283
14	56	S. Nakano	Honda	1'35.389
15	24	T. Elias	Honda	1'35.632
16	6	M. Tamada	Yamaha	1'35.865
17	4	A. Barros	Ducati	1'35.897
18	80	Ku. Roberts	KR212V	1'36.605
19	65	A. Hofmann	Ducati	1'36.659

RACE: 28 laps = 117.040 km

1	Casey Stoner	44'34.720 (157.528 km/h)
2	Chris Vermeulen	+ 4''851
3	John Hopkins	+ 16''002
4	Marco Melandri	+ 22''737
5	Loris Capirossi	+ 24''787
6	Carlos Checa	+ 34''986
7	Toni Elias	+ 40''896
8	Anthony West	+ 41''774
9	Colin Edwards	+ 47''146
10	Shinya Nakano	+ 48''808
11	Alex Hofmann	+ 49''299
12	Sylvain Guintoli	+ 1'09.176
13	Nicky Hayden	+ 1'20.424
14	Makoto Tamada	+ 1'34.223
15	Kurtis Roberts	+ 1 lap

Fastest lap
Stoner, in 1'34.649 (158.987 km/h).
Record (new circuit)

Outright fastest lap
Stoner, in 1'33.918 (160.224 km/h/2007).

CHAMPIONSHIP

1	C. Stoner	271 (8 wins)
2	V. Rossi	186 (3 wins)
3	D. Pedrosa	168 (1 win)
4	C. Vermeulen	144 (1 win)
5	J. Hopkins	140
6	M. Melandri	126
7	C. Edwards	100
8	L. Capirossi	98
9	N. Hayden	92
10	A. Barros	83

VICTIM OF A MECHANICAL FAILURE, ANDREA DOVIZIOSO SEES HIS LAST CHANCE OF THE TITLE VANISH

RUNNERS AND RIDERS
After somehow surviving the Brno warm-up, Taro Sekiguchi is naturally enough not present. On the Monday and Tuesday after Brno, Alvaro Bautista and Thomas Luthi stayed on in the Czech Republic to get to know the 2008 Aprilia 250 RSA, a bike that the Swiss rider decides to use immediately, to learn as much as possible about it.

QUALIFYING
Once again the two best riders in the category are out to enjoy themselves, with Lorenzo demonstrating his panache and Dovizioso his consistency. Ten riders are covered by less than eight tenths and on Sunday, Alex de Angelis wheels out a bike painted in the colours of his home country, the Republic of San Marino.

START
Dovizioso shows he has the sharpest reflexes, ahead of Lorenzo, Barbera, Kallio and Bautista. Crossing the line for the first time, the Italian heads the championship leader by 172 thousandths.

LAP 3
Barbera surprises Lorenzo for second place. Simoncelli retires.

LAP 4
Lorenzo gets back his position, but Dovizioso has not been waiting for him and now leads his great rival by 7 tenths.

LAP 6
For the last two laps, eighth placed

Beautiful backdrop to some great scraps. Above, the one between Barbera and Luthi for third place. Below, the aborted one between Dovizioso and Lorenzo, as the Italian's Honda has just given up the ghost.

Luthi has been the quickest man on track. He has closed to 3.153 of the leader..

LAP 10
Bautista falls, having just passed Barbera, but the reigning 125 champion gets going again.

HALF-DISTANCE (13 LAPS)
Dovizioso and Lorenzo, separated by 118 thousandths, have made the break, heading third placed Kallio by 2.312 seconds, with Barbera, H. Aoyama and De Angelis in hot pursuit. On the previous lap, Luthi made a mistake as he tried to attack De Angelis and is now 2 seconds behind the pack.

LAP 17
Lorenzo and Dovizioso swap places twice, with the latter coming off best.

LAP 18
This time, the world champion is back in charge. Hiroshi Aoyama closes on his team-mate Kallio.

LAP 19
Dovizioso did not deserve it, but his engine seized, which means that all at once, Lorenzo has a 2.534 second lead over the two KTMs. Luthi has closed up to Alex De Angelis' back wheel once again.

LAP 20
Luthi passes De Angelis.

LAP 22
Kallio is a faller.

LAP 23
All eyes are now on the scrap for third, between Barbera, Luthi and De Angelis.

FINISH (26 LAPS)
With an advantage of over 4 seconds going into the final lap, Lorenzo has nothing to worry about. Barbera has the last word when it comes to third place.

CHAMPIONSHIP
The gap is now 54 points, which means Jorge Lorenzo has two races in hand over Alex De Angelis, with five rounds to go.

GP SAN MARINO| 2nd September 2007 | Misano | 4.180 m

STARTING GRID

1	1	J. Lorenzo	Aprilia	1'38.395
2	34	A. Dovizioso	Honda	1'38.558
3	80	H. Barberá	Aprilia	1'38.733
4	4	H. Aoyama	KTM	1'38.826
5	36	M. Kallio	KTM	1'39.007
6	19	A. Bautistá	Aprilia	1'39.023
7	12	T. Lüthi	Aprilia	1'39.031
8	60	J. Simón	Honda	1'39.087
9	58	M. Simoncelli	Gilera	1'39.180
10	3	A. De Angelis	Aprilia	1'39.182
11	73	S. Aoyama	Honda	1'39.506
12	55	Y. Takahashi	Honda	1'39.694
13	41	A. Espargaro	Aprilia	1'40.056
14	15	R. Locatelli	Gilera	1'40.206
15	32	F. Lai	Aprilia	1'40.329
16	8	R. Wilairot	Honda	1'40.408
17	16	J. Cluzel	Aprilia	1'40.768
18	50	E. Laverty	Honda	1'40.912
19	28	D. Heidolf	Aprilia	1'41.290
20	17	K. Abraham	Aprilia	1'41.545
21	7	E. Vazquez	Aprilia	1'41.717
22	25	A. Baldolini	Aprilia	1'41.749
23	45	D. Linfoot	Aprilia	1'42.426
24	10	I. Toth	Aprilia	1'42.944
25	64	O. Menghi	Aprilia	1'44.745

RACE: 26 laps = 108.680 km

1	Jorge Lorenzo	42'54.427 (151.974 km/h)
2	Hiroshi Aoyama	+ 3''578
3	Hector Barbera	+ 7''041
4	Thomas Lüthi	+ 7''213
5	Alex De Angelis	+ 7''664
6	Shuhei Aoyama	+ 36''234
7	Roberto Locatelli	+ 36''918
8	Alvaro Bautistá	+ 36''936
9	Yuki Takahashi	+ 37''142
10	Julian Simón	+ 40''293
11	Jules Cluzel	+ 51''720
12	Aleix Espargaro	+ 56''620
13	Ratthapark Wilairot	+ 1'00.060
14	Karel Abraham	+ 1'01.500
15	Eugene Laverty	+ 1'09.950
16	Efren Vazquez	+ 1'10.059
17	Imre Toth	+ 1 lap
18	Omar Menghi	+ 1 lap

Fastest lap
H. Aoyama, in 1'38.074 (153.435 km/h).
Record (new circuit).

Outright fastest lap
H. Aoyama, in 1'38.074 (153.435 km/h/2007).

CHAMPIONSHIP

1	J. Lorenzo	241 (8 wins)
2	A. De Angelis	187
3	A. Dovizioso	186 (2 wins)
4	A. Bautistá	135 (1 win)
5	H. Barberá	119
6	H. Aoyama	108 (1 win)
7	M. Kallio	94
8	T. Lüthi	85
9	J. Simón	75
10	S. Aoyama	72

PASINI IS THE WINNER BUT A VERY GOOD DAY TOO FOR TALMACSI

RUNNERS AND RIDERS
Five riders have wild cards and not all of them are Italian, as we have Germany's Stefan Bradl on parade. Among the list of new finds is a familiar name: Biaggi, or Federico Biaggi to be precise, who is Max's nephew, looked after by his grandfather, the dad of the former four times world champion.

QUALIFYING
Just one qualifying session, which does not change much, as the dominant forces in the series find themselves at the front as usual. The Czech, Lukas Pesek, who has just been confirmed as a 250 runner for 2008, takes the third pole of his career, by 3 thousandths of a second. Faubel, Pasini and Talmacsi complete the front row.

START
Pasini is impeccable, charging off ahead of Faubel, Corsi, Pesek and Talmacsi. Sandi does not make it round the opening lap, which Pasini rattles off with a 2 tenths lead over Faubel. There's already a first break in the pack after the ninth placed Ranseder.

LAP 3
The pace increases and the lead group has peeled into two: Pasini, Faubel, Corsi, Talmacsi and Pesek out in front, with Koyama sixth, a second down, in company with Gadea, De Rosa and Ranseder.

LAP 4
Faubel takes the lead, then it's Corsi. As these two fight, it allows Koyama and Gadea to catch up with the lead

Above, a Biaggi in the race - Federico, Max's nephew. On left, Pasini flies to another win. At KTM, the kids, Steve Bonsey and Randy Krummenacher carry on with their apprenticeship.

pack.
LAP 8
Pasini has made the break and has just set the fastest race lap, crossing the line 847 thousandths ahead of Corsi.

HALF-DISTANCE (12 LAPS)
Pasini, who was born just fifteen kilometres from the Misano circuit, now leads Corsi by 1.933. Then come Faubel, Pesek and Talmacsi. Koyama has dropped back once again, almost 2 seconds off the group, with Gadea all over his back wheel.

LAP 17
Pasini is still in total control. It's a game of cat and mouse for second place, while the elbows are out in the tussle for eighth spot between a group of ten riders all within less than 3 seconds.

LAP 21
Pesek is a faller and Koyama narrowly avoids the Derbi on the deck. Now there are only three fighting for second place, but over 5 seconds behind Pasini

LAP 22
It was always going to end in tears: Corsi and Faubel collide because of a mistake from the series leader and Talmacsi is very lucky to avoid them.

FINISH (23 LAPS)
Pasini cruises home in triumph and his fans are waiting for him at the edge of the track with a ...deckchair! Talmacsi could not have asked for more, as Faubel gets going again, but finishes outside the points.

CHAMPIONSHIP
Of course it has all gone swimmingly for Talmacsi who is back in the lead by a small 10 point margin over team-mate Faubel. Koyama is third, but 40 points down.

GP SAN MARINO | 2nd September 2007 | Misano | 4.180 m

STARTING GRID

1	52	L. Pesek	Derbi	1'43.370
2	55	H. Faubel	Aprilia	1'43.373
3	75	M. Pasini	Aprilia	1'43.381
4	14	G. Talmacsi	Aprilia	1'43.541
5	24	S. Corsi	Aprilia	1'43.611
6	71	T. Koyama	KTM	1'43.695
7	12	E. Rabat	Honda	1'44.095
8	11	S. Cortese	Aprilia	1'44.095
9	38	B. Smith	Honda	1'44.385
10	33	S. Gadea	Aprilia	1'44.529
11	63	M. Di Meglio	Honda	1'44.546
12	60	M. Ranseder	Derbi	1'44.635
13	35	R. De Rosa	Aprilia	1'44.762
14	44	P. Espargaro	Aprilia	1'44.895
15	6	J. Olivé	Aprilia	1'44.917
16	34	R. Krummenacher	KTM	1'44.928
17	17	S. Bradl	Aprilia	1'44.966
18	18	N. Terol	Derbi	1'45.054
19	27	S. Bianco	Aprilia	1'45.071
20	8	L. Zanetti	Aprilia	1'45.074
21	20	R. Tamburini	Aprilia	1'45.191
22	29	A. Iannone	Aprilia	1'45.396
23	42	S. Sancioni	Aprilia	1'45.627
24	53	S. Grotzkyj	Aprilia	1'45.719
25	77	D. Aegerter	Aprilia	1'45.782
26	15	F. Sandi	Aprilia	1'45.821
27	7	A. Masbou	Honda	1'45.856
28	22	P. Nieto	Aprilia	1'45.861
29	51	S. Bonsey	KTM	1'45.911
30	87	R. Lacalendola	Aprilia	1'46.107
31	37	J. Litjens	Honda	1'46.183
32	80	F. Biaggi	Friba	1'46.513
33	99	D. Webb	Honda	1'46.614
34	13	D. Lombardi	Honda	1'46.777
35	56	H. Van Den Berg	Aprilia	1'46.833
36	95	R. Muresan	Derbi	1'46.890
37	79	F. Lamborghini	Aprilia	1'47.147

RACE: 23 laps = 96.140 km

1	Mattia Pasini		39'47.944 (144.938 km/h)
2	Gabor Talmacsi		+ 4''774
3	Tomoyoshi Koyama		+ 8''576
4	Sergio Gadea		+ 15''819
5	Pol Espargaro		+ 23''972
6	Randy Krummenacher		+ 25''159
7	Stefan Bradl		+ 25''391
8	Bradley Smith		+ 25''513
9	Raffaele De Rosa		+ 25''994
10	Michael Ranseder		+ 26''239
11	Esteve Rabat		+ 26''693
12	Joan Olivé		+ 26''972
13	Mike Di Meglio		+ 27''493
14	Andrea Iannone		+ 32''894
15	Sandro Cortese		+ 39''305
16	Lorenzo Zanetti		+ 40''035
17	Hector Faubel		+ 40''125
18	Nicolas Terol		+ 40''157
19	Roberto Tamburini		+ 48''291
20	Lukas Pesek		+ 49''621
21	Alexis Masbou	+ 50''496
22	Simone Sancioni	+ 57''519
23	Dominique Aegerter	+ 57''666
24	Ferruccio Lamborghini	+ 59''680
25	Roberto Lacalendola	+ 1'05.109
26	Steve Bonsey	+ 1'05.276
27	Joey Litjens	+ 1'08.757
28	Simone Grotzkyj	+ 1'10.395
29	Robert Muresan	+ 1'18.572
30	Daniel Webb	+ 1'20.963
31	Hugo Van Den Berg	+ 1'21.676
32	Federico Biaggi	+ 1'54.228

Fastest lap
Pasini, in 1'42.811 (146.365 km/h).
Record (new circuit).

Outright fastest lap
Pasini, in 1'42.811 (146.365 km/h).

CHAMPIONSHIP

1	G. Talmacsi	189 (2 wins)
2	H. Faubel	179 (3 wins)
3	T. Koyama	145 (1 win)
4	L. Pesek	129 (1 win)
5	S. Corsi	119 (1 win)
6	S. Gadea	118 (1 win)
7	M. Pasini	111 (3 wins)
8	P. Espargaro	83
9	B. Smith	82
10	J. Olivé	76

The win is only a matter of honour: Valentino Rossi wins for the fourth time this season.

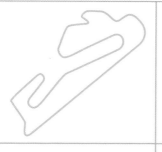

14

ROSSI:

IT'S ALL VERY WELL...

....BUT POINTLESS. THE YAMAHA RIDER
NEVER GIVES UP WITHOUT A FIGHT. HE
TAKES NINE POINTS OFF STONER...BUT
HE IS STILL 76 DOWN

THE RACE

THE KING'S LAST STAND

Rossi, oh how we love him: dominant on track, proud on the victory lap and a sprayer of champagne from the topmost step of the podium

He so needed to make sure, so needed to reassure himself. Of course, deep down, he knew that he was still the rider he always was and his skills had not vanished with one stroke of a magic wand waved by the sharp toothed members of the Italian tax service. He knew it, we knew it, the whole world knew it. Nevertheless, he had to prove it and secure his position. The important thing in this 2007 championship where tyre companies were playing an ever more important role, was to find an arena where Michelin could return to the position that the French company had held for such a long time, as the outright dominant force in the sport.

Estoril, tucked away in the most westerly corner of Europe would be the scene, this September weekend. Everything was in place for Valentino Rossi to return to his usual role. Right from the start of qualifying, the Michelin riders were on the pace, with the only Bridgestone runner to mix it with them

being world championship leader, Casey Stoner, who could take the crown at this round, with four more races still to go. Hayden took pole, which was a good sign for Rossi, who had understood that he might actually find himself some opportunistic allies in this race, such as Pedrosa who is close by. This is all good news, very good news, if it were not for doubts that even Valentino himself seemed aware of the night before the race. "I know we will be on the pace, but I am also worried that we might have concerns in the second half of the race." And worse than that, although beaten in the scrap for pole position, on Saturday morning, Casey Stoner put together a run of 27 laps on the same set of tyres at a mind blowing pace.

Place your bets ladies and gentlemen, the croupier has tossed the little white ball into the roulette wheel and it is yet again a classis number that is going to come out as the winner: 46, pair, white with a blue strip, a bit of yellow on the head.

King Valentino Rossi won his last stand, beating not only Casey Stoner, but Daniel Pedrosa too and so he can once again side saddle ride his Yamaha M1 as the king completes his lap of honour. Therefore, in one fell swoop and even if Valentino Rossi knows it will not change much in the current situation, be it financial or sporting, his terrible summer can be put behind him. Of course, the vulpine money men had to have their say again a few days earlier. They swarmed into a former stable converted into a home, which houses a true museum of GP bikes; Rossi's private collection. Of course, Casey Stoner's comfortable position at the top of the points table has not really been challenged. But all the same, Rossi had needed a race like this, a win like this, a boost like this.

Only the day before, his mate, his idol, rally driver Colin McRae, had been killed piloting his helicopter. Rossi had just paid homage to him in the best way possible, with a win.

A MICHELIN DOUBLE THANKS TO ROSSI AND PEDROSA

RUNNERS AND RIDERS

No changes, although Fiat-Yamaha team manager, Davide Brivio explains Rossi's mechanical failure at Misano. "It was not the new pneumatic valve system, but a mechanical component located in the bottom end of the engine which broke, but orders from the Japanese mean I can say no more about it."

QUALIFYING

Michelin is working harder than ever and the results are evident, as Stoner is the only Bridgestone runner in the top eight. The ever increasing importance of tyres is underlined by the fact that Tamada is fourth and

Guintoli is eighth on their Dunlops. Pole? For the very first time this season it goes to the still reigning world champion, Nicky Hayden.

START

Stoner, Pedrosa, Hayden and Melandri lead off the line ahead of Rossi. Stoner completes the first lap with a 373 thousandth lead over Pedrosa, who is pursued by Hayden and Rossi.

LAP 3

Stoner sets the tone with a lead over Pedrosa extended to 576 thousandths. Rossi has passed Hayden to go third, 1.357 off the lead.

LAP 7

A great contest as Pedrosa comes alongside Stoner down the main straight and is the last to brake. The Spaniard is thus in the lead and Rossi, who has just set the race fastest lap, is 272 thousandths off the Ducati.

LAP 9

Rossi passes Stoner and helps himself to Pedrosa's position at the end of the straight.

LAP 12

Hofmann, who had started from pit lane, retires. Hayden has closed to 1.5 seconds off Stoner.

HALF-DISTANCE (14 LAPS)

Still Rossi. Pedrosa is second at 184 thousandths. Stoner is third at 5 tenths, with Hayden 1.321 off the championship leader.

LAP 17

Dani Pedrosa recaptures the lead taking Rossi with him but not Stoner.

LAP 20

Randy de Puniet retires.

LAP 22

Guintoli pits and rejoins the race. At the front, Hayden is again almost 2 seconds behind Stoner.

LAP 23

Barros retires.

LAP 24

Rossi retakes the lead with a truly amazing move, but Pedrosa fights back. In eighth place, Tamada is a faller.

LAP 27

At his second attempt, also very impressive, Rossi is back in front with 170 thousandths in hand going into the final lap.

FINISH (28 LAPS)

The crowd goes wild as Rossi has returned to form, showing all his old panache and putting behind him any stories about a millionaire and his fiscal worries.

CHAMPIONSHIP

Stoner is still in the driving seat with a 76 point lead. At Motegi, in one week's time, he can even afford to lose one point to Rossi, but no more, if he is to take the title before "his" grand prix.

The intense scrap between Pedrosa and Rossi would finish in victory for the Italian (above.) On right, all smiles, Sylvain Guintoli, one of the sensations of qualifying.

GP PORTUGAL | 16th September 2007 | Estoril | 4.182 m

STARTING GRID

1	1	N. Hayden	Honda	1'36.301
2	27	C. Stoner	Ducati	1'36.341
3	46	V. Rossi	Yamaha	1'36.576
4	6	M. Tamada	Yamaha	1'36.736
5	26	D. Pedrosa	Honda	1'36.829
6	5	C. Edwards	Yamaha	1'36.904
7	33	M. Melandri	Honda	1'37.157
8	50	S. Guintoli	Yamaha	1'37.189
9	24	T. Elias	Honda	1'37.246
10	21	J. Hopkins	Suzuki	1'37.280
11	7	C. Checa	Honda	1'37.296
12	71	C. Vermeulen	Suzuki	1'37.365
13	56	S. Nakano	Honda	1'37.530
14	4	A. Barros	Ducati	1'37.550
15	65	L. Capirossi	Ducati	1'37.733
16	13	A. West	Kawasaki	1'37.885
17	65	A. Hofmann	Ducati	1'37.959
18	14	R. De Puniet	Kawasaki	1'38.271
19	80	Ku. Roberts	KR212V	1'39.017

RACE: 28 laps = 117.096 km

1	Valentino Rossi	45'49.911 (153.294 km/h)
2	Daniel Pedrosa	+ 0''175
3	Casey Stoner	+ 1''477
4	Nicky Hayden	+ 12''951
5	Marco Melandri	+ 17''343
6	John Hopkins	+ 18''857
7	Carlos Checa	+ 31''524
8	Toni Elias	+ 40''535
9	Loris Capirossi	+ 43''107
10	Colin Edwards	+ 44''674
11	Shinya Nakano	+ 45''403
12	Anthony West	+ 54''562
13	Chris Vermeulen	+ 1'00.002
14	Sylvain Guintoli	+ 1 lap

Fastest lap
Hayden, in 1'37.493 (154.423 km/h). New record.
Previous: Ke. Roberts, in 1'37''914 (153.759 km/h/2006).

Outrigth fastest lap
Rossi, in 1'36.200 (156.498 km/h/2006).

CHAMPIONSHIP

1	C. Stoner	287 (8 wins)
2	V. Rossi	211 (4 wins)
3	D. Pedrosa	188 (1 win)
4	J. Hopkins	150
5	C. Vermeulen	147 (1 win)
6	M. Melandri	137
7	C. Edwards	106
8	L. Capirossi	105
9	N. Hayden	105
10	A. Barros	83

SECOND WIN FOR THE ROOKIE, ALVARO BAUTISTA

RUNNERS AND RIDERS

Taro Sekiguchi is still missing from the grid. Worth noting the presence of the Chinese Zonghsen team and three familiar wild cards in this category: the Spaniards Molina and Barragan and Englishman Lawrence.

QUALIFYING

It's all a bit twitchy in the class that has most evolved this year. Saturday's key session ended in chaos and recrimination, with Lorenzo having to shell out for a 5000 dollar fine and some bitter words were exchanged: "If Mr. Lorenzo wants to be all alone on track, he should hire a circuit. Unfortunately for him, there are thirty of us racing here," comments his "enemy" Hector Barbera, something of a specialist of the slipstreamers art. In contrast to all this fuss, Dovizioso goes about his business in a calm fashion and takes pole position.

START

Dovizioso, Lorenzo and Kallio are the lead trio off the grid. Simon passes the KTM rider and completes the first lap in third place. At the front, Dovizioso has put 421 thousandths between himself and Lorenzo.

LAP 2

Roberto Locatelli falls.

LAP 3

Takahashi falls from thirteenth spot.

LAP 5

Kallio is touring round. The lead pair of Dovizioso and Lorenzo now head third placed Simon by 1.899. Back up

Simon, Kallio and Barbera (above) fight tooth and nail. Opposite, the second crowning of the reigning 125 world champion, Bautista. His predecessor, Thomas Luthi consoles himself with his fiancée, the lovely Fabienne Kropf.

to seventh, Bautista is the quickest man on track.

LAP 7

Bautista continues to string together a series of fastest laps and he is now fourth.

LAP 8

Bautista is third, dragging along a group made up of Barbera, the Aoyama brothers, Simon, De Angelis and Luthi.

HALF-DISTANCE (13 LAPS)

Still Dovizioso, whose lead over Lorenzo is now 933 thousandths. Bautista is third, with Barbera still fourth ahead of De Angelis and Luthi.

LAP 14

Bautista continues to shine and is within 2 tenths of Lorenzo.

LAP 17

Bautista passes Lorenzo on the straight and then Dovizioso at the chicane. He leads!

LAP 19

Lorenzo realises he is powerless against the Bautista-Dovizioso duo. Shuhei Aoyami retires.

LAP 23

Hiroshi Aoyama retires, so both KTMs are out. At the front, Bautista, who has once again beaten the lap record, leads Dovizioso by 1.187. Luthi has passed De Angelis for fourth spot.

FINISH (26 LAPS)

Well done Mister Bautista! The 125 world champion scores his second win in his new class and Dovizioso and Lorenzo could only admire his handiwork. A nice race also from Thomas Luthi, who came out on top in his duel with De Angelis.

CHAMPIONSHIP

Although beaten, Lorenzo still leads Dovizioso by 51 points, or the equivalent of two races. There are still four to go.

GP PORTUGAL | 16th September 2007 | Estoril | 4.182 m

STARTING GRID

1	34	A. Dovizioso	Honda	1'40.355
2	1	J. Lorenzo	Aprilia	1'40.480
3	80	H. Barberá	Aprilia	1'40.699
4	36	M. Kallio	KTM	1'40.851
5	4	H. Aoyama	KTM	1'40.856
6	19	A. Bautistá	Aprilia	1'40.884
7	60	J. Simón	Honda	1'41.093
8	3	A. De Angelis	Aprilia	1'41.100
9	55	Y. Takahashi	Honda	1'41.157
10	12	T. Lüthi	Aprilia	1'41.176
11	58	M. Simoncelli	Gilera	1'41.370
12	73	S. Aoyama	Honda	1'41.531
13	15	R. Locatelli	Gilera	1'41.552
14	41	A. Espargaro	Aprilia	1'42.200
15	32	F. Lai	Aprilia	1'42.334
16	28	D. Heidolf	Aprilia	1'43.074
17	50	E. Laverty	Honda	1'43.132
18	8	R. Wilairot	Honda	1'43.150
19	7	E. Vazquez	Aprilia	1'43.336
20	10	I. Toth	Aprilia	1'43.664
21	17	K. Abraham	Aprilia	1'43.703
22	16	J. Cluzel	Aprilia	1'43.981
23	25	A. Baldolini	Aprilia	1'44.069
24	45	D. Linfoot	Aprilia	1'44.539
25	31	A. Molina	Aprilia	1'44.570
26	89	H. Chow	Aprilia	1'47.044

Not qualified:

84	L. Lawrence	Aprilia	1'48.335
53	S. Barragan	Honda	1'49.307
88	Z. Wang	Aprilia	1'49.413

RACE: 26 laps = 108.732 km

1	Alvaro Bautistá	43'56.458 (148.470 km/h)
2	Andrea Dovizioso	+ 4''367
3	Jorge Lorenzo	+ 6''148
4	Thomas Lüthi	+ 12''685
5	Hector Barberá	+ 13''411
6	Alex De Angelis	+ 13''440
7	Marco Simoncelli	+ 30''322
8	Julian Simón	+ 30''634
9	Fabrizio Lai	+ 1'12.253
10	Karel Abraham	+ 1'12.319
11	Dirk Heidolf	+ 1'14.060
12	Aleix Espargaro	+ 1'14.159
13	Jules Cluzel	+ 1'14.575
14	Eugene Laverty	+ 1'30.978
15	Imre Toth	+ 1 lap
16	Alvaro Molina	+ 1 lap
17	Ho Wan Chow	+ 2 laps

Fastest lap

Bautistá, in 1'40.521 (149.771 km/h). New record.
Previous: H. Aoyama, in 1'41''676 (148.070 km/h/2006).

Outright fastest lap

Dovizioso, in 1'40.355 (150.019 km/h/2007).

CHAMPIONSHIP

1	J. Lorenzo	257 (8 wins)
2	A. Dovizioso	206 (2 wins)
3	A. De Angelis	197
4	A. Bautistá	160 (2 wins)
5	H. Barberá	130
6	H. Aoyama	108 (1 win)
7	T. Lüthi	98
8	M. Kallio	94
9	J. Simón	83
10	S. Aoyama	72

THE TURN OF FAUBEL AND ALSO POL ESPARGARO

RUNNERS AND RIDERS
Four riders have wild cards, including one Portuguese, Ivo Relvas, and Louis Rossi, one of the revelations of the French championship this year. We already know Ricard Cardus and even better established is Pere Tutusaus, who this year is fighting for the Spanish title with Germany's Stefan Bradl, the latter replacing Dutchman Van Den Berg in the Blusens Aprilia squad.

QUALIFYING
Yet another pole for Mattia Pasini, who makes the most of a fall for Pesek, but also of the tension that now exists within the Bancaja Aspar team: Faubel is "only" eighth. Exploit of the day comes from Sandro Cortese, the German of Italian origins who rides for the Emmi-Caffe Latte team who qualifies fifth. Local rider Relvas does not make it through the qualifying cut.

START
A super start from Pasini ahead of Espargaro, Corsi and Faubel. First time round, the dominant yet unlucky force of the season already has a lead of 763 thousandths over the first of his pursuers, Simone Corsi.

LAP 2
Faubel has helped himself to second place and, more importantly is within 3 tenths of Pasini. Corsi hangs on, but already a gap has grown to the chasing pack.

LAP 5
Pasini, Faubel and Corsi are within 5 tenths. Behind them, Talmacsi leads the pursuers, but 2 seconds down.

LAP 8
Pasini has built himself a small 7 tenths cushion and Talmacsi has closed to one second off third spot.

LAP 10
Cortese and Ranseder are fallers after scrapping over eleventh place.

LAP 11
The leader, Mattia Pasini is a faller but rejoins. Talmacsi is back in touch and so now there are once again three men fighting for the win.

HALF-DISTANCE (12 LAPS)
Corsi leads Faubel by 181 thousandths, while Talmacsi is third. Olive is now fourth with Espargaro in pursuit. Gadea who reached the halfway point in fifth place stops shortly afterwards with technical problems.

LAP 14
Talmacsi, Faubel, Corsi, Espargaro and Olive: that is the leading quintet all within a second.

LAP 17
Little Espargaro leads.

FINISH (23 LAPS:
The five lead riders are within 996 thousandths going into the final lap. Olive and Corsi are the first to drop back. Talmacsi goes ahead at the chicane, but Faubel, well placed in the slipstream, makes the most of the tow to take the win.

CHAMPIONSHIP:
209 for Talmacsi, 204 for the winner on the day, Faubel: there will be no time for boredom on track over the next few weeks, nor in the backrooms of the team run by "Aspar" Martinez.

The new star of Spanish motorcycling, Pol Espargaro (no. 44 in the wake of future winner, Hector Faubel) takes his first podium. On right, a new Rossi called Louis, a Frenchman.

GP PORTUGAL | 16th September 2007 | Estoril | 4.182 m

STARTING GRID

1	75	M. Pasini	Aprilia	1'44.675
2	52	L. Pesek	Derbi	1'44.933
3	24	S. Corsi	Aprilia	1'45.158
4	14	G. Talmacsi	Aprilia	1'45.176
5	11	S. Cortese	Aprilia	1'45.288
6	33	S. Gadea	Aprilia	1'45.339
7	44	P. Espargaro	Aprilia	1'45.365
8	55	H. Faubel	Aprilia	1'45.378
9	17	S. Bradl	Aprilia	1'45.479
10	6	J. Olivé	Aprilia	1'45.621
11	71	T. Koyama	KTM	1'45.695
12	34	R. Krummenacher	KTM	1'45.970
13	18	N. Terol	Derbi	1'45.971
14	63	M. Di Meglio	Honda	1'46.010
15	38	B. Smith	Honda	1'46.048
16	29	A. Iannone	Aprilia	1'46.062
17	12	E. Rabat	Honda	1'46.164
18	35	R. De Rosa	Aprilia	1'46.192
19	60	M. Ranseder	Derbi	1'46.374
20	7	A. Masbou	Honda	1'46.374
21	22	P. Nieto	Aprilia	1'46.756
22	8	L. Zanetti	Aprilia	1'46.798
23	27	S. Bianco	Aprilia	1'46.869
24	77	D. Aegerter	Aprilia	1'46.982
25	20	R. Tamburini	Aprilia	1'47.183
26	37	J. Litjens	Honda	1'47.215
27	95	R. Muresan	Derbi	1'47.351
28	15	F. Sandi	Aprilia	1'47.375
29	99	D. Webb	Honda	1'47.520
30	13	D. Lombardi	Honda	1'47.874
31	30	P. Tutusaus	Aprilia	1'48.003
32	51	S. Bonsey	KTM	1'48.236
33	53	S. Grotzkyj	Aprilia	1'48.697
34	62	L. Rossi	Honda	1'49.679
35	86	R. Cardus	Aprilia	1'50.854

Not qualified:

	61	I. Relvas	Aprilia	1'52.088

RACE: 23 laps = 96.186 km

1	Hector Faubel	40'46.337 (141.546 km/h)
2	Gabor Talmacsi	+ 0''132
3	Pol Espargaro	+ 0''235
4	Simone Corsi	+ 1''001
5	Joan Olivé	+ 1''188
6	Stefan Bradl	+ 7''579
7	Tomoyoshi Koyama	+ 8''297
8	Mattia Pasini	+ 8''957
9	Raffaele De Rosa	+ 8''984
10	Randy Krummenacher	+ 14''052
11	Esteve Rabat	+ 14''123
12	Bradley Smith	+ 18''145
13	Lukas Pesek	+ 21''118
14	Alexis Masbou	+ 31''521
15	Stefano Bianco	+ 31''612
16	Mike Di Meglio	+ 31''648
17	Lorenzo Zanetti	+ 31''945
18	Andrea Iannone	+ 31''986
19	Federico Sandi	+ 44''317
20	Daniel Webb	+ 1'01.566
21	Simone Grotzkyj	+ 1'03.909
22	Roberto Tamburini	+ 1'04.002
23	Robert Muresan	+ 1'06.216
24	Louis Rossi	+ 1'09.350

Fastest lap
Talmacsi, in 1'45.027 (143.345 km/h). New record.
Previous: Bautistá, in 1'45.746 (142.371 km/h/2006).

Outright fastest lap
Pasini, in 1'44.675 (143.828 km/h).

CHAMPIONNAT

1	G. Talmacsi	209 (2 wins)
2	H. Faubel	204 (4 wins)
3	T. Koyama	154 (1 win)
4	L. Pesek	132 (1 win)
5	S. Corsi	132 (1 win)
6	M. Pasini	119 (3 wins)
7	S. Gadea	118 (1 win)
8	P. Espargaro	99
9	J. Olivé	87
10	B. Smith	86

Adriana Stoner can give back husband Casey his wedding ring: as of now she is married to a world champion.

15

THE CHAMPION
IS CALLED STONER!

AT THE END OF A RACE FULL OF
INCIDENT, THE AUSTRALIAN TAKES
THE TITLE AT THE FIRST
OPPORTUNITY

THE RACE

STONER'S BEST SHOT

Rossi tried in vain to put the pressure on. Casey is ready for the family photo, with his wife, Adriana and his parents, Colin and Bronwyn, before having a quiet moment with his beloved.

It had seemed he had a fever, and he was fed up with always being asked the same questions about his almost insolent domination of the 2007 MotoGP World Championship. Who was winning? The Ducati Desmosedici? The fantastic Bridgestone tyres? Or did it have a little bit to do with Casey Stoner after all? He seemed to be at the end of his tether, perfect prey in fact for the cold predators that are Rossi and Pedrosa. Then, as he awoke on the morning of Sunday 23 September, he realised immediately that the weather had decided to play a role and not just as a blue sky spectator, but as a key player. The rain was falling and with it a more serious risk of falling and a greater chance of uncertainty. This rain that came and went meant the track was changing and drying. It also meant that Casey Stoner was about to kick the decisive penalty shoot out shot in what was effectively going to be a lottery.

If he seems to be showing signs of pressure, once the lights went green, he is once again in total control of his art and of the situation. He starts off as a front runner with Melandri and Rossi as the path he must take became clearer. The first to change bikes start coming down pit lane, but he stays out as does Rossi as the two men stalk one another. Stoner will go on to stop at the right moment: "it's the team who told me when to come in to pit and it all went perfectly," he said after the race. "It was too late to go for the win, but it was enough to shake off Valentino, the only man who could stop him, but who had to make a further stop, in the grasp of problems that were more psychological than technical. It is 14h48 on this Sunday 23 September 2007 as Casey Stoner finishes sixth in the Japanese GP, his "worst" result of the season, but it is enough to make the dream come true. His young wife Adriana kisses her in-laws, Colin and Bronwyn. Casey is still on his Ducati on his slowing down lap. He looks at the sky and grabs an Australian flag. His predecessor, Nicky Hayden stops alongside him in a symbolic handing over of power. As for Valentino

Rossi, he hardly glances at the hero of the day. For the second year in a row, the king of motorcycle racing in the modern era is beaten.

The emotion is too much for Casey and he cries under his crash helmet. He knows that his immediate future is out of his control: podium, interviews, press conference, party, photos. A beer Casey? "One or two, maybe…" That afternoon, while the "red team" celebrate, he holds Adriana in his arms. Underneath the podium, following a well practiced routine, Casey has pulled off his gloves, handed them to his wife, who smiles as she replaces her beloved's wedding ring that has united them since the start of the year. It's a gold ring that Stoner never removes except when racing his motorbike.

It's a gold ring for a superb exploit. The most coveted motorcycling world title has gone to a rider of a European manufacturer, here in Motegi in Honda's backyard. It's a nice little snub to arrogance don't you think?

CAPIROSSI, OR THE VICTORIOUS LOOK OF THE MAN WHO DEVELOPED THE DESMOSEDICI

RUNNERS AND RIDERS

There was plenty going on the night of the Portuguese GP, as Germany's Alexander Hofmann was shown the door with immediate effect and here, is replaced by Shinichi Ito, Ducati-Bridgestone's test rider. A third Kawasaki is entered for Akira Yanagawa and a third Suzuki for Kousuke Akiyoshi.

QUALIFYING

Stoner is suffering a fever, De Puniet only just misses out on a front row slot and there are three Michelin riders in

the top three, on the day when a bombshell drops. Not only has HRC president, Masumi Hamane admitted he has been in touch with Bridgestone, but more than that, Carmelo Ezpeleta, the Dorna boss is close to switching to a sole tyre supplier, having come under pressure from Pedrosa and Rossi.

START

It had rained in the morning and so everyone starts on grooved rubber. West moves on the line, Pedrosa takes the lead ahead of Elias, Hayden and Stoner. The Spaniard rattles off the opening lap with a 481 thousandths edge over West and 1"183 over Stoner. Rossi is seventh.

LAP 2

At the exact moment that West takes the lead, it is announced he has jumped the start. Casey Stoner passes Pedrosa.

LAP 4

West rumbles down pit lane for his penalty. Stoner finds himself back in the lead, with Melandri hanging onto to his pillion pad.

LAP 7

Hayden and Guintoli change bikes.

LAP 9

Capirossi, Vermeulen and Barros are now on slicks. Guintoli sets the fastest lap, three seconds quicker than the leaders.

HALF-DISTANCE (12 LAPS)

Rossi has just passed Stoner. In front, Melandri is in the lead with a 1.833 seconds lead over the Yamaha rider, followed by Stoner at 6 tenths. Pedrosa is 3.245 away. Including Edwards in fifth place, all these riders are still on rain tyres.

LAP 13

It's very heated between Melandri and Rossi. Pedrosa has passed Stoner for

third place. Melandri stops as does Casey Stoner.

LAP 15

Rossi changes bikes, Pedrosa falls and Capirossi finds himself in the lead.

LAP 17

Rossi pits for a second time and a close-up shot of the Stoner garage reveals the Casey clan looking as though they are beginning to believe in it. Rossi is only fifteenth.

LAP 18

Capirossi has a 14 second lead over the De Puniet-Elias duo. Guintoli is fourth and the quickest man on track.

FINISH (24 LAPS)

It's a great story for the man who was at the root of Ducati's triumph, Loris Capirossi. The Italian takes top honours for a third consecutive time at Motegi on the day his young team-mate is crowned as world champion.

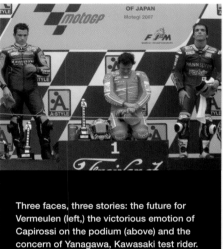

Three faces, three stories: the future for Vermeulen (left,) the victorious emotion of Capirossi on the podium (above) and the concern of Yanagawa, Kawasaki test rider.

GP JAPAN | 23rd September 2007 | Motegi | 4.801 m

STARTING GRID

Pos	No	Rider	Bike	Time
1	26	D. Pedrosa	Honda	1'45.864
2	46	V. Rossi	Yamaha	1'46.255
3	1	N. Hayden	Honda	1'46.575
4	14	R. De Puniet	Kawasaki	1'46.643
5	24	T. Elias	Honda	1'46.804
6	13	A. West	Kawasaki	1'46.912
7	5	C. Edwards	Yamaha	1'46.997
8	65	L. Capirossi	Ducati	1'47.047
9	27	C. Stoner	Ducati	1'47.121
10	33	M. Melandri	Honda	1'47.136
11	21	J. Hopkins	Suzuki	1'47.163
12	56	S. Nakano	Honda	1'47.295
13	64	K. Akiyoshi	Suzuki	1'47.316
14	7	C. Checa	Honda	1'47.334
15	4	A. Barros	Ducati	1'47.367
16	6	M. Tamada	Yamaha	1'47.714
17	71	C. Vermeulen	Suzuki	1'47.914
18	50	S. Guintoli	Yamaha	1'48.085
19	87	A. Yanagawa	Kawasaki	1'48.569
20	72	S. Ito	Ducati	1'49.548
21	80	Ku. Roberts	KR212V	1'50.035

RACE: 24 laps = 115.224 km

Pos	Rider	Time/Gap
1	Loris Capirossi	47'05.484 (146.808 km/h)
2	Randy De Puniet	+ 10''853
3	Toni Elias	+ 11''526
4	Sylvain Guintoli	+ 12''192
5	Marco Melandri	+ 28''569
6	Casey Stoner	+ 31''179
7	Anthony West	+ 50''001
8	Alex Barros	+ 52''343
9	Nicky Hayden	+ 53''629
10	John Hopkins	+ 59''715
11	Chris Vermeulen	+ 1'02.804
12	Makoto Tamada	+ 1'09.313
13	Valentino Rossi	+ 1'09.699
14	Colin Edwards	+ 1'11.735
15	Shinichi Ito	+ 1'12.290
16	Shinya Nakano	+ 1'32.979
17	Akira Yanagawa	+ 1 lap
18	Carlos Checa	+ 1 lap

Fastest lap

Elias, in 1'50.718 (156.104 km/h).
Record: Rossi, in 1'47''288 (161.095 km/h/2006).

Outright fastest lap

Capirossi, in 1'45.724 (163.478 km/h/2006).

CHAMPIONSHIP

Pos	Rider	Points
1	C. Stoner	297 (8 wins)
2	V. Rossi	214 (4 wins)
3	D. Pedrosa	188 (1 win)
4	J. Hopkins	156
5	C. Vermeulen	152 (1 win)
6	M. Melandri	148
7	L. Capirossi	130 (1 win)
8	N. Hayden	112
9	C. Edwards	108
10	A. Barros	91

Dovizioso gives Kallio a champagne shower: the Finn in action opposite, avoided all the traps, including that of the first corner (above.)

ANOTHER "DEBUTANT", BUT THIS TIME IT'S KALLIO!

RUNNERS AND RIDERS

The paddock is delighted to see Taro Sekiguchi, the miraculous survivor of Brno. The Campetella rider has to get about using crutches. There are four wild cards, including Takumi Takahashi (brother of the other one) and an old favourite, Youichi Ui (Yamaha.)

QUALIFYING

A first pole for Shuhei Aoyama, who hangs onto Dovizioso in the final seconds of qualifying. Lorenzo is third, ahead of Barbera.

START

It has not rained since midway through the 125 race, but the track is still damp. A super start from Shuhei Aoyama and also from Dovizioso, who leads at the first split. Baldolini and Vazquez fall right from the start, while Dovizioso heads the first lap with a lead of 1"389 over the chasing group, dragged along by the two KTMs.

LAP 3

Still Dovizioso now with a lead of 655 thousandths over H. Aoyama. Yuki Takahashi is now third at 1"291, with Kallio in attendance. Barbera is a solitary fifth.

LAP 6

Dovizioso, Yuki Takahashi, (whose brother has just fallen,) H. Aoyama, Barbera and Kallio: the lead five are covered by 1"717. Behind them Simoncelli is over six seconds down. Lorenzo is fighting for second place with Luthi.

LAP 8

It is hotting up at the front as Y. Takahashi has taken the lead from Barbera and Dovizioso. At the same time, the two KTM riders are back in touch.

LAP 9

Bautista goes straight on into the gravel trap and rejoins twentieth.

HALF-DISTRANCE (12 LAPS)

The racing line is drying out more and more and Takahashi makes the most of it. He now leads Kallio by 2.156 seconds, with the Finn still fighting off Barbera, H. Aoyama and Dovizioso. Simon is sixth, but over 16 seconds down.

LAP 14

Dovizioso has closed up to Kallio, while H. Aoyama and Barbera have dropped back.

LAP 17

Dovizioso passes Kallio but he is overtaken again before taking the lead once more! The top four are separated by 606 thousandths as they cross the line.

LAP 19

Yuki Takahashi goes off the track, rejoining fifth. Out in front, Kallio leads H. Aoyama.

LAP 22

Hiroshi Aoyama falls having just been passed by Dovizioso.

FINISH (23 LAPS)

Kallio leads Dovizioso by precisely 999 thousandths going into the final lap. He does a magnificent job to take his first victory in the class. Dovizioso is second, with Barbera completing the podium trio.

CHAMPIONSHIP

There are only 36 points separating Lorenzo and Dovizioso, the latter with every passing day regretting his mechanical failure at Misano.

GP JAPAN | 23rd September 2007 | Motegi | 4.801 m

STARTING GRID

1	73	S. Aoyama	Honda	1'51.327
2	34	A. Dovizioso	Honda	1'51.466
3	1	J. Lorenzo	Aprilia	1'51.765
4	80	H. Barberá	Aprilia	1'51.828
5	36	M. Kallio	KTM	1'52.053
6	4	H. Aoyama	KTM	1'52.169
7	60	J. Simón	Honda	1'52.261
8	55	Y. Takahashi	Honda	1'52.328
9	3	A. De Angelis	Aprilia	1'52.329
10	12	T. Lüthi	Aprilia	1'52.441
11	19	A. Bautistá	Aprilia	1'52.711
12	58	M. Simoncelli	Gilera	1'52.825
13	15	R. Locatelli	Gilera	1'52.830
14	8	R. Wilairot	Honda	1'54.124
15	32	F. Lai	Aprilia	1'54.418
16	20	T. Takahashi	Honda	1'54.487
17	75	Y. Ui	Yamaha	1'54.779
18	25	A. Baldolini	Aprilia	1'54.914
19	17	K. Abraham	Aprilia	1'55.032
20	28	D. Heidolf	Aprilia	1'55.182
21	50	E. Laverty	Honda	1'55.352
22	41	A. Espargaro	Aprilia	1'55.451
23	10	I. Toth	Aprilia	1'55.485
24	7	E. Vazquez	Aprilia	1'55.690
25	16	J. Cluzel	Aprilia	1'56.042
26	77	Y. Hamamoto	Yamaha	1'56.692
27	45	D. Linfoot	Aprilia	1'56.705
28	76	S. Oikawa	Yamaha	1'56.973

RACE: 23 laps = 110.423 km

1	Mika Kallio	48'28.585 (136.672 km/h)	
2	Andrea Dovizioso	+ 4''893	
3	Hector Barberá	+ 21''527	
4	Yuki Takahashi	+ 23''488	
5	Alex De Angelis	+ 25''378	
6	Julian Simón	+ 42''264	
7	Marco Simoncelli	+ 48''782	
8	Hiroshi Aoyama	+ 57''782	
9	Shuhei Aoyama	+ 1'09.049	
10	Thomas Lüthi	+ 1'10.837	
11	Jorge Lorenzo	+ 1'13.035	
12	Seijin Oikawa	+ 1'26.371	
13	Jules Cluzel	+ 1'36.236	
14	Youichi Ui	+ 1'47.098	
15	Alvaro Bautistá	+ 1'50.081	
16	Roberto Locatelli	+ 1'58.741	
17	Aleix Espargaro	+ 2'06.782	
18	Imre Toth	+ 2'10.415	
19	Eugene Laverty	+ 1 lap	
20	Yuki Hamamoto	+ 1 lap	

Fastest lap

Dovizioso, in 2'04.160 (139.204 km/h).
Record: Nakano, in 1'52''253 (153.970 km/h/2000).

Outright fastest lap

S. Aoyama, in 1'51.327 (155.250 km/h/2007).

CHAMPIONSHIP

1	J. Lorenzo	262 (8 wins)
2	A. Dovizioso	226 (2 wins)
3	A. De Angelis	208
4	A. Bautistá	161 (2 wins)
5	H. Barberá	146
6	M. Kallio	119 (1 win)
7	H. Aoyama	116 (1 win)
8	T. Lüthi	104
9	J. Simón	93
10	S. Aoyama	79

BETWEEN TALMACSI AND FAUBEL, THE TOING AND FROING CONTINUES

RUNNERS AND RIDERS

The Dutchman Joey Litjens is not on parade; having suffered concussion at the Portuguese GP, he has, on instructions from his doctor, opted out of the long haul flight. He is not replaced. A Japanese tradition, there is a Yamaha on track in the hands of Nayuta Mizuna, one of the five Japanese riders with a wild card.

QUALIFYING:

And it's number eight for Mattia Pasini, who is still the class of the field, despite some problems on the first day. Winner last year and literally raised up by his fans, Koyama (KTM) is second, ahead of the two title contenders, Talmacsi and Faubel, in that order.

START

Pasini scoots off in the lead ahead of Koyama and Faubel. Tomizawa is a faller at the first corner, while Pasini finishes the opening lap with a lead of 1.144 over an "Aspar" trio made up of Talmacsi, Faubel and Gadea. Having dominated the morning warm-up, France's Mike Di Meglio is already seventh.

LAP 4

Di Meglio is the quickest man on track, fifth at 2.851 seconds off the leader, who is still Pasini. Germany's Sandro Cortese falls on the main straight.

LAP 6

De Rosa, who was sixth having set the fastest race lap up to that point, falls. A bit later, it's Gadea's turn to hit the deck, rejoining in sixteenth place.

LAP 7

Pesek is a faller, having been fifth, but he gets going again.

LAP 8

Pasini and Talmacsi are wheel to wheel and have managed to pull out a lead of 1.804 over another duo made up of Faubel and Di Meglio.

HALF-DISTANCE (10 LAPS)

Pasini and Talmacsi are inseparable (248 thousandths,) Di Meglio is third at 2"105, but Faubel has dropped back. Rabat and Smith hit the dirt.

LAP 13

Pesek is a faller for the second time in this race.

LAP 15

Di Meglio surprises Talmacsi for second place, but falls a bit later. He picks up his bike and restarts in fourth place.

LAP 18

Pol Espargaro is a faller, having been eighth.

FINISH (21 LAPS)

With a lead of over 4 seconds going into the final lap, Pasini makes no mistake of it and takes his fourth win of the season. Even though he was none too keen on racing in the wet, he has come out of it remarkably well, which is not the case for everyone.

CHAMPIONSHIP

Talmacsi has a good day at the office, as he almost doubles his lead over Hector Faubel: it is now nine points. Koyama, who finished way down, is 73 points off the leader and is therefore no longer mathematically capable of taking the title, even if his chances were a bit slim.

While Pol Espargaro (opposite) learns about racing in the rain, Pasini (right) wins for the fourth time this season and Dominique Aegerter (no 77 above) produces his best performance in GP racing.

GP JAPAN | 23rd September 2007 | Motegi | 4.801 m

STARTING GRID

1	75	M. Pasini	Aprilia	1'57.301
2	71	T. Koyama	KTM	1'57.892
3	14	G. Talmacsi	Aprilia	1'58.175
4	55	H. Faubel	Aprilia	1'58.571
5	38	B. Smith	Honda	1'58.752
6	24	S. Corsi	Aprilia	1'58.764
7	6	J. Olivé	Aprilia	1'58.958
8	52	L. Pesek	Derbi	1'58.981
9	35	R. De Rosa	Aprilia	1'59.073
10	11	S. Cortese	Aprilia	1'59.206
11	33	S. Gadea	Aprilia	1'59.259
12	63	M. Di Meglio	Honda	1'59.316
13	17	S. Bradl	Aprilia	1'59.346
14	18	N. Terol	Derbi	1'59.377
15	12	E. Rabat	Honda	1'59.496
16	44	P. Espargaro	Aprilia	1'59.603
17	34	R. Krummenacher	KTM	1'59.615
18	8	L. Zanetti	Aprilia	1'59.639
19	29	A. Iannone	Aprilia	1'59.639
20	22	P. Nieto	Aprilia	1'59.752
21	60	M. Ranseder	Derbi	2'00.087
22	7	A. Masbou	Honda	2'00.364
23	27	S. Bianco	Aprilia	2'00.420
24	20	R. Tamburini	Aprilia	2'00.570
25	51	S. Bonsey	KTM	2'00.836
26	77	D. Aegerter	Aprilia	2'00.935
27	53	S. Grotzkyj	Aprilia	2'01.457
28	95	R. Muresan	Derbi	2'01.587
29	99	D. Webb	Honda	2'01.786
30	58	S. Tomizawa	Honda	2'01.947
31	59	I. Namihira	Honda	2'01.966
32	74	K. Watanabe	Honda	2'01.978
33	13	D. Lombardi	Honda	2'02.056
34	15	F. Sandi	Aprilia	2'02.096
35	57	Y. Yanagisawa	Honda	2'02.127
36	69	N. Mizuno	Yamaha	2'03.964

RACE: 21 laps = 100.821 km

1	Mattia Pasini	46'29.900 (130.096 km/h)
2	Gabor Talmacsi	+ 2''985
3	Hector Faubel	+ 22''405
4	Mike Di Meglio	+ 33''751
5	Joan Olivé	+ 37''351
6	Simone Corsi	+ 39''062
7	Pablo Nieto	+ 44''488
8	Sergio Gadea	+ 48''901
9	Michael Ranseder	+ 50''672
10	Andrea Iannone	+ 56''674
11	Dominique Aegerter	+ 1'03.588
12	Lukas Pesek	+ 1'10.334
13	Daniel Webb	+ 1'14.579
14	Tomoyoshi Koyama	+ 1'19.549
15	Stefan Bradl	+ 1'23.255
16	Roberto Tamburini	+ 1'28.289
17	Nicolas Terol	+ 1'30.061
18	Kazuma Watanabe	+ 1'30.554
19	Randy Krummenacher	+ 1'35.406
20	Nayuto Mizuno	+ 1'42.793
21	Alexis Masbou	+ 2'05.969
22	Shouya Tomizawa	+ 4 laps

Fastest lap

De Rosa, in 2'10.998 (131.937 km/h).
Record: Kallio, in 1'57.886 (146.886 km/h/2006).

Outright fastest lap

Pasini, in 1'56.954 (147.781 km/h).

CHAMPIONSHIP

1	G. Talmacsi	229 (2 wins)
2	H. Faubel	220 (4 wins)
3	T. Koyama	156 (1 win)
4	M. Pasini	144 (4 wins)
5	S. Corsi	142 (1 win)
6	L. Pesek	136 (1 win)
7	S. Gadea	126 (1 win)
8	P. Espargaro	99
9	J. Olivé	98
10	B. Smith	86

A champion at home: Casey Stoner and the unique backdrop that is Phillip Island.

STONER, BUT ALSO DUCATI

THE CROWD WAS HERE TO
CELEBRATE THE NEW WORLD
CHAMPION. A CROWD WHO
ADMIRED FANTASTIC 1-2 DUCATI

THE RACE

PASSION ACCORDING TO LORIS CAPIROSSI

Always smiling, always as effective in a race, Loris Capirossi was an important part of the Stoner-Ducati success story

The pizzeria on a corner of the seafront road at Cowes is still there. Every year, the owner is happy to meet up again with his regulars, including a certain Loris Capirossi. He was here on 16 September 1990, no less than seventeen years ago now, to celebrate taking his first world title! "I remember the party very well, even if, at the time, I didn't understand the importance of the event. I knew I had won, but I did not realise the significance of it."

Seventeen years later, on 14 September, Loris Capirossi once again stood on the Phillip Island podium. He was on the second step, alongside world champion Casey Stoner. Looking down from the balcony, Capirossi smiled as he could guess that the same questions would be coming his way as usual: how does he keep going? How, seventeen years after

his first win at the highest level, does he still win? How did the adolescent of 1990 become a mature man, married, a father to little Ricardo since the start of the year, how does he keep going? "Of course, you need real determination to keep going this long in this game. And to tell you the truth, I am proud of this record, because I honestly think that no one will beat it in the future. Just think, for example it would mean that Rossi would have to keep racing for another six years in GP. My secret? It is simple and that's why I can tell you. It's enjoyment! I always said I would carry on riding as long as I derived pleasure from it and today, when I get on a racing bike, I have as much fun as I did a very long time ago!"

He loves it to such an extent that, next year, the valiant Loris will take on a new challenge with Suzuki, having already done his time in the blue riband category with Yamaha, Honda and, above all, Ducati. Because on a day that is not like any other for him - "every time I come to Phillip Island the emotions come back" - Capirossi not only ensured that the Reds got a one-two finish, he above all offered his soon to be ex-

employers the Constructors' World Championship and the teams' title as well. It is all very significant for a man who, over the past five years, symbolised the human side of the European challenge to Japanese technology, a match which Ducati had finally won, going up against the Goliaths of the Land of the Rising Sun.

Of course, while Loris can be seen as Ducati's ambassador, most of the winning was done not by him, but by a very young rider, in the shape of Casey Stoner. Frustrating for the older man? "Of course, over the past five years, I built up close links to the members of the team, but as jealousy is not part of my character, I am totally delighted with Casey's title."

It is a triumph and it takes nothing away from Stoner's immense achievement to say that Loris Capirossi contributed to it in no small way. "What happened this year? Simple, while I had the impression at the start of it all that the Desmosedici 1000 was made for me, I didn't have the same feeling with the 800." Stoner did not need to be asked twice…

Homage: Chris Vermeulen and Barry Sheene's son on the retro liveried Suzuki. On right, another total success for Casey Stoner.

AT PHILLIP ISLAND IT WAS THE DUCATIS WITH THE OTHERS NOWHERE

RUNNERS AND RIDERS

The paddock, especially Rossi, for whom he was an idol, is in a state of shock after the death a week before this Australian GP, of Norifume Abe, killed in a road traffic accident in Japan. The tyre tangle continues apace after Motegi and now it seems the pendulum is swinging towards keeping two tyre suppliers. In the D'Antin camp, Englishman Chaz Davies rides what was Hofmann's bike up to the Portuguese GP. The works Yamahas carry the Abarth colours; Vermeulen's Suzuki

has a retro design in honour of Barry Sheene.

QUALIFYING

Second consecutive pole for Pedrosa. The Suzukis are suffering, Capirossi confirms his return to a state of grace and Barros, who is in a difficult position, as it is Checa who will replace Toseland in superbikes, sets a good seventh fastest time.

START

Stoner, Hayden and Pedrosa all make better starts than Rossi. The new world champion finishes the first lap 318 thousandths ahead of Hayden and 759 ahead of Pedrosa.

LAP 4

Stoner and Hayden are wheel to wheel. Rossi is third, 1.328 down, ahead of Melandri, who had started from twelfth on the grid and has just set the fastest race lap, with Pedrosa hanging in there.

LAP 9

Stoner ups the pace and Hayden now trails by 5 tenths. Rossi is third at 1.911 seconds off the leader. Pedrosa has pulled out a one second advantage over Melandri.

LAP 10

Hayden seems to have engine problems, so Stoner has escaped. Rossi is second, but 2.873 off the national hero.

HALF-DISTANCE (13 LAPS)

It had seemed likely and now it's happened, as Nicky Hayden's engine has just given up the ghost. Out in front, Stoner leads Rossi by precisely 4.007 seconds, with Pedrosa a further 1.234 behind. There is a nice duel going on for fourth place between Melandri and Capirossi.

LAP 17

Stoner carries on his merry way, while Pedrosa has closed right up to

Rossi, as Capirossi catches out Melandri.

LAP 19

Super Capirossi: 17 years after winning his first world title, at this very circuit, the Italian takes two moves to sweep past first Pedrosa and then Rossi to go second. Barros has dealt with Melandri to take fifth place.

FINISH (27 LAPS)

A lead of more than 7 seconds over his team-mate going into the final lap, the world champion celebrates his title in the best possible way with a win on home soil. The crowd goes wild and the fans invade the track to gather underneath the podium.

CHAMPIONSHIP

Capirossi has done very well, as he is now right there with Hopkins, Vermeulen and Melandri in the battle for fourth place.

GP AUSTRALIA | **14th October 2007** | **Phillip Island** | **4.448 m**

STARTING GRID

1	26	D. Pedrosa	Honda	1'29.201
2	46	V. Rossi	Yamaha	1'29.419
3	27	C. Stoner	Ducati	1'29.816
4	1	N. Hayden	Honda	1'29.932
5	65	L. Capirossi	Ducati	1'30.090
6	14	R. De Puniet	Kawasaki	1'30.110
7	4	A. Barros	Ducati	1'30.325
8	56	S. Nakano	Honda	1'30.612
9	50	S. Guintoli	Yamaha	1'30.621
10	13	A. West	Kawasaki	1'30.649
11	5	C. Edwards	Yamaha	1'30.676
12	33	M. Melandri	Honda	1'31.078
13	7	C. Checa	Honda	1'31.203
14	21	J. Hopkins	Suzuki	1'31.386
15	6	M. Tamada	Yamaha	1'31.595
16	71	C. Vermeulen	Suzuki	1'31.810
17	57	C. Davies	Ducati	1'32.043
18	24	T. Elias	Honda	1'32.442
19	80	Ku. Roberts	KR212V	1'32.948

RACE: 27 laps = 120.096 km

1	Casey Stoner	41'12.244 (174.879 km/h)
2	Loris Capirossi	+ 6''763
3	Valentino Rossi	+ 10''038
4	Daniel Pedrosa	+ 11''663
5	Alex Barros	+ 19''475
6	Randy De Puniet	+ 27''313
7	John Hopkins	+ 29''243
8	Chris Vermeulen	+ 34''833
9	Colin Edwards	+ 35''073
10	Marco Melandri	+ 36''971
11	Carlos Checa	+ 37''721
12	Anthony West	+ 38''426
13	Shinya Nakano	+ 47''430
14	Sylvain Guintoli	+ 54''324
15	Toni Elias	+ 1'10.471
16	Makoto Tamada	+ 1'12.904
17	Kurtis Roberts	+ 1'13.020

Fastest lap

Rossi, in 1'30.801 (176.350 km/h).
Record: Melandri, in 1'30.332 (177.266 km/h/2005).

Outright fastest lap

Hayden, in 1'29.020 (179.878 km/h/2006).

CHAMPIONSHIP

1	C. Stoner	322 (9 wins)
2	V. Rossi	230 (4 wins)
3	D. Pedrosa	201 (1 win)
4	J. Hopkins	165
5	C. Vermeulen	160 (1 win)
6	M. Melandri	154
7	L. Capirossi	150 (1 win)
8	C. Edwards	115
9	N. Hayden	112
10	A. Barros	102

JORGE LORENZO ALONE IN A CLASS OF HIS OWN

RUNNERS AND RIDERS

One invited rider, China's Chow, and a brave comeback for Japan's Sekiguchi, who miraculously survived the Brno warm-up. Something new in the Sicilia team, as the Englishman, Linfoot is replaced by Sandi, who had been racing until now in the 125 class.

QUALIFYING

Jorge Lorenzo is totally dominant, given that every time he gets on his bike, he takes at least 8 tenths out of his closest pursuer. That's the situation on Friday and Saturday, in both cases ahead of Barbera, whose qualifying ends with a high speed dismount in the first braking area. Victim of another frightening fall is Locatelli: the Italian who had been seriously injured at Jerez at the start of the season, gets away with bruises. Luthi has a high speed crash in the warm-up.

START

A super start for Lorenzo, ahead of Dovizioso, Bautista, De Angelis and Luthi. Crossing the line for the first time, the world champion heads his only challenger, Dovizioso, by 7 tenths! Barbera fails to finish the first lap.

LAP 2

Kallio falls.

LAP 3

Lorenzo now has a lead of 2.672 seconds over the man heading the chasing group, Bautista. Keeping him company are Dovizioso, Simoncelli, De Angelis, Shuhei Aoyama and Luthi.

Thomas Luthi plays with the seagulls: the Swiss rider missed out on a first podium because of engine problems. On right, Lorenzo the pirate has won again. Above, Dovizioso has not yet abdicated the title. Although…

LAP 6

Simoncelli gets it wrong and drops two places.

LAP 8

Shuhei Aoyama goes off on the grass. His brother Hiroshi and Simon have joined the chasing group, which already trails Lorenzo by 9 seconds.

HALF-DISTANCE (12 LAPS)

Lorenzo is majestic, leading Bautista by 12.645 seconds. Next up are Dovizioso and Luthi, who will go ahead a bit further on. Further back, Simon and H. Aoyama are not far behind.

LAP 15

Behind Lorenzo, Bautista and Luthi are fighting for second spot. Dovizioso is fourth, eight seconds off the Swiss rider.

LAP 18

Dovizioso and H. Aoyama have caught up, bringing Simon with them.

LAP 19

Bautista seems to have handling problems. Dovizioso has passed Thomas Luthi.

LAP 21

Still Lorenzo of course. Luthi is now second ahead of Bautista and Dovizioso.

FINISH (25 LAPS)

Five of them are scrapping over the last two podium places, separated by 9 tenths. In the end it goes to Bautista and Dovizioso. Luthi has been heroic, as his bike had carburation problems all race long when going down the straight. He finishes fifth, having been "forgotten" by Aoyama's KTM in the last few metres.

CHAMPIONSHIP

A lead of 45 points, with 50 still up for grabs: Lorenzo is not yet a two times world champion, but …

GP AUSTRALIA | 14th October 2007 | Phillip Island | 4.448 m

STARTING GRID

1	1	J. Lorenzo	Aprilia	1'32.884
2	80	H. Barberá	Aprilia	1'33.770
3	19	A. Bautistá	Aprilia	1'33.820
4	3	A. De Angelis	Aprilia	1'33.824
5	58	M. Simoncelli	Gilera	1'33.854
6	4	H. Aoyama	KTM	1'33.932
7	34	A. Dovizioso	Honda	1'34.153
8	12	T. Lüthi	Aprilia	1'34.185
9	60	J. Simón	Honda	1'34.299
10	73	S. Aoyama	Honda	1'34.412
11	36	M. Kallio	KTM	1'34.527
12	55	Y. Takahashi	Honda	1'34.990
13	15	R. Locatelli	Gilera	1'35.372
14	41	A. Espargaro	Aprilia	1'35.788
15	16	J. Cluzel	Aprilia	1'35.860
16	32	F. Lai	Aprilia	1'35.903
17	28	D. Heidolf	Aprilia	1'36.238
18	10	I. Toth	Aprilia	1'36.463
19	25	A. Baldolini	Aprilia	1'36.512
20	7	E. Vazquez	Aprilia	1'36.842
21	17	K. Abraham	Aprilia	1'37.076
22	11	T. Sekiguchi	Aprilia	1'37.106
23	8	R. Wilairot	Honda	1'37.376
24	50	E. Laverty	Honda	1'37.476
25	21	F. Sandi	Aprilia	1'37.623
26	89	H. Chow	Aprilia	1'38.981

RACE: 25 laps = 111.200 km

1	Jorge Lorenzo	39'25.727 (169.216 km/h)
2	Alvaro Bautistá	+ 19''634
3	Andrea Dovizioso	+ 19''724
4	Hiroshi Aoyama	+ 19''797
5	Thomas Lüthi	+ 20''066
6	Julian Simón	+ 21''045
7	Marco Simoncelli	+ 32''960
8	Shuhei Aoyama	+ 33''043
9	Alex De Angelis	+ 33''051
10	Yuki Takahashi	+ 44''814
11	Roberto Locatelli	+ 48''733
12	Jules Cluzel	+ 54''010
13	Karel Abraham	+ 1'03.218
14	Aleix Espargaro	+ 1'09.368
15	Dirk Heidolf	+ 1'17.807
16	Eugene Laverty	+ 1'21.239
17	Fabrizio Lai	+ 1'31.245
18	Taru Sekiguchi	+ 1'33.575
19	Ratthapark Wilairot	+ 1'33.916
20	Federico Sandi	+ 1 lap

Fastest lap

Lorenzo, in 1'33.761 (170.783 km/h).
Record: Porto, in 1'33''381 (171.478 km/h/2004).

Outright fastest lap

Porto, in 1'32.099 (173.865 km/h/2004).

CHAMPIONSHIP

1	J. Lorenzo	287 (9 wins)
2	A. Dovizioso	242 (2 wins)
3	A. De Angelis	215
4	A. Bautistá	181 (2 wins)
5	H. Barberá	146
6	H. Aoyama	129 (1 win)
7	M. Kallio	119 (1 win)
8	T. Lüthi	115
9	J. Simón	103
10	S. Aoyama	87

PESEK THE WINNER, FAUBEL IS WITHIN A POINT OF TALMACSI

RUNNERS AND RIDERS

Stefano Bianco is replaced by the Australian Glenn Scott. In the Skilled camp, Ferruccio Lamborghini is going to finish the season instead of Sandi, who has now gone to the 250 class. Three riders have wild cards, including the Leigh-Smith brothers, Blake and Jackson: for Blake, the elder, this is not his first GP and he has actually taken part this year in several rounds of the German championship. Only Scott will make it through qualifying.

QUALIFYING

Alright then, we won't trot out that old "but who do you think took pole?" For the ninth time this year, it's Mattia Pasini who picks up the watch that comes as a prize for being quickest. The surprise comes in the form of the second placed rider, De Rosa, beaten by just 26 thousandths. He pips Pesek, who had a technical problem on his number one bike, by 2 thousandths.

START

Although qualified second, De Rosa starts from the pits. It's Koyama who takes off in the lead ahead of Pasini and Faubel. The Japanese rider finishes the first lap with a lead of 82 thousandths over Pasini and 90 over Pesek.

LAP 2

Pasini has taken control of the situation, ahead of Pesek and Faubel, who passes everyone at the end of the main straight.

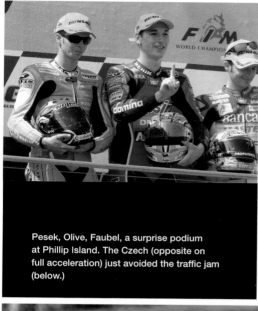

Pesek, Olive, Faubel, a surprise podium at Phillip Island. The Czech (opposite on full acceleration) just avoided the traffic jam (below.)

LAP 5

Eleven of them are wheel to wheel with just 1.469 seconds between the leader, Pasini and eleventh placed Cortese. Behind them, the chasing group led by Switzerland's Krummenacher trails by 3 seconds.

LAP 6

De Rosa retires. Talmacsi has taken the lead.

LAP 11

The Austrian Ranseder is a faller, having been ninth. Pasini leads once again.

HALF-DISTANCE (12 LAPS)

As is nearly always the case at Phillip Island, no one ever manages to make a real break. Therefore there are nine of them in 1.463 seconds: Pesek, Faubel, Rabat, Olive, Koyama, Gadea, Pasini, Talmacsi and Cortese, with Corsi 7 seconds adrift of the pack.

LAP 15

We will never know if Pesek was given advice by the man who will be his 250 team-mate next year - in 2005, Luthi won out on his own at Phillip Island - but here we have the Czech with a 6 tenths lead over his closest pursuer, who is now Faubel.

LAP 17

Tried but failed, as Faubel is now out in front and it is his turn to try, in vain, to get away.

FINISH (23 LAPS)

Nine riders in 1.008 going into the final lap. Pesek takes charge and will hold his own to the flag, which he takes ahead of Olive and Faubel. Talmacsi, the championship leader is "only" eighth.

CHAMPIONSHIP

Faubel has closed to within a point of Talmacsi: it's going to be touch and go between the two team-mates in Malaysia and then Valencia.

GP AUSTRALIA | 14th October 2007 | Phillip Island | 4.448 m

STARTING GRID

1	75	M. Pasini	Aprilia	1'38.078
2	35	R. De Rosa	Aprilia	1'38.104
3	52	L. Pesek	Derbi	1'38.106
4	71	T. Koyama	KTM	1'38.382
5	24	S. Corsi	Aprilia	1'38.528
6	55	H. Faubel	Aprilia	1'38.587
7	33	S. Gadea	Aprilia	1'38.974
8	6	J. Olivé	Aprilia	1'38.977
9	14	G. Talmacsi	Aprilia	1'39.134
10	11	S. Cortese	Aprilia	1'39.189
11	12	E. Rabat	Honda	1'39.354
12	63	M. Di Meglio	Honda	1'39.477
13	38	B. Smith	Honda	1'39.697
14	8	L. Zanetti	Aprilia	1'39.708
15	60	M. Ranseder	Derbi	1'39.750
16	22	P. Nieto	Aprilia	1'39.775
17	44	P. Espargaro	Aprilia	1'39.797
18	51	S. Bonsey	KTM	1'39.945
19	18	N. Terol	Derbi	1'39.983
20	34	R. Krummenacher	KTM	1'40.305
21	7	A. Masbou	Honda	1'40.377
22	29	A. Iannone	Aprilia	1'40.424
23	37	J. Litjens	Honda	1'40.544
24	53	S. Grotzkyj	Aprilia	1'40.659
25	99	D. Webb	Honda	1'41.197
26	17	S. Bradl	Aprilia	1'41.240
27	13	D. Lombardi	Honda	1'41.476
28	77	D. Aegerter	Aprilia	1'41.949
29	20	R. Tamburini	Aprilia	1'42.330
30	79	F. Lamborghini	Aprilia	1'42.612
31	68	G. Scott	Aprilia	1'43.415

Not qualified:

	70	B. Leigh-Smith	Honda	1'44.971
	96	R. Moller	Honda	1'45.536
	73	J. Leigh-Smith	Honda	1'48.459
	95	R. Muresan	Derbi	2'13.903

RACE: 23 laps = 102.304 km

1	Lukas Pesek	38'03.020 (161.318 km/h)
2	Joan Olivé	+ 0''090
3	Hector Faubel	+ 0''190
4	Simone Corsi	+ 0''405
5	Esteve Rabat	+ 0''915
6	Tomoyoshi Koyama	+ 1''315
7	Mattia Pasini	+ 1''316
8	Gabor Talmacsi	+ 1''371
9	Sergio Gadea	+ 1''457
10	Sandro Cortese	+ 14''652
11	Pol Espargaro	+ 21''745
12	Randy Krummenacher	+ 22''687
13	Nicolas Terol	+ 26''491
14	Mike Di Meglio	+ 26''563
15	Steve Bonsey	+ 37''823
16	Bradley Smith	+ 37''981
17	Joey Litjens	+ 40''406
18	Lorenzo Zanetti	+ 40''453
19	Dominique Aegerter	+ 44''271
20	Andrea Iannone	+ 44''831
21	Simone Grotzkyj	+ 51''482

22	Michael Ranseder	+ 1'01.153
23	Roberto Tamburini	+ 1'03.614
24	Dino Lombardi	+ 1'18.524
25	Ferruccio Lamborghini	+ 1'37.558
26	Glenn Scott	+ 1 lap

Fastest lap
Talmacsi, in 1'38.061 (163.294 km/h).
Record: Bautistá, in 1'36.927 (165.204 km/h/2006).

Outright fastest lap
Kallio, in 1'36.625 (165.721 km/h/2006).

CHAMPIONSHIP

1	G. Talmacsi	237 (2 wins)
2	H. Faubel	236 (4 wins)
3	T. Koyama	166 (1 win)
4	L. Pesek	161 (2 wins)
5	S. Corsi	155 (1 win)
6	M. Pasini	153 (4 wins)
7	S. Gadea	133 (1 win)
8	J. Olivé	118
9	P. Espargaro	104
10	B. Smith	86

A familiar image this year: Casey Stoner at speed, alone on track.

17

21st October 2007

MALAYSIA SEPANG

ROSSI, WHERE IS HE,
THE HERO WITHOUT REPROACH?

WHILE CASEY STONER ONCE AGAIN
WINS AS HE PLEASES, VALENTINO
CELEBRATES HIS FIFTH PLACE AS
THOUGH IT WAS A VICTORY

THE RACE

MIRROR, MIRROR, WHO IS THE BEST OF ALL...

"Mirror mirror on the wall, who is the fairest of them all..." the once cheeky Rossi, the triumphant Rossi has given way to a lad caught up in blackmail, who gets stuck behind others (here it is West) that he used to dish out lessons to in the past.

For years now, every morning, he could ask his mirror who was the best; the best at everything, riding, racecraft, dealing with the press, promoting his image. Yes, every morning, the mirror would have said: "But it's you of course Valentino, you know very well that you don't need me to confirm it for you."

Valentino Rossi used to win races - he does so less often now - and lots of money - still no problems in that area at least. Or maybe... He was the crowd's favourite and it was easy to fall for his charms, seeing his touches of genius when it came to handling the media with his quick wit. On top of that, Valentino was ready to take on more complex challenges, as when he left the champion maker that was the works HRC team to join Yamaha that had not won any titles for ten years! Remember that one hundred percent Rossi panache, saying goodbye to Honda but also taking his technical team, the winning force, with him? It

was huge and of course, he was going to win.

"Mirror, dear mirror, where did it all go?" Of course there is still the unrivalled track record, the fact that his media persona has lifted motorcycle grands prix out of their specialist media doldrums. There is still all that left, as well as huge sums of money that are attracting the attention of the Italian tax authorities, who knows why.

But, as for the rest, where is the Rossi who could succeed in the most difficult challenges, now that he seems to have gone from being for so long the master to now being the moaner: "If Bridgestone don't give me tyres next year, ciao, I'm off!" Where is the rider who always hated losing and who, this Sunday at the end of October in Sepang, hugs every member of his crew when he gets back to the pits, even though he only finished fifth?

Where is the unbeatable Rossi? Because,

now we see he has his weak points. It seems he was treating everyone as fools by claiming he was living in London and hiding away his millions. This is the Rossi who today, having failed to find a way to beat the Casey Stoner - Ducati Desmosedici - Bridgestone trio, has a rant at Michelin his tyre supplier.

This is not the Rossi of old. Of course, it is well known that when one wants to shoot one's horse one claims it has colic. So, it is up to him to get what he wants for 2008 and prove that this year was a glitch. If he does not manage it, then all that will be left will be the image of someone who resembles the man he complained about so much over the past few years, Massimiliano "Max" Biaggi, the man who railed against everyone as he refused to admit that a new generation had arrived. Strange don't you think that the two most popular riders of the past fifteen years seem to be mimicking one another?

AND THAT'S TEN FOR STONER! DE PUNIET A BRILLIANT FOURTH

RUNNERS AND RIDERS

Suzuki test rider, Nobuatsu Aoki has a wild card, riding the company's 2008 prototype and he is the only one of the current bunch of riders to have already run on the new Sepang surface (on a superbike.) All the talk is still about tyres and the decision concerning 2008, which should have been made on the Saturday of this GP, has been put back a week. Once again, the name of Max Biaggi is doing the rounds and this time rumour has it that Fausto Gresini is in touch with the man who has just lost his world superbike ride. Now, everything is being done to persuade the money men.

QUALIFYING

Another pole for Pedrosa, but those watching carefully could see that the Stoner-Bridgestone combo is working the most effectively. Melandri completes the front row, with the two Kawasakis on the second row, with Rossi "only" ninth.

START

Stoner, Pedrosa and De Puniet are the immediate lead trio, ahead of Melandri and Elias. The world champion completes the opening lap with 91 thousandths over Pedrosa and 601 ahead of De Puniet. Rossi is tenth.

LAP 2

West is informed he jumped the start whereas in fact, he parked on the wrong grid slot, unused to the MotoGP grid having three per line, unlike the four for the 125 and 250 classes.

LAP 4

Stoner, Pedrosa, De Puniet and Melandri: the top four are covered by 1.150 seconds.

LAP 5

West comes in for his "drive through," Melandri has passed De Puniet.

LAP 8

Stoner ups the pace, Pedrosa is now 460 thousandths behind. Rossi is fifth.

LAP 9

Melandri gets by Pedrosa and is 8 tenths behind Stoner.

HALF-DISTANCE (10 LAPS)

Stoner now has 1.401 in hand over Melandri, who has Pedrosa glued to his back wheel. De Puniet is a second off in fourth, with Rossi fifth, 2.997 behind the Frenchman.

LAP 12

Hayden gets it wrong braking for the final turn and drops down to tenth.

LAP 15

Yet another fastest lap for Stoner, beating the outright lap record on his 800! He now leads by 1.899.

FINISH (21 LAPS)

How can one put this? It was a touch dull with hardly any change of position among the top three. In the battle for fourth, De Puniet controlled Rossi's climb up the order - the Michelins weren't bad towards the end of the race! The Frenchman runs out of fuel on the slowing down lap.

CHAMPIONSHIP

Stoner is no longer the topic of the day. Instead, there is the fact that with 241 points, Rossi is now 24 ahead of Pedrosa for the runner-up slot. It's going to be a fun time in Valencia in the battle for fourth place between Melandri, Hopkins and Vermeulen.

A perfect start from Casey Stoner, who would stay out in front of the opposition until the flag. The opposition included a very good showing from Randy De Puniet (opposite.)

GP MALAYSIA | 21st October 2007 | Sepang | 5.548 m

STARTING GRID

1	26	D. Pedrosa	Honda	2'01.877
2	27	C. Stoner	Ducati	2'01.918
3	33	M. Melandri	Honda	2'01.944
4	14	R. De Puniet	Kawasaki	2'02.107
5	13	A. West	Kawasaki	2'02.202
6	1	N. Hayden	Honda	2'02.225
7	71	C. Vermeulen	Suzuki	2'02.301
8	24	T. Elias	Honda	2'02.432
9	46	V. Rossi	Yamaha	2'02.466
10	21	J. Hopkins	Suzuki	2'02.697
11	65	L. Capirossi	Ducati	2'02.708
12	4	A. Barros	Ducati	2'03.022
13	5	C. Edwards	Yamaha	2'03.040
14	56	S. Nakano	Honda	2'03.233
15	50	S. Guintoli	Yamaha	2'03.408
16	7	C. Checa	Honda	2'03.525
17	57	C. Davies	Ducati	2'04.197
18	6	M. Tamada	Yamaha	2'04.314
19	9	N. Aoki	Suzuki	2'04.604
20	80	Ku. Roberts	KR212V	2'05.404

RACE: 21 laps = 116.508 km

1	Casey Stoner	43'04.405 (162.292 km/h)
2	Marco Melandri	+ 1''701
3	Daniel Pedrosa	+ 2''326
4	Randy De Puniet	+ 3''765
5	Valentino Rossi	+ 4''773
6	Toni Elias	+ 17''667
7	Chris Vermeulen	+ 20''950
8	John Hopkins	+ 22''198
9	Nicky Hayden	+ 22''450
10	Colin Edwards	+ 29''746
11	Loris Capirossi	+ 34''923
12	Alex Barros	+ 35''667
13	Nobuatsu Aoki	+ 44''113
14	Carlos Checa	+ 44''486
15	Anthony West	+ 49''658
16	Shinya Nakano	+ 51''726
17	Chaz Davies	+ 58''905
18	Makoto Tamada	+ 59''596
19	Sylvain Guintoli	+ 1'23.119
20	Kurtis Roberts	+ 1'50.960

Fastest lap
Stoner, in 2'02.108 (163.566 km/h). New record.
Ancien: Capirossi, in 2'02.127 (163.541 km/h/2006)

Outright fastest lap
Rossi, in 2'00.605 (165.605 km/h/2006).

CHAMPIONSHIP

1	C. Stoner	347 (10 wins)
2	V. Rossi	241 (4 wins)
3	D. Pedrosa	217 (1 win)
4	M. Melandri	174
5	J. Hopkins	173
6	C. Vermeulen	169 (1 win)
7	L. Capirossi	155 (1 win)
8	C. Edwards	121
9	N. Hayden	119
10	A. Barros	106

LORENZO IS CHAMPION SAYS THE MATHS

RUNNERS AND RIDERS

An Indonesian rider is on the list of starters, Doni Tata Pradita, whom we have already seen in the past in the 125 class. He is riding a Yamaha, entered by his country's importer. No change otherwise among the contracted riders.

QUALIFYING

Lorenzo marks his turf right from the first day, but there is a surprise in store for the Aprilia troops on Saturday, when the two KTM riders, Hiroshi Aoyama and Mika Kallio sneak up to take the two best slots. The top six - H. Aoyama, Kallio, Lorenzo, Dovizioso, Bautista and Luthi - are covered by a mere 510 thousandths.

START

Dovizioso gets the best start ahead of Kallio, Lorenzo, Barbera and Luthi. The Italian completes Lap 1 with a lead of 875 thousandths over the Finn, who is in front of Lorenzo.

LAP 4

Lorenzo has found a way through Kallio's armour and sets the fastest race lap as he moves to within 1.930 of the leader.

LAP 5

Bautista and Luthi manage to shake themselves loose from the two KTMs (fastest lap for the Swiss who now finds himself third.)

LAP 7

Bautista retires (engine.) The Lorenzo-Luthi duo has closed to 1.685 off Dovizioso.

HALF-DISTANCE (10 LAPS)

Dovizioso is still holding them off, but his lead over Lorenzo is down to only 349 thousandths. Luthi is third, 7 tenths behind the world champion. Kallio is fourth, heading the chasing pack that is 2.276 behind the Swiss rider.

LAP 11

Lorenzo takes the lead. Alex de Angelis is a faller.

LAP 13

Dovizioso hangs onto Lorenzo's back wheel. Kallio and Aoyama have closed to 1.1 off Luthi for third place.

LAP 14

Now it is the two KTMs that are quickest on track. Lorenzo and Dovizioso narrowly avoid being reduced to pedestrians while Luthi is only fifth now.

LAP 16

Dovizioso retakes the lead, but Hiroshi Aoyama is less than a second behind. Luthi is in trouble, having chosen too soft tyres and is down to sixth.

LAP 18

The two KTMs have caught the Dovizioso-Lorenzo battle and Barbera is not far off either.

LAP 19

Kallio tries a suicidal move at the last hairpin and knocks Dovizioso over.

FINISH (20 LAPS)

H. Aoyama has made the most of the previous lap's coming together and sets the fastest race lap on the final lap. Barbera is second ahead of Lorenzo, world champion for the second time.

CHAMPIONSHIP

Lorenzo can well transform himself into a boxer as he is world champion for the second consecutive year. Hats off to Dovizioso who fought right to the bitter end, in what was an unequal contest against Aprilia.

The boxer Jorge Lorenzo picked up the last points he needed at the end of a race with Dovizioso, H. Aoyama, Kallio and Barbera that was rather "hot." The race was won (on right) by the Japanese KTM rider.

GP MALAYSIA | 21st October 2007 | Sepang | 5.548 m

STARTING GRID

1	4	H. Aoyama	KTM	2'07.429
2	36	M. Kallio	KTM	2'07.461
3	1	J. Lorenzo	Aprilia	2'07.621
4	34	A. Dovizioso	Honda	2'07.675
5	19	A. Bautistá	Aprilia	2'07.785
6	12	T. Lüthi	Aprilia	2'07.939
7	80	H. Barberá	Aprilia	2'08.148
8	60	J. Simón	Honda	2'08.496
9	3	A. De Angelis	Aprilia	2'08.745
10	15	R. Locatelli	Gilera	2'08.953
11	58	M. Simoncelli	Gilera	2'09.557
12	55	Y. Takahashi	Honda	2'09.570
13	17	K. Abraham	Aprilia	2'10.501
14	41	A. Espargaro	Aprilia	2'10.549
15	8	R. Wilairot	Honda	2'10.587
16	73	S. Aoyama	Honda	2'10.664
17	25	A. Baldolini	Aprilia	2'10.685
18	16	J. Cluzel	Aprilia	2'10.698
19	28	D. Heidolf	Aprilia	2'10.854
20	50	E. Laverty	Honda	2'10.926
21	32	F. Lai	Aprilia	2'11.110
22	7	E. Vazquez	Aprilia	2'11.176
23	21	F. Sandi	Aprilia	2'11.333
24	10	I. Toth	Aprilia	2'11.596
25	11	T. Sekiguchi	Aprilia	2'12.051
26	35	D. Pradita	Yamaha	2'14.439

RACE: 20 laps = 110.960 km

1	Hiroshi Aoyama	43'09.316 (154.270 km/h)
2	Hector Barberá	+ 2''251
3	Jorge Lorenzo	+ 2''957
4	Mika Kallio	+ 2''965
5	Thomas Lüthi	+ 7''305
6	Julian Simón	+ 8''747
7	Roberto Locatelli	+ 16''105
8	Marco Simoncelli	+ 26''101
9	Yuki Takahashi	+ 28''032
10	Aleix Espargaro	+ 34''754
11	Andrea Dovizioso	+ 35''888
12	Karel Abraham	+ 42''514
13	Shuhei Aoyama	+ 48''020
14	Alex Baldolini	+ 48''058
15	Dirk Heidolf	+ 49''190
16	Ratthapark Wilairot	+ 49''273
17	Eugene Laverty	+ 53''468
18	Taru Sekiguchi	+ 1'02.665
19	Jules Cluzel	+ 1'15.625
20	Fabrizio Lai	+ 1'17.024
21	Imre Toth	+ 1'32.646

Fastest lap

H. Aoyama, in 2'08.266 (155.713 km/h).
Record: Pedrosa, in 2'08.015 (156.019 km/h/2004).

Outright fastest lap

Porto, in 2'06.940 (157.340 km/h/2004).

CHAMPIONSHIP

1	J. Lorenzo	303 (9 wins)
2	A. Dovizioso	247 (2 wins)
3	A. De Angelis	215
4	A. Bautistá	181 (2 wins)
5	H. Barberá	166
6	H. Aoyama	154 (2 wins)
7	M. Kallio	132 (1 win)
8	T. Lüthi	126
9	J. Simón	113
10	M. Simoncelli	95

A full grid and an ongoing fight...but this time it was just for second place. Because Gabor Talmacsi, a muscular man (on right) managed to run a solitary race out in front.

BY SCORING 9 POINTS MORE THAN FAUBEL, TALMACSI MAKES THE BREAK

RUNNERS AND RIDERS

The French Federation team had obtained a wild card for Louis Rossi, but the young hopeful was seriously injured the previous Sunday in the Italian championship final (a broken tibia and fibula) and so it is Cyril Carrillo, who this year competed in the Red Bull "Rookie Cup" who made his GP debut. Bianco is back.

QUALIFYING

It rains at the end of Friday morning and the first qualifying session is held on a track that improves with every passing lap. Nieto tries a gamble, fitting mixed tyres with a few minutes to go and takes provisional pole by 2.7 seconds from his closest pursuer, the inevitable Pasini! Faubel, who had technical problems is not qualified by the end of Friday, but he takes pole on Saturday, ahead of Talmacsi and two neophytes at this performance level, Cortese and Pol Espargaro.

START

Espargaro is the promptest out of the blocks, but he gets it wrong in the first braking area. Pasini makes the most of it to take the lead ahead of Corsi and Talmacsi. Ranseder fails to finish the first lap, which Talmacsi completes with a lead of 391 thousandths over Faubel.

LAP 4

Talmacsi steps up the pace and he now has 1.306 in hand over Pasini

and Faubel, who are being caught by Corsi.

LAP 6

Faubel is down to fourth. Pasini in second place is 2.542 off Talmacsi.

LAP 8

Talmacsi has doubled his lead. Behind him, six of them are fighting over the runner up slot: Corsi, Faubel, Pasini, Olive, Cortese and Koyama.

HALF-DISTANCS (10 LAPS)

Talmacsi still leads with 6.720 seconds in hand over a frantic pack (Gadea has now joined the group) scrapping over second place. At this point, Olive is winning this battle, from Pasini and Corsi.

LAP 14

No change for Talmacsi. In the pack, Espargaro has closed on Cortese and will soon pass him.

LAP 16

Faubel is keen to avoid the often uncontrolled fight that is the final lap and so he takes second place. At the same moment, Pol Espargaro falls.

LAP 18

Surprise, surprise: it's Koyama who takes the lead of the pursuing group.

FINISH (19 LAPS)

Talmacsi goes into the final lap with 8.136 in hand over Koyama, who leads the pair of Olive-Faubel by 1.372. Cortese does not finish as he falls. Faubel is third.

CHAMPIONSHIP

There are two points separating Talmacsi and Faubel going into the final race. Which means that if the Spaniard wins in Valencia, the Hungarian has to finish at least third, in which case he would take the title by one little point!

GP MALAYSIA | 21st October 2007 | Sepang | 5.548 m

STARTING GRID

1	55	H. Faubel	Aprilia	2'13.327
2	14	G. Talmacsi	Aprilia	2'13.443
3	11	S. Cortese	Aprilia	2'14.141
4	44	P. Espargaro	Aprilia	2'14.166
5	24	S. Corsi	Aprilia	2'14.347
6	71	T. Koyama	KTM	2'14.440
7	52	L. Pesek	Derbi	2'14.630
8	6	J. Olivé	Aprilia	2'14.723
9	22	P. Nieto	Aprilia	2'14.738
10	75	M. Pasini	Aprilia	2'14.798
11	33	S. Gadea	Aprilia	2'14.967
12	7	A. Masbou	Honda	2'15.061
13	18	N. Terol	Derbi	2'15.385
14	35	R. De Rosa	Aprilia	2'15.476
15	38	B. Smith	Honda	2'15.635
16	60	M. Ranseder	Derbi	2'15.676
17	12	E. Rabat	Honda	2'15.835
18	63	M. Di Meglio	Honda	2'15.895
19	17	S. Bradl	Aprilia	2'16.150
20	20	R. Tamburini	Aprilia	2'16.483
21	29	A. Iannone	Aprilia	2'16.546
22	77	D. Aegerter	Aprilia	2'16.778
23	34	R. Krummenacher	KTM	2'16.822
24	27	S. Bianco	Aprilia	2'16.835
25	99	D. Webb	Honda	2'16.866
26	8	L. Zanetti	Aprilia	2'17.267
27	37	J. Litjens	Honda	2'17.616
28	51	S. Bonsey	KTM	2'17.772
29	36	C. Carrillo	Honda	2'18.030
30	53	S. Grotzkyj	Aprilia	2'18.420
31	95	R. Muresan	Derbi	2'19.004
32	13	D. Lombardi	Honda	2'19.189
33	79	F. Lamborghini	Aprilia	2'19.972

RACE: 19 laps = 105.412 km

1	Gabor Talmacsi	42'50.831 (147.611 km/h)	
2	Tomoyoshi Koyama	à 6''753	
3	Hector Faubel	+ 7''793	
4	Joan Olivé	+ 8''180	
5	Sergio Gadea	+ 8''947	
6	Lukas Pesek	+ 9''935	
7	Simone Corsi	+ 10''132	
8	Mattia Pasini	+ 10''335	
9	Bradley Smith	+ 23''426	
10	Alexis Masbou	+ 24''808	
11	Nicolas Terol	+ 24''909	
12	Pablo Nieto	+ 26''194	
13	Stefan Bradl	+ 29''490	
14	Mike Di Meglio	+ 29''775	
15	Esteve Rabat	+ 31''011	
16	Stefano Bianco	+ 35''455	
17	Randy Krummenacher	+ 35''829	
18	Andrea Iannone	+ 54''666	
19	Lorenzo Zanetti	+ 56''956	
20	Simone Grotzkyj	+ 57''356	
21	Roberto Tamburini	+ 1'05.426	
22	Daniel Webb	+ 1'08.541	
23	Robert Muresan	+ 1'08.549	
24	Joey Litjens	+ 1'19.477	
25	Cyrill Carillo	+ 1'22.382	
26	Steve Bonsey	+ 1'30.374	
27	Ferruccio Lamborghini	+ 1'33.736	
28	Raffaele De Rosa	+ 1'41.013	

Fastest lap

Talmacsi, in 2'13.987 (149.065 km/h).
Record: Bautistá, in 2'13.118 (150.038 km/h/2006).

Outright fastest lap

Dovizioso, in 2'12.684 (150.529 km/h/2004).

CHAMPIONSHIP

1	G. Talmacsi	262 (3 wins)
2	H. Faubel	252 (4 wins)
3	T. Koyama	186 (1 win)
4	L. Pesek	171 (2 wins)
5	S. Corsi	164 (1 win)
6	M. Pasini	161 (4 wins)
7	S. Gadea	144 (1 win)
8	J. Olivé	131
9	P. Espargaro	104
10	B. Smith	93

Dani Pedrosa on a wild charge in front of his home crowd: even world champion Casey Stoner knew better than to interfere.

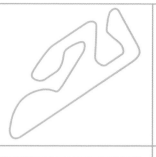

18

HONDA AND MICHELIN:
A WARNING

DOMINATED ALL SEASON LONG BY THE
DUCATI-BRIDGESTONE PAIRING, DANIEL
PEDROSA MARKED EVERYONE'S CARD
IN READINESS FOR 2008

THE RACE

ROSSI, AN INFERNAL YEAR - THE END

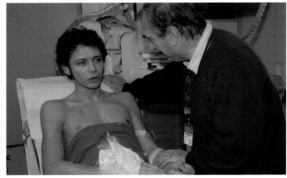

Poor Valentino Rossi: having suffered a painful fall on Saturday at the start of qualifying, he stopped in the race, let down by his Yamaha M1. For the first time since the start of his GP career, he failed to finish the championship in the top two.

Saturday, 3 November 2007, Cheste, 13h59. The image keeps going round on a loop. We are with Valentino Rossi on his bike, although a bike is not the right word to describe what looks more like a wild horse gone mad, bucking and rearing, just waiting for the rider to let go of the reins. But the horse is angry as the rider won't give up. Then after a second or two comes the crash, the sparks and a shot showing just the road and then the camera stops working. The Yamaha M1 is just a twisted wreck, broken and crushed.

The rider, where is the rider? There he is, on all fours at the edge of the track. He gets up in a flash and dashes away from the scene of the crash. He holds his right hand with his left and he is grimacing. Now, he leans on a pile of tyres and tries to get his bearings. A few seconds later and the rescue crews get their act together. Seconds become minutes and the ambulance arrives. Valentino Rossi takes off his helmet to reveal a face

drained of colour. He is in pain. Cheste, on Saturday 3 November 2007, 13h59: a strange way to end this terrible year. Is it the last drama of the year? Rossi does not know what awaits him still…

Outside the circuit medical centre, a crowd has gathered. The ambulance stops, as Dr. Claudio Costa waves his arms about. Valentino Rossi gets out, revealing an ice pack on his right hand. He walks through a pack of photographers, onlookers and fans dressed in yellow, who all want to know what's going on. Now he climbs the steps leading into the mobile clinic as the motor drives fire off like machine guns. No one is taking a blind bit of notice about what is happening on track. After a short while, the verdict is given: he has a fracture in the metacarpuses. No complications are expected as a result of the pains at the base of the back. Valentino Rossi will decide tomorrow morning whether or not he will start the last GP of the 2007 season."

Sunday 4 November 2007, Cheste, 10h00.

Valentino Rossi smiles into the camera, with Doctor Costa standing next to him in the Yamaha pit. No way is the king going to stand down. Firstly, because he has never done i before at any point in his career, and also because there's the matter of one little point he needs to score to ensure his place as runner-up to Casey Stoner in the championship.

Same day, same place, 14h00. Rossi is on the back row, which is a surprising image for Valentino's 192nd GP start. Surely nothing worse can happen now. There is no logical reason why he cannot make sure of this all important fifteenth place. Hard to think he was about to be hit by even more bad luck on the eighteenth lap as the Yamaha hiccoughs. Rossi has understood that the engine noise is worrying and that it is all over. For the first time since 1996, his first GP season, when he finished ninth in the 125 class, he would not finish in the top two in the championship! Farewell 2007. Here's to 2008?

PEDROSA THE HERO AT HOME. ROSSI GRITTED HIS TEETH UNTIL HIS ENGINE LET HIM DOWN

RUNNERS AND RIDERS

The day before first qualifying, Carlos Checa and Alexandre Barros bid their farewells to GP racing. Next year, the Spaniard will join the Ten Kate team in world superbikes, but the Brazilian has not yet finalised his plans. "If I find a good ride in superbikes, I'll take it, but if not, there are other interesting things I can do."

QUALIFYING

Pedrosa takes yet another pole position but that is by no means the news of the day. At precisely 13h59 on

Saturday 3 November 2007, Valentino Rossi takes a frightening tumble, from which he gets up with a triple fracture to his right hand. His bleak and black year was determined to haunt him right to the final GP of the season. Chaz Davies (Ducati D'Antin) falls on Friday and decides not to race, because of injuries to the right hand and wrist.

START

A super Stoner gets a textbook start: at the first split, he already has over 7 tenths in hand over Pedrosa. At the end of the opening lap, the Spaniard has closed to 368 thousandths. Hayden is third, ahead of Hopkins, Melandri and Capirossi. Having started from the back row, Rossi is seventeenth.

LAP 3

Only Pedrosa can hang onto Stoner's coat tails. Behind them, Hayden is

already 2 seconds off his team-mate.

LAP 4

Hopkins is third.

LAP 5

Lap record for Pedrosa, who will pass Stoner at the end of the main straight.

LAP 7

Hayden has slipped to fifth, as Melandri has found a way past.

LAP 10

Kurtis Roberts retires. At the front, Pedrosa has one second in hand over Stoner.

HALF-DISTANCE (15 LAPS)

Dani Pedrosa is on top of his game and now leads Stoner by 1.863. Hopkins is third, but already 6 seconds adrift of the world champion. In fifteenth place, Valentino Rossi makes sure of the single point he needs to hang onto second place in the world championship.

LAP 18

Rossi is in trouble and is only sixteenth

and therefore no longer championship runner-up!

LAP 19

Rossi pits and retires (engine.)

LAP 26

Capirossi passes Hayden and finds himself fifth. The American immediately comes under pressure from Vermeulen, who gets by one lap later.

FINISH (30 LAPS)

The 132,500 spectators at the track today are happy in the sunshine: Dani Pedrosa is the clear winner in front of his home fans.

CHAMPIONSHIP

The incredible has thus been played out in two acts: after the qualifying crash, Rossi is hit with a failure which means that for the first time since 1996, his first GP season in 125, he fails to finish in the top two in the world championship!

Is Pedrosa on form? Talk about understatement! The Spaniard's dominance has no effect on the good mood of Sylvain Guintoli. As for Casey Stoner, he is rather thoughtful.

GP VALENCIA | 4th November 2007 | Cheste | 4.005 m

STARTING GRID

1	26	D. Pedrosa	Honda	1'31.517
2	27	C. Stoner	Ducati	1'31.603
3	1	N. Hayden	Honda	1'31.903
4	14	R. De Puniet	Kawasaki	1'31.963
5	50	S. Guintoli	Yamaha	1'32.074
6	6	M. Tamada	Yamaha	1'32.151
7	21	J. Hopkins	Suzuki	1'32.165
8	65	L. Capirossi	Ducati	1'32.261
9	7	C. Checa	Honda	1'32.273
10	33	M. Melandri	Honda	1'32.367
11	71	C. Vermeulen	Suzuki	1'32.617
12	4	A. Barros	Ducati	1'32.714
13	56	S. Nakano	Honda	1'32.730
14	24	T. Elias	Honda	1'32.790
15	5	C. Edwards	Yamaha	1'33.021
16	13	A. West	Kawasaki	1'33.231
17	46	V. Rossi	Yamaha	1'33.290
18	80	Ku. Roberts	KR212V	1'33.431
19	57	C. Davies	Ducati	1'34.436 (*)

(*): C. Davies (GB, Ducati), injured on Friday, he had to withdraw.

RACE: 30 laps = 120.150 km

1	Daniel Pedrosa	46'43.533 (154.283 km/h)
2	Casey Stoner	+ 5''447
3	John Hopkins	+ 20''404
4	Marco Melandri	+ 24''827
5	Loris Capirossi	+ 25''804
6	Chris Vermeulen	+ 25''862
7	Alex Barros	+ 29''470
8	Nicky Hayden	+ 30''333
9	Randy De Puniet	+ 30''895
10	Toni Elias	+ 31''030
11	Sylvain Guintoli	+ 38''763
12	Carlos Checa	+ 42''506
13	Colin Edwards	+ 46''572
14	Shinya Nakano	+ 50''220
15	Makoto Tamada	+ 56''879
16	Anthony West	+ 1'15.369

Outright fastest lap:
Rossi, en 1'31.002 (158.436 km/h/2006).

CHAMPIONSHIP

1	C. Stoner	367 (10 wins)
2	D. Pedrosa	242 (2 wins)
3	V. Rossi	241 (4 wins)
4	J. Hopkins	189
5	M. Melandri	187
6	C. Vermeulen	179 (1 win)
7	L. Capirossi	166 (1 win)
8	N. Hayden	127
9	C. Edwards	124
10	A. Barros	115

Fastest lap:
Pedrosa, in 1'32.748 (155.453 km/h). New record.
Previous: Capirossi, in 1'32.924 (155.159 km/h/2006)

AND NUMBER TWO FOR KALLIO, WHILE A GREAT WILD CARD, DEBON, IS ON THE PODIUM

RUNNERS AND RIDERS

This is the final appearance in the category for Lorenzo, Dovizioso and De Angelis. Aprilia test rider, Alex Debon has a wild card, like his fellow countrymen, Molina and Barragan as well as the German, Sommer.

QUALIFYING

Mika Kallio is having a good end to the season, taking pole position after having a few problems on the first day, as happened in Malaysia. Tough times for Luthi, who was seventh on Friday but is unable to improve on that time on Saturday. The first row

is completed by Lorenzo, Takahashi and Simoncelli, who is the first rider to have tested Dainese's new airbag system "in the field."

START

Kallio has the quickest reflexes, but Barbera finds a way past at the first corner, just before Lorenzo moves into the lead. Lai does not go far, as he falls. Crossing the line for the first time, Lorenzo has a lead of 196 thousandths over Barbera, who is followed by Dovizioso, Kallio and Bautista.

LAP 3

Dovizioso is second, 223 thousandths off Lorenzo.

LAP 6

Lorenzo, Dovizioso, Kallio, Barbera, De Angelis, Debon, Bautista, Simon and Simoncelli: nine of them covered by 1.708 seconds.

LAP 8

De Angelis has helped himself to

second place. Kallio and Dovizioso are still hanging on.

LAP 9

Simoncelli goes off into a gravel trap.

LAP 10

De Angelis has taken the lead.

HALF-DISTANCE (13 LAPS)

De Angelis recalls that it was here in Valencia, twelve months ago, that he took his only world championship win. He leads Bautista by 1.591, who is fighting with Dovizioso and Kallio. Lorenzo is now only eighth.

LAP 16

Fastest race lap for De Angelis: his lead is 2.057 seconds.

LAP 19

Now it is Bautista who is the fastest man on the track. Kallio is with him, but Dovizioso has been dropped.

LAP 21

Bautista is a faller.

LAP 22

Kallio is 1.261 off Alex de Angelis.

Debon is about to pass Dovizioso for third place.

LAP 24

The gap between De Angelis and Kallio is now down to 547 thousandths.

LAP 26

Kallio has got by and embarks on the final lap with a lead of 178 thousandths over De Angelis.

FINISH (27 LAPS)

A superb Kallio takes his second victory in this category, after the win in Japan. Debon does well to get to the podium.

CHAMPIONSHIP

Lorenzo, Dovizioso and De Angelis fill the top three slots and next year we will find them all in MotoGP. Therefore, 2008 will see a new generation, featuring the likes of Bautista and Kallio who both won twice this year.

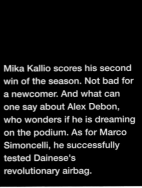

Mika Kallio scores his second win of the season. Not bad for a newcomer. And what can one say about Alex Debon, who wonders if he is dreaming on the podium. As for Marco Simoncelli, he successfully tested Dainese's revolutionary airbag.

GP VALENCIA | 4th November 2007 | Cheste | 4.005 m

STARTING GRID

1	36	M. Kallio	KTM	1'35.166
2	1	J. Lorenzo	Aprilia	1'35.333
3	55	Y. Takahashi	Honda	1'35.623
4	58	M. Simoncelli	Gilera	1'35.712
5	80	H. Barberá	Aprilia	1'35.727
6	19	A. Bautistá	Aprilia	1'35.766
7	60	J. Simón	Honda	1'35.958
8	6	A. Debón	Aprilia	1'35.962
9	3	A. De Angelis	Aprilia	1'35.985
10	34	A. Dovizioso	Honda	1'35.985
11	4	H. Aoyama	KTM	1'36.077
12	73	S. Aoyama	Honda	1'36.103
13	41	A. Espargaro	Aprilia	1'36.318
14	12	T. Lüthi	Aprilia	1'36.344
15	15	R. Locatelli	Gilera	1'36.688
16	32	F. Lai	Aprilia	1'37.580
17	16	J. Cluzel	Aprilia	1'37.680
18	28	D. Heidolf	Aprilia	1'37.770
19	8	R. Wilairot	Honda	1'37.792
20	25	A. Baldolini	Aprilia	1'37.922
21	17	K. Abraham	Aprilia	1'38.090
22	11	T. Sekiguchi	Aprilia	1'38.557
23	7	E. Vazquez	Aprilia	1'38.589
24	31	A. Molina	Aprilia	1'38.683
25	21	F. Sandi	Aprilia	1'38.904
26	50	E. Laverty	Honda	1'38.919
27	10	I. Toth	Aprilia	1'39.080
28	53	S. Barragan	Honda	1'40.427
29	18	J. Sommer	Honda	1'41.692

RACE: 27 laps = 108.135 km

1	Mika Kallio	43'28.349 (149.246 km/h)
2	Alex De Angelis	+ 0''371
3	Alex Debón	+ 6''797
4	Andrea Dovizioso	+ 6''880
5	Hector Barberá	+ 12''767
6	Julian Simón	+ 13''030
7	Jorge Lorenzo	+ 14''751
8	Yuki Takahashi	+ 16''437
9	Thomas Lüthi	+ 16''551
10	Hiroshi Aoyama	+ 20''223
11	Marco Simoncelli	+ 23''626
12	Aleix Espargaro	+ 31''805
13	Roberto Locatelli	+ 34''310
14	Alex Baldolini	+ 58''825
15	Ratthapark Wilairot	+ 58''845
16	Dirk Heidolf	+ 59''688
17	Shuhei Aoyama	+ 1'01.510
18	Efren Vazquez	+ 1'19.620
19	Taru Sekiguchi	+ 1'20.598
20	Federico Sandi	+ 1'24.412
21	Eugene Laverty	+ 1'27.529
22	Alvaro Molina	+ 1 lap
23	Imre Toth	+ 1 lap
24	Santiago Barragan	+ 1 lap

Fastest lap
Kallio, in 1'35.659 (150.722 km/h). New record.
Previous: Pedrosa, in 1'35.792 (150.513 km/h/2005).

Outright fastest lap
H. Aoyama, in 1'35.109 (151.594 km/h/2006).

CHAMPIONSHIP

1	J. Lorenzo	312 (9 wins)
2	A. Dovizioso	260 (2 wins)
3	A. De Angelis	235
4	A. Bautistá	181 (2 wins)
5	H. Barberá	177
6	H. Aoyama	160 (2 wins)
7	M. Kallio	157 (2 wins)
8	T. Lüthi	133
9	J. Simón	123
10	M. Simoncelli	97

FAUBEL TRIED EVERYTHING BUT GABOR TALMACSI, THE BOXER, FOUGHT HIM OFF

RUNNERS AND RIDERS

All eyes are on the title fight between Talmacsi and Faubel. Five wild cards have been dealt, including one for the young Japanese rider, Takaaki Nakagami, who turned 15 in February and is learning the job in Spain. The Japanese consider he is the worthy successor to the late lamented Daijiro Kato.

QUALIFYING

The situation is clear between the last two men still in the running for the title and the final battle begins with the very first free practice session. And it's Talmacsi who comes off best, eventually getting the better of Faubel, having had to give best to the Spaniard on Friday afternoon. Gadea follows his two team-mates and one has to wonder if the third man in the "Aspar" Martinez outfit favours either one of the two contenders.

START

Espargaro goes off in the lead, ahead of Nieto, Smith, Talmacsi, Corsi, Cortese, Gadea and Faubel. The young Spaniard finishes the first lap 123 thousandths ahead of Nieto, while Maestro does not go any further.

LAP 2

Talmacsi takes the lead and crosses the line with a 7 tenths lead over Nieto, who is pursued by Faubel. Bradl is a faller.

LAP 3

Faubel is second, but Talmacsi has stepped up the pace once again. His lead is 1.122 seconds.

LAP 6

Pesek has found a way past Nieto and the Czech is third. At the sharp end, Faubel has closed to within 920 thousandths of Talmacsi.

LAP 8

De Rosa is a faller. There are less than four tenths between the only two men who can be crowned. Olive is touring.

LAP 9

Faubel crosses the line first but Talmacsi counter attacks just at the moment when Faubel slows, trying to let the chasing group catch up! Cortese falls.

HALF-DISTANCE (12 LAPS)

68 thousandths between Talmacsi and Faubel. Pasini, Nieto and Pesek have closed to 3.880 seconds off the two leaders who are mounting attack after attack on one another. Faubel's plan is clearly to provoke his rival and above all, to make it easier for the others to catch up. Between these two groups is Olive, who is a lap down but that doesn't stop him from joining in the scrap!

LAP 14

Faubel makes a mistake and is 7 tenths off.

LAP 20

Faubel has fought his way back again and the two leaders narrowly avoid a collision. His pursuers, Gadea, Pasini and Pesek, are 2 seconds down.

FINISH (24 LAPS)

Talmacsi embarks on the final lap leading Faubel by 123 thousandths, with Gadea in attendance. Faubel goes by at the final corner and wins by 185 thousandths from a fantastic Talmacsi and a very spectacular Gadea.

CHAMPIONSHIP

With a margin of five points, Gabor Talmacsi becomes the first Hungarian to win a world title.

A nice triple for the Aspar Martinez team, even if Gabor Talmacsi would maybe have preferred something a bit calmer for his title win. Because it has to be said that Faubel tried everything to sink his rival, but in vain. As for Pesek, his 125 career is over.

GP VALENCIA | 4th November 2007 | Cheste | 4.005 m

STARTING GRID

1	14	G. Talmacsi	Aprilia	1'39.029
2	55	H. Faubel	Aprilia	1'39.402
3	33	S. Gadea	Aprilia	1'39.745
4	52	L. Pesek	Derbi	1'39.792
5	22	P. Nieto	Aprilia	1'39.877
6	24	S. Corsi	Aprilia	1'40.000
7	18	N. Terol	Derbi	1'40.048
8	75	M. Pasini	Aprilia	1'40.059
9	44	P. Espargaro	Aprilia	1'40.279
10	11	S. Cortese	Aprilia	1'40.287
11	12	E. Rabat	Honda	1'40.488
12	38	B. Smith	Honda	1'40.528
13	6	J. Olivé	Aprilia	1'40.551
14	17	S. Bradl	Aprilia	1'40.660
15	71	T. Koyama	KTM	1'40.743
16	60	M. Ranseder	Derbi	1'40.927
17	34	R. Krummenacher	KTM	1'40.951
18	7	A. Masbou	Honda	1'40.999
19	27	S. Bianco	Aprilia	1'41.161
20	98	T. Nakagami	Honda	1'41.200
21	63	M. Di Meglio	Honda	1'41.222
22	35	R. De Rosa	Aprilia	1'41.291
23	77	D. Aegerter	Aprilia	1'41.321
24	8	L. Zanetti	Aprilia	1'41.327
25	29	A. Iannone	Aprilia	1'41.344
26	20	R. Tamburini	Aprilia	1'41.349
27	51	S. Bonsey	KTM	1'41.600
28	99	D. Webb	Honda	1'41.843
29	95	R. Muresan	Derbi	1'42.171
30	76	I. Maestro	Aprilia	1'42.257
31	78	D. Saez	Aprilia	1'42.378
32	37	J. Litjens	Honda	1'42.420
33	30	P. Tutusaus	Aprilia	1'42.567
34	13	D. Lombardi	Honda	1'43.075
35	53	S. Grotzkyj	Aprilia	1'43.276
36	79	F. Lamborghini	Aprilia	1'43.335
37	40	A. Gyorfi	Aprilia	1'43.807

RACE: 24 laps = 96.120 km

1	Hector Faubel	40'14.228 (143.330 km/h)
2	Gabor Talmacsi	+ 0''185
3	Sergio Gadea	+ 0''286
4	Mattia Pasini	+ 0''826
5	Lukas Pesek	+ 0''878
6	Esteve Rabat	+ 5''850
7	Pablo Nieto	+ 9''038
8	Bradley Smith	+ 13''034
9	Tomoyoshi Koyama	+ 20''734
10	Pol Espargaro	+ 21''002
11	Nicolas Terol	+ 21''344
12	Simone Corsi	+ 32''078
13	Michael Ranseder	+ 39''542
14	Alexis Masbou	+ 39''548
15	Randy Krummenacher	+ 39''706
16	Steve Bonsey	+ 39''880
17	Stefano Bianco	+ 40''877
18	Dominique Aegerter	+ 40''998
19	Roberto Tamburini	+ 44''169
20	Andrea Iannone	+ 44''173
21	Daniel Webb	+ 54''912
22	Robert Muresan	+ 1'09.235
23	Mike Di Meglio	+ 1'12.208
24	Joey Litjens	+ 1'12.315
25	Dino Lombardi	+ 1'12.770
26	Daniel Saez	+ 1'12.786
27	Pere Tutusaus	+ 1'12.868
28	Ferruccio Lamborghini	+ 1'16.195
29	Alen Gyorfi	+ 1'38.850
30	Joan Olivé	+ 1 lap

Fastest lap

Faubel, in 1'39.380 (145.079 km/h). New record.
Previous: Faubel, in 1'39.574 (144.796 km/h/2006).

Outright fastest lap

Talmacsi, in 1'39.029 (145.029 km/h/2007).

CHAMPIONSHIP

1	G. Talmacsi	282 (3 wins)
2	H. Faubel	277 (5 wins)
3	T. Koyama	193 (1 win)
4	L. Pesek	182 (2 wins)
5	M. Pasini	174 (4 wins)
6	S. Corsi	168 (1 win)
7	S. Gadea	160 (1 win)
8	J. Olivé	131
9	P. Espargaro	110
10	B. Smith	101

1			2	3	4	5	6	7	8	9	10
1	STONER CASEY	AUS	367	18	5	12	10	14	18	1	-
2	PEDROSA DANIEL	ESP	242	18	5	11	2	8	15	1	3
3	ROSSI VALENTINO	ITA	241	18	4	11	4	8	15	1	3
4	HOPKINS JOHN	USA	189	18	-	1	-	4	17	2	-
5	MELANDRI MARCO	ITA	187	17	-	2	-	3	17	2	-
6	VERMEULEN CHRIS	AUS	179	18	1	3	1	4	17	1	-
7	CAPIROSSI LORIS	ITA	166	18	-	-	1	3	14	1	4
8	HAYDEN NICKY	USA	127	18	1	5	-	3	14	3	3
9	EDWARDS COLIN	USA	124	18	2	5	-	2	16	2	2
10	BARROS ALEX	BRÉ	115	18	-	-	-	1	14	3	4
11	DE PUNIET RANDY	FRA	108	18	-	2	-	1	11	2	7
12	ELIAS TONI	ESP	104	15	-	-	-	2	12	2	3
13	HOFMANN ALEX	ALL	65	12	-	-	-	-	10	5	2
14	CHECA CARLOS	ESP	65	18	-	2	-	-	11	6	4
15	WEST ANTHONY	AUS	59	11	-	-	-	-	10	7	-
16	GUINTOLI SYLVAIN	FRA	50	18	-	-	-	-	15	4	1
17	NAKANO SHINYA	JAP	47	18	-	-	-	-	13	10	3
18	TAMADA MAKOTO	JAP	38	18	-	-	-	-	12	8	1
19	ROBERTS KURTIS	USA	10	13	-	-	-	-	5	12	5
20	HAYDEN ROGER LEE	USA	6	1	-	-	-	-	1	10	-
21	FABRIZIO MICHEL	ITA	6	1	-	-	-	-	1	10	-
22	GONZALES-NIETO F.	ESP	5	1	-	-	-	-	1	11	-
23	JACQUE OLIVIER	FRA	4	4	-	-	-	-	1	12	1
24	ROBERTS JR KENNY	USA	4	7	-	-	-	-	1	13	2
25	AOKI NOBUATSU	JAP	3	1	-	-	-	-	1	13	-
26	ITO SHINICHI	JAP	1	1	-	-	-	-	1	15	-

1 Final Championship Classification **2** Number of points **3** Number of qualifications (out of 17 GP) **4** Number of pole positions **5** Number of front row starts **6** Number of victories **7** Number of podiums **8** Score points (top 15) **9** Best race finish **10** Number of retirements

FINAL CONSTRUCTOR'S WORLDS CHAMPIONSHIP CLASSIFICATION

1	DUCATI	394
2	HONDA	313
3	YAMAHA	283
4	SUZUKI	241
5	KAWASAKI	144
6	KR212V	14

ROOKIE OF THE YEAR

1	GUINTOLI SYLVAIN	50

FINAL TEAMS WORLDS CHAMPIONSHIP CLASSIFICATION

1	DUCATI MARLBORO TEAM	533
2	REPSOL HONDA TEAM	369
3	RIZLA SUZUKI MOTOGP	368
4	FIAT YAMAHA TEAM	365
5	HONDA GRESINI	297
6	PRAMAC D'ANTIN	181
7	KAWASAKI RACING TEAM	176
8	DUNLOP YAMAHA TECH 3	88
9	HONDA LCR	65
10	KONICA MINOLTA HONDA	47
11	TEAM ROBERTS	14

1			2	3	4	5	6	7	8	9	10
1	LORENZO JORGE	ESP	312	17	9	16	9	12	16	1	1
2	DOVIZIOSO ANDREA	ITA	260	17	2	11	2	10	16	1	1
3	DE ANGELIS ALEX	RSM	235	17	1	6	-	8	16	2	1
4	BAUTISTÁ ALVARO	ESP	181	17	1	6	2	7	12	1	4
5	BARBERÁ HECTOR	ESP	177	17	-	9	-	5	14	2	3
6	AOYAMA HIROSHI	JAP	160	17	1	3	2	4	12	1	4
7	KALLIO MIKA	FIN	157	17	2	5	2	4	11	1	6
8	LÜTHI THOMAS	SUI	133	17	-	2	-	-	13	4	4
9	SIMÓN JULIAN	ESP	123	17	-	4	-	-	14	5	3
10	SIMONCELLI MARCO	ITA	97	17	-	1	-	-	12	6	5
11	TAKAHASHI YUKI	JAP	90	15	-	1	-	-	11	4	4
12	AOYAMA SHUHEI	JAP	90	17	1	2	-	-	13	5	2
13	LOCATELLI ROBERTO	ITA	59	13	-	-	-	-	9	6	2
14	LAI FABRIZIO	ITA	49	17	-	-	-	-	10	9	4
15	ESPARGARO ALEIX	ESP	47	17	-	-	-	-	11	10	2
16	ABRAHAM KAREL	TCH	31	17	-	-	-	-	10	10	5
17	WILAIROT RATTHA.	THA	30	17	-	-	-	-	9	8	3
18	DEBÒN ALEX	ESP	27	4	-	2	-	2	2	3	1
19	WEST ANTHONY	AUS	25	7	-	-	-	-	5	9	1
20	HEIDOLF DIRK	ALL	24	17	-	-	-	-	8	10	4
21	CLUZEL JULES	FRA	19	17	-	-	-	-	6	11	4
22	BALDOLINI ALEX	ITA	18	17	-	-	-	-	8	13	6
23	SEKIGUCHI TARO	JAP	13	13	-	-	-	-	6	12	2
24	LINFOOT DAN	GB	7	7	-	-	-	-	1	9	5
25	LAVERTY EUGENE	IRL	6	17	-	-	-	-	4	14	3
26	OIKAWA SEIJIN	JAP	4	1	-	-	-	-	1	12	-
27	UI YOUICHI	JAP	2	1	-	-	-	-	1	14	-
28	TOTH IMRE	HON	2	17	-	-	-	-	2	15	4
29	VAZQUEZ EFREN	ESP	1	10	-	-	-	-	1	15	5
30	TIZÓN ARTURO	ESP	1	6	-	-	-	-	1	15	3

1 Final Championship Classification 2 Number of points 3 Number of qualifications (out of 17 GP) 4 Number of pole positions 5 Number of front row starts
6 Number of victories 7 Number of podiums 8 Score points (top 15) 9 Best race finish 10 Number of retirements

FINAL CONSTRUCTOR'S WORLDS CHAMPIONSHIP CLASSIFICATION

1	APRILIA	387
2	HONDA	275
3	KTM	226
4	GILERA	116
5	YAMAHA	4

ROOKIE OF THE YEAR

1	BAUTISTÁ ALVARO	181
2	KALLIO MIKA	157
3	LÜTHI THOMAS	133
4	SIMÓN JULIAN	123
5	LAI FABRIZIO	49
6	ESPARGARO ALEIX	47
7	ABRAHAM KAREL	31
8	W. RATTHAPARK	30
9	LAVERTY EUGENE	6
10	TOTH IMRE	2

MICHEL MÉTRAUX TROPHY (BEST PRIVATE RIDER)

1	LAI FABRIZIO	ITA	49
2	ESPARGARO ALEIX	ESP	47
3	ABRAHAM KAREL	TCH	31
4	WILAIROT RATTHA.	THA	30
5	WEST ANTHONY	AUS	25
6	HEIDOLF DIRK	ALL	24
7	CLUZEL JULES	FRA	19
8	BALDOLINI ALEX	ITA	18
9	SEKIGUCHI TARO	JAP	13
10	LINFOOT DAN	GB	7
11	LAVERTY EUGENE	IRL	6
12	TOTH IMRE	HON	2
13	TIZÓN ARTURO	ESP	1

1			2	3	4	5	6	7	8	9	10
1	TALMACSI GABOR	HON	282	17	5	14	3	10	16	1	1
2	FAUBEL HECTOR	ESP	277	17	2	12	5	13	15	1	1
3	KOYAMA TOMOYOSHI	JAP	193	17	-	5	1	6	15	1	2
4	PESEK LUKAS	TCH	182	17	1	8	2	6	14	1	1
5	PASINI MATTIA	ITA	174	17	9	12	4	5	11	1	6
6	CORSI SIMONE	ITA	168	17	-	4	1	2	15	1	2
7	GADEA SERGIO	ESP	160	17	-	4	1	3	12	1	5
8	OLIVÉ JOAN	ESP	131	17	-	-	-	2	13	2	1
9	ESPARGARO PO	ESP	110	17	-	1	-	1	13	3	4
10	SMITH BRADLEY	GB	101	16	-	3	-	1	13	3	1
11	RABAT ESTEVE	ESP	74	15	-	-	-	1	12	3	3
12	RANSEDER MICHAEL	AUT	73	17	-	-	-	-	13	7	2
13	KRUMMENACHER RA.	SUI	69	17	-	-	-	1	12	3	-
14	CORTESE SANDRO	ALL	66	17	-	1	-	-	10	7	5
15	NIETO PABLO	ESP	57	17	-	-	-	-	9	6	6
16	DE ROSA RAFFAELE	ITA	56	17	-	2	-	-	8	4	7
17	DI MEGLIO MIKE	FRA	42	15	-	1	-	-	9	4	2
18	BRADL STEFAN	ALL	39	9	-	-	-	-	7	6	2
19	ZANETTI LORENZO	ITA	30	17	-	-	-	-	7	7	2
20	IANNONE ANDREA	ITA	26	17	-	-	-	-	7	9	3
21	MASBOU ALEXIS	FRA	25	17	-	-	-	-	7	10	4
22	TEROL NICOLAS	ESP	19	17	-	-	-	-	5	11	2
23	AEGERTER DOMINI.	SUI	7	17	-	-	-	-	3	11	3
24	BIANCO STEFANO	ITA	7	15	-	-	-	-	3	11	6
25	BONSEY STEVE	USA	4	17	-	-	-	-	2	13	5
26	WEBB DANIEL	GB	3	16	-	-	-	-	1	13	4
27	FROEHLICH GEORG	ALL	2	1	-	-	-	-	1	14	-
28	JEREZ ENRIQUE	ESP	2	2	-	-	-	-	1	14	-
29	GROTZKYJ SIMONE	ITA	1	17	-	-	-	-	1	15	6

1 Final Championship Classification **2** Number of points **3** Number of qualifications (out of 17 GP) **4** Number of pole positions **5** Number of front row starts
6 Number of victories **7** Number of podiums **8** Score points (top 15) **9** Best race finish **10** Number of retirements

FINAL CONSTRUCTOR'S WORLDS CHAMPIONSHIP CLASSIFICATION

1	APRILIA	410
2	DERBI	199
3	KTM	196
4	HONDA	146

ROOKIE OF THE YEAR

1	ESPARGARO POL	ESP	110
2	RABAT ESTEVE	ESP	74
3	KRUMMENACHER	SUI	69
4	AEGERTER SUI	SUI	7
5	BONSEY STEVE	USA	4
6	WEBB DANIEL	GB	3

MICHEL MÉTRAUX TROPHY (BEST PRIVATE RIDER)

1	TALMACSI GABOR	HON	282	9	RABAT ESTEVE	ESP	74	17	MASBOU ALEXIS	FRA	25
2	FAUBEL HECTOR	ESP	277	10	RANSEDER MICHAEL	AUT	73	18	AEGERTER DOMINI.	SUI	7
3	PASINI MATTIA	ITA	174	11	CORTESE SANDRO	ALL	66	19	BIANCO STEFANO	ITA	7
4	CORSI SIMONE	ITA	168	12	NIETO PABLO	ESP	57	20	WEBB DANIEL	GB	3
5	GADEA SERGIO	ESP	160	13	DE ROSA RAFFAELE	ITA	56	21	GROTZKYJ SIMONE	ITA	1
6	OLIVÉ JOAN	ESP	131	14	DI MEGLIO MIKE	FRA	42				
7	ESPARGARO POL	ESP	110	15	ZANETTI LORENZO	ITA	30				
8	SMITH BRADLEY	GB	101	16	IANNONE ANDREA	ITA	26				

Superbike champion for a second time, the Englishman James Toseland will race in GP next year.

THE RESULTS
OF THE CHAMPIONSHIPS

THE MOST EXTENSIVE STATISTICS SECTION
ON THE MARKET, FROM
THE SUPERBIKE WORLD CHAMPIONSHIP
TO THE SWISS CHAMPIONSHIP, VIA
GERMANY, FRANCE, ITALY, THE
UNITED STATES, GREAT BRITAIN AND SPAIN.

SUPERBIKE WORLD CHAMPIONSHIP

24th February - Doha - Qatar

Race I: 1. M. Biaggi (I, Suzuki), 18 laps, 36'10.115 (160.648 km/h); 2. J. Toseland (GB, Honda), 1.483; 3. L. Lanzi (I, Ducati), 13.906; 4. Y. Kagayama (J, Suzuki), 14.819; 5. T. Bayliss (AUS, Ducati), 17.305; 6. M. Neukirchner (D, Suzuki), 24.931; 7. R. Rolfo (I, Honda), 25.165; 8. N. Haga (J, Yamaha), 27.320; 9. T. Corser (AUS, Yamaha), 31.237; 10. R. Xaus (E, Ducati), 31.669; 11. S. Martin (AUS, Honda), 42.355; 12. S. Nakatomi (J, Yamaha), 46.845; 13. A. Polita (I, Suzuki), 59.207; 14. J. Smrz (CZ, Ducati), 1'00.296; 15. D. Ellison (GB, Ducati), 1'21.043. 17 finishers. Fastest lap: M. Biaggi (I, Suzuki), 1'59.275 (162.381 km/h).

Race II: 1. J. Toseland (GB, Honda), 18 laps, 36'09.433 (160.698 km/h); 2. M. Biaggi (I, Suzuki), 0.738; 3. T. Corser (AUS, Yamaha), 7.386; 4. N. Haga (J, Yamaha), 14.984; 5. A. Gonzales-Nieto (E, Kawasaki), 15.033; 6. Y. Kagayama (J, Suzuki), 15.911; 7. L. Lanzi (I, Ducati), 16.664; 8. T. Bayliss (AUS, Ducati), 23.249; 9. R. Xaus (E, Ducati), 24.282; 10. M. Neukirchner (D, Suzuki), 33.480; 11. R. Laconi (F, Kawasaki), 34.004; 12. M. Fabrizio (I, Honda), 37.297; 13. J. Brookes (AUS, Honda), 42.064; 14. K. Muggeridge (AUS, Honda), 42.359; 15. A. Polita (I, Suzuki), 46.206. 20 finishers. Fastest lap: M. Biaggi (I, Suzuki), 1'59.194 (162.491 km/h).

4th March - Phillip Island - Australia

Race I: 1. T. Bayliss (AUS, Ducati), 22 laps, 34'11.276 (171.622 km/h); 2. J. Toseland (GB, Honda), 2.096; 3. M. Biaggi (I, Suzuki), 10.143; 4. N. Haga (J, Yamaha), 18.923; 5. T. Corser (AUS, Yamaha), 19.742; 6. L. Lanzi (I, Ducati), 24.765; 7. R. Xaus (E, Ducati), 27.404; 8. M. Neukirchner (D, Suzuki), 34.614; 9. A. Gonzales-Nieto (E, Kawasaki), 35.339; 10. S. Martin (AUS, Honda), 36.238; 11. R. Rolfo (I, Honda), 38.067; 12. J. Brookes (AUS, Honda), 47.078; 13. S. Nakatomi (J, Yamaha), 58.571; 14. J. Smrz (CZ, Ducati), 1'08.000; 15. A. Polita (I, Suzuki), 1'22.584. 18 finishers. Fastest lap: T. Corser (AUS, Yamaha), 1'31.826 (174.264 km/h).

Race II: 1. J. Toseland (GB, Honda), 22 laps, 34'16.990 (171.145 km/h); 2. T. Bayliss (AUS, Ducati), 0.274; 3. N. Haga (J, Yamaha), 6.916; 4. M. Biaggi (I, Suzuki), 7.013; 5. T. Corser (AUS, Yamaha), 7.052; 6. R. Xaus (E, Ducati), 23.176; 7. L. Lanzi (I, Ducati), 26.471; 8. M. Neukirchner (D, Suzuki), 26.486; 9. M. Fabrizio (I, Honda), 26.501; 10. R. Rolfo (I, Honda), 37.936; 11. J. Smrz (CZ, Ducati), 41.308; 12. J. Brookes (AUS, Honda), 48.672; 13. S. Nakatomi (I, Yamaha), 48.717; 14. A. Gonzales-Nieto (E, Kawasaki), 1'13.095; 15. A. Polita (I, Suzuki), 1'13.882. 16 finishers. Fastest lap: N. Haga (J, Yamaha), 1'32.621 (172.769 km/h).

1st April - Donington Park - Europe

Race I: 1. J. Toseland (GB, Honda), 23 laps, 35'28.222 (156.518 km/h); 2. T. Corser (AUS, Yamaha), 1.368; 3. M. Biaggi (I, Suzuki), 2.448; 4. N. Haga (J, Yamaha), 9.249; 5. L. Lanzi (I, Ducati), 18.028; 6. A. Gonzales-Nieto (E, Kawasaki), 18.956; 7. R. Laconi (F, Kawasaki), 29.998; 8. M. Neukirchner (D, Suzuki), 30.296; 9. R. Rolfo (I. Honda), 30.525; 10. J. Smrz (CZ, Ducati), 36.661; 11. K. Muggeridge (AUS, Honda), 39.389; 12. J. Brookes (AUS, Honda), 48.045; 13. M. Fabrizio (I, Honda), 51.290; 14. G. Bussei (I, Ducati), 51.402; 15. D. Ellison (GB, Ducati), 1'00.156. 19 finishers. Fastest lap: T. Bayliss (AUS, Ducati), 1'31.575 (158.152 km/h).

Race II: 1. N. Haga (J, Yamaha), 23 laps, 35'26.734 (156.627 km/h); 2. M. Biaggi (I, Suzuki), 0.111; 3. T. Corser (AUS, Yamaha), 1.100; 4. R. Xaus (E, Ducati), 5.927; 5. L. Lanzi (I, Ducati), 9.834; 6. R. Laconi (F, Kawasaki), 12.203; 7. R. Rolfo (I, Honda), 22.287; 8. J. Smrz (CZ, Ducati), 30.060; 9. K. Muggeridge (AUS, Honda), 37.734; 10. M. Neukirchner (D, Suzuki), 39.893; 11. G. Bussei (I, Ducati), 41.524; 12. M. Fabrizio (I, Honda), 45.617; 13. S. Martin (AUS, Honda), 52.547; 14. S. Nakatomi (J, Yamaha), 1'01.669; 15. J. Brookes (AUS, Honda), 1'20.586. 17 finishers. Fastest lap: N. Haga (J, Yamaha), 1'31.634 (158.051 km/h).

15th April - Valencia - Spain

Race I: 1. R. Xaus (E, Ducati), 23 laps, 37'14.606 (148.399 km/h); 2. N. Haga (J, Yamaha), 1.997; 3. T. Bayliss (AUS, Ducati), 6.330; 4. T. Corser (AUS, Yamaha), 8.780; 5. J. Toseland (GB, Honda), 17.040; 6. L. Lanzi (I, Ducati), 24.272; 7. M. Fabrizio (I, Honda), 25.822; 8. M. Biaggi (I, Suzuki), 26.087; 9. J. Brookes (AUS, Honda), 28.778; 10. R. Rolfo (I, Honda), 32.754; 11. R. Laconi (F, Kawasaki), 37.084; 12. M. Neukirchner (D, Suzuki), 37.141; 13. G. Bussei (I, Ducati), 37.563; 14. J. Smrz (CZ, Ducati), 38.544; 15. Y. Kagayama (J, Suzuki), 53.049. 15 finishers. Fastest lap: T. Bayliss (AUS, Ducati), 1'36.092 (150.044 km/h).

Race II: 1. J. Toseland (GB, Honda), 23 laps, 37'02.596 (149.201 km/h); 2. M. Biaggi (I, Suzuki), 0.287; 3. N. Haga (J, Yamaha), 0.375; 4. R. Xaus (E, Ducati), 6.637; 5. L. Lanzi (I, Ducati), 7.991; 6. T. Bayliss (AUS, Ducati), 10.210; 7. J. Brookes (AUS, Honda), 10.861; 8. R. Laconi (F, Kawasaki), 14.366; 9. T. Corser (AUS, Yamaha), 15.511; 10. M. Neukirchner (D, Suzuki), 19.716; 11. M. Fabrizio (I, Honda), 25.287; 12. R. Rolfo (I, Honda), 26.437; 13. Y. Kagayama (J, Suzuki), 34.992; 14. C. Morales (E, Yamaha), 39.987; 15. G. Bussei (I, Ducati), 42.445. 17 finishers. Fastest lap: N. Haga (J, Yamaha), 1'35.746 (150.586 km/h).

29th April - Assen - Netherlands

Race I: 1. J. Toseland (GB, Honda), 22 laps, 37'02.097 (162.349 km/h); 2. N. Haga (J, Yamaha), 0.663; 3. R. Xaus (E, Ducati), 3.698; 4. T. Bayliss (AUS, Ducati), 7.134; 5. L. Lanzi (I, Ducati), 9.312; 6. M. Biaggi (I, Suzuki), 9.534; 7. Y. Kagayama (J, Suzuki), 18.286; 8. A. Gonzales-Nieto (E, Kawasaki), 18.403; 9. R. Rolfo (I, Honda), 19.873; 10. M. Neukirchner (D, Suzuki), 22.914; 11. J. Smrz (CZ, Ducati), 29.602; 12. M. Fabrizio (I, Honda), 40.961; 13. S. Nakatomi (J, Yamaha), 41.008; 14. D. Ellison (GB, Ducati), 1'12.714; 15. M. Svoboda (CZ, Yamaha), 2 laps. 16 finishers. Fastest lap: T. Bayliss (AUS, Ducati), 1'39.906 (164.134 km/h).

Race II: 1. T. Bayliss (AUS, Ducati), 22 laps, 36'54.133 (162.933 km/h); 2. J. Toseland (GB, Honda), 0.009; 3. M. Biaggi (I, Suzuki), 7.439; 4. T. Corser (AUS, Yamaha), 12.379; 5. R. Rolfo (I, Honda), 23.052; 6. M. Fabrizio (I, Honda), 23.158; 7. M. Neukirchner (D, Suzuki), 23.311; 8. A. Gonzales-Nieto (E, Kawasaki), 24.147; 9. J. Smrz (CZ, Ducati), 29.660; 10. R. Laconi (F, Kawasaki), 32.301; 11. Y. Kagayama (J, Suzuki), 32.389; 12. S. Nakatomi (J, Yamaha), 39.091; 13. J. Brookes (AUS, Honda), 39.128; 14. L. Morelli (I, Ducati), 1 lap; 15. M. Svoboda (CZ, Yamaha). 16 finishers. Fastest lap: N. Haga (J, Yamaha), 1'39.770 (164.358 km/h).

13th May - Monza - Italy

Race I: 1. N. Haga (J, Yamaha), 18 laps, 32'04.428 (195.064 km/h); 2. T. Bayliss (AUS, Ducati), 8.403; 3. M. Biaggi (I, Suzuki), 9.703; 4. J. Toseland (GB, Honda), 13.587; 5. T. Corser (AUS, Yamaha), 14.898; 6. Y. Kagayama (J, Suzuki), 14.954; 7. L. Lanzi (I, Ducati), 19.517; 8. M. Fabrizio (I, Honda), 24.120; 9. K. Muggeridge (AUS, Honda), 24.682; 10. M. Neukirchner (D, Suzuki), 29.197; 11. J. Brookes (AUS, Honda), 32.654; 12. R. Xaus (E, Ducati), 34.054; 13. M. Borciani (I, Ducati), 37.386; 14. A. Polita (I, Suzuki), 37.704; 15. J. Smrz (CZ, Ducati), 41.377. 17 finishers. Fastest lap: M. Biaggi (I, Suzuki), 1'46.172 (196.425 km/h).

Race II: 1. N. Haga (J, Yamaha), 18 laps, 32'05.318 (194.974 km/h); 2. J. Toseland (GB, Honda), 2.691; 3. T. Bayliss (AUS, Ducati), 2.841; 4. R. Rolfo (I, Honda), 3.188; 5. M. Biaggi (I, Suzuki), 3.551; 6. T. Corser (AUS, Yamaha), 13.034; 7. Y. Kagayama (J, Suzuki), 17.246; 8. R. Laconi (I, Kawasaki), 18.410; 9. K. Muggeridge (AUS, Honda), 29.017; 10. J. Smrz (CZ, Ducati), 29.686; 11. M. Fabrizio (I, Honda), 30.371; 12. M. Neukirchner (D, Suzuki), 31.982; 13. R. Xaus (E, Ducati), 32,165; 14. R. Pietri (VEN, Yamaha), 1'32.292; 15. D. Ellison (GB, Ducati), 1'41.840. 15 finishers. Fastest lap: N. Haga (J, Yamaha), 1'46.064 (196.625 km/h).

27th May - Silverstone - Great Britain

Race I: 1. T. Bayliss (AUS, Ducati), 28 laps, 46'02.875 (129.919 km/h); 2. N. Haga (J, Yamaha), 2.035; 3. T. Corser (AUS, Yamaha), 4.568; 4. R. Rolfo (I, Honda), 50.039; 5. R. Laconi (F, Kawasaki), 1'09.634; 6. M. Biaggi (I, Suzuki), 1'20.982; 7. L. Lanzi (I, Ducati), 1'33.061; 8. J. Toseland (GB, Honda), 1 lap; 9. R. Xaus (E, Ducati); 10. M. Neukirchner (D, Suzuki); 11. V. Iannuzzo (I, Kawasaki); 12. L. Morelli (I, Honda); 13. S. Nakatomi (J, Yamaha), 2 laps. 13 finishers. Fastest lap: N. Haga (J, Yamaha), 1'37.005 (132.154 km/h). Race II: Annulée en raison des conditions météorologiques.

17th June - San Marino - Misano

Race I: 1. T. Bayliss (AUS, Ducati), 24 laps, 38'52.856 (154.811 km/h); 2. T. Corser (AUS, Yamaha), 2.374; 3. Y. Kagayama (J, Suzuki), 8.965; 4. J. Toseland (GB, Honda), 11.110; 5. R. Rolfo (I, Honda), 18.709; 6. L. Lanzi (I, Ducati), 20.467; 7. R. Laconi (F, Kawasaki), 22.072; 8. R. Xaus (E, Ducati), 25.424; 9. M. Neukirchner (D, Suzuki), 30.891; 10. J. Smrz (CZ, Ducati), 37.724; 11. M. Borciani (I, Ducati), 44.898; 12. M. Sanchini (I, Kawasaki), 1'01.538; 13. L. Morelli (I, Honda), 1'37.781; 14. D. Ellison (GB, Ducati), 1 lap; 15. C. Zaiser (A, MV-Agusta). 15 finishers. Fastest lap: N. Haga (J, Yamaha), 1'36.356 (156.171 km/h)

Race II: 1. T. Bayliss (AUS, Ducati), 24 laps, 38'43.506 (155.434 km/h); 2. N. Haga (J, Yamaha), 2.537; 3. M. Biaggi (I, Suzuki), 6.386; 4. Y. Kagayama (J, Suzuki), 8.905; 5. T. Corser (AUS, Yamaha), 9.130; 6. J. Toseland (GB, Honda), 13.967; 7. R. Xaus (E, Ducati), 16.708; 8. R. Rolfo (I, Honda), 16.781; 9. L. Lanzi (I, Ducati), 17.312; 10. M. Neukirchner (D, Suzuki), 33.065; 11. R. Laconi (F, Kawasaki), 33.605; 12. A. Gonzales-Nieto (E, Kawasaki), 41.251; 13. J. Smrz (CZ, Ducati), 42.723; 14. S. Nakatomi (J, Yamaha), 56.644; 15. M. Sanchini (I, Kawasaki), 1'00.739. 19 finishers. Fastest lap: T. Bayliss (AUS, Ducati), 1'36.022 (156.714 km/h).

22nd July - Brno - Czech Republic

Race I: 1. J. Toseland (GB, Honda), 20 laps, 41'02.730 (157.961 km/h); 2. M. Biaggi (I, Suzuki), 0.237; 3. Y. Kagayama (J, Suzuki), 1.185; 4. N. Haga (J, Yamaha), 2.403; 5. R. Rolfo (I, Honda), 3.472; 6. M. Fabrizio (I, Honda), 3.758; 7. T. Corser (AUS, Yamaha), 18.235; 8. L. Lanzi (I, Ducati), 19.653; 9. M. Neukirchner (D, Suzuki), 22.230; 10. S. Nakatomi (J, Yamaha), 31.662; 11. R. Laconi (F, Kawasaki), 32.796; 12. R. Xaus (E, Ducati), 47.360; 13. V. Iannuzzo (I, Kawasaki), 1'01.983; 14. J. Drazdak (CZ, Yamaha), 1'02.052; 15. S. Cruciani (I, Suzuki), 1'48.872. 15 finishers. Fastest lap: N. Haga (J, Yamaha), 2'01.543 (160.032 km/h).

Race II: 1. M. Biaggi (I, Suzuki), 19 laps, 38'53.022 (158.406 km/h); 2. J. Toseland (GB, Honda), 1.510; 3. M. Fabrizio (I, Honda), 5.419; 4. N. Haga (J, Yamaha), 6.765; 5. R. Rolfo (I, Honda), 7.910; 6. T. Bayliss (AUS, Ducati), 9.241; 7. L. Lanzi (I, Ducati), 19.424; 8. A. Gonzales-Nieto (E, Kawasaki), 24.191; 9. S. Nakatomi (J, Yamaha), 26.680; 10. R. Xaus (E, Ducati), 28.095; 11. K. Muggeridge (AUS, Honda), 33.256; 12. M. Neukirchner (D, Suzuki), 33.352; 13. J. Smrz (CZ, Ducati), 33.495; 14. R. Laconi (F, Kawasaki), 40.453; 15. V. Iannuzzo (I, Kawasaki), 57.284. 18 finishers. Fastest lap: T. Corser (AUS, Yamaha), 2'00.674 (161.185 km/h).

5th August - Brands Hatch - Great Britain

Race I: 1. J. Toseland (GB, Honda), 25 laps, 36'35.120 (151.782 km/h); 2. T. Corser (AUS, Yamaha), 1.554; 3. M. Biaggi (I, Suzuki), 2.917; 4. R. Xaus (E, Ducati), 10.202; 5. M. Fabrizio (I, Honda), 14.133; 6. R. Rolfo (I, Honda), 14.323; 7. N. Haga (J, Yamaha), 19.380; 8. R. Laconi (F, Kawasaki), 22.676; 9. L. Lanzi (I, Ducati), 24.259; 10. M. Neukirchner (D, Suzuki), 24.423; 11. S. Martin (AUS, Yamaha), 33.365; 12. A. Gonzales-Nieto (E, Kawasaki), 33.373; 13. S. Nakatomi (J, Yamaha), 33.548; 14. J. Smrz (CZ, Ducati), 48.283; 15. M. Nutt (GB, Yamaha), 1'04.655. 18 finishers. Fastest lap: N. Haga (J, Yamaha), 1'26.590 (153.912 km/h).

Race II: 1. J. Toseland (GB, Honda), 25 laps, 36'34.177 (151.847 km/h); 2. N. Haga (J, Yamaha), 1.686; 3. T. Corser (AUS, Yamaha), 1.760; 4. M. Fabrizio (I, Honda), 8.456; 5. Y. Kagayama (J, Suzuki), 8.988; 6. R. Xaus (E, Ducati), 9.470; 7. T. Bayliss (AUS, Ducati), 18.313; 8. M. Biaggi (I, Suzuki), 19.116; 9. R. Laconi (F, Kawasaki), 20.501; 10. M. Neukirchner (D, Suzuki), 20.586; 11. R. Rolfo (I, Honda), 21.808; 12. L. Lanzi (I, Ducati), 24.883; 13. A. Gonzales-Nieto (E, Kawasaki), 31.988; 14. K. Muggeridge (AUS, Honda), 33.253; 15. S. Nakatomi (J, Yamaha), 36.868. 18 finishers. Fastest lap: J. Toseland (GB, Honda), 1'26.689 (153.736 km/h).

9th September - Lausitz - Germany

Race I: 1. N. Haga (J, Yamaha), 24 laps, 40'02.923 (153.353 km/h); 2. M. Biaggi (I, Suzuki), 11.007; 3. T. Corser (AUS, Yamaha), 11.628; 4. T. Bayliss (AUS, Ducati), 22.156; 5. R. Rolfo (I, Honda), 26.082; 6. R. Laconi (F, Kawasaki), 26.381; 7. A. Gonzales-Nieto (E, Kawasaki), 36.870; 8. L. Lanzi (I, Ducati), 43.465; 9. J. Toseland (GB, Honda), 44.258; 10. K. Muggeridge (AUS, Honda), 45.233; 11. S. Nakatomi (J, Yamaha), 52.563; 12. R. Xaus (E, Ducati), 1'01.959; 13. J. Smrz (CZ, Ducati), 1'17.989; 14. S. Martin (AUS, Suzuki), 1'19.224; 15. Y. Tiberio (F, Honda), 1'36.627. 16 finishers. Fastest lap: N. Haga (J, Yamaha), 1'39.033 (155.039 km/h).

Race II: 1. T. Bayliss (AUS, Ducati), 24 laps, 39'49.291 (154.228 km/h); 2. N. Haga (J, Yamaha), 1.353; 3. M. Biaggi (I, Suzuki), 13.001; 4. J. Toseland (GB, Honda), 14.641; 5. T. Corser (AUS, Yamaha), 15.210; 6. R. Xaus (E, Ducati), 25.830; 7. R. Rolfo (I, Honda), 29.752; 8. A. Gonzales-Nieto (E, Kawasaki), 29.947; 9. M. Neukirchner (D, Suzuki), 30.552; 10. K. Muggeridge (AUS, Honda), 33.815; 11. R. Laconi (F, Kawasaki), 39.323; 12. L. Lanzi (I, Ducati), 42.592; 13. M. Fabrizio (I, Honda), 50.755; 14. S. Martin (AUS, Suzuki), 53.598; 15. S. Nakatomi (J, Yamaha), 56.284. 19 finishers. Fastest lap: N. Haga (J, Yamaha), 1'38.622 (155.685 km/h).

30 September - Vallelunga - Italy

Race I: 1. M. Biaggi (I, Suzuki), 24 laps, 39'24.967 (150.152 km/h); 2. T. Bayliss (AUS, Ducati), 5.638; 3. J. Toseland (GB, Honda), 7.452; 4. N. Haga (J, Yamaha), 10.079; 5. M. Fabrizio (I, Honda), 22.257; 6. L. Lanzi (I, Ducati), 25.662; 7. R. Laconi (F, Kawasaki), 34.811; 8. A. Gonzales-Nieto (E, Kawasaki), 38.075; 9. S. Nakatomi (J, Yamaha), 39.070; 10. V. Iannuzzo (I, Kawasaki), 47.702; 11. J. Smrz (CZ, Ducati), 47.806; 12. M. Borciani (I, Ducati), 53.488; 13. K. Muggeridge (AUS, Honda), 54.509; 14. S. Martin (AUS, Suzuki), 1'01.967; 15. Y. Tiberio (F, Honda), 1'08.291. 17 finishers. Fastest lap: N. Haga (J, Yamaha), 1'37.419 (151.880 km/h).

Race II: 1. T. Bayliss (AUS, Ducati), 24 laps, 39'30.861 (149.778 km/h); 2. M. Biaggi (I, Suzuki), 1.431; 3. N. Haga (J, Yamaha), 4.466; 4. T. Corser (AUS, Yamaha), 13.766; 5. R. Rolfo (I, Honda), 20.848; 6. R. Xaus (E, Ducati), 21.930; 7. L. Lanzi (I, Ducati), 29.847; 8. A. Gonzales-Nieto (E, Kawasaki), 29.986; 9. S. Nakatomi (J, Yamaha), 40.126; 10. M. Neukirchner (D, Suzuki), 40.733; 11. J. Toseland (GB, Honda), 42.544; 12. V. Iannuzzo (I, Kawasaki), 54.504; 13. K. Muggeridge (AUS, Honda), 55.024; 14. S. Martin (AUS, Suzuki), 55.304; 15. Y. Tiberio (F, Honda), 59.781. 19 finishers. Fastest lap: M. Biaggi (I, Suzuki), 1'37.727 (151.401 km/h).

7 October - Magny-Cours - France

Race I: 1. N. Haga (J, Yamaha), 23 laps, 38'33.762 (157.851 km/h); 2. T. Bayliss (AUS, Ducati), 2.770; 3. T. Corser (AUS, Yamaha), 3.735; 4. M. Neukirchner (D, Suzuki), 8.570; 5. A. Gonzales-Nieto (E, Kawasaki), 12.925; 6. M. Biaggi (I, Suzuki), 13.283; 7. J. Toseland (GB, Honda), 16.395; 8. R. Xaus (E, Ducati), 22.581; 9. R. Laconi (F, Kawasaki), 22.828; 10. R. Rolfo (I, Honda), 32.729; 11. S. Nakatomi (J, Yamaha), 38.305; 12. K. Muggeridge (AUS, Honda), 53.685; 13. Y. Tiberio (F, Honda), 53.799; 14. M. Fabrizio (I, Honda), 53.915; 15. G. Dietrich (F, Suzuki), 56.474. 16 finishers. Fastest lap: M. Neukirchner (D, Suzuki), 1'39.844 (159.044 km/h).

Race II: 1. N. Haga (J, Yamaha), 23 laps, 38'35.353 (157.743 km/h); 2. M. Biaggi (I, Suzuki), 3.518; 3. A. Gonzales-Nieto (E, Kawasaki), 9.142; 4. T. Corser (AUS, Yamaha), 9.257; 5. T. Bayliss (AUS, Ducati), 12.825; 6. J. Toseland (GB, Honda), 19.316; 7. R. Rolfo (I, Honda), 20.994; 8. R. Laconi (F, Kawasaki), 22.452; 9. M. Fabrizio (I, Honda), 22.505; 10. R. Xaus (E, Ducati), 28.352; 11. K. Muggeridge (AUS, Honda), 44.333; 12. Y. Tiberio (F, Honda), 48.077; 13. G. Dietrich (F, Suzuki), 1'23.307; 14. L. Morelli (I, Honda), 1'23.826; 15. D. Ellison (GB, Ducati), 1'37.631. 15 finishers. Fastest lap: M. Biaggi (I, Suzuki), 1'40.040 (158.733 km/h).

FINAL CLASSIFICATION

1. James Toseland (GB)	Honda	415 points
2. Noriyuki Haga (J)	Yamaha	413
3. Massimiliano Biaggi (I)	Suzuki	397

4. T. Bayliss (AUS, Ducati), 372; 5. T. Corser (AUS, Yamaha), 296; 6. R. Xaus (E, Ducati), 201; 7. L. Lanzi (I, Ducati), 192; 8. R. Rolfo (I, Honda), 192; 9. M. Neukirchner (D, Suzuki), 149; 10. R. Laconi (F, Kawasaki), 137; 11. M. Fabrizio (I, Honda), 132; 12. A. Gonzales-Nieto (E, Kawasaki), 125; 13. Y. Kagayama (J, Suzuki), 116; 14. J. Smrz (CZ, Ducati), 66; 15. S. Nakatomi (J, Yamaha), 66. 34 finishers.

CONSTRUCTORS

1. Yamaha	467 points
2. Honda	439
3. Ducati	439

4. Suzuki, 419; 5. Kawasaki, 192; 6. MV-Agusta, 1. 6 finishers.

SUPERSPORT WORLD CHAMPIONSHIP

24th February - Doha - Qatar

1. K. Sofuoglu (TUR, Honda), 18 laps, 37'22.52 (155.466 km/h); 2. K. Curtain (AUS, Yamaha), 3.413; 3. K. Fujiwara (J, Honda), 6.228; 4. F. Foret (F, Kawasaki), 13.759; 5. P. Riba Cabana (E, Kawasaki), 13.857; 6. R. Harms (DK, Honda), 14.534; 7. M. Roccoli (I, Yamaha), 18.650; 8. G. Nannelli (I, Ducati), 18.776; 9. B. Veneman (NL, Suzuki), 19.291; 10. V. Kallio (SF, Suzuki), 20.595; 11. J. Fores (E, Honda), 20.817; 12. C. Jones (GB, Honda), 22.398; 13. L. Alfonsi (I, Honda), 26.903; 14. D. Salom Fuentes (E, Yamaha), 28.568; 15. G. Vizziello (I, Yamaha), 34.516. 24 finishers. Fastest lap: S. Charpentier (F, Honda), 2'02.949 (157.529 km/h).

4th March - Phillip Island - Australia

1. F. Foret (F, Kawasaki), 21 laps, 33'46.218 (165.847 km/h); 2. K. Sofuoglu (TUR, Honda), 0.704; 3. B. Parkes (AUS, Yamaha), 2.243; 4. S. Charpentier (F, Honda), 6.415; 5. K. Fujiwara (J, Honda), 15.085; 6. P. Riba Cabana (E, Kawasaki), 15.192; 7. R. Harms (DK, Honda), 22.846; 8. B. Veneman (NL, Suzuki), 24.509; 9. L. Alfonsi (I, Honda), 26.146; 10. Y. Tiberio (F, Honda), 29.413; 11. K. Curtain (AUS, Yamaha), 29.706; 12. G. Leblanc (F, Honda), 29.759; 13. S. Gimbert (F, Yamaha), 35.318; 14. C. Jones (GB, Honda), 43.153; 15. D. Salom Fuentes (E. Yamaha), 43.410. 29 finishers. Fastest lap: S. Charpentier (F, Honda), 1'34.976 (168.485 km/h).

1st April - Donington Park - Europe

1. K. Sofuoglu (TUR, Honda), 22 laps, 34'56.601 (151.971 km/h); 2. R. Harms (DK, Honda), 0.764; 3. K. Fujiwara (J, Honda), 1.343; 4. C. Jones (GB, Honda), 10.215; 5. S. Sanna (I, Honda), 12.135; 6. D. Giugliano (I, Kawasaki), 12.982; 7. Y. Tiberio (F, Honda), 16.642; 8. M. Roccoli (I, Yamaha), 16.664; 9. D. Checa (E, Yamaha), 22.965; 10. G. Nannelli (I, Ducati), 23.852; 11. S. Gimbert (F, Yamaha), 24.862; 12. G. Vizziello (I, Yamaha), 26.053; 13. D. Salom Fuentes (E, Yamaha), 26.512; 14. B. Veneman (NL, Suzuki), 29.445; 15. P. Riba Cabana (E, Kawasaki), 29.448. 22 finishers. Fastest lap: K. Fujiwara (J, Honda), 1'33.848 (154.322 km/h).

15th April - Valencia - Spain

1. K. Sofuoglu (TUR, Honda), 23 laps, 38'08.523 (144.903 km/h); 2. A. Pitt (AUS, Honda), 4.911; 3. G. Nannelli (I, Ducati), 5.200; 4. F. Foret (F, Kawasaki), 5.619; 5. B. Parkes (AUS, Yamaha), 12.776; 6. D. Salom (E, Yamaha), 14.913; 7. M. Roccoli (I, Yamaha), 15.178; 8. J. Lascorz (E, Honda), 25.356; 9. V. Kallio (SF, Suzuki), 28.454; 10. C. Jones (GB, Honda), 29.885; 11. G. Vizziello (I, Yamaha), 30.422; 12. D. Giugliano (I, Kawasaki), 30.810; 13. L. Alfonsi (I, Honda), 31.204; 14. D. Checa (E, Yamaha), 35.273; 15. S. Gimbert (F, Yamaha), 37.610. 26 finishers. Fastest lap: K. Fujiwara (J, Suzuki), 1'37.570 (147.771 km/h).

29th April - Assen - Netherlands

1. K. Sofuoglu (TUR, Honda), 21 laps, 36'04.418 (159.100 km/h); 2. A. Pitt (AUS, Honda), 4.043; 3. F. Foret (F, Kawasaki), 5.479; 4. B. Veneman (NL, Suzuki), 8.140; 5. D. Salom (E, Yamaha), 8.900; 6. S. Charpentier (F, Honda), 11.090; 7. D. Checa (E, Yamaha), 14.847; 8. V. Kallio (SF, Suzuki), 19.545; 9. G. Giugliano (I, Kawasaki), 19.880; 10. S. Martin (AUS, Yamaha), 20.084; 11. L. Alfonsi (I, Honda), 21.940; 12. P. Riba Cabana (E, Kawasaki), 26.792; 13. S. Sanna (I, Honda), 36.477; 14. M. Roccoli (I, Yamaha), 37.156; 15. A. Vos (NL, Honda), 39.459. 29 finishers. Fastest lap: K. Sofuoglu (TUR, Honda), 1'42.096 (160.614 km/h).

13th May - Monza - Italy

1. K. Sofuoglu (TUR, Honda), 16 laps, 29'44.471 (186.989 km/h); 2. F. Foret (F, Kawasaki), 3.992; 3. A. West (AUS, Yamaha), 4.043; 4. G. Nannelli (I, Ducati), 4.598; 5. B. Veneman (NL, Suzuki), 8.348; 6. K. Fujiwara (J, Honda), 10.323; 7. Y. Tiberio (F, Honda), 22.621; 8. L. Alfonsi (I, Honda), 25.613; 9. D. Salom (E, Yamaha), 25.668; 10. S. Sanna (I, Honda), 25.702; 11. M. Roccoli (I, Yamaha), 25.857; 12. P. Riba Cabana (E, Kawasaki), 26.562; 13. V. Kallio (SF, Suzuki), 26.618; 14. D. Checa (E, Yamaha), 31.074; 15. J. Lascorz (E, Honda), 33.737. 25 finishers. Fastest lap: K. Sofuoglu (TUR, Honda), 1'50.550 (188.646 km/h).

27th May - Silverstone - Great Britain

1. A. West (AUS, Yamaha), 22 laps, 39'16.245 (119.695 km/h); 2. R. Harms (DK, Honda), 33.477; 3. K. Fujiwara (J, Honda), 48.057; 4. F. Foret (F, Kawasaki), 51.777; 5. G. Vizziello (I, Yamaha), 54.295; 6. M. Lagrive (F, Honda), 1'01.579; 7. J. Fores (E, Honda), 1'37.576; 8. L. Alfonsi (I, Honda), 1'52.106; 9. J. Enjolras (F, Yamaha), 1'53.184; 10. B. Veneman (NL, Suzuki), 1 lap; 11. M. Praia (POR, Honda); 12. S. Gimbert (F, Yamaha); 13. J. Günther (D, Honda); 14. G. Leblanc (F, Honda); 15. J. Lascorz (E, Honda). 19 finishers. Fastest lap: A. West (AUS, Yamaha), 1'44.188 (123.043 km/h).

17th June - San Marino - Misano

1. A. West (AUS, Yamaha), 22 laps, 36'47.866 (149.944 km/h); 2. B. Parkes (AUS, Yamaha), 4.197; 3. K. Sofuoglu (TUR, Honda), 4.340; 4. M. Roccoli (I, Yamaha), 15.123; 5. R. Harms (DK, Honda), 18.429; 6. S. Sanna (I, Honda), 18.741; 7. J. Fores (E, Honda), 18.915; 8. K. Fujiwara (J, Honda), 25.082; 9. G. Vizziello (I, Yamaha), 30.240; 10. S. Charpentier (F, Honda), 31.633; 11. Y. Tiberio (F, Honda), 32.743; 12. M. Lagrive (F, Honda), 33.093; 13. B. Veneman (NL, Suzuki), 33.592; 14. S. Gimbert (F, Yamaha), 35.678; 15. G. Boccolini (I, Kawasaki), 37.193. 25 finishers. Fastest lap: A. West (AUS, Yamaha), 1'39.109 (151.833 km/h).

22nd July - Brno - Czech Republic

1. K. Sofuoglu (TUR, Honda), 18 laps, 38'09.132 (152.946 km/h); 2. C. Jones (GB, Honda), 11.313; 3. F. Foret (F, Kawasaki), 17.527; 4. M. Roccoli (I, Yamaha), 17.566; 5. J. Brookes (AUS, Honda), 18.109; 6. K. Fujiwara (J, Honda), 20.163; 7. D. Checa (E, Yamaha), 20.541; 8. S. Charpentier (F, Honda), 23.448; 9. S. Gimbert (F, Yamaha), 23.855; 10. B. Veneman (NL, Suzuki), 25.863; 11. V. Kallio (SF, Suzuki), 25.961; 12. J. O'Halloran (AUS, Yamaha), 32.323; 13. B. Parkes (AUS, Yamaha), 33.714; 14. L. Alfonsi (I, Honda), 34.462; 15. G. Nannelli (I, Ducati), 34.578. 25 finishers. Fastest lap: K. Sofuoglu (TUR, Honda), 2'06.089 (154.262 km/h).

5th August - Brands Hatch - Great Britain

1. B. Parkes (AUS, Yamaha), 23 laps, 34'34.688 (147.745 km/h); 2. K. Sofuoglu (TUR, Honda), 3.658; 3. M. Roccoli (I, Yamaha), 5.556; 4. R. Harms (DK, Honda), 5.573; 5. T. Hill (GB, Yamaha), 6.506; 6. F. Foret (F, Kawasaki), 10.113; 7. L. Alfonsi (I, Honda), 10.414; 8. B. Veneman (NL, Suzuki), 14.236; 9. P. Riba Cabana (E, Kawasaki), 15.978; 10. M. Lagrive (F, Honda), 18.424; 11. G. Vizziello (I, Yamaha), 25.083; 12. J. Lascorz (E, Honda), 25.154; 13. S. Gimbert (F, Yamaha), 25.442; 14. G. Leblanc (F, Honda), 28.957; 15. M. Sanchini (I, Honda), 36.557. 24 finishers. Fastest lap: B. Parkes (AUS, Yamaha), 1'29.021 (149.708 km/h).

9th September - Lausitz - Germany

1. B. Parkes (AUS, Yamaha), 23 laps, 39'25.235 (§49.305 km/h); 2. K. Sofuoglu (TUR, Honda), 1.987; 3. M. Lagrive (F, Honda), 23.435; 4. C. Jones (GB, Honda), 27.912; 5. T. Hill (GB, Yamaha), 29.090; 6. D. Checa (E, Yamaha), 29.286; 7. M. Roccoli (I, Yamaha), 29.299; 8. J. Lascorz (E, Honda), 32.114; 9. S. Charpentier (F, Honda), 39.210; 10. B. Veneman (NL, Suzuki), 41.226; 11. G. Nannelli (I, Ducati), 41.520; 12. S. Gimbert (F, Yamaha), 42.239; 13. G. Vizziello (I, Yamaha), 43.801; 14. S. Sanna (I, Honda), 53.049; 15. S. Nebel (D, Kawasaki), 56.907. 25 finishers. Fastest lap: K. Sofuoglu (TUR, Honda), 1'41.946 (150.609 km/h).

30th September - Vallelunga - Italy

1. K. Sofuoglu (TUR, Honda), 17 laps, 28'42.956 (145.989 km/h); 2. C. Jones (GB, Honda), 0.181; 3. J. Lascorz (E, Honda), 5.822; 4. B. Parkes (AUS, Yamaha), 7.063; 5. G. Vizziello (I, Yamaha), 15.412; 6. M. Lagrive (F, Honda), 17.246; 7. A. Tode (D, Honda), 18.062; 8. S. Sanna (I, Honda), 18.565; 9. S. Charpentier (F, Honda), 20.676; 10. K. Fujiwara (J, Honda), 20.909; 11. G. Gowland (GB, Honda), 24.514; 12. V. Kallio (SF, Suzuki), 25.772; 13. S. Gimbert (F, Yamaha), 26.529; 14. F. Foret (F, Kawasaki), 26.643; 15. D. Checa (E, Yamaha), 26.999. 21 finishers. Fastest lap: K. Sofuoglu (TUR, Honda), 1'40.231 (147.619 km/h).

7 October - Magny-Cours - France

1. K. Sofuoglu (TUR, Honda), 22 laps, 37'55.892 (153.501 km/h); 2. B. Parkes (AUS, Yamaha), 2.794; 3. C. Jones (GB, Honda), 11.135; 4. G. Vizziello (I, Yamaha), 11.551; 5. T. Hill (GB, Yamaha), 12.359; 6. D. Checa (E, Yamaha), 16.473; 7. J. Brookes (AUS, Honda), 17.861; 8. K. Fujiwara (J, Honda), 22.019; 9. G. Leblanc (F, Honda), 22.540; 10. M. Roccoli (I, Yamaha), 22.640; 11. S. Gimbert (F, Yamaha), 23.534; 12. A. Tode (D, Honda), 29.480; 13. S. Sanna (I, Honda), 40.098; 14. K. Foray (F, Honda), 40.283; 15. D. Perret (F, Kawasaki), 42.882. 23 finishers. Fastest lap: K. Sofuoglu (TUR, Honda), 1'42.740 (154.561 km/h).

FINAL CLASSIFICATION

1. Kenan Sofuoglu (TUR)Honda		276 points
2. Broc Parkes (AUS)	Yamaha	133
3. Fabien Foret (F)	Kawasaki	128

4. K. Fujiwara (J, Honda), 101; 5. C. Jones (GB, Honda), 94; 6. M. Roccoli (I, Yamaha), 90; 7. R. Harms (DK, Honda), 83; 8. B. Veneman (NL, Suzuki), 79; 9. A. West (AUS, Yamaha), 66; 10. G. Vizziello (I, Yamaha), 60; 11. S. Charpentier (F, Honda), 51; 12. D. Checa-Carrera (E, Yamaha), 50; 13. G. Nannelli (I, Ducati), 49; 14. M. Lagrive (F, Honda), 46; 15. L. Alfonsi (I, Honda), 45. 42 finishers.

CONSTRUCTORS

1. Honda 296 points
2. Yamaha 228
3. Kawasaki 141
4. Suzuki, 81; 5. Ducati, 49. 5 finishers.

ENDURANCE WORLD CHAMPIONSHIP

21st-22nd April - Le Mans 24 Hours - France

1. Costes/Dietrich/Neukirchner (F/F/D, Suzuki), 818 laps, 24 h 01'40.609 (142.303 km/h); 2. Philippe/Da Costa/M. Lagrive (F, Suzuki), 1'19.938; 3. Plater/Mazuecos/Giabbani (GB/E/F, Kawasaki), 1 lap; 4. Gimbert/D. Checa/Four (F/E/F, Yamaha), 7 laps; 5. Jerman/Scarnato/D. Cudlin (SLO/F/AUS, Yamaha), 8 laps; 6. F. Foray/Jonchière/Selhall (F, Suzuki), 23 laps; 7. J. Smrz/Cogan/Nebel (CZ/F/D, Yamaha), 27 laps; 8. Moreno/Lalevée/Dos Santos (F, Yamaha), 30 laps; 9. Nowland/Richards/Van Keymeulen (AUS/GB/B, Yamaha), 30 laps; 10. Molinier/Pialoux/Brière (F, Suzuki), 21 laps; 11. Jadoul/Fastre/Lannod (F, Kawasaki), 36 laps; 12. Henry/Parisse/Gueno (F, Honda), 38 laps; 13. Depoorter/Fischer/Marey (F, Yamaha), 39 laps; 14. Haquin/Labussière/Guittet (F, Kawasaki), 40 laps; 15. Penna/Le Bail/D'Anton (SF/F/F, Suzuki). 32 finishers.

5th May - 6 Hours of Albacete - Spain

1. Plater/Giabbani/Mazuecos (GB/F/E, Kawasaki), 227 laps, 6 h 01'27.173; 2. Phillipe/Lagrive/Da Costa (F, Suzuki), 1 lap; 3. Tomas/Casas/Fouloi (E/E/F, Yamaha), 3 laps; 4. Cardoso/Silva (E, Kawasaki), 5 laps; 5. Morillon/Muff/Saiger (F/CH/A, Kawasaki); 6. Tsujimura/Sugai (J, Honda), 6 laps; 7. Nigon/Millet/Contente (F, Yamaha), 7 laps; 8. Molinier/Pialoux/Brière (F, Suzuki), 8 laps; 9. Jerman/Scarnato/D. Cudlin (SLO/F/AUS, Yamaha), 9 laps; 10. Andersson/Notman/Carlberg (S/GB/S, Suzuki), 11 laps; 11. Tessari/Gruy/Ricci (I, Yamaha); 12. Chêne/Kokes/Grosjean (F/GB/CH, Kawasaki); 13. Lagrive/Genestier/Rulfo (F, Suzuki); 14. Lalevée/Dos Santos/Tachon (F, Yamaha); 15. Hutchins/Ulmann/A. Cudlin (GB/D/AUS, Kawasaki), 12 laps. 34 finishers.

29 juillet - 8 Hours of Suzuka - Japan

1. Kagayama/Akiyoshi (J, Suzuki), 216 laps, 8 h 01'35.077 (156.650 km/h); 2. Okada/C. Checa (J/E, Honda), 2'01.484; 3. Teshima/Ito (J, Honda), 1 lap; 4. Watanabé/Sakai (J, Suzuki); 5. Yamaguchi/Camier (J/GB, Honda), 4 laps; 6. K. Tokudome/Kamada (J, Honda), 5 laps; 7. Philippe/M. Lagrive/Da Costa (F, Suzuki), 6 laps; 8. Iwata/Sugai/Platacis (J/J/D, Honda); 9. Stauffer/Abé (USA/J, Yamaha); 10. Takeda/Tsuda (J, Honda), 7 laps; 11. Noda/Yamamoto (J, Honda); 12. Yunoki/Morii (J, Honda), 8 laps; 13. Eguchi/Tsuruta (J, Kawasaki), 9 laps; 14. Suzuki/T. Takahashi (J, Honda), 10 laps; 15. Nowland/Richards/Nebel (AUS/AUS/D, Yamaha). 59 finishers.

11-12 août - 24 Hours of Oschersleben - Germany

1. Philippe/M. Lagrive/Da Costa (F, Suzuki), 905 laps, 24 h 01'14.798 (139.240 km/h); 2. Plater/Giabbani/Mazuecos (GB/F/E, Kawasaki), 12 laps; 3. Jerman/Martin/D. Cudlin (SLO/AUS/AUS,Yamaha), 20 laps; 4. Morillon/Muff/Saiger (F/CH/A, Kawasaki), 27 laps; 5. Hinterreiter/Penzkofer/Barth (D, BMW), 32 laps; 6. Chêne/Kokes/Grosjean (F/GB/CH, Kawasaki), 34 laps; 7. Hutchins/A. Cudlin/Giuseppetti (GB/AUS/D, Kawasaki), 35 laps; 8. Jadoul/Fastre/La Undo (F, Kawasaki), 37 laps; 9. Öttl/Cooper/Nion (D/GB/F, BMW); 10. Nigon/J. Millet/Contente (F, Yamaha), 39 laps; 11. Seidel/Meyer/Raub (D, Honda), 45 laps; 12. Belleza/Arnoldi/Cordara (I, Yamaha), 51 laps; 13. Hepelmann/Krächter/Wrede (D, Suzuki), 52 laps ; 14. S. Hernandez/Guersilolon/Donischal (F, Suzuki), 53 laps; 15. Jaulneau/Louvel/Grilli (F, Suzuki), 62 laps. 32 finishers.

15 -16 September- Bol d'Or - France

1. D. Checa/Gimbert/Four (E/F/F, Yamaha), 801 laps, 24 h 00'21.085; 2. Philippe/M. Lagrive/Da Costa (F, Suzuki), 7 laps; 3. Costes/Dietrich/M. Neukirchner (F/F/D, Suzuki), 10 laps; 4. Nowland/Richards/Vallcañeras (AUS/AUS/E, Yamaha), 12 laps; 5. Fremy/Fastre/Leblanc (F, Yamaha), 19 laps; 6. Protat/Ribalta/Bouan (F/E/F, Honda), 22 laps; 7. J. Millet/Brivet/Auger (F, Yamaha), 29 laps; 8. F. Foray/Jonchière/Delhalle (F, Suzuki), 30 laps; 9. Molinier/Pialoux/Brière (F, Suzuki), 32 laps; 10. Hernandez/Guersillon/Ulmann (F, Suzuki), 33 laps; 11. Jaulneau/Louvel/Grilli (F, Suzuki), 37 laps; 12. Haquin/Labussière/Guittet (F, Kawasaki); 13. Jadoul/Lerat-Vanstaen/Lannoo (F/F/B, Kawasaki), 38 laps; 14. C. Michel/Fissette/Bocquet (F/B/F, Suzuki), 41 laps; 15. Devoyon/F. Jond/Monot (F, Suzuki), 47 laps. 30 finishers.

10 novembre - 8 Hours of Losail - Qatar

1. Philippe/M. Lagrive (F, Suzuki), 222 laps, 8 h 00'30.281 (157,712 km/h); 2. Martin/Jerman/D. Cudlin (AUS/SLO/AUS, Yamaha), 54.584; 3. Silva Aberola/Carrasco/Naimi (E/E/Q, Kawasasi), 3 laps; 4. Molinier/Pialoux/Brière (F, Suzuki), 5 laps; 5. Tessari/P. Ricci/Gruy (I, Yamaha); 6. J. Millet/Brivet/Fernandes (F/F/P, Yamaha); 7. Hinterreiter/Cooper/Al-Abdulla (D/GB/Q, BMW), 6 laps; 8. T. Andersson/Young/A. Notman (S/GB/GB, Suzuki); 9. Nowland/Richards/Plater (AUS/AUS/GB, Yamaha), 7 laps; 10. P. Piot/Miksovsky/Verboven (F/POL/B, Yamaha); 11. Dos Santos/Baratin/Huvier (F, Yamaha), 8 laps; 12. Devoyon/F. Jond (F, Suzuki); 13. Fisher/Kokes/Grosjean (F/GB/CH, Kawasaki); 14. Jaulneau/Louvel/Jonchière (F, Suzuki), 10 laps; 15. Hoogenraad/Velthuijzen/Van Vossel (NL, Yamaha), 15 laps. 25 finishers.

CLASSEMENT FINAL

1. Suzuki Endurance Racing Team 1	165 points
2. Kawasaki Motor France	75
3. Yamaha Austria Racing Team	74

4. Suzuki Endurance Racing Team 2, 57; 5. Endurance Moto 38, 55; 6. Yamaha Phase One Endurance, 54; 7. Yamaha GMT 94, 53; 8. Bolliger Switzerland Kawasaki, 43; 9. Team 18 Sapeurs Pompiers, 42; 10. FCC TSR, 40. 36 finishers.

THE RESULTS OF THE OTHER CHAMPIONSHIPS

FIM SUPERSTOCK CUP 1000

1st April - Donington Park - Europe

1. N. Canepa (I, Ducati), 8 laps, 12'46.272 (151.203 km/h); 2. C. Corti (I, Yamaha), 0.147; 3. D. Van Keymeulen (B, Yamaha), 0.983; 4. M. Aitchison (AUS, Suzuki), 2.355; 5. M. Baiocco (I, Yamaha), 4.199; 6. I. Dionisi (I, Suzuki), 6.635; 7. X. Siméon (B, Suzuki), 6.927; 8. A. Tode (D, Honda), 9.402; 9. S. Morais (RSA, Ducati), 10.150; 10. R. Mähr (A, Yamaha), 10.846; 11. M. Jerman (SLO, Yamaha), 11.145; 12. D. Giuseppetti (Dm Yamaha), 11.578; 13. M. Rohtlaan (EST, Honda), 11.922; 14. C. Tangre (F, Yamaha), 16.027; 15. N. Moore (USA, Ducati), 18.843. 31 finishers. Fastest lap: M. Pirro (I, Yamaha), 1'34.653 (153.009 km/h).

15th April - Valencia - Spain

1. M. Aitchison (AUS, Suzuki), 10 laps, 18'04.561 (132.939 km/h); 2. M. Pirro (I, Yamaha), 0.566; 3. N. Canepa (I, Ducati), 8.556; 4. M. Baiocco (I, Yamaha), 12.741; 5. I. Dionisi (I, Suzuki), 13.883; 6. X. Siméon (B, Suzuki), 14.606; 7. R. Mähr (A, Yamaha), 15.604; 8. M. Smrz (CZ, Honda), 23.290; 9. C. Tangre (F, Yamaha), 25.733; 10. M. Jerman (SLO, Yamaha), 26.178; 11. C. Corti (I, Yamaha), 26.428; 12. D. Sacchetti (I, MV-Agusta), 29.667; 13. S. Morais (RSA, Ducati), 33.732; 14. M. Rothlaan (EST, Honda), 34.541; 15. A. Tode (D, Honda), 41.693. 30 finishers. Fastest lap: C. Corti (I, Yamaha), 1'43.040 (139.926 km/h).

29th April - Assen - Netherlands

1. M. Pirro (I, Yamaha), 13 laps, 22'27.536 (158.195 km/h); 2. C. Corti (I, Yamaha), 0.092; 3. D. Van Keymeulen (B, Yamaha), 0.513; 4. I. Dionisi (I, Suzuki), 9.257; 5. M. Baiocco (I, Yamaha), 13.319; 6. N. Canepa (I, Ducati), 14.996; 7. B. Roberts (AUS, Ducati), 15.569; 8. X. Siméon (B, Suzuki), 15.796; 9. M. Smrz (CZ, Honda), 19.816; 10. D. Dell'Omo (I, MV-Agusta), 20.396; 11. R. Schouten (NL, Yamaha), 27.508; 12. R. Ter Braake (NL, Kawasaki), 28.404; 13. R. Mähr (A, Yamaha), 30.659; 14. C. Tangre (F, Yamaha), 30.863; 15. M. Rothlaan (EST, Honda), 35.346. 34 finishers. Fastest lap: D. Van Keymeulen (B. Yamaha), 1'42.548 (159.906 km/h).

13th May - Monza - Italy

1. M. Baiocco (I, Yamaha), 11 laps, 20'19.109 (188.173 km/h); 2. M. Aitchison (AUS, Suzuki), 0.004; 3. I. Dionisi (I, Suzuki), 0.136; 4. D. Van Keymeulen (B, Yamaha), 0.510; 5. X. Siméon (B, Suzuki), 5.949; 6. M. Jerman (SLO, Yamaha), 7.712; 7. S. Morais (RSA, Ducati), 8.132; 8. R. Mähr (A, Yamaha), 14.693; 9. D. Dell'Omo (I, MV-Agusta), 14.743; 10. N. Canepa (I, Ducati), 15.193; 11. D. Sutter (CH, Yamaha), 20.413; 12. A. Tode (D, Honda), 20.731; 13. C. Tangre (F, Yamaha), 21.135; 14. M. Rothlaan (EST, Honda), 21.565; 15. B. Roberts (AUS, Ducati), 21.794. 29 finishers. Fastest lap: M. Aitchison (AUS, Suzuki), 1'49.575 (190.324 km/h).

27th May - Silverstone - Great Britain

1. B. Roberts (AUS, Ducati), 10 laps, 17'54.454 (119.313 km/h); 2. M. Aitchison (AUS, Suzuki), 3.270; 3. M. Smrz (CZ, Honda), 9.170; 4. X. Siméon (B, Suzuki), 14.674; 5. M. Pirro (I, Yamaha), 20.559; 6. M. Baiocco (I, Yamaha), 26.737; 7. C. Tangre (F, Yamaha), 27.183; 8. L. Napoleone (I, MV-Agusta), 27.437; 9. A. Badovini (I, MV-Agusta), 32.785; 10. C. Corti (I, Yamaha), 34.403; 11. L. Baroni (I, Ducati), 37.299; 12. I. Dionisi (I, Suzuki), 37.586; 13. N. Canepa (I, Ducati), 40.906; 14. M. Jerman (SLO, Yamaha), 46.422; 15. D. Giuseppetti (D, Yamaha), 58.452. 35 finishers. Fastest lap: M. Smrz (CZ, Honda), 1'44.768 (122.362 km/h).

17th June - San Marino - Misano

1. M. Baiocco (I, Yamaha), 9 laps, 15'06.692 (149.369 km/h); 2. X. Siméon (B, Suzuki), 0.581; 3. I. Dionisi (I, Suzuki), 10.969; 4. C. Corti (I, Yamaha), 12.790; 5. N. Canepa (I, Ducati), 13.188; 6. S. Morais (RSA, Ducati), 13.527; 7. M. Aitchison (AUS, Suzuki), 14.415; 8. D. Sutter (CH, Yamaha), 17.010; 9. R. Mähr (A, Yamaha), 17.015; 10. B. Roberts (AUS, Ducati), 18.154; 11. A. Tode (D, Honda), 19.638; 12. L. Biliotti (I, MV-Agusta), 23.353; 13. M. Pirro (I, Yamaha), 23.435; 14. M. Smrz (CZ, Honda), 28.126; 15. O. Depoorter (B, Yamaha), 30.456. 31 finishers. Fastest lap: X. Siméon (B, Suzuki), 1'39.337 (151.484 km/h).

22nd July - Brno - Czech Republic

1. X. Siméon (B, Suzuki), 12 laps, 25'31.786 (152.377 km/h); 2. M. Baiocci (I, Yamaha), 0.882; 3. C. Corti (I, Yamaha), 3.644; 4. M. Aitchison (AUS, Suzuki), 3.793; 5. M. Pirro (I, Yamaha), 5.219; 6. R. Mähr (A, Yamaha), 7.111; 7. N. Canepa (I, Ducati), 7.585; 8. D. Van Keymeulen (B, Yamaha), 8.411; 9. I. Dionisi (I, Suzuki), 8.855; 10. M. Smrz (CZ, Honda), 14.651; 11. D. Giuseppetti (D, Yamaha), 17.738; 12. D. Sacchetti (I, MV-Agusta), 18.739; 13. B. Nemeth (H, Suzuki), 19.273; 14. D. Dell'Omo (I., MV-Agusta), 21.973; 15. T. Gieseler (D, Yamaha), 22.166. 28 finishers. Fastest lap: C. Corti (I, Yamaha), 2'06.093 (154.258 km/h).

5th August - Brands Hatch - Great Britain

1. N. Canepa (I, Ducati), 14 laps, 21'07.922 (147.155 km/h); 2. X. Siméon (B, Suzuki), 0.654; 3. C. Corti (I, Yamaha), 2.212; 4. M. Baiocco (I, Yamaha), 2.394; 5. B. Roberts (AUS, Ducati), 3.130; 6. A. Badovini (I, MV-Agusta), 3.566; 7. I. Dionisi (I, Suzuki), 4.640; 8. M. Aitchison (AUS, Suzuki), 5.763; 9. M. Pirro (I, Yamaha), 10.051; 10. A. Tode (D, Honda), 10.284; 11. M. Smrz (CZ, Honda), 13.642; 12. S. Morais (RSA, Ducati), 14.439; 13. D. Sacchetti (I, MV-Agusta), 20.329; 14. D. Dell'Omo (I, MV-Agusta), 25.853; 15. B. Burrell (GB, Honda), 25.994. 31 finishers. Fastest lap: M. Aitchison (AUS, Suzuki), 1'29.317 (149.212 km/h).

9 September - Lausitz - Germany

1. D. Van Keymeulen (B, Yamaha), 14 laps, 24'20.075 (147.223 km/h); 2. N. Canepa (I, Ducati), 0.194; 3. C. Corti (I, Yamaha), 0.527; 4. M. Aitchison (AUS, Suzuki), 0.556; 5. X. Siméon (B, Suzuki), 2.410; 6. A. Tode (D, Honda), 6.044; 7. A. Badovini (I, MV-Agusta), 9.485; 8. M. Baiocco (I, Yamaha), 9.658; 9. I. Dionisi (I, Suzuki), 11.106; 10. D. Giuseppetti (D, Yamaha), 13.086; 11. R. Mähr (A, Yamaha), 19.819; 12. S. Morais (RSA, Ducati), 20.115; 13. M. Smrz (CZ, Honda), 20.442; 14. D. Dell'Omo (I, MV-Agusta), 27.882; 15. M. Rothlaan (Est, Honda), 28.010.32 finishers. Fastest lap: M. Aitchison (AUS, Suzuki), 1'43.076 (148.958 km/h).

30th September - Vallelunga - Italy

1. C. Corti (I, Yamaha), 13 laps, 22'08.540 (144.781 km/h); 2. N. Canepa (I, Ducati), 0.817; 3. A. Badovini (I, MV-Agusta), 2.884; 4. B. Roberts (AUS, Ducati), 4.678; 5. X. Siméon (B, Suzuki), 7.058; 6. M. Baiocco (I, Yamaha), 8.232; 7. I. Dionisi (I, Suzuki), 8.502; 8. M. Pirro (I, Yamaha), 13.352; 9. F. Foray (F, Yamaha), 14.351; 10. R. Mähr (A, Yamaha), 15.598; 11. D. Van Keymeulen (B, Yamaha), 15.884; 12. L. Verdini (I, Yamaha), 22.010; 13. D. Sutter (CH, Yamaha), 23.933; 14. D. Giuseppetti (D, Yamaha), 24.169; 15. B. Nemeth (H, Suzuki), 27.124. 27 finishers. Fastest lap: N. Canepa (I, Ducati), 1'40.925 (146.604 km/h).

7th October - Magny-Cours - France

1. A. Badovini (I, MV-Agusta), 12 laps, 20'51.999 (152.201 km/h); 2. C. Corti (I, Yamaha), 0.084; 3. N. Canepa (I, Ducati), 1.071; 4. L. Scassa (I, MV-Agusta), 2.416; 5. M. Aitchison (AUS, Suzuki), 2.591; 6. F. Foray (F, Yamaha), 3.352; 7. I. Dionisi (I, Suzuki), 3.648; 8. D. Giuseppetti (D, Yamaha), 13.925; 9. M. Baiocco (I, Yamaha), 14.175; 10. R. Mähr (A, Yamaha), 14.346; 11. M. Smrz (CZ, Honda), 14.542; 12. M. Rothlaan (EST, Honda), 19.327; 13. A. Jenkinson (GB, Suzuki), 22.833; 14. C. Brivet (F, Suzuki), 23.348; 15. F. Millet (F, MV-Agusta), 24.159. Fastest lap: A. Badovini (I, MV-Agusta), 1'43.567 (153.327 km/h).

FINAL CLASSIFICATION

1. Niccolò Canepa (I)	Ducati	161 points
2. Claudio Corti (I)	Yamaha	157
3. Matteo Baiocco (I)	Yamaha	153

4. X. Siméon (B, Suzuki), 138; 5. M. Aitchison (AUS, Suzuki), 132; 6. I. Dionisi (I, Suzuki), 111; 7. M. Pirro (I, Yamaha), 85; 8. D. Van Keymeulen (B, Yamaha), 83; 9. A. Badovini (I, MV-Agusta), 67; 10. B. Roberts (AUS, Ducati), 65; 11. R. Mähr (A, Yamaha), 60; 12. M. Smrz (CZ, Honda), 52; 13. S. Morais (RSA, Ducati), 37; 14. A. Tode (D, Honda), 34: 15. D. Giuseppetti (D, Yamaha), 26. 37 finishers.

CONSTRUCTORS

1. Yamaha	232 points
2. Suzuki	191
3. Ducati	186

4. MV-Agusta, 93; 5. Honda, 75; 6. Kawasaki, 4. 6 finishers.

SIDE-CARS WORLD CUP

13th May - Schleiz - Germany

Race I: 1. T. Reeves/Farrance (GB, LCR-Suzuki), 3 laps, 4'38.286 (147.668 km/h); 2. Päivärinta/Karttiala (SF, LCR-Suzuki), 0.443; 3. Schlosser/Hänni (CH, LCR-Suzuki), 1.535; 4. Delannoy/Cluze (F, LCR-Suzuki), 2.102; 5. Moser/Wäfler (A/CH, LCR-Honda), 6.826; 6. Schofield/Thomas (GB, LCR-Suzuki), 18.298. 6 finishers.

Race II: 1. Schlosser/Hänni (CH, LCR-Suzuki), 22 laps, 34'01.996 (147.581 km/h); 2. Delannoy/Cluze (F, LCR-Suzuki), 6.819; 3. B. Birchall/T. Birchall (GB, LCR-Suzuki), 16.180; 4. Päivärinta/Karttiala (SF, LCR-Suzuki), 16.691; 5. Norbury/Knapton (GB, Windle-Suzuki), 21.933; 6. Gällros/Stevens (S/GB, LCR-Suzuki), 1'07.331 7. T. Reeves/Farrance (GB, LCR-Suzuki), 1'23.253; 8. Molyneux/Long (GB, Windle-Suzuki), 1'32.083; 9. Schofield/Thomas (GB, LCR-Suzuki), 1 lap; 10. Spendal/Pickering (SLO/GB, LCR-Suzuki); 11. Jones/Lake (GB, LCR-Suzuki), 2 laps; 12. Horner/Barrett (GB, LCR-Suzuki); 13. Treasure/Cornwall (AUS, LCR-Suzuki); 14. Sellar/Abrahams (AUS/NZ, LCR-Suzuki), 3 laps; 15. Percy/Hildebrand (GB/D, LCR-Suzuki), 6 laps. 15 finishers.

10th June - Brands Hatch - Great Britain

1. Päivärinta/Karttiala (SF, LCR-Suzuki), 36 laps, 29'27.897 (141.410 km/h); 2. T. Reeves/Farrance (GB, LCR-Suzuki), 1.118; 3. S. Hegarty/M. Hegarty (GB, LCR-Suzuki), 30.261; 4. Delannoy/Cluze (F, LCR-Suzuki), 36.332; 5. B. Birchall/T. Birchall (GB, LCR-Suzuki), 40.778; 6. Norbury/Knapton (GB, Windle-Suzuki), 1'02.462; 7. Moser/Wäfler (A/CH, LCR-Honda), 1 lap; 8. M. Grabmüller/B. Grabmüller (A, LCR-Suzuki); 9. Molyneux/Long (GB, Windle-Suzuki); 10. Gällros/Stevens (S/GB, LCR-Suzuki); 11. Schofield/Graham (GB, LCR-Suzuki); 12. Morrissey/P. Biggs (GB, LCR-Suzuki); 13. Schlosser/Hänni (CH, LCR-Suzuki); 14. Horner/Barrett (GB, LCR-Suzuki), 2 laps; 15. Spendal/Pickering (SLO/GB, LCR-Suzuki). 16 finishers.

30th June - Assen - Netherlands

1. Päivärinta/Karttiala (SF, LCR-Suzuki), 22'43.409; 2. T. Reeves/Farrance (GB, LCR-Suzuki), 8.818; 3. Delannoy/Cluze (F, LCR-Suzuki), 15.296; 4. B. Birchall/T. Birchall (GB, LCR-Suzuki), 39.111; 5. Schlosser/Hänni (CH, LCR-Suzuki), 49.977; 6. S. Hegarty/M. Hegarty (GB, LCR-Suzuki), 59.708; 7. M. Grabmüller/B. Grabmüller (A, LCR-Suzuki), 1'02.440; 8. Laidlow/Graham (GB, LCR-Suzuki), 1'09.682; 9. Moser/Wäfler (A/CH, LCR-Honda), 1'31.516; 10. Gatt/Randall (GB, LCR-Suzuki), 1'50.815; 11. Baer/De Haas (F/NL, LCR-Suzuki), 2'16.007; 12. Treasure/Cornwell (AUS, LCR-Suzuki), 1 lap; 13. Spendal/Pickering (SLO/GB, LCR-Suzuki); 14. Percy/Hildebrand (GB, LCR-Suzuki); 15. Green/Two (GB, LCR-Suzuki). 20 finishers.

15th July - Sachsenring - Germany

Race I: 1. T. Reeves/Farrance (GB, LCR-Suzuki), 11 laps, 16'32.615 (147.453 km/h); 2. Schlosser/Hänni (CH, LCR-Suzuki), 0.098; 3. Päivärinta/Karttiala (SF, LCR-Suzuki), 2.608; 4. Delannoy/Cluze (F, LCR-Suzuki), 2.850; 5. B. Birchall/T. Birchall (GB, LCR-Suzuki), 13.189; 6. Gatt/Randall (GB, LCR-Suzuki), 24.005; 7. Moser/Wäfler (A/CH, LCR-Honda), 25.422; 8. M. Grabmüller/B. Grabmüller (A, LCR-Suzuki), 31.108; 9. Gällros/Stevens (S/GB, LCR-Suzuki), 31.877; 10. Molyneux/Long (GB, LCR-Suzuki), 32.423; 11. Laidlow/Graham (GB, LCR-Suzuki), 34.035; 12. Spendal/Pickering (SLO/GB, LCR-Suzuki), 34.219; 13. Treasure/Cornwall (AUS, LCR-Suzuki), 1'02.806; 14. Baer/Aa Itor (F/SF, LCR-Suzuki), 1'29.072; 15. Shand/Becker (GB/D, LCR-Suzuki), 1'29.808. 17 finishers.

Race II: 1. Päivärinta/Karttiala (SF, LCR-Suzuki), 22 laps, 33'15.298 (145.714 km/h); 2. T. Reeves/Farrance (GB, LCR-Suzuki), 17.892; 3. Moser/Wäfler (A/CH, LCR-Honda), 52.325; 4. S. Hegarty/M. Hegarty (GB, LCR-Suzuki), 58.883; 5. Gällros/Stevens (S/GB, LCR-Suzuki), 1'25.156; 6. Schofield/Barrett (GB, LCR-Suzuki), 1'30.502; 7. Spendal/Pickering (SLO/GB, LCR-Suzuki), 1 lap; 8. Treasure/Cornwall (AUS, LCR-Suzuki), 1 lap; 9. Remse/Bajde (SLO, LCR-Yamaha), 1 lap; 10. Baer/Aa Itor (F/SF, LCR-Suzuki), 1 lap; 11. Shand/Becker (GB/D, LCR-Suzuki), 2 laps; 12. Horner/Charlwood (GB, LCR-Suzuki), 2 laps. 12 finishers.

22nd July - Salzburgring - Autriche

Race I: 1. T. Reeves/Farrance (GB, LCR-Suzuki), 10 laps, 14'11.261 (179.900 km/h); 2. Päivärinta/Karttiala (SF, LCR-Suzuki), 2.232; 3. Schlosser/Hänni (CH, LCR-Suzuki), 6.690; 4. B. Birchall/T. Birchall (GB, LCR-Suzuki), 9.200; 5. Delannoy/Cluze (F, LCR-Suzuki), 12.66; 6. Gatt/Randall (GB, LCR-Suzuki), 28.865; 7. Schofield/Barrett (GB, LCR-Suzuki), 31.193; 8. Moser/Wäfler (A/CH, LCR-Honda), 32.769; 9. S. Hegarty/M. Hegarty (GB, LCR-Suzuki), 48.377; 10. Gällros/Stevens (S/GB, LCR-Suzuki), 52.204; 11. Molyneux/Long (GB, LCR-Suzuki), 1'08.671; 12. Percy/Hildebrand (GB/D, LCR-Suzuki), 1'14.377; 13. Remse/Bajde (SLO, LCR-Yamaha), 1.14.559; 14. J. Jones/Ziegler (GB, LCR-Suzuki), 1 lap. 14 finishers.

Race II: 1. T. Reeves/Farrance (GB, LCR-Suzuki), 20 laps, 28'13.441 (180.900 km/h); 2. B. Birchall/T. Birchall (GB, LCR-Suzuki),0.930; 3. Schlosser/Hänni (CH, LCR-Suzuki), 5.937; 4. Delannoy/Cluze (F, LCR-Suzuki), 25.159; 5. Schofield/Barrett (GB, LCR-Suzuki), 49.916; 6. Norbury/Knapton (GB, Windle-Suzuki), 52.603; 7. S. Hegarty/M. Hegarty (GB, LCR-Suzuki), 59.727; 8. Gatt/Randall (GB, LCR-Suzuki), 1'00.357; 9. Moser/Wäfler (A/CH, LCR-Honda), 1'01.419; 10. Gällros/Stevens (S/GB, LCR-Suzuki), 1'25.250; 11. Treasure/Cornwell (AUS, LCR-Suzuki), 1 lap; 12. Molyneux/Long (GB, LCR-Suzuki); 13. Horner/Charlwood (GB, LCR-Suzuki); 14. J. Jones/Ziegler (GB, LCR-Suzuki); 15. Percy/Hildebrand (GB/D, LCR-Suzuki), 2 laps. 15 finishers.

19th August - Grobnik - Croatia

Race I: 1. T. Reeves/Farrance (GB, LCR-Suzuki), 3 laps, 4'41.453; 2. Päivärinta/Karttiala (SF, LCR-Suzuki), 0.265; 3. Schlosser/Hänni (CH, LCR-Suzuki), 6.839; 4. B. Birchall/T. Birchall (GB, LCR-Suzuki), 8.080; 5. S. Hegarty/M. Hegarty (GB, LCR-Suzuki), 8.140; 6. Molyneux/Patridge(GB, LCR-Suzuki), 11.303. 6 finishers.

Race II: 1. Delannoy/Cluze (F, LCR-Suzuki), 20 laps, 31.35.389; 2. B. Birchall/T. Birchall (GB, LCR-Suzuki), 4.575; 3. T. Reeves/Farrance (GB, LCR-Suzuki), 19.436; 4. Norbury/Knapton (GB, Windle-Suzuki), 41.251; 5. Schlosser/Hänni (CH, LCR-Suzuki), 1'07.875; 6. Gällros/Stevens (S/GB, LCR-Suzuki), 1'28.658; 7. Spendal/Long (CZ/GB, LCR-Suzuki). 1'28.848; 8. Moser/Wäfler (A/CH, LCR-Honda), 1.30.402; 9. Ducouret/Gandois (F, LCR-Suzuki), 1 lap; 10. Percy/Hildebrand (GB/D, LCR-Suzuki); 11. Green/Two (GB, LCR-Honda), 2 laps. 11 finishers.

9th September - Le Mans - France

1. T. Reeves/Farrance (GB, LCR-Suzuki), 15 laps, 25'52.847 (145,360 km/h); 2. B. Birchall/T. Birchall (GB, LCR-Suzuki), 0.938; 3. Päivärinta/Karttiala (SF, LCR-Suzuki), 2.962; 4. Delannoy/Cluze (F, LCR-Suzuki), 13.255; 5. Schlosser/Hänni (CH, LCR-Suzuki), 21.461; 6. Molyneux/Sayle (GB, LCR-Suzuki), 41.296; 7. Gatt/Randall (GB, LCR-Suzuki), 45.985; 8. S. Hegarty/M. Hegarty (GB, LCR-Suzuki), 49.594; 9. Moser/Wäfler (A/CH, LCR-Honda), 50.679; 10. Schoffield/Barrett (GB, LCR-Suzuki), 51.706; 11. M. Grabmüller/B. Grabmüller (A, LCR-Suzuki), 1'10.260; 12. Le Bail/Huet (F, LCR-Yamaha), 1'30.457; 13. Ducouret/Gandois (F, LCR-Suzuki), 1'40.282; 14. Horner/Charlwood (GB, LCR-Suzuki), 1'40.619; 15. Treasure/Endeveled (AUS/NL, LCR-Suzuki), 1 lap. 19 finishers.

FINAL CLASSIFICATION

1. T. Reeves/P. Farrance (GB)	LCR-Suzuki	235 points
2. P. Päivärinta/T. Karttiala (SF)	LCR-Suzuki	180
3. M. Schlosser/A. Hänni (CH)	LCR-Suzuki	145

4. S. Delannoy/G. Cluze (F, LCR-Suzuki), 144; 5. B. Birchall/T. Birchall (GB, LCR-Suzuki), 137; 6. J.

Moser/U. Wäfler (A/CH, LCR-Honda), 86; 7. S. Hegarty/M. Hegarty (GB, LCR-Suzuki), 80; 8. B. Gällros/W. Stevens (S/GB, LCR-Suzuki), 72; 9. S. Norbury/P. Knapton (GB, Windle-Suzuki), 58; 10. A. Schofield/Thomas/L. Barrett (GB, LCR-Suzuki), 58; 11. D. Molyneux/P. Long/M. Partridge/D. Sayle (GB, LCR-Suzuki), 55; 12. R. Gatt/P. Randall (GB, LCR-Suzuki), 44; 13. M. Spendal/M. Pickering/P. Long (SLO/GB/GB, LCR-Suzuki), 35; 14. A. Treasure/B. Cornwell/K. Endeveled (AUS/AUS/NL, LCR-Suzuki), 32; 15. M. Grabmüller/B. Grabmüller (A, LCR-Suzuki), 30. 28 finishers.

EUROPEAN CHAMPIONSHIP

125 cc

20th May- Vallelunga - Italy

1. Lamborghini (I, Aprilia), 16 laps, 28'51.728 (136.705 km/h); 2. F. Biaggi (I, Aprilia), 0.099; 3. Gyorfi (H, Aprilia), 1.112; 4. Palumbo (I, Aprilia), 2.430; 5. Miralles (E, Aprilia), 5.344; 6. Mosca (I, Aprilia), 12.715; 7. G. Gnani (I, Gnani), 23.445; 8. A. Rodriguez (E, Aprilia), 25.749; 9. Siegert (D, Aprilia), 38.338; 10. Manfrinati (I, Honda), 39.529; 11. Passeri (I, Aprilia), 45.390; 12. Mattiello (I, Honda), 45.915; 13. Y. Freymond (CH, Honda), 54.905; 14. Pavan (I, Honda), 1'06.352; 15. Krajci (SLO, Honda), 1'37.887. 16 finishers.

17th June - Rijeka - Croatia

1. Gyorfi (H, Aprilia), 15 laps, 24'08.503 (155.382 km/h); 2. Conti (I, Honda), 3.315; 3. G. Gnani (I, Gnani), 3.775; 4. Vivarelli (I, Honda), 9.156; 5. Caiani (CH, Honda), 25.193; 6. Siegert (D, Aprilia), 33.156; 7. Y. Freymond (CH, Honda), 34.919; 8. Kornfeil (CZ, Honda), 34.963; 9. Pavan (I, Honda), 40.260; 10. Nesic (SRB, Honda), 40,330; 11. Krajci (SLO, Honda), 57.617; 12. Attila (H, FGR), 58.534; 13. Majek (CZ, FGR), 1'09.133; 14. K. Pesek (CZ, Honda), 1'33.109; 15. Kovacs (H, Honda), 1 lap.

8th July- Most - Czech Republic

1. G. Gnani (I, Gnani), 30'19.951; 2. Vivarelli (I, Honda), 0.187; 3. Sembera (CZ, Honda), 12.305; 4. Conti (I, Honda), 12.401; 5. Pavan (I, Honda), 28.161; 6. Kornfeil (CZ, Honda), 40.157; 7. Fagerhaug (N, Honda), 41.171; 8. Manfrinati (I, Honda), 54.256; 9. Y. Freymond (CH, Honda), 54.262; 10. Siegert (D, Aprilia), 54.421; 11. Touskova (CZ, Honda), 57.681; 12. Nesic (SRB, Honda), 57.713; 13. Krajci (SK, Honda), 1'32.742; 14. K. Pesek (CZ, Honda), 3 laps. 14 finishers.

29th July- Karlskoga - Sweden

1. Gyorfi (H, Aprilia), 28 laps, 32'33.847 (123.817 km/h); 2. Conti (I, Honda), 0.161; 3. Vivarelli (I, Honda), 1.252; 4. Karlsen (N, Honda), 8.386; 5. Gull (S, Honda), 8.740; 6. G. Gnani (I, Gnani), 33.210; 7. Kuparinen (SF, Honda), 45.854; 8. Y. Freymond (CH, Honda), 46.604; 9. Sembera (CZ, Honda), 46.732; 10. Siegert (D, Aprilia), 1'06.984; 11. Kainulainen (SF, Honda), 1'08.126; 12. Carlsson (S, Honda), 1 lap; 13. Nielsen (DK, Honda); 14. Möller (DK, Honda); 15. Berntsson (S, Honda), 2 laps. 16 finishers.

21st October- Cartagena - Spain

1. Mossey (GB, Aprilia), 20 laps, 33'32.056 (125,450 km/h); 2. Saez (E, Aprilia), 1.644; 3. J. Miralles Jnr (E, Aprilia), 21.569; 4. A. Rodriguez (E, Aprilia), 27.104; 5. Vivarelli (I, Honda), 27.313; 6. Debise (F, Honda), 32.514; 7. Conti (I, Honda), 41.978; 8. Hübsch (E, Aprilia), 42.789; 9. Borch (N, Honda), 42.938; 10. Kreuziger (D, Aprilia), 43.072; 11. Gyorfi (H, Aprilia), 57.955; 12. Gnani (I, Gnani), 58.212; 13. Sembera (CZ, Honda), 58.376; 14. R.-R. Fernandez (E, Aprilia), 1'19.516; 15. Muñoz (E, Aprilia), 1'32.614. 22 finishers.

FINAL CLASSIFICATION

1. Alen Gyorfi (H)	Aprilia	71 points
2. Gabriele Gnani (I)	Gnani	64
3. Michele Conti (I)	Honda	62

4. N. Vivarelli (I, Honda), 60; 5. T. Siegert (D, Aprilia), 29; 6. J. Miralles Jnr (E, Aprilia), 27; 7. Y. Freymond (CH, Honda), 27; 8. L. Sembera (CZ, Honda), 26; 9. L. Mossey (GB, Aprilia), 25; 10. F. Lamborghini (I, Aprilia), 25; 11. A. Rodriguez (E, Aprilia), 21; 12. D. Saez Romas (E, Aprilia), 20; 13. F. Mandatori (I, Aprilia), 20; 14. F. Pavan (I, Honda), 20; 15. J. Knorfeil (CZ, Honda), 18. 42 finishers.

250 cc

20th May - Vallelunga - Italy

1. Molina (E, Aprilia), 19 laps, 33'10.166 (141.256 km/h); 2. Petrini (I, Honda), 10.553; 3. Smees (NL, Aprilia), 20.040; 4. Marchetti (I, Aprilia), 45.135; 5. Markham (GB, Yamaha), 49.790; 6. Roelofs (NL, Honda), 49.979; 7. Sawford (GB, Yamaha), 53.932; 8. Kohlinger (D, Honda), 54.327; 9. Orlandini (I, Yamaha), 54.772; 10. Kenchington (GB, Yamaha), 55.157; 11. Pavone (I, Aprilia), 1'01.107; 12. Binucci (I, Yamaha), 1'01.245; 13. Lucchetti (I, Aprilia), 1'10.580; 14. Heierli (CH, Honda), 1'11.977; 15. Anhetti (I, Yamaha), 1'21.728. 24 finishers.

17th June - Rijeka - Croatia

1. Molina (E, Aprilia), 17 laps, 26'18.110 (161.367 km/h); 2. Menghi (I, Aprilia), 24.887; 3. Smees (NL, Aprilia), 25'149; 4. Petrini (I, Honda), 39.283; 5. Walther (D, Honda), 48.772; 6. Markham (GB, Yamaha), 51.373; 7. Pavone (I, Aprilia), 51.503; 8. Kohlinger (D, Honda), 1'08.084; 9. Orlandini (I, Yamaha), 1'08.390; 10. Heierli (CH, Honda), 1'15.733; 11. J. Mayer (CZ, Honda), 1'26.276; 12. Binucci (I, Honda), 1'27.908; 13. Senk (SLO, Honda), 1'27.982; 14. Engerisser (A, Yamaha), 1'38.319; 15. Leonhardt (D, Aprilia), 1 lap. 15 finishers.

8th July - Most - Czech Republic

1. Molina (E, Aprilia), 30'29.163; 2. Petrini (I, Honda), 3.967; 3. Sommer (D, Honda), 12.544; 4. Smees (NL, Aprilia), 27.042; 5. Menghi (I, Aprilia), 37.046; 6. Markham (GB, Yamaha), 37.221; 7. Gevers (NL, Aprilia), 57.294; 8. Velthuijzen (NL, Honda), 1'11.465; 9. Kohlinger (D, Honda), 1'12.173; 10. Lawrence (GB, Aprilia), 1'16.342; 11. Binucci (I, Honda), 1'16.653; 12. Heierli (CH, Honda), 1'17.738; 13. Orlandini (I, Yamaha), 1'26.000; 14. J. Mayer (CZ, Honda), 1'26.218; 15. Voit (D, Honda), 1 lap. 22 finishers.

29th July - Karlskoga - Sweden

1. Watz (S, ISR-Honda), 32 laps, 36'26.838 (126.429 km/h); 2. Petrini (I, Honda), 5.169; 3. Smees (NL, Aprilia), 5.262; 4. Gevers (NL, Aprilia), 33.275; 5. Walther (D, Honda), 38.379; 6. Dobrich (S, Aprilia), 39.368; 7. Menghi (I, Aprilia), 49.245; 8. Roelofs (NL, Honda), 49.341; 9. Lawrence (GB, Aprilia), 59.902; 10. Köhlinger (D, Honda), 1 lap; 11. Corneliusson (S, Honda); 12. Larsson (S, Honda), 2 laps; 13. Sjögren (S, Honda); 14. Robin (S, Aprilia); 15. Ahlberg (SF, Honda). 15 finishers.

21st October - Cartagena - Spain

1. Markham (GB, Yamaha), 24 laps, 43'42.265 (115,510 km/h); 2. Sommer (D, Honda), 4.317; 3. Smees (NL, Aprilia), 16.990; 4. Walther (D, Honda), 45.336; 5. Menghi (I, Aprilia), 52.753; 6. Roelofs (NL, Honda), 1'05.860; 7. Köhlinger (D, Honda), 1'11.116; 8. Petrini (I, Honda), 1'13.410; 9. Molina (E, Aprilia), 1'13.512; 10. Dickinson (GB, Honda), 1'16.595; 11. Oid (D, Honda), 1'16.757; 12. Lawrence (GB, Aprilia), 1'16.944; 13. Heierli (CH, Honda), 1 lap. 13 finishers.

FINAL CLASSIFICATION

1. Alvaro Molina (E)	Aprilia	82 points
2. Marco Petrini (I)	Honda	81
3. Hans Smees (NL)	Aprilia	77

4. T. Markham (GB, Yamaha), 56; 5. O. Menghi (I, Aprilia), 51; 6. O. Köhlinger (D, Honda), 38; 7. J. Sommer (D, Honda), 36; 8. T. Walther (D, Honda), 35; 9. J. Roelofs (NL, Honda), 28; 10. F. Watz (S, ISR), 25; 11. R. Gevers (NL, Aprilia), 22; 12. E. Orlandini (I, Yamaha), 17; 13. L. Lawrence (GB, Aprilia), 17; 14. R. Heierli (CH, Honda), 15; 15. M. Pavone (I, Aprilia), 14. 34 finishers.

SUPERSPORT 600

20th May- Vallelunga - Italy

1. Marrancone (I, Yamaha), 19 laps, 32'49.116 (142.766 km/h); 2. Giansanti (I, Yamaha), 5.252; 3. Giugovaz (I, Triumph), 9.255; 4. F. Gentile (I, Triumph), 25.461; 5. Ruggiero (I, Yamaha), 40.186; 6. Tarizzo (I, Honda), 46.541; 7. Filla (CZ, Yamaha), 49.214; 8. Rous (CZ, Yamaha), 50.448; 9. Cajback (S, Honda), 56.416; 10. Bostjan (SLO, Yamaha), 56.644; 11. Vigilucci (I, Honda), 59.821; 12. Roncoroni (I, Yamaha), 1'01.796; 13. Pascota (I, Yamaha), 1'17.996; 14. Anello (I, Honda), 1'20.210; 15. Valjan (HR, Yamaha), 1'22.424. 16 finishers.

17th June - Rijeka - Croatia

1. Tarizzo (I, Honda), 17 laps, 26'27.389 (160.693 km/h); 2. Valjan (HR, Yamaha), 0.062; 3. Radek Rous (CZ, Yamaha), 0.640; 4. Pintar (SLO, Yamaha), 0.772; 5. Filla (CZ, Yamaha), 14.969; 6. Bittman (CZ, Honda), 15.666; 7. Marrancone (I, Yamaha), 15.976; 8. Ruggiero (I, Yamaha), 41.073; 9. Pasciuta (ROU, Yamaha), 48.830; 10. Pagnoni (I, Honda), 48.891; 11. Roncoroni (I, Yamaha), 1'04.622; 12. De Marco (I, Honda), 1'15.637; 13. Broz (CZ, Kawasaki), 1'34.646; 14. Kraplikhin (RUS, Yamaha), 1 lap. 14 finishers.

8th July- Most - Czech Republic

1. Radek Rous (CZ, Yamaha), 35'44.445; 2. Marrancone (I, Yamaha), 0.356; 3. Filla (CZ, Yamaha), 6.363; 4. Tarizzo (I, Honda), 12.788; 5. Bittman (CZ, Honda), 13.158; 6. Manici (I, Yamaha), 31.702; 7. Cajback (S, Honda), 31.796; 8. Roncoroni (I, Yamaha), 44.488; 9. Pasciuta (ROU, Yamaha), 1'06.329; 10. Jezek (CZ, Kawasaki), 1'08.757; 11. Ruggiero (I, Yamaha), 1'19.584; 12. Carniglia (I, Kawasaki), 1'25.738; 13. Broz (CZ, Kawasaki), 1'29.066; 14. Valjan (HR, Yamaha), 1'29.077; 15. Domke (D, Honda), 1 lap. 16 finishers.

29th July- Karlskoga - Sweden

1. Kubberöd (N, Honda), 32 laps, 36'14.564 (127.143 km/h); 2. Pekkanen (SF, Triumph), 5.830; 3. Cajback (S, Honda), 21.247; 4. Filla (CZ, Yamaha), 24.214; 5. Solberg (N, Yamaha), 25.465; 6. Tarizzo (I, Honda), 25.717; 7. Rönning (N, Yamaha), 37.874; 8. Aarnio (SF, Yamaha), 37.944; 9. Valjan (HR, Yamaha), 41.045; 10. Roncoroni (I, Yamaha), 46.302; 11. Marrancone (I, Yamaha), 53.647; 12. Rado. Rous (CZ, Yamaha), 1'04.311; 13. Nieminen (SF, Suzuki), 1'07.065; 14. Bostjan (SLO, Yamaha), 1 lap; 15. Ruggiero (I, Yamaha). 15 finishers.

21st October- Cartagena - Spain

1. Pellizzon (I, Triumph), 24 laps, 39'54.078 (126.520 km/h); 2. Perret (F, Honda), 2.765; 3. Giugovaz (I, Triumph), 3.878; 4. Tarizzo (I, Honda), 12.395; 5. Marrancone (I, Yamaha), 12.859; 6. Filla (CZ, Yamaha), 26.125; 7. Tirado Martin (E, Yamaha), 29.820; 8. Roncoroni (I, Yamaha), 48.920; 9. Azcona Zapico (E, Honda), 49.355; 10. Pintar (SLO, Yamaha), 59.314; 11. Kubberöd (N, Honda), 59.595; 12. Valjan (HR, Yamaha), 1 lap; 13. Broz (CZ, Kawasaki); 14. Pozdeneev (RUS, Yamaha), 2 laps. 14 finishers.

FINAL CLASSIFICATION

1. Guglielmo Tarizzo (I)	Honda	71 points
2. Danilo Marrancone (I)	Yamaha	70
3. Michal Filla (CZ)	Yamaha	59

4. Rade. Rous (CZ, Yamaha), 53; 5. L. Valjan (HR, Yamaha), 34; 6. D. Giugovaz (I, Triumph), 32; 7. N. Cajback (S, Honda), 32; 8. M. Roncoroni (I, Yamaha), 31; 9. D. Kubberöd (N, Honda), 30; 10. B. Pintar (SLO, Yamaha), 27; 11. F. Pellizzon (I, Triumph), 25; 12. V. Bittman (CZ, Honda), 21; 13. D. Perret (F, Honda), 20; 14. P. Pekkanen (SF, Triumph), 20; 15. M. Giansanti (I, Yamaha), 20. 36 finishers.

STOCKSPORT 600

20th May- Vallelunga - Italy

1. Petrucci (I, Yamaha), 19 laps, 33'19.909 (140.568 km/h); 2. Meschini (I, Yamaha), 20.265; 3. Spigariol (I, Yamaha), 21.819; 4. Casadei (RSM, Yamaha), 24.760; 5. Chmielewski (POL, Suzuki), 25.229; 6. Spjeldnes (N, Yamaha), 34.020; 7. Lovino (I, Honda), 37.170; 8. Szkopek (POL, Yamaha), 37.468; 9. Zappa (I, Honda), 39.030; 10. Menghi (I, Yamaha), 40.090; 11. Erbacci (I, Yamaha), 40.194; 12. Guerra (E, Yamaha), 40.522; 13. R. Rossi (I, Yamaha), 55.447; 14. Bezshlyaga (RUS, Yamaha), 1'08.258; 15. Svitok (SLO, Kawasaki), 1'12.306. 23 finishers.

17th June - Rijeka - Croatia

1. Veghini (I, Triumph), 17 laps, 26'46.385 (158.792 km/h); 2. Emili (I, Kawasaki), 0.069; 3. Spigariol (I, Yamaha), 4.631; 4. Di Vora (I, Yamaha), 6.807; 5. Casadei (RSM. Yamaha), 16.339; 6. Kemenovic (CZ, Honda), 29.159; 7. Spjeldnes (N, Yamaha), 29.562; 8. Chmielewski (POL, Suzuki), 36.067; 9. Kalab (CZ, Yamaha), 36.074; 10. Erbacci (I, Yamaha), 39.259; 11. Menghi (I, Yamaha). 52.890; 12. Zappa (I, Honda), 52.900; 13. Bezshlyaga (RUS, Yamaha), 57.601; 14. Vrdoljak (HR, Honda), 1'11.634; 15. Arnautovic (SLO, Kawasaki), 1'11.643. 19 finishers.

8th July- Most - Czech Republic

1. Pellizzon (I, Triumph), 36'10.749; 2. Barone (I, Honda), 6.201; 3. Vostarek (CZ, Honda), 11.710; 4. Casadei (I, Yamaha), 24.477; 5. Spjeldnes (N, Yamaha), 32.726; 6. Ouda (CZ, Honda), 34.669; 7. Spigariol (I, Yamaha), 39.179; 8. I. Kalab (CZ, Yamaha), 39.339; 9. Drobny (CZ, Yamaha), 48.555; 10. Monto (E, Yamaha), 48.816; 11. Holubec (CZ, Yamaha), 48.930; 12. Menghi (I, Yamaha), 51.003; 13. Bezshlyaga (RUS, Yamaha), 56.908; 14. Huylebroeck (B, Triumph), 1'23.493; 15. Dokoupil (CZ, Honda), 1'38.793. 25 finishers.

29th July- Karlskoga - Sweden

1. Spjeldnes (N, Yamaha), 32 laps, 36'16.133 (127.051 km/h); 2. Pellizzon (I, Triumph), 15.170; 3. Chmielevski (POL, Suzuki), 21.708; 4. Johansson (S, Yamaha), 26.006; 5. Spigariol (I, Yamaha), 47.843; 6. Casadei (RSM, Yamaha), 50.300; 7. Rönning (N, Yamaha), 51.074; 8. J. Andersson (S, Yamaha), 1'01.699; 9. O. Persson (S, Honda), 1'04.330; 10. S. Harms (DK, Honda), 1'05.784; 11. J. Persson (S, Honda), 1 lap; 12. Huylebroeck (B, Triumph); 13. Hakansson (S, Honda); 14. Rasmussen (DK, Kawasaki); 15. Dizerens (N, Yamaha). 21 finishers.

21st October- Cartagena - Spain

1. Spjeldnes (N, Yamaha), 23 laps, 48'33.303 (99,640 km/h); 2. Ballestreros (E, Suzuki), 5.289; 3. F. Menghi (I, Yamaha), 10.240; 4. Masoni (I, Triumph), 13.978; 5. Capel (E, Yamaha), 40.900; 6. I. Kalab (CZ, Yamaha), 51.049; 7. Plassen (N, Suzuki), 1 lap; 8. Monto (E, Yamaha); 9. Chmielevski (POL, Suzuki); 10. Dizerens (N, Yamaha); 11. Spigariol (I, Yamaha), 2 laps. 11 finishers.

FINAL CLASSIFICATION

1. Helge Spjeldnes (N)	Yamaha	80 points
2. Olmo Spigariol (I)	Yamaha	57
3. Michele Casadei (I)	Yamaha	47

4. F. Pellizzon (I, Triumph), 45; 5. A. Chmielevski (POL, Suzuki), 42; 6. F. Menghi (I, Yamaha), 31; 7. D. Veghini (I, Triumph), 25; 8. D. Petrucci (I, Yamaha), 25; 9. I. Kalab (CZ, Yamaha), 25; 10. S. Ballestreros (E, Suzuki), 20; 11. G. Barone (I, Honda), 20; 12. M. Emili (I, Kawasaki), 20; 13. F. Meschini (I, Yamaha), 20; 14. P. Vostarek (CZ, Honda), 16; 15. M.-A. Monto (E, Yamaha), 14. 42 finishers.

SUPERSTOCK 600

1st April - Donington Park - Europe

1. Magnoni (I, Yamaha), 10 laps, 16'16.888 (148.254 km/h); 2. Antonelli (I, Honda), 0.528; 3. Colucci (I, Ducati), 0.858; 4. Barrier (F, Yamaha), 5.043; 5. Berger (F, Yamaha), 5.813; 6. Ten Napel (NL, Yamaha), 13.795; 7. Gines (F, Yamaha), 14.052; 8. Savary (CH, Yamaha), 17.746; 9. Costantini (I, Honda), 19.978; 10. G. Rea (GB, Suzuki), 23.865; 11. Black (GB, Yamaha), 23.978; 12. Sigloch (D, Yamaha), 24.109; 13. Barone (I, Honda), 27.954; 14. Junod (CH, Kawasaki), 29.050; 15. Beretta (I, Suzuki), 29.574. 28 finishers.

15th April - Valencia - Spain

1. Berger (F, Yamaha), 11 laps, 20'28.806 (129.067 km/h); 2. Ten Napel (NL, Yamaha), 9.517; 3. G. Rea (GB, Suzuki), 10.893; 4. Sigloch (D, Yamaha), 12.592; 5. Colucci (I, Ducati), 12.889; 6. Beretta (I, Suzuki), 28.944; 7. Magnoni (I, Yamaha), 30.303; 8. La Marra (I, Honda), 31.130; 9. Antonelli (I, Honda), 31.879; 10. Pedro Subirats (E, Yamaha), 38.671; 11. Savary (CH, Yamaha), 45.870; 12. Tirsgaard (DK, Suzuki), 52.047; 13. Lonbois (B, Suzuki), 52.237; 14. Srdanov (NL, Yamaha), 52.870; 15. Sembera (CZ, Honda), 53.057. 28 finishers.

THE RESULTS OF THE OTHER CHAMPIONSHIPS

29th April - Assen - Netherlands
1. Antonelli (I, Honda), 10 laps, 17'45.988 (153.829 km/h); 2. Barrier (F, Yamaha), 0.156; 3. Berger (F, Yamaha) 0.572; 4. Black (GB, Yamaha), 0.691; 5. Magnoni (I, Yamaha), 5.776; 6. Ten Napel (NL, Yamaha), 7.373; 7. Savary (CH, Yamaha), 7.666; 8. Gines (F, Yamaha), 7.935; 9. Sigloch (D, Yamaha), 8.245; 10. Sembera (CZ, Honda), 8.459; 11. Beretta (I, Suzuki), 10.979; 12. Vostarek (CZ, Honda), 12.181; 13. Pedro Subirats (E, Yamaha), 17.887; 14. Barone (I, Honda), 25.874; 15. Junod (CH, Kawasaki), 26.016. 30 finishers.

13th May- Monza - Italy
1. Magnoni (I, Yamaha), 8 laps, 15'28.902 (179.608 km/h); 2. Black (GB, Yamaha), 0.079; 3. Bussolotti (I, Yamaha), 0.232; 4. Barrier (F, Yamaha), 0.426; 5. Colucci (I, Ducati), 0.493; 6. Berger (F, Yamaha), 0.632; 7. Antonelli (I, Honda), 1.220; 8. Sigloch (D, Yamaha), 1.483; 9. Ten Napel (NL, Yamaha), 5.284; 10. Gines (F, Yamaha), 5.396; 11. Savary (CH, Yamaha), 10.013; 12. Costantini (I, Honda), 15.779; 13. Tirsgaard (DK, Suzuki), 19.736; 14. G. Rea (GB, Suzuki), 19.934; 15. Pedro Subirats (E, Yamaha), 19.999. 26 finishers.

27th May- Silverstone - Great Britain
Race cancelled due to weather conditions.

17th June - San Marino - Misano
1. Berger (F, Yamaha), 10 laps, 17'04.734 (146.848 km/h); 2. Magnoni (I, Yamaha), 0.596; 3. Bussolotti (I, Yamaha), 7.742; 4. Gregorini (I, Yamaha), 7.903; 5. Antonelli (I, Honda), 8.293; 6. Tirsgaard (DK, Suzuki), 14.342; 7. Costantini (I, Honda), 14.711; 8. Sigloch (D, Yamaha), 14.950; 9. Beretta (I, Suzuki), 15.423; 10. Savary (CH, Yamaha), 18.944; 11. Ten Napel (NL, Yamaha), 19.259; 12. Vostarek (CZ, Honda), 19.289; 13. Sembera (CZ, Honda), 28.474; 14. Lonbois (B, Suzuki), 28.793; 15. G. Rea (GB, Suzuki), 30.060. 27 finishers.

22nd July- Brno - Czech Republic
1. Colucci (I, Ducati), 6 laps, 13'02.268 (149.188 km/h); 2. Barrier (F, Yamaha), 0.190; 3. Berger (F, Yamaha), 2.847; 4. Ten Napel (NL, Yamaha), 3.121; 5. Antonelli (I, Honda), 6.966; 6. Black (GB, Yamaha), 10.484; 7. Savary (CH, Yamaha), 10.870; 8. Magnoni (I, Yamaha), 11.283; 9. Costantini (I, Honda), 11.505; 10. Vostarek (CZ, Honda), 11.716; 11. G. Rea (GB, Suzuki), 12.039; 12. Bonastre (E, Yamaha), 12.919; 13. Leeson (RSA, Suzuki), 13.078; 14. Jezek (CZ, Kawasaki), 14.079; 15. Beretta (I, Suzuki), 14.358. 32 finishers.

5th August - Brands Hatch - Great Britain
Race I: 1. Berger (F, Yamaha), 11 laps, 16'59.101 (143.851 km/h); 2. Colucci (I, Ducati), 0.617; 3. Magnoni (I, Yamaha), 2.777; 4. Antonelli (I, Hona), 2.877; 5. Black (GB, Yamaha), 5.582; 6. Barrier (F, Yamaha), 5.752; 7. Savary (CH, Yamaha), 6.371; 8. Lonbois (B, Suzuki), 9.989; 9. Sembera (CZ, Honda), 11.984; 10. Beretta (I, Suzuki), 12.746; 11. G. Rea (GB, Suzuki), 13.331; 12. Hunt (GB, Honda), 14.602; 13. Barone (I, Honda), 18.665; 14. Gault (GB, Suzuki), 21.843; 15. Jezek (CZ, Kawasaki), 22.106. 25 finishers.
Race II: 1. Berger (F, Yamaha), 11 laps, 16'56.852 (144.170 km/h); 2. Antonelli (I, Honda), 0.308; 3. Black (GB, Yamaha), 2.337; 4. Magnoni (I, Yamaha), 10.998; 5. Savary (CH, Yamaha), 11.615; 6. Lonbois (B, Suzuki), 11.785; 7. Beretta (I, Suzuki), 14.004; 8. Costantini (I, Honda), 14.079; 9. Bonastre (E, Yamaha), 14.255; 10. Ten Napel (NL, Yamaha), 14.414; 11. Barone (I, Honda), 16.344; 12. Hunt (GB, Honda), 16.513; 13. G. Rea (GB, Suzuki), 22.585; 14. Vostarek (CZ, Honda), 24.610; 15. Leonov (RUS, Yamaha), 26.250. 26 finishers.

9th September- Lausitz - Germany
1. Lonbois (B, Suzuki), 11 laps, 23'35.097 (119.352 km/h); 2. Black (GB, Yamaha), 5.506; 3. Jezek (CZ, Kawasaki), 45.007; 4. Hellyer (RSA, Kawasaki), 46.247; 5. Gines (F, Yamaha), 58.007; 6. Berger (F, Yamaha), 1'00.471; 7. Hunt (GB, Honda), 1'02.387; 8. Guerra (E, Yamaha), 1'04.751; 9. Beretta (I, Suzuki), 1'08.785; 10. Antonelli (I, Honda), 1'35.456; 11. Johansson (S, Yamaha), 1'41.049; 12. Magnoni (I, Yamaha), 1'47.220; 13. Srdanov (NL, Yamaha), 1'48.535; 14. La Marra (I, Honda), 1'49.272; 15. Ten Napel (NL, Yamaha), 1'50.365. 18 finishers.

30th September- Vallelunga - Italy
1. Ten Napel (NL, Yamaha), 10 laps, 17'20.455 (142.207 km/h); 2. Antonelli (I, Honda), 0.879; 3. Berger (F, Yamaha), 1.627; 4. Beretta (I, Suzuki), 4.889; 5. Magnoni (I, Yamaha), 4.995; 6. Bussolotti (I, Yamaha), 5.065; 7. Barrier (F, Yamaha), 12.362; 8. Petrucci (I, Yamaha), 12.677; 9. Black (GB, Yamaha), 13.041; 10. Lonbois (B, Suzuki), 13.243; 11. Savary (CH, Yamaha), 13.760; 12. Gines (F, Yamaha), 13.791; 13. Sembera (CZ, Honda), 16.821; 14. Morelli (I, Yamaha), 17.087; 15. Vostarek (CZ, Honda), 18.205. 30 finishers.

7th October- Magny-Cours - France
1. Berger (F, Yamaha), 10 laps, 17'40.422 (149.748 km/h); 2. Antonelli (I, Honda), 2.522; 3. Black (GB, Yamaha), 7.775; 4. Magnoni (I, Yamaha), 12.461; 5. Ten Napel (NL, Yamaha), 12.617; 6. Barrier (F, Yamaha), 12.670; 7. Savary (CH, Yamaha), 12.970; 8. Beretta (I, Suzuki), 13.970; 9. Lonbois (B, Suzuki), 14.396; 10. Pouhair (F, Yamaha), 15.118; 11. Vostarek (CZ, Honda), 15.449; 12. Maurin (F, Kawasaki), 19.413; 13. G. Rea (GB, Suzuki), 19.734; 14. Sembera (CZ, Honda), 27.240; 15. Leeson (RSA, Suzuki), 27.919. 28 finishers.

FINAL CLASSIFICATION

1. Maxime Berger (F)	Yamaha	204 points
2. Andrea Antonelli (I)	Honda	162
3. Michele Magnoni (I)	Yamaha	155

4. G. Black (GB, Yamaha), 118; 5. R. Ten Napel (NL, Yamaha), 108; 6. S. Barrier (F, Yamaha), 95; 7. D. Colucci (I, Ducati), 83; 8. M. Savary (CH, Yamaha), 76; 9. D. Beretta (I, Suzuki), 67; 10. V. Lonbois (B, Suzuki), 61; 11. M. Bussolotti (I, Yamaha), 42; 12. G. Rea (GB, Suzuki), 41; 13. D. Sigloch (D, Yamaha), 40; 14. M. Gines (F,Yamaha), 38; 15. R. Costantini (I, Honda), 35. 37 finishers.

USA CHAMPIONSHIP

SUPERSPORT

10th March - Daytona
1. R.-L. Hayden (Kawasaki); 2. Hacking (Kawasaki); 3. T. Hayden (Suzuki); 4. Barnes (Suzuki); 5. Hayes (Honda); 6. Attard (Kawasaki); 7. Rapp (Kawasaki); 8. C. Davies (GB, Yamaha); 9. May (Suzuki); 10. C. West (Yamaha).

22nd April - Birmingham
1. Hayes (Honda); 2. Herrin (Yamaha); 3. Rapp (Kawasaki); 4. Aa. Gobert (AUS, Honda); 5. R.-L. Hayden (Kawasaki); 6. T. Hayden (Suzuki); 7. Attard (Kawasaki); 8. C. West (Yamaha); 9. Young (Suzuki); 10. Eslick (Suzuki).

29th April - Fontana
1. Hacking (Kawasaki); 2. Hayes (Honda); 3. R.-L. Hayden (Kawasaki); 4. Rapp (Kawasaki); 5. Barnes (Suzuki); 6. T. Hayden (Suzuki); 7. May (Suzuki); 8. Eslick (Suzuki); 9. C. Davies (GB, Yamaha); 10. C. West (Yamaha).

20th May - Sonoma
1. Hayes (Honda); 2. Hacking (Kawasaki); 3. R.-L. Hayden (Kawasaki); 4. Davies (GB, Yamaha); 5. Herrin (Yamaha); 6. Rapp (Kawasaki); 7. May (Suzuki); 8. Aa. Gobert (AUS, Honda); 9. Attard (Kawasaki); 10. T. Hayden (Suzuki).

3rd June - Elkhart Lake
1. Aa. Gobert (AUS, Honda); 2. Hacking (Kawasaki); 3. R.-L. Hayden (Kawasaki); 4. Hayes (Honda); 5. Young (Suzuki); 6. T. Hayden (Suzuki); 7. C. Davies (GB, Yamaha); 8. Rapp (Kawasaki); 9. May (Suzuki); 10. Elleby (Honda).

24th June - Tooele
1. Hacking (Kawasaki); 2. May (Suzuki); 3. Cardeñas (COL, Suzuki); 4. Aa. Gobert (AUS, Honda); 5. R.-L. Hayden (Kawasaki); 6. Herrin (Yamaha); 7. Hayes (Honda); 8. Peris (Yamaha); 9. C. Davies (GB, Yamaha); 10. Rapp (Kawasaki).

22nd July - Laguna Seca
1. R.-L. Hayden (Kawasaki); 2. Herrin (Yamaha); 3. Rapp (Kawasaki); 4. Hacking (Kawasaki); 5. May (Suzuki); 6. Aa. Gobert (AUS, Honda); 7. Cardeñas (COL, Suzuki); 8. Young (Suzuki); 9. Attard (Kawasaki); 10. T. Hayden (Suzuki).

5th August - Lexington
Race annulée en raison des conditions atmosphériques.

19th August - Alton
1. Hayes (Honda); 2. Cardeñas (COL, Suzuki); 3. Hacking (Kawasaki); 4. R.-L. Hayden (Kawasaki); 5. May (Suzuki); 6. C. Davies (GB, Yamaha); 7. Rapp (Kawasaki); 8. Peris (Yamaha); 9. Wood (Yamaha); 10. Moore (Kawasaki).

2nd September - Road Atlanta
1. Hayes (Honda); 2. Hacking (Kawasaki); 3. R.-L. Hayden (Kawasaki); 4. Cardeñas (COL, Suzuki); 5. Herrin (Yamaha); 6. Young (Suzuki); 7. Rapp (Kawasaki); 8. Peris (Yamaha); 9. C. West (Yamaha); 10. Beck (Suzuki).

16th September - Laguna Seca
1. Herrin (Yamaha); 2. Hacking (Kawasaki); 3. Cardeñas (COL, Suzuki); 4. Attard (Kawasaki); 5. R-.L. Hayden (Kawasaki); 6. Young (Suzuki); 7. Aa. Gobert (AUS, Honda); 8. T. Hayden (Suzuki); 9. Carter (Yamaha); 10. Rapp (Kawasaki).

FINAL CLASSIFICATION

1. Roger-Lee Hayden	Kawasaki	297 points
2. Jamie Hacking	Kawasaki	294
3. Joshua Hayes	Honda	261

4. S. Rapp (Kawasaki), 247; 5. T. Hayden (Suzuki), 216; 6. B. Young (Suzuki), 212; 7. J. Herrin (Yamaha), 208; 8. G. May (Suzuki), 181; 9. B. Attard (Kawasaki), 178; 10. Aa. Gobert (AUS, Honda), 174. 83 finishers.

SUPERSTOCK

10th March - Daytona
1. Spies (Suzuki); 2. B. Bostrom (Yamaha); 3. May (Suzuki); 4. Yates (Suzuki); 5. Eslick (Suzuki); 6. Ulrich (Suzuki); 7. Young (Suzuki); 8. Jensen (Suzuki); 9. Palmer (Suzuki); 10. Haner (Suzuki).

22nd April - Birmingham
1. Yates (Suzuki); 2. Holden (Suzuki); 3. B. Bostrom (Yamaha); 4. Spies (Suzuki); 5. Eslick (Suzuki); 6. Young (Suzuki); 7. May (Suzuki); 8. Ulrich (Suzuki); 9. Cardeñas (COL, Kawasaki); 10. Jensen (Suzuki).

29th April - Fontana
1. Spies (Suzuki); 2. Holden (Suzuki); 3. Yates (Suzuki); 4. B. Bostrom (Yamaha); 5. May (Suzuki); 6. Eslick (Suzuki); 7. Cardeñas (COL, Kawasaki); 8. Jensen (Suzuki); 9. Young (Suzuki); 10. Pietri (VEN, Suzuki).

20th May - Sonoma
1. Spies (Suzuki); 2. May (Suzuki); 3. B. Bostrom (Yamaha); 4. Eslick (Suzuki); 5. Young (Suzuki); 6. Ulrich (Suzuki); 7. Yates (Suzuki); 8. Jensen (Suzuki); 9. Pietri (VEN, Suzuki); 10. Curtis (Suzuki).

3rd June - Elkhart Lake
1. Spies (Suzuki); 2. May (Suzuki); 3. Jensen (Suzuki); 4. B. Bostrom (Yamaha); 5. Haner (Suzuki); 6. Holden (Suzuki); 7. Pietri (VEN, Suzuki); 8. Yates (Suzuki); 9. Weber (Suzuki); 10. Young (Suzuki).

24th June - Tooele
1. Spies (Suzuki); 2. B. Bostrom (Yamaha); 3. Yates (Suzuki); 4. Pietri (VEN, Suzuki); 5. Eslick (Suzuki); 6. Jensen (Suzuki); 7. Ulrich (Suzuki); 8. Lewin (Suzuki); 9. Szwarc (Suzuki); 10. Call (Suzuki).

5th August - Lexington
Race annulée en raison des conditions atmosphériques.

19th August - Alton
1. Spies (Suzuki); 2. Yates (Suzuki); 3. Holden (Suzuki); 4. B. Bostrom (Yamaha); 5. Young (Suzuki); 6. Eslick (Suzuki); 7. Ulrich (Suzuki); 8. Thompson (Suzuki); 9. Jensen (Suzuki); 10. Mason (Suzuki).

2nd September - Road Atlanta
1. Spies (Suzuki); 2. B. Bostrom (Yamaha); 3. May (Suzuki); 4. Holden (Suzuki); 5. Stauffer (Yamaha); 6. Young (Suzuki); 7. Mason (Suzuki); 8. Jensen (Suzuki); 9. Weber (Suzuki); 10. Pietri (Suzuki).

16th September - Laguna Seca
1. Holden (Suzuki); 2. Yates (Suzuki); 3. B. Bostrom (Yamaha); 4. Stauffer (Yamaha); 5. May (Suzuki); 6. Young (Suzuki); 7. Thompson (Suzuki); 8. Eslick (Suzuki); 9. Ulrich (Suzuki); 10. Pietri (VEN, Suzuki).

FINAL CLASSIFICATION

1. Ben Spies	Suzuki	292 points
2. Ben Bostrom	Yamaha	264
3. Aaron Yates	Suzuki	251

4. G. May (Suzuki), 229; 5. S. Jensen (Suzuki), 207; 6. C. Ulrich (Suzuki), 203; 7. D. Eslick (Suzuki), 198; 8. B. Young (Suzuki), 194; 9. J. Holden (Suzuki), 183; 10. R. Pietri (VEN, Suzuki), 155. 71 finishers.

SUPERBIKE

10th March - Daytona
1. Spies (Suzuki); 2. Mi. Duhamel (CAN, Honda); 3. Zemke (Honda); 4. Yanagawa (J, Kawasaki); 5. May (Suzuki); 6. Di Salvo (Yamaha); 7. Holden (Suzuki); 8. T. Hayden (Suzuki); 9. J. Ellison (GB, Honda); 10. Mladin (AUS, Suzuki).

22nd April - Birmingham
Race I: 1. Mladin (AUS, Suzuki); 2. Spies (Suzuki); 3. Mi. Duhamel (CAN, Honda); 4. Yates (Suzuki); 5. T. Hayden (Suzuki); 6. Zemke (Honda); 7. Hacking (Kawasaki); 8. E. Bostrom (Yamaha); 9. Di Salvo (Yamaha); 10. J. Ellison (GB, Honda).
Race II: 1. Mladin (AUS, Suzuki); 2. Spies (Suzuki); 3. Mi. Duhamel (CAN, Honda); 4. T. Hayden (Suzuki); 5. Yates (Suzuki); 6. E. Bostrom (Yamaha); 7. Di Salvo (Yamaha); 8. Hacking (Kawasaki); 9. R.-L. Hayden (Kawasaki); 10. Zemke (Honda).

29th April - Fontana
Race I: 1. Spies (Suzuki); 2. Mladin (AUS, Suzuki); 3. E. Bostrom (Yamaha); 4. T. Hayden (Suzuki); 5. Mi. Duhamel (CAN, Honda); 6. Zemke (Honda); 7. Yates (Suzuki); 8. R.-L. Hayden (Kawasaki); 9. Di Salvo (Yamaha); 10. Lynn (MV-Agusta).
Race II: 1. Mladin (AUS, Suzuki); 2. Spies (Suzuki); 3. E. Bostrom (Yamaha); 4. T. Hayden (Suzuki); 5. Zemke (Honda); 6. Mi. Duhamel (CAN, Honda); 7. R.-L. Hayden (Kawasaki); 8. Hacking (Kawasaki); 9. Yates (Suzuki); 10. Di Salvo (Yamaha).

20th May - Sonoma
Race I: 1. Mladin (AUS, Suzuki); 2. Spies (Suzuki); 3. Mi. Duhamel (CAN, Honda); 4. Di Salvo (Yamaha); 5. Zemke (Honda); 6. R.-L. Hayden (Kawasaki); 7. T. Hayden (Suzuki); 8. Hacking (Kawasaki); 9. J. Ellison (GB, Honda); 10. Lynn (MV-Agusta).

Race II: 1. Mladin (AUS, Suzuki); 2. Spies (Suzuki); 3. Zemke (Honda); 4. Mi. Duhamel (CAN, Honda); 5. T. Hayden (Suzuki); 6. Di Salvo (Yamaha); 7. E. Bostrom (Yamaha); 8. J. Ellison (GB, Honda); 9. Holden (Suzuki); 10. Hacking (Kawasaki).

3rd June - Elkhart Lake
Race I: 1. Mladin (AUS, Suzuki); 2. Spies (Suzuki); 3. T. Hayden (Suzuki); 4. Mi. Duhamel (CAN, Honda); 5. Zemke (Honda); 6. E. Bostrom (Yamaha); 7. R.-L. Hayden (Kawasaki); 8. Di Salvo (Yamaha); 9. Hacking (Kawasaki); 10. Holden (Suzuki).
Race II: 1. Spies (Suzuki); 2. Hacking (Kawasaki); 3. Mladin (AUS, Suzuki); 4. Yates (Suzuki); 5. J. Ellison (GB, Honda); 6. Zemke (Honda); 7. Holden (Suzuki); 8. Haner (Suzuki); 9. E. Bostrom (Yamaha); 10. Jones (Honda).

24th June - Tooele
Race I: 1. Spies (Suzuki); 2. Mladin (AUS, Suzuki); 3. Zemke (Honda); 4. R.-L. Hayden (Kawasaki); 5. Mi. Duhamel (CAN, Honda); 6. Hacking (Kawasaki); 7. T. Hayden (Suzuki); 8. Yates (Suzuki); 9. Di Salvo (Yamaha); 10. J. Ellison (GB, Honda).
Race II: 1. Spies (Suzuki); 2. Zemke (Honda); 3. Mi. Duhamel (CAN, Honda); 4. Mladin (AUS, Suzuki); 5. R.-L. Hayden (Kawasaki); 6. T. Hayden (Suzuki); 7. Di Salvo (Yamaha); 8. Yates (Suzuki); 9. Hacking (Kawasaki); 10. Scassa (I, MV-Agusta).

22nd July - Laguna Seca
1. Spies (Suzuki); 2. Mladin (AUS, Suzuki); 3. Yates (Suzuki); 4. Mi. Duhamel (CAN, Honda); 5. Hodgson (GB, Honda); 6. Hacking (Kawasaki); 7. Di Salvo (Yamaha); 8. Holden (Suzuki); 9. E. Bostrom (Yamaha); 10. J. Ellison (GB, Honda).

5th August - Lexington
Race I: 1. Mladin (AUS, Suzuki); 2. Spies (Suzuki); 3. Mi. Duhamel (CAN, Honda); 4. Yates (Suzuki); 5. R.-L. Hayden (Kawasaki); 6. E. Bostrom (Yamaha); 7. Di Salvo (Yamaha); 8. Zemke (Honda); 9. T. Hayden (Suzuki); 10. J. Ellison (GB, Honda).
Race II: 1. Mladin (AUS, Suzuki); 2. Spies (Suzuki); 3. Hacking (Kawasaki); 4. Yates (Suzuki); 5. Zemke (Honda); 6. Mi. Duhamel (CAN, Honda); 7. E. Bostrom (Yamaha); 8. R.-L. Hayden (Kawasaki); 9. T. Hayden (Suzuki); 10. Lynn (MV-Agusta).

19th August - Alton
Race I: 1. Mladin (AUS, Suzuki); 2. Spies (Suzuki); 3. Hacking (Kawasaki); 4. Yates (Suzuki); 5. R.-L. Hayden (Kawasaki); 6. E. Bostrom (Yamaha); 7. Di Salvo (Yamaha); 8. Zemke (Honda); 9. T. Hayden (Suzuki); 10. J. Ellison (GB, Honda).
Race II: 1. Mladin (AUS, Suzuki); 2. Spies (Suzuki); 3. Yates (Suzuki); 4. Hacking (Kawasaki); 5. T. Hayden (Suzuki); 6. Zemke (Honda); 7. Scassa (I, MV-Agusta); 8. Lynn (MV-Agusta); 9. Holden (Suzuki); 10. R.-L. Hayden (Kawasaki).

2nd September - Road Atlanta
Race I: 1. Mladin (AUS, Suzuki); 2. Spies (Suzuki); 3. Hacking (Kawasaki); 4. Yates (Suzuki); 5. Zemke (Honda); 6. R.-L. Hayden (Kawasaki); 7. Lynn (MV-Agusta); 8. Scassa (I, MV-Agusta); 9. Holden (Suzuki); 10. T. Hayden (Suzuki).
Race II: 1. Mladin (AUS, Suzuki); 2. Spies (Suzuki); 3. Hacking (Kawasaki); 4. Yates (Suzuki); 5. R.-L. Hayden (Kawasaki); 6. Zemke (Honda); 7. T. Hayden (Suzuki); 8. J. Ellison (GB, Honda); 9. Holden (Suzuki); 10. E. Bostrom (Yamaha).

16th September - Laguna Seca
1. Spies (Suzuki); 2. Mladin (AUS, Suzuki); 3. Yates (Suzuki); 4. Zemke (Honda); 5. E. Bostrom (Yamaha); 6. T. Hayden (Suzuki); 7. Di Salvo (Yamaha); 8. J. Ellison (GB, Honda); 9. Holden (Suzuki); 10. Lynn (MV-Agusta).

FINAL CLASSIFICATION
1. Ben Spies — Suzuki — 652 points
2. Mat Mladin (AUS) — Suzuki — 651
3. Jake Zemke — Honda — 468
4. A. Yates (Suzuki), 465; 5. T. Hayden (Suzuki), 454; 6. J. Hacking (Kawasaki), 403; 7. E. Bostrom (Yamaha), 362; 8. M. Duhamel (CAN, Honda), 360; 9. J. Di Salvo (Yamaha), 359; 10. R.-L. Hayden (Kawasaki), 344. 55 finishers.

FORMULA XTREME

10th March - Daytona 200
1. Rapp (Kawasaki); 2. Attard (Kawasaki); 3. Barnes (Suzuki); 4. C. Davies (GB, Yamaha); 5. Di Salvo (Yamaha); 6. Hayes (Honda); 7. Picotte (Suzuki); 8. Elleby (Honda); 9. Day (Yamaha); 10. Pintar (SLO, Yamaha).

22nd April - Birmingham
1. Hayes (Honda); 2. Aa. Gobert (AUS, Honda); 3. Rapp (Kawasaki); 4. Craggill (AUS, Ducati); 5. Andrews (Honda); 6. Pegram (Ducati); 7. Elleby (Honda); 8. C. West (Yamaha); 9. Crevier (Yamaha); 10. Anthony (Yamaha).

29th April - Fontana
1. Hayes (Honda); 2. Aa. Gobert (AUS, Honda); 3. Pegram (Ducati); 4. C. Davies (GB, Yamaha); 5. Barnes (Suzuki); 6. Rapp (Kawasaki); 7. Long (Yamaha); 8. Perez (Yamaha); 9. Toye (Yamaha); 10. Carlotta (Suzuki).

20th May - Sonoma
1. Hayes (Honda); 2. Aa. Gobert (AUS, Honda); 3. Rapp (Kawasaki); 4. Attard (Kawasaki); 5. Pegram (Ducati); 6. Craggill (AUS, Ducati); 7. C. West (Yamaha); 8. Perez (Yamaha); 9. Fong (Suzuki); 10. Andrews (Honda).

3rd June - Elkhart Lake
1. Hayes (Honda); 2. Rapp (Kawasaki); 3. Cardeñas (COL, Suzuki); 4. Aa. Gobert (AUS, Honda); 5. Pegram (Ducati); 6. Craggill (AUS, Ducati); 7. Attard (Kawasaki); 8. Andrews (Honda); 9. C. West (Yamaha); 10. Herrmann (Suzuki).

24th June - Tooele
1. Aa. Gobert (AUS, Honda); 2. Hayes (Honda); 3. C. Davies (GB, Yamaha); 4. Attard (Kawasaki); 5. Cardeñas (COL, Suzuki); 6. Rapp (Kawasaki); 7. Peris (Yamaha); 8. Elleby (Honda); 9. C. West (Yamaha); 10. Andrews (Honda).

5th August - Lexington
1. Hayes (Honda); 2. Attard (Kawasaki); 3. Davies (GB, Yamaha); 4. Aa. Gobert (AUS, Honda); 5. Pegram (Ducati); 6. Craggill (AUS, Ducati); 7. Andrews (Honda); 8. Elleby (Honda); 9. Rapp (Kawasaki); 10. Peris (Yamaha).

19th August - Alton
1. Hayes (Honda); 2. Pegram (Ducati); 3. Craggill (AUS, Ducati); 4. Attard (Kawasaki); 5. Cardeñas (COL, Suzuki); 6. C. Davies (GB, Yamaha); 7. Rapp (Kawasaki); 8. Aa. Gobert (AUS, Honda); 9. C. West (Yamaha); 10. Wood (Yamaha).

2nd September - Road Atlanta
1. Hayes (Honda); 2. Attard (Kawasaki); 3. Craggill (AUS, Ducati); 4. Rapp (Kawasaki); 5. Cardeñas (COL, Suzuki); 6. Davies (GB, Yamaha); 7. Pegram (Ducati); 8. Andrews (Honda); 9. Elleby (Honda); 10. C. West (Yamaha).

16th September - Laguna Seca
1. Aa. Gobert (AUS, Honda); 2. Pegram (Ducati); 3. Rapp (Kawasaki); 4. Cardeñas (COL, Suzuki); 5. Peris (Yamaha); 6. Davies (GB, Yamaha); 7. Andrews (Honda); 8. C. West (Yamaha); 9. Elleby (Honda); 10. Attard (Kawasaki).

FINAL CLASSIFICATION
1. Joshua Hayes — Honda — 324 points
2. Steve Rapp — Kawasaki — 279
3. Aaron Gobert (AUS) — Honda — 247
4. L. Pegram (Ducati), 244; 5. B. Attard (Kawasaki), 231; 6. C. Davies (GB, Yamaha), 206; 7. R. Andrews (Honda), 179; 8. M. Craggill (AUS, Ducati), 162; 9. C. West (Yamaha); 10. B. Fong (Suzuki), 155. 91 finishers.

GERMAN CHAMPIONSHIP

125

29th April - Lausitz
1. Fröhlich (Honda); 2. Schrötter (Honda); 3. Wirsing (Honda); 4. Martinez-Gomez (E, Aprilia); 5. Unger (Aprilia); 6. Fritz (Honda); 7. Leigh-Smith (AUS, Honda); 8. Kreuziger (Aprilia); 9. Eckner (Honda); 10. Reichenwallner (CH, Aprilia).

20th May - Oschersleben
1. Fröhlich (Honda); 2. Wirsing (Honda); 3. Kreuziger (Aprilia); 4. Puffe (Aprilia); 5. Eckner (Honda); 6. Unger (Aprilia); 7. Reichenwallner (CH, Aprilia); 8. Hübsch (Aprilia); 9. Dubbink (NL, Honda); 10. Kartheininger (Honda).

3rd June - Assen - Netherlands
1. Fröhlich (Honda); 2. Fritz (Honda); 3. Unger (Aprilia); 4. Schrötter (Honda); 5. Wirsing (Honda); 6. Lässer (Honda); 7. Dubbink (NL, Honda); 8. Györfi (H, Aprilia); 9. Van Der Mark (NL, Honda); 10. Reichenwallner (CH, Aprilia).

24th June - Nürburgring
1. Fröhlich (Honda); 2. Lässer (Honda); 3. Unger (Aprilia); 4. Leigh-Smith (AUS, Honda); 5. Hübsch (Aprilia); 6. Eckner (Honda); 7. Puffe (Aprilia); 8. Schrötter (Honda); 9. Iwema (NL, Honda); 10. Van Der Mark (NL, Honda).

8th July - Salzburgring - Autriche
1. Folger (Honda); 2. Fröhlich (Honda); 3. Fritz (Honda); 4. Lässer (Honda); 5. Iwema (NL, Honda); 6. Hübsch (Aprilia); 7. Kartheininger (Honda); 8. B. Chesaux (CH, Aprilia); 9. Unger (Aprilia); 10. Dubbink (NL, Honda).

5th August - Schleiz
1. Wirsing (Honda); 2. Fritz (Honda); 3. Hübsch (Aprilia); 4. Unger (Aprilia); 5. Lässer (Honda); 6. Schrötter (Honda); 7. Leigh-Smith (AUS, Honda); 8. Eckner (Honda); 9. Reichenwallner (CH, Aprilia); 10. B. Chesaux (CH, Aprilia).

2nd September - Most - Czech Republic
1. Fröhlich (Honda); 2. Wirsing (Honda); 3. Leigh-Smith (AUS, Honda); 4. Fritz (Honda); 5. Hübsch (Aprilia); 6. Schrötter (Honda); 7. B. Chesaux (Aprilia); 8. Unger (Aprilia); 9. Dubbink (NL, Honda); 10. Eckner (Honda).

16th September - Hockenheim
1. Fröhlich (Honda); 2. Folger (Honda); 3. Lässer (Honda); 4. Fritz (Honda); 5. Schrötter (Honda); 6. Hübsch (Aprilia); 7. Leigh-Smith (AUS, Honda); 8. Wirsing (Honda); 9. Unger (Aprilia); 10. B. Chesaux (CH, Aprilia).

FINAL CLASSIFICATION
1. Georg Fröhlich — Honda — 170 points
2. Toni Wirsing — Honda — 100
3. Marvin Fritz — Honda — 94
4. P. Unger (Aprilia), 90; 5. M. Schrötter (Honda), 74; 6. E. Hübsch (Aprilia), 74; 7. R. Lässer (Honda), 70; 8. B. Leigh-Smith (AUS, Honda), 61; 9. S. Eckner (Honda), 53; 10. J. Folger (Honda), 45. 26 finishers.

SUPERSPORT

29th April - Lausitz
Race I: 1. Kaufmann (Suzuki); 2. Diss (F, Kawasaki); 3. Penzkofer (Triumph); 4. Phillip (DK, Suzuki); 5. Ahnendrop (NL, Yamaha); 6. Harding (DK, Suzuki); 7. Peh (Michels (Suzuki); 9. Le Grelle (B, Honda); 10. P. Hafenegger (Triumph).
Race II: 1. Penzkofer (Triumph); 2. Diss (F, Kawasaki); 3. Phillip (DK, Suzuki); 4. Tirsgaard (DK, Yamaha); 5. Ahnendrop (NL, Yamaha); 6. Richter (Honda); 7. Peh (Suzuki); 8. Solberg (N, Yamaha); 9. Kaulamo (SF, Yamaha); 10. Kellner (Suzuki).

20th May - Oschersleben
Race I: 1. Ivanov (RUS, Yamaha); 2. Kaufmann (Suzuki); 3. Diss (F, Kawasaki); 4. Van Ginhoven (NL, Ducati); 5. Knobloch (A, Yamaha); 6. Tirsgaard (DK, Yamaha); 7. Phillip (DK, Suzuki); 8. Ahnendrop (NL, Yamaha); 9. Michels (Suzuki); 10. Hommel (Honda).
Course II: 1. Diss (F, Kawasaki); 2. Ahnendrop (NL, Yamaha); 3. Kaufmann (Suzuki); 4. Knobloch (A, Yamaha); 5. Van Ginhoven (NL, Ducati); 6. Hafenegger (Triumph); 7. Reichelt (Kawasaki); 8. Michels (Suzuki); 9. Phillip (DK, Suzuki); 10. Hommel (Honda).

3rd June - Assen - Netherlands
1. Ivanov (RUS, Yamaha); 2. LeGrelle (B, Honda); 3. Phillip (DK, Suzuki); 4. Knobloch (A, Yamaha); 5. Diss (Kawasaki); 6. Ahnendrop (NL, Yamaha); 7. Hafenegger (Triumph); 8. Kaufmann (Suzuki); 9. Solberg (N, Yamaha); 10. Hommel (Honda).

24th June - Nürburgring
1. Hafenegger (Triumph); 2. Knobloch (A, Yamaha); 3. Kaufmann (Suzuki); 4. Diss (F, Kawasaki); 5. Ahnendrop (NL, Yamaha); 6. Minnerop (Yamaha); 7. Reichelt (Kawasaki); 8. Solberg (N, Yamaha); 9. Raschle (CH, Yamaha); 10. Eckhardt (Yamaha).

8th July - Salzburgring - Autriche
Race I: 1. Knobloch (A, Yamaha); 2. Kaufmann (Suzuki); 3. Diss (F, Kawasaki); 4. Ahnendrop (NL, Yamaha); 5. Fuchs (Triumph); 6. Michels (Suzuki); 7. Hommel (Honda); 8. Eckhardt (Yamaha); 9. Reichelt (Kawasaki); 10. Richter (Honda).
Race II: 1. Knobloch (A, Yamaha); 2. Kaufmann (Suzuki); 3. Diss (F, Kawasaki); 4. Hafenegger (Triumph); 5. Ahnendrop (NL, Yamaha); 6. Eckhardt (Yamaha); 7. Hommel (Honda); 8. Michels (Suzuki); 9. Minnerop (Yamaha); 10. Le Grelle (B, Honda).

5th August - Schleiz
Race I: 1. Penzkofer (Triumph); 2. Kaufmann (Suzuki); 3. Hafeneger (Triumph); 4. Knobloch (A, Yamaha); 5. Diss (F, Kawasaki); 6. Ahnendrop (NL, Yamaha); 7. Richter (Honda); 8. Phillip (DK, Suzuki); 9. Peh (Suzuki); 10. Reichelt (Kawasaki).
Race II: 1. Penzkofer (Triumph); 2. Knobloch (A, Yamaha); 3. Hafeneger (Triumph); 4. Kaufmann (Suzuki); 5. Phillip (DK, Suzuki); 6. Richter (Honda); 7. Eckhardt (Yamaha); 8. Michels (Suzuki); 9. Hommel (Honda); 10. Raschle (CH, Kawasaki).

2nd September - Most - Czech Republic
Race I: 1. Penzkofer (Triumph); 2. Ivanov (RUS, Yamaha); 3. Diss (F, Kawasaki); 4. Van Ginhoven (NL, Ducati); 5. Hommel (Honda); 6. Eckhardt (Yamaha); 7. Kaufmann (Suzuki); 8. Raschle (CH, Kawasaki); 9. Peh (Suzuki); 10. Jespersen (DK, Honda).
Race II: 1. Ivanov (RUS, Yamaha); 2. Hommel (Honda); 3. Penzkofer (Triumph); 4. Knobloch (A,

Yamaha); 5. Hafenegger (Triumph); 6. Diss (F, Kawasaki); 7. Richter (Honda); 8. Kaufmann (Suzuki); 9. Michels (Suzuki); 10. Van Ginhoven (NL, Ducati).

16th September - Hockenheim
1. Knobloch (A, Yamaha); 2. Diss (F, Kawasaki); 3. Hafenegger (Triumph); 4. Kellner (Triumph); 5. Eckhardt (Yamaha); 6. Phillip (DK, Suzuki); 7. Ahnendrop (NL, Yamaha); 8. Ritzmayer (H, Suzuki); 9. Solberg (N, Yamaha); 10. Peh (Suzuki).

FINAL CLASSIFICATION
1. Sébastien Diss (F)   Kawasaki   189 points
2. Günther Knobloch (A) Yamaha   184
3. Herbert Kaufmann   Suzuki   172
4. P. Hafenegger (Triumph), 125; 5. R. Penzkofer (Triumph), 124; 6. S. Ahnendrop (NL, Yamaha), 115; 7. K. Phillip (DK, Suzuki), 92; 8. V. Ivanov (RUS, Yamaha), 82; 9. S. Hommel (Honda), 77; 10. S. Michels (Suzuki), 68. 31 finishers.

SUPERBIKE

29th April - Lausitz
Race I: 1. Meklau (A, Suzuki); 2. Andersen (N, Honda); 3. Stamm (CH, Suzuki); 4. Bauer (A, Honda); 5. Nebel (Suzuki); 6. Eismann (MV-Agusta); 7. Daemen (B, Honda); 8. Von Hammerstein (Suzuki); 9. Wegscheider (I, Suzuki); 10. Willemsen (LUX, Suzuki).
Race II: 1. Teuchert (Suzuki); 2. Meklau (A, Suzuki); 3. Stamm (CH, Suzuki); 4. Daemen (B, Honda); 5. Nebel (Suzuki); 6. Bauer (A, Honda); 7. Eismann (MV-Agusta); 8. Von Hammerstein (Suzuki); 9. Berthelsen (N, Suzuki); 10. Wegscheider (I, Suzuki).

20th May - Oschersleben
Race I: 1. Bauer (A, Honda); 2. Andersen (N, Honda); 3. Stamm (CH, Suzuki); 4. Daemen (B, Honda); 5. Nebel (Suzuki); 6. M. Neukirchner (Suzuki); 7. Teuchert (MV-Agusta); 8. Meklau (A, Suzuki); 9. Lammert (Suzuki); 10. Von Hammerstein (Suzuki).
Race II: 1. Bauer (A, Honda); 2. Andersen (N, Honda); 3. M. Neukirchner (Suzuki); 4. Daemen (B, Honda); 5. Meklau (A, Suzuki); 6. Nebel (Suzuki); 7. Teuchert (MV-Agusta); 8. Schulten (Kawasaki); 9. Lammert (Suzuki); 10. Von Hammerstein (Suzuki).

3rd June - Assen - Netherlands
Race I: 1. Bauer (A, Honda); 2. Stamm (CH, Suzuki); 3. Teuchert (MV-Agusta); 4. Daemen (B, Honda); 5. Meklau (A, Suzuki); 6. Nebel (Suzuki); 7. Lammert (Suzuki); 8. Veneman (NL, Suzuki); 9. Johnson (AUS, Yamaha); 10. Wegscheider (I, Suzuki).
Race II: 1. Neukirchner (Suzuki); 2. Bauer (A, Honda); 3. Andersen (N, Honda); 4. Teuchert (MV-Agusta); 5. Veneman (NL, Suzuki); 6. Daemen (B, Honda); 7. Meklau (A, Suzuki); 8. Stamm (CH, Suzuki); 9. Nebel (Suzuki); 10. Lammert (Suzuki).

24th June - Nürburgring
Race I: 1. Bauer (A, Honda); 2. Daemen (B, Honda); 3. Andersen (N, Honda); 4. Teuchert (MV-Agusta); 5. Vos (NL, Honda); 6. Lammert (Suzuki); 7. Nebel (Suzuki); 8. Meklau (A, Suzuki); 9. Stamm (CH, Suzuki); 10. Johnson (AUS, Yamaha).
Race II: 1. Bauer (A, Honda); 2. Teuchert (MV-Agusta); 3. Nebel (Suzuki); 4. Lammert (Suzuki); 5. Meklau (A, Suzuki); 6. Stamm (CH, Suzuki); 7. Schulten (Kawasaki); 8. Mizera (F, Honda); 9. Van Steenbergen (NL, Honda); 10. Wegscheider (I, Suzuki).

8th July - Salzburgring - Autriche
Race I: 1. Neukirchner (Suzuki); 2. Bauer (A, Honda); 3. Daemen (B, Honda); 4. Teuchert (MV-Agusta); 5. Nebel (Suzuki); 6. Andersen (N, Honda); 7. Stamm (CH, Suzuki); 8. Schulten (Kawasaki); 9. Lammert (Suzuki); 10. Meklau (A, Suzuki).
Race II: 1. Neukirchner (Suzuki); 2. Teuchert (MV-Agusta); 3. Bauer (A, Honda); 4. Daemen (B, Honda); 5. Nebel (Suzuki); 6. Schulten (Kawasaki); 7. Meklau (A, Suzuki); 8. Stamm (CH, Suzuki); 9. Wegscheider (I, Suzuki); 10. Andersen (N, Honda).

5th August - Schleiz
Race I: 1. Bauer (A, Honda); 2. Andersen (N, Honda); 3. Meklau (A, Suzuki); 4. Nebel (Suzuki); 5. Schulten (Kawasaki); 6. Lammert (Suzuki); 7. Von Hammerstein (Suzuki); 8. Eismann (MV-Agusta); 9. Kerkhoven (NL, Yamaha); 10. Berthelsen (N, Suzuki).
Race II: 1. Meklau (A, Suzuki); 2. Andersen (N, Honda); 3. Bauer (A, Honda); 4. Lammert (Suzuki); 5. Nebel (Suzuki); 6. Schulten (Kawasaki); 7. Von Hammerstein (Suzuki); 8. Berthelsen (N, Suzuki); 9. Manz (Suzuki); 10. Skach (Suzuki).

2nd September - Most - Czech Republic
Race I: 1. Meklau (A, Suzuki); 2. Andersen (N, Honda); 3. Teuchert (MV-Agusta); 4. Lammert (Suzuki); 5. Daemen (B, Honda); 6. Nebel (Suzuki); 7. Bauer (A, Honda); 8. Schulten (Kawasaki); 9. Stamm (CH, Suzuki); 10. Von Hammerstein (Suzuki).
Race II: 1. Lammert (Suzuki); 2. Teuchert (MV-Agusta); 3. Nebel (Suzuki); 4. Meklau (A, Suzuki); 5. Daemen (B, Honda); 6. Bauer (A, Honda); 7. T. Lauslehto (Suzuki); 8. Von Hammerstein (Suzuki); 9. Eismann (MV-Agusta); 10. Leuthard (CH, Yamaha).

16th September - Hockenheim
Race I: 1. Bauer (A, Honda); 2. Daemen (B, Honda); 3. Vos (NL, Honda); 4. Andersen (N, Honda); 5. Nebel (Suzuki); 6. Lammert (Suzuki); 7. Stamm (CH, Suzuki); 8. Lindström (S, Yamaha); 9. Schulten (Kawasaki); 10. Lozano (E, Honda).
Race II: 1. Daemen (B, Honda); 2. Andersen (N, Honda); 3. Teuchert (MV-Agusta); 4. Lammert (Suzuki); 5. Nebel (Suzuki); 6. Stamm (CH, Suzuki); 7. Schulten (Kawasaki); 8. Lozano (E, Honda); 9. T. Lauslehto (SF, Suzuki); 10. Vos (NL, Honda).

FINAL CLASSIFICATION
1. Martin Bauer (A)   Honda   293 points
2. Kai-Borre Andersen (N) Honda   204
3. Andreas Meklau (A)   Suzuki   199
4. J. Teuchert (MV-Agusta), 190; 5. W. Daemen (B, Honda), 188; 6. S. Nebel (Suzuki), 183; 7. D. Lammert (Suzuki), 151; 8. R. Stamm (CH, Suzuki), 139; 9. M. Neukirchner (Suzuki), 101; 10. M. Schulten (Kawasaki), 88. 27 finishers.

SIDE-CARS

29th April - Lausitz
1. Schlosser/Hänni (CH, Suzuki); 2. Roscher/Hildebrandt (Suzuki); 3. Hainbucher/Adelsberger (A, Suzuki); 4. Schröder/Burkard (CH, Suzuki); 5. Kornas/Stepien (RSR); 6. Reuterholt/Ikonen (S, Suzuki); 7. Kiser/Näf (CH, Kawasaki); 8. Brändle/Fritz (CH, Suzuki); 9. Nagel/Knoof (Suzuki); 10. Rutz/Aeberli (CH, Yamaha).

20th May - Oschersleben
1. Hainbucher/Adelsberger (A, Suzuki); 2. Kornas/Stepien (RSR); 3. Hock/Becker (Honda); 4. Schröder/Burkard (CH, Suzuki); 5. Göttlich/Koloska (Suzuki); 6. Eilers/Freund (Honda); 7. Brändle/Fritz (CH, Suzuki); 8. Bereuter/Hofer (CH, Swissauto); 9. Kiser/Näf (CH, Kawasaki); 10. Nagel/Knoof (Suzuki).

3rd June - Assen - Netherlands
1. Hainbucher/Adelsberger (A, Suzuki); 2. Reuterholt/Ikonen (S, Suzuki); 3. Schlosser/Hänni (CH, Suzuki); 4. Kornas/Stepien (RSR); 5. Göttlich/Koloska (Suzuki); 6. Schröder/Burkard (CH, Suzuki); 7. Eilers/Freund (Honda); 8. Hock/Becker (Honda); 9. Brändle/Fritz (CH, Suzuki); 10. Nagel/Knoof (Suzuki).

24th June - Nürburgring
1. Schlosser/Hänni (CH, Suzuki); 2. Roscher/Hildebrand (Suzuki); 3. Hainbucher/Adelsberger (A, Suzuki); 4. Schröder/Burkard (CH, Suzuki); 5. Eilers/Freund (Honda); 6. Bevers/Vermeer (NL, Yamaha); 7. Bereuter/Hofer (CH, Swissauto); 8. Nicholson/Van Lith (NL, Yamaha); 9. S. Dodd/D. Dodd (GB, Yamaha); 10. Nagel/Knoof (Suzuki).

8th July - Salzburgring - Autriche
1. Schlosser/Hänni (CH, Suzuki); 2. Roscher/Hildebrand (Suzuki); 3. M. Grabmüller/B. Grabmüller (A, Suzuki); 4. Hainbucher/Adelsberger (A, Suzuki); 5. Schröder/Burkard (CH, Suzuki); 6. Moser/Wäfler (A/CH, Honda); 7. Kornas/Stepien (RSR); 8. Eilers/Freund (Honda); 9. Ozimo/Zanarini (I, LCR); 10. Bereuter/Hofer (CH, Swissauto).

5th August - Schleiz
1. Schlosser/Hänni (CH, Suzuki); 2. Roscher/Hildebrand (Suzuki); 3. Kornas/Stepien (RSR); 4. Göttlich/Koloska (Suzuki); 5. Hock/Becker (Honda); 6. Hainbucher/Adelsberger (A, Suzuki); 7. Schröder/Burkard (CH, Suzuki); 8. Reuterholt/Ikonen (S, Suzuki); 9. Bevers/Vermeer (NL, RCN); 10. Ozimo/Zanarini (I, LCR).

2nd September - Most - Czech Republic
1. Schlosser/Hänni (CH, Suzuki); 2. Roscher/Hildebrand (Suzuki); 3. Hainbucher/Adelsberger (A, Suzuki); 4. Hock/Becker (Honda); 5. Kornas/Stepien (RSR); 6. Göttlich/Koloska (Suzuki); 7. Reuterholt/Ikonen (S, Suzuki); 8. Schröder/Burkard (CH, Suzuki); 9. Klaffenböck/Parzer (A, Honda) ; 10. Eilers/Freund (Honda).

16th September - Hockenheim
1. Roscher/Hildebrand (Suzuki); 2. Schlosser/Hänni (CH, Suzuki); 3. Göttlich/Koloska (Suzuki); 4. Hock/Becker (Honda); 5. Eilers/Freund (Honda); 6. Hainbucher/Adelsberger (A, Suzuki); 7. Bevers/Vermeer (NL, RCN); 8. Brändle/Helbig (CH, Suzuki); 9. S. Dodd/D. Dodd (GB, Yamaha); 10. Nicholson/Van Lith (NL, Suzuki).

FINAL CLASSIFICATION
1. Schlosser/Hänni (CH) Suzuki   161 points
2. Hainbucher/Adelsberger (A)   Suzuki   134
3. Roscher/Hildebrand   Suzuki   125
4. Kornas/Stepien (RSR), 82; 5. Schröder/Burkard (CH, Suzuki), 79; 6. Hock/Becker (Honda), 66; 7. Göttlich/Koloska (Suzuki), 64; 8. Brändle/Helbig (CH, Suzuki), 61; 9. Eilers/Freund (Honda), 58; 10. Reuterholt/Ikonen (S, Suzuki). 18 finishers.

SPAIN CHAMPIONSHIP

125
2006

19th November - Valencia
1. Rabat (Honda); 2. Jerez (Aprilia); 3. P. Espargaro (Derbi); 4. Masbou (F, Honda); 5. R. Krummenacher (CH, KTM); 6. Tutusaus (Derbi); 7. Webb (GB, Honda); 8. Hernandez Jnr (Aprilia); 9. Folger (D, Honda); 10. E. Vazquez (Honda).

26th November - Jerez de la Frontera
1. Rabat (Honda); 2. Folger (D, Honda); 3. Redding (GB, Honda); 4. Marquez (Honda); 5. Masbou (F, Honda); 6. Hernandez (Aprilia); 7. E. Vazquez (Honda); 8. Coghlan (GB, Honda); 9. Jerez (Aprilia); 10. Tuñez (Aprilia).

FINAL CLASSIFICATION
1. Pol Espargaro   Derbi   141 points
2. Esteve Rabat   Honda   121
3. Jonas Folger (D)   Honda   80
4. K. Coghlan (GB, Honda), 77; 5. E. Jerez (Aprilia), 64; 6. P. Tutusaus (Derbi), 57; 7. E. Vazquez (Honda), 51; 8. M. Marquez (Honda), 48; 9. S. Redding (GB, Honda), 46; 10. R. Cardus (Derbi), 43.

2007

29th April - Albacete
1. Tutusaus (Aprilia); 2. Jerez (Honda); 3. Maestro (Honda); 4. E. Vazquez (Aprilia); 5. S. Bradl (D, Aprilia); 6. J. Salom (Aprilia); 7. Saez (Aprilia); 8. Moncayo (Aprilia); 9. Nakagami (J, Honda); 10. Marquez (KTM).

27th May - Catalunya
1. S. Bradl (D, Aprilia); 2. E. Vazquez (Aprilia); 3. L. Salom (Aprilia); 4. Tutusaus (Aprilia); 5. J. Fernandez (Aprilia); 6. Nakagami (J, Honda); 7. Fröhlich (D, Honda); 8. Tuñez (Aprilia); 9. Redding (GB, Aprilia); 10. Moncayo (Aprilia).

17th June - Jerez de la Frontera
1. Marquez (KTM); 2. Tutusaus (Aprilia); 3. S. Bradl (D, Aprilia); 4. Redding (GB, Aprilia); 5. Maestro (Aprilia); 6. Salom (Aprilia); 7. Saez (Aprilia); 8. Tuñez (Aprilia); 9. Lacalendola (I, Aprilia); 10. Eitzinger (A, Honda).

29th July - Valencia
1. S. Bradl (D, Aprilia); 2. Redding (GB, Aprilia); 3. Nakagami (J, Honda); 4. Maestro (Aprilia); 5. Tutusaus (Aprilia); 6. E. Vazquez (Aprilia); 7. R. Cardus (Aprilia); 8. Fröhlich (D, Honda); 9. Saez (Aprilia); 10. J. Fernandez (Aprilia).

7th October - Albacete
1. Redding (GB, Aprilia); 2. E. Vazquez (Aprilia); 3. Moncayo (Aprilia); 4. S. Bradl (D, Aprilia); 5. Folger (D, Honda); 6. Nakagami (J, Honda); 7. Tutusaus (Aprilia); 8. Maestro (Aprilia); 9. Saez (Aprilia); 10. Salom (Aprilia).
(*) The two last races (Valencia on 18 November and Jerez de la Frontera on the 25) took place after printing of "The Motorcycle Yearbook" had been completed.

SUPERSPORT
2006

19th November - Valencia
1. Fores (Yamaha); 2. Salom (Yamaha); 3. Bonastre (Yamaha); 4. Torres (Yamaha); 5. Lascorz (Honda); 6. Leblanc (F, Honda); 7. Barragan (Honda); 8. Carrasco (Honda); 9. Hidalgo (Honda); 10. Arcas (Yamaha).

26th November - Jerez de la Frontera
1. Salom (Yamaha); 2. Fores (Yamaha); 3. Bonastre (Yamaha); 4. Piñera (Suzuki); 5. Gómez (Honda); 6. Almeda (Yamaha); 7. Barragan (Honda); 8. Lascorz (Honda); 9. Hidalgo (Honda); 10. Gowland (GB, Honda).

FINAL CLASSIFICATION
1. David Salom   Yamaha   126 points
2. Adrián Bonastre   Yamaha   116
3. Javier Fores   Yamaha   95
4. J. Lascorz (Honda), 75; 5. J. Torres (Yamaha), 64; 6. V. Carrasco (Honda), 49; 7. J.-L. Carrión (Honda), 46; 8. R. Gómez (Honda), 45; 9. S. Barragan (Honda), 40; 10. D. Piñera (Suzuki), 31.

2007

29th April - Albacete

1. R. Gomez (Suzuki); 2. Bonastre (Yamaha); 3. Gowland (GB, Honda); 4. Carrion (Honda); 5. Almeda (Kawasaki); 6. Arcas (Honda); 7. A. Rodriguez (Yamaha); 8. Aguilar (Honda); 9. Alabarce (Kawasaki); 10. Barragan (Honda).

27th May - Catalunya
1. A. Rodriguez (Yamaha); 2. R. Gomez (Suzuki); 3. Gowland (GB, Honda); 4. Almeda (Kawasaki); 5. Bonastre (Yamaha); 6. Alabarce (Kawasaki); 7. Hidalgo (Honda); 8. Bonache (Suzuki); 9. Caus (Yamaha); 10. Valls (Suzuki).

17th June - Jerez de la Frontera
1. A. Rodriguez (Yamaha); 2. Gowland (GB, Honda); 3. Bonastre (Yamaha); 4. R. Gomez (Suzuki); 5. Bonache (Suzuki); 6. Hidalgo (Honda); 7. Alabarce (Kawasaki); 8. Arcas (Honda); 9. Rivas (Suzuki); 10. Carrion (Honda).

29th July - Valencia
1. Lascorz (Honda); 2. A. Rodriguez (Yamaha); 3. R. Gomez (Suzuki); 4. X. Fores (Honda); 5. Gowland (GB, Honda); 6. Alabarce (Kawasaki); 7. Arcas (Honda); 8. Hidalgo (Honda); 9. Carrion (Honda); 10. Aguilar (Honda).

7th October - Albacete
1. Bonastre (Yamaha); 2. Arcas (Honda); 3. Bonache (Suzuki); 4. Alabarce (Kawasaki); 5. Rivas (Suzuki); 6. M. Hernandez Jnr (Kawasaki); 7. Gowland (GB, Honda); 8. Barragan (Honda); 9. Moreno (Yamaha); 10. Cortes (Yamaha).
(*) The two last races (Valencia on 18 November and Jerez de la Frontera on the 25) took place after printing of "The Motorcycle Yearbook" had been completed.

FORMULA EXTREME
2006
19th November - Valencia
1. Morales (Yamaha); 2. De Gea (Honda); 3. Del Amor (Honda); 4. Fuertes (Suzuki); 5. Monge (Yamaha); 6. I. Silvá (Kawasaki); 7. J.-O. Fernandez (Yamaha); 8. Mazuecos (Kawasaki); 9. B. Martinez (Yamaha); 10. Casas (Suzuki).

26th November - Jerez de la Frontera
1. Morales (Yamaha); 2. Mazuecos (Kawasaki); 3. Sardá (Yamaha); 4. J.-O. Fernandez (Yamaha); 5. Ribalta (Suzuki); 6. Casas (Suzuki); 7. J.-E. Gomez (Honda); 8. Monge (Yamaha); 9. Fuertes (Suzuki); 10. D. Lozano (Honda).

FINAL CLASSIFICATION
1. José De Gea — Honda — 128 points
2. Carmelo Morales — Yamaha — 120
3. Javier Del Amor — Honda — 85
4. J.-O. Fernandez (Yamaha), 83; 5. J. Sardá (Yamaha), 75; 6. J. Monge (Yamaha), 70; 7. I. Silvá (Kawasaki), 67; 8. J. Mazuecos (Kawasaki), 64; 9. D. Lozano (Honda), 42; 10. S. Fuertes (Suzuki), 40.

2007
29th April - Albacete
1. De Gea (Suzuki); 2. Morales (Yamaha); 3. Del Amor (Honda); 4. Torres (Yamaha); 5. Sarda (Suzuki); 6. Mazuecos (Suzuki); 7. Carrasco (Honda); 8. Cardoso (Kawasaki); 9. Lozano (Honda); 10. Casas (Yamaha).

27th May - Catalunya
1. Morales (Yamaha); 2. De Gea (Suzuki); 3. Sardá (Suzuki); 4. Del Amor (Yamaha); 5. Torres (Yamaha); 6. Fuertes (Suzuki); 7. Lozano (Honda); 8. Luis (Yamaha); 9. Monge (Honda); 10. Casas (Yamaha).

17th June - Jerez de la Frontera
1. Morales (Yamaha); 2. De Gea (Suzuki); 3. Del Amor (Honda); 4. Cardoso (Yamaha); 5. Lozano (Honda); 6. Fuertes (Suzuki); 7. Rocamora (Yamaha); 8. Noyes (Suzuki); 9. Casas (Yamaha); 10. Silvá (Kawasaki).

29th July - Valencia
1. De Gea (Suzuki); 2. Del Amor (Honda); 3. Sardá (Suzuki); 4. Fuertes (Suzuki); 5. Lozano (Honda); 6. Mazuecos (Kawasaki); 7. Torres (Yamaha); 8. Noyes (Suzuki); 9. I. Silvá (Kawasaki); 10. Vallcañeras (Yamaha).

7th October - Albacete
1. Morales (Yamaha); 2. De Gea (Suzuki); 3. Del Amor (Yamaha); 4. Torres (Yamaha); 5. Mazuecos (Kawasaki); 6. Cardoso (Yamaha); 7. Fuertes (Suzuki); 8. K. Noyes (Suzuki); 9. B. Martinez (Yamaha); 10. Carrasco (Honda).
(*) The two last races (Valencia on 18 November and Jerez de la Frontera on the 25) took place after printing of "The Motorcycle Yearbook" had been completed.

FRANCE CHAMPIONSHIP

125
25th March - Le Mans
1. Ale. Michel (Aprilia); 2. L. Rossi (Honda); 3. Le Coquen (Honda); 4. Cartron (Honda); 5. Debise (Honda); 6. Dunikowski (Honda); 7. Pagaud (Honda); 8. G. Le Badezet (Honda); 9. Bonnet (Honda); 10. Maitre (Honda).

15th April - Lédenon
1. Ale. Michel (Aprilia); 2. Maitre (Honda); 3. L. Rossi (Honda); 4. Dunikowski (Honda); 5. Pagaud (Honda); 6. Quellet (Honda); 7. Chamignon (Aprilia); 8. Rouvière (Honda); 9. Major (Honda); 10. Loiseau (Honda).

29th April - Nogaro
1. Maitre (Honda); 2. L. Rossi (Honda); 3. J. Petit (Honda); 4. Debise (Honda); 5. Dunikowski (Honda); 6. Pagaud (Honda); 7. Loiseau (Honda); 8. Le Coquen (Honda); 9. Major (Honda); 10. Chenard (Honda).

13th May - Le Vigeant
1. Debisse (Honda); 2. J. Petit (Honda); 3. Pagaud (Honda); 4. Ale. Michel (Aprilia); 5. Maitre (Honda); 6. Cartron (Honda); 7. Le Coquen (Honda); 8. Loiseau (Honda); 9. Major (Honda); 10. Rouvière (Honda).

17th June - Lédenon
1. Ale. Michel (Aprilia); 2. Dunikowski (Honda); 3. L. Rossi (Honda); 4. J. Petit (Honda); 5. Loiseau (Honda); 6. Pagaud (Honda); 7. Le Coquen (Honda); 8. Quellet (Honda); 9. Major (Honda); 10. Debise (Honda).

8th July - Albi
1. Masbou (Honda); 2. Dunikowski (Honda); 3. Ale. Michel (Aprilia); 4. J. Petit (Honda); 5. L. Rossi (Honda); 6. Pagaud (Honda); 7. Debise (Honda); 8. Baillot (Honda); 9. Rouvière (Honda); 10. Bonnet (Honda).

29th July - Magny-Cours
1. Leigh-Smith (AUS, Honda); 2. Le Coquen (Honda); 3. Dunikowski (Honda); 4. L. Rossi (Honda); 5. Debise (Honda); 6. Pagaud (Honda); 7. Szalai (Honda); 8. Maitre (Honda); 9. Bonnet (Honda); 10. Baillot

(Honda).

FINAL CLASSIFICATION
1. Alexis Michel — Aprilia — 104 points
2. Louis Rossi — Honda — 99
3. Clément Dunikowski — Honda — 94
4. V. Debise (Honda), 77; 5. R. Pagaud (Honda), 77; 6. R. Maitre (Honda), 71; 7. S. Le Coquen (Honda), 67; 8. J. Petit (Honda), 62; 9. A. Loiseau (Honda), 34; 10. T. Rouvière (Honda), 31. 28 finishers.

SUPERSPORT
25th March - Le Mans
1. A. Vincent (Yamaha); 2. M. Lagrive (Suzuki); 3. K. Foray (Triumph); 4. Mizera (Yamaha); 5. Y. Lussiana (Yamaha); 6. Lefort (Yamaha); 7. Marsac (Yamaha); 8. Bouffier (Kawasaki); 9. Le Grelle (B, Honda); 10. D'Orgeix (Honda).

15th April - Lédenon
1. K. Foray (Triumph); 2. A. Vincent (Yamaha); 3. Perret (Kawasaki); 4. Lefort (Yamaha); 5. Andrieu (Yamaha); 6. Bouffier (Kawasaki); 7. D'Orgeix (Honda); 8. Polesso (Yamaha); 9. Marsac (Yamaha); 10. Brian (Honda).

29th April - Nogaro
1. Perret (Kawasaki); 2. D'Orgeix (Honda); 3. Andrieu (Yamaha); 4. K. Foray (Triumph); 5. Lefort (Yamaha); 6. Brian (Honda); 7. Marsac (Yamaha); 8. Lussiana (Yamaha); 9. Ruiz (Kawasaki); 10. Stey (Honda).

13th May - Le Vigeant
1. K. Foray (Triumph); 2. Perret (Kawasaki); 3. D'Orgeix (Honda); 4. Andrieu (Yamaha); 5. Marsac (Yamaha); 6. Lussiana (Yamaha); 7. A. Vincent (Yamaha); 8. Lefort (Yamaha); 9. Brian (Honda); 10. Bouffier (Kawasaki).

17th June - Lédenon
1. K. Foray (Triumph); 2. A. Vincent (Yamaha); 3. Andrieu (Yamaha); 4. Perret (Kawasaki); 5. D'Orgeix (Honda); 6. Lussiana (Yamaha); 7. Bouffier (Kawasaki); 8. Brian (Honda); 9. Ruiz (Kawasaki); 10. Lefort (Yamaha).

8th July - Albi
1. Perret (Kawasaki); 2. A. Vincent (Yamaha); 3. K. Foray (Triumph); 4. Gines (Triumph); 5. D'Orgeix (Honda); 6. Brian (Honda); 7. Lefort (Yamaha); 8. Stey (Honda); 9. Lussiana (Yamaha); 10. Andrieu (Yamaha).

29 July - Magny-Cours
1. Perret (Kawasaki); 2. A. Vincent (Yamaha); 3. Barrier (Honda); 4. Andrieu (Yamaha); 5. K. Foray (Triumph); 6. Brian (Honda); 7. Gines (Triumph); 8. D'Orgeix (Honda); 9. Lefort (Yamaha); 10. Mizera (Yamaha).

FINAL CLASSIFICATION
1. Kenny Foray — Triumph — 132 points
2. David Perret — Kawasaki — 125
3. Arnaud Vincent — Yamaha — 115
4. J. D'Orgeix (Honda), 81; 5. M. Andrier (Yamaha), 80; 6. G. Lefort (Yamaha), 64; 7. L. Brian (Honda), 52; 8. Y. Lussiana (Yamaha), 51; 9. C. Bouffier (Kawasaki), 40; 10. D. Marsac (Yamaha), 36. 27 finishers.

SUPERBIKE
25th March - Le Mans
1. Dietrich (Suzuki); 2. Four (Yamaha); 3. Giabbani (Kawasaki); 4. F. Foray (Suzuki); 5. Delhalle (Suzuki); 6. Piot (Yamaha); 7. Bouan (Yamaha); 8. Jonchière (Suzuki); 9. Huvier (Yamaha); 10. Fremy (Yamaha).

15th April - Lédenon
1. Four (Yamaha); 2. Piot (Yamaha); 3. Metro (Ducati); 4. F. Foray (Suzuki); 5. Bouan (Yamaha); 6. Giabbani (Kawasaki); 7. Dietrich (Suzuki); 8. Nigon (Yamaha); 9. J. Millet (Yamaha); 10. Delhalle (Suzuki).

29th April - Nogaro
1. Bouan (Yamaha); 2. Dietrich (Suzuki); 3. F. Foray (Suzuki); 4. Giabbani (Kawasaki); 5. Piot (Yamaha); 6. Delhalle (Suzuki); 7. Nigon (Yamaha); 8. Muscat (Ducati); 9. Metro (Ducati); 10. Tangre (Suzuki).

13th May - Le Vigeant
1. Four (Yamaha); 2. Nigon (Yamaha); 3. Bouan (Yamaha); 4. Piot (Yamaha); 5. Dietrich (Suzuki); 6. Giabbani (Kawasaki); 7. F. Foray (Suzuki); 8. Duterne (MV-Agusta); 9. Tangre (Suzuki); 10. Protat (Ducati).

17th June - Lédenon
1. Dietrich (Suzuki); 2. Four (Yamaha); 3. F. Foray (Suzuki); 4. Muscat (Ducati); 5. Giabbani (Kawasaki); 6. Nigon (Yamaha); 7. Metro (Ducati); 8. J. Millet (Yamaha); 9. Protat (Ducati); 10. Bouan (Yamaha).

8th July - Albi
1. Piot (Yamaha); 2. Four (Yamaha); 3. Dietrich (Suzuki); 4. Bouan (Yamaha); 5. Nigon (Yamaha); 6. F. Foray (Suzuki); 7. Giabbani (Kawasaki); 8. Metro (Ducati); 9. De Carolis (Honda); 10. Tangre (Suzuki).

29th July - Magny-Cours
1. Dietrich (Suzuki); 2. Giabbani (Kawasaki); 3. Four (Yamaha); 4. F. Foray (Suzuki); 5. Piot (Yamaha); 6. Metro (Ducati); 7. Marchand (Yamaha); 8. De Carolis (Honda); 9. Duterne (MV-Agusta); 10. Bouan (Yamaha).

FINAL CLASSIFICATION
1. Guillaume Dietrich — Suzuki — 131 points
2. Olivier Four — Yamaha — 129
3. Patrick Piot — Yamaha — 98
4. F. Foray (Suzuki), 90; 5. G. Giabbani (Kawasaki), 89; 6. D. Bouan (Yamaha), 86; 7. E. Nigon (Yamaha), 64; 8. T. Metro (Ducati), 50; 9. A. Delhalle (Suzuki), 40; 10. L. De Carolis (Honda), 27. 29 finishers.

SIDE-CARS
25th March - Le Mans
1. Delannoy/Cluze (Suzuki); 2. Le Bail/Chaigneau (Suzuki); 3. Ducouret/Gandois (Suzuki); 4. S. Bessy/R. Bessy (Suzuki); 5. Bourc'his/Scellier (Honda); 6. Brunazzi/Le Croq (Suzuki); 7. F. Leblond/S. Leblond (Suzuki); 8. Marzelle/Lavidalie (Suzuki); 9. Baer/Hullois (Suzuki); 10. Herman/Bajus (Yamaha).

15th April - Lédenon
Race I: 1. Delannoy/Cluze (Suzuki); 2. Le Bail/Chaigneau (Suzuki); 3. Baer/Hullois (Suzuki); 4. Barbier/Mignon (Suzuki); 5. Ducouret/Gandois (Suzuki); 6. Beneteau/Chaussade (Suzuki); 7. Gallerne/Lelias (Suzuki); 8. Brunazzi/Le Croq (Suzuki); 9. Marzelle/Lavidalie (Suzuki); 10. Bajus/Darras (Kawasaki).
Race II: 1. Delannoy/Cluze (Suzuki); 2. Baer/Hullois (Suzuki); 3. Le Bail/Chaigneau (Suzuki); 4. Barbier/Mignon (Suzuki); 5. Ducouret/Gandois (Suzuki); 6. Gallerne/Lelias (Suzuki); 7. S. Bessy/R. Bessy (Suzuki); 8. Brunazzi/Le Croq (Suzuki); 9. Beneteau/Chaussade (Suzuki); 10. Marzelle/Lavidalie (Suzuki).

29th April - Nogaro
Race I: 1. Delannoy/Cluze (Suzuki); 2. Baer/Dury (Suzuki); 3. S. Bessy/R. Bessy (Suzuki); 4. Barbier/Chaperon (Suzuki); 5. Ducouret/Gandois (Suzuki); 6. Marzelle/Lavidalie (Suzuki); 7. J.-C.

Huet/J. Huet (Yamaha); 8. Gallerne/Lelias (Suzuki); 9. Bourc'his/Scellier (Honda); 10. F. Lebond/S. Leblond (Honda).
Race II: 1. Delannoy/Cluze (Suzuki); 2. Le Bail/Chaigneau (Suzuki); 3. Baer/Dury (Suzuki); 4. S. Bessy/R. Bessy (Suzuki); 5. Ducouret/Gandois (Suzuki); 6. Barbier/Chaperon (Suzuki); 7. Beneteau/Chaussade (Suzuki) ; 8. Marzelle/Lavidalie (Suzuki); 9. Bourc'his/Scellier (Honda); 10. Gallerne/Lelias (Suzuki).

13th May - Le Vigeant
Race I: 1. Le Bail/Chaigneau (Suzuki); 2. S. Bessy/R. Bessy (Suzuki); 3. Marzelle/Lavidalie (Suzuki); 4. Barbier/Chaperon (Suzuki); 5. Beneteau/Chaussade (Suzuki); 6. Brunazzi/Le Croq (Suzuki); 7. Bourch'is/Darras (Honda); 8. F. Leblond/S. Leblond (Honda); 9. Geffray/Mairot (Kawasaki); 10. Guigue/Théveneau (Suzuki).
Race II: 1. Le Bail/Chaigneau (Suzuki); 2. S. Bessy/R. Bessy (Suzuki); 3. Marzelle/Lavidalie (Suzuki); 4. Ducouret/Gandois (Suzuki); 5. Brunazzi/Le Croq (Suzuki); 6. Beneteau/Chaussade (Suzuki); 7. Bourch'is/Darras (Honda); 8. F. Leblond/S. Leblond (Honda); 9. Geffray/Mairot (Kawasaki); 10. Guigue/Théveneau (Suzuki).

17th June - Lédenon
Race I: 1. LeBail/Chaigneau (Suzuki); 2. Baer/Hullois (Suzuki); 3. Delannoy/Cluze (Suzuki); 4. Barbier/Chaperon (Suzuki); 5. Marzelle/Lavidalie (Suzuki); 6. Beneteau/Chaussade (Suzuki); 7. Brunazzi/Le Croq (Suzuki); 8. Ducouret/Gandois (Suzuki); 9. Gallerne/Lelias (Suzuki); 10. Guigue/Théveneau (Suzuki).
Race II: 1. LeBail/Chaigneau (Suzuki); 2. Delannoy/Cluze (Suzuki); 3. Baer/Hullois (Suzuki); 4. Barbier/Chaperon (Suzuki); 5. Ducouret/Gandois (Suzuki); 6. Marzelle/Lavidalie (Suzuki); 7. Beneteau/Chaussade (Suzuki); 8. Brunazzi/Le Croq (Suzuki); 9. Gallerne/Lelias (Suzuki); 10. Bourch'is/Scellier (Honda).

8th July - Albi
Race I: 1. Ducouret/Gandois (Suzuki); 2. S. Bessy/R. Bessy (Suzuki); 3. Baer/Dury (Suzuki); 4. Marzelle/Lavidalie (Suzuki); 5. Beneteau/Chaussade (Suzuki); 6. Barbier/Chaperon (Suzuki); 7. Bourch'is/Scellier (Suzuki); 8. Guigue/Théveneau (Suzuki); 9. Vannier/Leber (Suzuki); 10. Geffray/Mairot (Kawasaki).
Race II: 1. Le Bail/Chaigneau (Suzuki); 2. S. Bessy/R. Bessy (Suzuki); 3. Ducouret/Gandois (Suzuki); 4. Barbier/Chaperon (Suzuki); 5. Baer/Dury (Suzuki); 6. Marzelle/Lavidalie (Suzuki); 7. Beneteau/Chaussade (Suzuki); 8. Bourch'is/Scellier (Honda); 9. Gallerne/Lelias (Suzuki) ; 10. Guigue/Théveneau (Suzuki).

29th July - Magny-Cours
Race I: 1. Ducouret/Gandois (Suzuki); 2. Le Bail/Chaigneau (Suzuki); 3. Barbier/Chaperon (Suzuki); 4. Baer/Dury (Suzuki); 5. Marzelle/Lavidalie (Suzuki); 6. Brunazzi/Le Croq (Suzuki); 7. R. Poret/V. Poret (Suzuki); 8. Bourch'is/Scellier (Honda); 9. Guigue/Théveneau (Suzuki); 10. F. Leblond/S. Leblond (Honda).
Race II: 1. Le Bail/Chaigneau (Suzuki); 2. Baer/Dury (Suzuki); 3. S. Bessy/R. Bessy (Suzuki); 4. Beneteau/Chaussade (Suzuki); 5. Marzelle/Lavidalie (Suzuki); 6. Barbier/Chaperon (Suzuki); 7. Brunazzi/Le Croq (Suzuki); 8. Gallerne/Lelias (Suzuki); 9. R. Poret/V. Poret (Suzuki); 10. Bourch'is/Scellier (Honda).

FINAL CLASSIFICATION
1. Le Bail/Chaigneau   Suzuki   130,5 points
2. Delannoy/Cluze   Suzuki   95,5
3. Baer/Dury   Suzuki   89,5
4. Ducouret/Gandois (Suzuki), 86,5; 5. S. Bessy/R. Bessy (Suzuki), 80,5; 6. Marzelle/Lavidalie (Suzuki), 72; 7. Barbier/Chaperon (Suzuki), 69,5; 8. Bourch'is/Scellier (Honda), 52,5; 9. Beneteau/Chaussade (Suzuki), 49,5; 10. Brunazzi/Le Croq (Suzuki), 45. 28 finishers.

GREAT BRITAIN CHAMPIONSHIP

125
1. Beech (Honda); 2. K. Coghlan (Honda); 3. A. Rogers (Honda); 4. R. Stewart (Honda); 5. Mossey (Honda); 6. L. Jones (Honda); 7. Hoyle (Honda); 8. D. Brown (Honda); 9. N. Coates (Honda); 10. Hayward (Honda).

15th April - Thruxton
1. Mossey (Honda); 2. L. Jones (Honda); 3. K. Coghlan (Honda); 4. N. Coates (Honda); 5. Beech (Honda); 6. Wilcox (Honda); 7. Ford (Honda); 8. Tinmouth (Honda); 9. Costello (Honda); 10. M. Hill (Honda).

29th April - Silverstone
1. L. Jones (Honda); 2. K. Coghlan (Honda); 3. Beech (Honda); 4. N. Coates (Honda); 5. Hayward (Honda); 6. Wilcox (Honda); 7. Rogers (Honda); 8. Ford (Honda); 9. Wright (Honda); 10. Lodge (Honda).

7th May - Oulton Park
1. L. Jones (Honda); 2. K. Coghlan (Honda); 3. Mossey (Aprilia); 4. Beech (Honda); 5. Stewart (Honda); 6. N. Coates (Honda); 7. Wilcox (Honda); 8. Hayward (Honda); 9. Costello (Honda); 10. Finlay (Honda).

20th May - Snetterton
1. Stewart (Honda); 2. Wilcox (Honda); 3. L. Jones (Honda); 4. K. Coghlan (Honda); 5. Hayward (Honda); 6. Hoyle (Honda); 7. Guiver (Honda); 7. Costello (Honda); 8. Mossey (Honda); 9. Malton (Honda); 10. Neate (Honda).

17th June - Mondello
1. N. Coates (Honda); 2. Stewart (Honda); 3. L. Jones (Honda); 4. Wilcox (Honda); 5. Rogers (Honda); 6. Hayward (Honda); 7. K. Coghlan (Honda); 8. Maguire (Honda); 9. Costello (Honda); 10. Wright (Honda).

1st July - Knockhill
1. K. Coghlan (Honda); 2. L. Jones (Honda); 3. Guiver (Honda); 4. Wilcox (Honda); 5. Stewart (Honda); 6. Rogers (Honda); 7. Costello (Honda); 8. Hayward (Honda); 9. Lodge (Honda); 10. Wright (Honda).

15th July - Oulton Park
1. Guiver (Honda); 2. L. Jones (Honda); 3. K. Coghlan (Honda); 4. Finlay (Honda); 5. Beech (Honda); 6. N. Coates (Honda); 7. Shorrock (Honda); 8. Costello (Honda); 9. Tinmouth (Honda); 10. Neate (Honda).

22nd July - Mallory Park
1. Beech (Honda); 2. L. Jones (Honda); 3. N. Coates (Honda); 4. Wilcox (Honda); 5. Costello (Honda); 6. Hayward (Honda); 7. K. Coghlan (Honda); 8. Guiver (Honda); 9. D. Brown (Honda); 10. Hoyle (Honda).

12th August - Croft
1. Stewart (Honda); 2. Wilcox (Honda); 3. L. Jones (Honda); 4. Hoyle (Honda); 5. Rogers (Honda); 6. Costello (Honda); 7. Wright (Honda); 8. D. Brown (Honda); 9. Guiver (Honda); 10. Ford (Honda).

27th August - Cadwell Park
1. Stewart (Honda); 2. Beech (Honda); 3. L. Jones (Honda); 4. Rogers (Honda); 5. K. Coghlan (Honda); 6. Hoyle (Honda); 7. D. Brown (Honda); 8. Guiver (Honda); 9. Hayward (Honda); 10. Finlay (Honda).

23rd September - Donington
1. Stewart (Honda); 2. L. Jones (Honda); 3. L. Rossi (F, Honda); 4. Beech (Honda); 5. Debise (F, Honda); 6. Rogers (Honda); 7. Hoyle (Honda); 8. Costello (Honda); 9. N. Coates (Honda); 10. Mossey (Honda).

14th October - Brands Hatch Indy
1. Jones (Honda); 2. Stewart (Honda); 3. Beech (Honda); 4. Hoyle (Honda); 5. Hayward (Honda); 6. N. Coates (Honda); 7. Costello (Honda); 8. Finlay (Honda); 9. D. Brown (Honda); 10. Hinton (Honda).

FINAL CLASSIFICATION
1. Luke Jones   Honda   249 points
2. Robbie Stewart   Honda   179
3. Kev Coghlan   Honda   162
4. A. Beech (Honda), 155; 5. N. Coates (Honda), 113; 6. M. Wilcox (Honda), 113; 7. T. Hayward (Honda), 92; 8. L. Costello (Honda), 87; 9. A. Rogers (Honda), 75; 10. R. Guiver (Honda), 73. 40 finishers.

SUPERSPORT

9th April - Brands Hatch GP
1. M. Laverty (Suzuki); 2. J. Robinson (Honda); 3. Lowry (Suzuki); 4. A. Walker (Honda): 5. Easton (Kawasaki); 6. McGuiness (Honda); 7. R. Cooper (Yamaha); 8. Neate (Honda); 9. Hutchinson (Honda); 10. Westmoreland (Honda).

15th April - Thruxton
1. M. Laverty (Suzuki); 2. J. Robinson (Honda); 3. McConnell (Yamaha); 4. Westmoreland (Honda); 5. Easton (Kawasaki); 6. Hutchinson (Honda); 7. Jessopp (Ducati); 8. D. Cooper (Honda); 9. Kennedy (Honda); 10. Lowes (Honda).

29th April - Silverstone
1. Hobbs (Honda); 2. Lowry (Suzuki); 3. M. Laverty (Suzuki); 4. Hutchinson (Honda); 5. Grant (Yamaha); 6. McGuiness (Honda); 7. McConnell (Yamaha); 8. Jessop (Ducati); 9. Easton (Kawasaki); 10. R. Cooper (Yamaha).

7th May - Oulton Park
1. Hobbs (Honda); 2. Lowry (Suzuki); 3. M. Laverty (Suzuki); 4. Sanders (Kawasaki); 5. McGuiness (Honda); 6. Grant (Yamaha); 7. Owens (Honda); 8. Young (Triumph); 9. J. Robinson (Honda); 10. Easton (Kawasaki).

20th May - Snetterton
1. Lowry (Suzuki); 2. M. Laverty (Suzuki); 3. Hobbs (Honda); 4. McConnell (Yamaha); 5. J. Robinson (Honda); 6. Young (Triumph); 7. Sanders (Kawasaki); 8. Westmoreland (Honda); 9. McGuiness (Honda); 10. T. Grant (Yamaha).

17th June - Mondello
1. Hobbs (Honda); 2. J. Robinson (Honda); 3. Lowry (Suzuki); 4. McGuiness (Honda); 5. Easton (Kawasaki); 6. Grant (Yamaha); 7. Fitzpatrick (Yamaha); 8. Westmoreland (Honda); 9. Jessop (Ducati); 10. Owens (Honda).

1st July - Knockhill
1. M. Laverty (Suzuki); 2. Young (Triumph); 3. Grant (Yamaha); 4. McConnell (Yamaha); 5. Lowry (Suzuki); 6. Jessop (Ducati); 7. Hobbs (Honda); 8. Hutchinson (Honda); 9. Amor (Honda); 10. Owens (Honda).

15th July - Oulton Park
1. Hutchinson (Honda); 2. McGuiness (Honda); 3. J. Robinson (Honda); 4. M. Laverty (Suzuki); 5. McConnell (Yamaha); 6. A. Walker (Honda); 7. Westmoreland (Honda); 8. Cooper (Honda); 9. Hobbs (Honda); 10. Dickinson (Honda).

22nd July - Mallory Park
1. M. Laverty (Suzuki); 2. Lowry (Suzuki); 3. Hobbs (Honda); 4. McConnell (Yamaha); 5. Hutchinson (Honda); 6. McGuiness (Honda); 7. Easton (Kawasaki); 8. Dickinson (Honda); 9. J. Robinson (Honda); 10. T. Grant (Yamaha).

12th August - Croft
1. McConnell (Yamaha); 2. Hobbs (Honda); 3. Lowry (Suzuki); 4. Hutchinson (Honda); 5. Easton (Kawasaki); 6. McGuiness (Honda); 7. T. Grant (Yamaha); 8. Westmoreland (Honda); 9. Young (Triumph); 10. A. Walker (Honda).

27th August - Cadwell Park
1. M. Laverty (Suzuki); 2. McConnell (Yamaha); 3. T. Grant (Yamaha); 4. McGuiness (Honda); 5. Jessopp (Ducati); 6. Hobbs (Honda); 7. Dickinson (Honda); 8. J. Robinson (Honda); 9. A. Walker (Honda); 10. Owens (Honda).

23rd September - Donington
1. M. Laverty (Suzuki); 2. Lowry (Suzuki); 3. McConnell (Yamaha); 4. McGuiness (Honda); 5. A. Walker (Honda); 6. Owens (Honda); 7. J. Robinson (Honda); 8. Dickinson (Honda); 9. Hillier (Kawasaki); 10. Grant (Yamaha).

14th October - Brands Hatch Indy
1. McConnell (Yamaha); 2. Hobbs (Honda); 3. M. Laverty (Suzuki); 4. Grant (Yamaha); 5. Brogan (Honda); 6. Lowry (Suzuki); 7. Owens (Honda); 8. J. Robinson (Honda); 9. Westmoreland (Honda); 10. Jessopp (Ducati).

FINAL CLASSIFICATION
1. Michael Laverty   Suzuki   231 points
2. Ian Lowry   Suzuki   179
3. Dennis Hobbs   Honda   173
4. B. McConnell (Yamaha), 161; 5. J. Robinson (Honda), 1? 6. J. McGuiness (Honda), 117; 7. T. Grant (Yamaha), 103; 8. I. Hutchinson (Honda), 96; 9. J. Westm and (Honda), 69; 10. S. Easton (Kawasaki), 66. 36 finishers.

SUPERSTOCK

9th April - Brands Hatch GP
1. G. Richards (AUS, Yamaha); 2. Kennaugh (SA, Yar , 3. Brogan (Honda); 4. Quigley (Suzuki); 5. B. Wilson (Suzuki); 6. Rose (Suzuki); 7. L. Jackson (Ya· ; 8. J. Laverty (Ducati); 9. A. Coates (Yamaha); 10. Murphy (Suzuki).

15th April - Thruxton
1. G. Richards (AUS, Yamaha); 2. Brogan (Hon ennaugh (SA, Yamaha) ; 4. Mainwaring (MV-Agusta) ; 5. L. Jackson (Yamaha) ; 6. Quigley (Suzu , 7. A. Coates (Yamaha) ; 8. J. Laverty (Ducati) ; 9. Clarke (Ducati) ; 10. B. Wilson (Suzuki).

29th April - Silverstone
1. Lennaugh (SA, Yamaha); 2. G. Richards (AUS, Yamaha); 3. Quigley (Suzuki); 4. B. Wilson (Suzuki); 5. Brogan (Honda); 6. Murphy (Suzuki); 7. Mainwaring (MV-Agusta); 8. Glynn (Yamaha); 9. L. Jackson (Yamaha); 10. J. Laverty (Ducati).

7th May - Oulton Park
1. Mainwaring (MV-Agusta); 2. G. Richards (AUS, Yamaha); 3. L. Jackson (Yamaha); 4. B. Wilson (Suzuki); 5. Quigley (Suzuki); 6. Murphy (Suzuki); 7. J. Laverty (Ducati); 8. Jenkinson (Suzuki); 9. Whitman (Suzuki); 10. Glynn (Yamaha).

20th May - Snetterton
1. G. Richards (AUS, Yamaha); 2. Kennaugh (SA, Yamaha); 3. J. Laverty (Ducati); 4. L. Jackson (Yamaha); 5. Jenkinson (Suzuki); 6. Mercer (Yamaha); 7. Kirkham (Yamaha); 8. Brogan (Yamaha); 9. Murphy (Suzuki); 10. Ventor (Suzuki).

17th June - Mondello
Race I: 1. Brogan (Honda); 2. B. Wilson (Suzuki); 3. Jenkinson (Suzuki); 4. Murphy (Suzuki); 5. L.

Jackson (Yamaha); 6. G. Johnson (Yamaha); 7. Kirkham (Yamaha); 8. J. Laverty (Ducati); 9. Rose (Suzuki); 10. Mercer (Yamaha).
Race II: 1. A. Coates (Yamaha); 2. G. Richards (AUS, Yamaha); 3. Brogan (Honda); 4. Seeley (Yamaha); 5. B. Wilson (Suzuki); 6. J. Laverty (Ducati); 7. Kirkham (Yamaha); 8. Mercer (Yamaha); 9. Rose (Suzuki); 10. L. Jackson (Yamaha).

1st July - Knockhill
Canceled.

15th July - Oulton Park
Canceled.

12th August - Croft
1. Neill (Suzuki); 2. Kirkham (Yamaha); 3. Seeley (Yamaha); 4. Kennaugh (Yamaha); 5. J. Laverty (Ducati); 6. L. Jackson (Yamaha); 7. Brogan (Honda); 8. Venter (Yamaha); 9. B. Roberts (AUS, Ducati); 10. Ingram (Suzuki).

27th August - Cadwell Park
1. B. Roberts (AUS, Ducati); 2. J. Laverty (Ducati); 3. G. Richards (AUS, Yamaha); 4. Kirkham (Yamaha); 5. Brogan (Honda); 6. Wilson (Suzuki); 7. L. Jackson (Yamaha); 8. Hegarty (Yamaha); 9. Hickman (Yamaha); 10. Seeley (Yamaha).

23rd September - Donington
Race I: 1. Kennaugh (Yamaha); 2. Kirkham (Yamaha); 3. Brogan (Honda); 4. G. Richards (AUS, Yamaha); 5. Wilson (Suzuki); 6. B. Roberts (AUS, Ducati); 7. Hickman (Yamaha); 8. Seeley (Yamaha); 9. Neill (Suzuki); 10. Venter (Yamaha).
Race II: 1. Kennaugh (Yamaha); 2. Kirkham (Yamaha); 3. G. Richards (AUS, Yamaha); 4. J. Laverty (Ducati); 5. B. Roberts (AUS, Ducati); 6. Brogan (Honda); 7. Neill (Suzuki); 8. Hickman (Yamaha); 9. Seeley (Yamaha); 10. Jenkinson (Suzuki).

14th October - Brands Hatch Indy
Race I: 1. J. Laverty (Ducati); 2. G. Richards (AUS, Yamaha); 3. Kirkham (Yamaha); 4. Brogan (Honda); 5. Wilson (Suzuki); 6. B. Roberts (AUS, Ducati); 7. L. Jackson (Yamaha); 8. Jenkinson (Suzuki); 9. Mainwaring (MV-Agusta); 10. Glynn (Yamaha).
Race II: 1. Brogan (Honda); 2. G. Richards (AUS, Yamaha); 3. Jenkinson (Suzuki); 4. J. Laverty (Ducati); 5. Kirkham (Yamaha); 6. L. Jackson (Yamaha); 7. B. Roberts (AUS, Ducati); 8. Kennaugh (Yamaha); 9. Buckles (MV-Agusta); 10. A. Seeley (Yamaha).

FINAL CLASSIFICATION

1. Glen Richards (AUS)	Yamaha	223 points
2. Steve Brogan	Honda	180
3. Hudson Kennaugh	Yamaha	154

4. J. Laverty (Ducati), 147; 5. J. Kirkham (Yamaha), 127; 6. L. Jackson (Yamaha), 111; 7. B. Wilson (Suzuki), 109; 8. B. Roberts (AUS, Ducati), 72; 9. A. Jenkinson (Suzuki), 67; 10. A. Seeley (Yamaha), 65. 40 finishers.

SUPERBIKE

9th April - Brands Hatch GP
Race I: 1. Lavilla (E, Ducati); 2. Camier (Honda); 3. J. Rea (Honda); 4. Byrne (Honda); 5. C. Walker (Suzuki); 6. L. Haslam (Ducati); 7. Sykes (Honda); 8. Kiyonari (J, Honda); 9. T. Hill (Yamaha); 10. Rutter (Kawasaki).
Race II: 1. Lavilla (E, Ducati); 2. J. Rea (Honda); 3. Camier (Honda); 4. L. Haslam (Ducati); 5. Sykes (Honda); 6. K. Harris (Honda); 7. Rutter (Kawasaki); 8. C. Walker (Suzuki); 9. Andrews (Yamaha); 10. Thomas (AUS, Suzuki).

15th April - Thruxton
Race I: 1. Lavilla (E, Ducati); 2. Camier (Honda); 3. Kiyonari (J, Honda); 4. Byrne (Honda); 5. Sykes (Honda); 6. L. Haslam (Ducati); 7. Crutchlow (Suzuki); 8. T. Hill (Yamaha); 9. C. Walker (Suzuki); 10. K. Harris (Honda).
Race II: 1. Lavilla (E, Ducati); 2. Kiyonari (Honda); 3. Byrne (Honda); 4. J. Rea (Honda); 5. Camier (Honda); 6. L. Haslam (Ducati); 7. Sykes (Honda); 8. Rutter (Kawasaki); 9. K. Harris (Honda); 10. T. Hill (Yamaha).

29th April - Silverstone
Race I: 1. Kiyonari (J, Honda); 2. J. Rea (Honda); 3. C. Walker (Suzuki); 4. Camier (Honda); 5. Lavilla (Ducati); 6. L. Haslam (Ducati); 7. Sykes (Honda); 8. T. Hill (Yamaha); 9. K. Harris (Honda); 10. Rutter (Kawasaki).
Race II: 1. Kiyonari (J, Honda); 2. Lavilla (E, Ducati); 3. J. Rea (Honda); 4. C. Walker (Suzuki); 5. L. Haslam (Ducati); 6. Sykes (Honda); 7. Crutchlow (Suzuki); 8. T. Hill (Yamaha); 9. Rutter (Kawasaki); 10. Bridewell (Suzuki).

7th May - Oulton Park
Race I: 1. Lavilla (E, Ducati); 2. L. Haslam (Ducati); 3. Kiyonari (J, Honda); 4. J. Rea (Honda); 5. Sykes (Honda); 6. Byrne (Honda); 7. Crutchlow (Suzuki); 8. Camier (Honda); 9. K. Harris (Honda); 10. Hill (Yamaha).
Race II: 1. Kiyonari (J, Honda); 2. Haslam (Ducati); 3. Byrne (Honda); 4. Lavilla (E, Ducati); 5. J. Rea (Honda); 6. Sykes (Honda); 7. Hill (Yamaha); 8. Camier (Honda); 9. C. Walker (Suzuki); 10. Thomas (AUS, Suzuki).

20th May - Snetterton
Race I: 1. Kiyonari (J, Honda); 2. J. Rea (Hc[illegible]da); 3. L. Haslam (Ducati); 4. Sykes (Honda); 5. Camier (Honda); 6. Lavilla (E, Ducati); 7. Hill (Yamal[illegible] 8. Crutchlow (Suzuki); 9. C. Walker (Suzuki); 10. Bridewell (Suzuki).
Race II: 1. Kiyonari (J, Honda); 2. J. Rea (Hc[illegible] 3. Byrne (Honda); 4. Sykes (Honda); 5. L. Haslam (Ducati); 6. Camier (Honda); 7. Hill (Yamaha), [illegible] Smart (Kawasaki); 9. C. Walker (Suzuki); 10. Bridewell (Suzuki).

17th June - Mondello
Race I: 1. L. Haslam (Ducati); 2. Byrne (Honda), [illegible]villa (E, Ducati); 4. J. Rea (Honda); 5. Kiyonari (J, Honda); 6. K. Harris (Honda); 7. Camier (Honda) [illegible]utchlow (Suzuki); 9. C. Walker (Suzuki); 10. Hill (Yamaha).
Race II: 1. J. Rea (Honda); 2. Byrne (Honda); 3. L[illegible] Ducati); 4. L. Haslam (Ducati); 5. Kiyonari (J, Honda); 6. Camier (Honda); 7. Sykes (Honda); 8. [illegible] (Honda); 9. Hill (Yamaha); 10. S. Smart (Kawasaki).

1st July - Knockhill
Race I: 1. J. Rea (Honda); 2. Kiyonari (J, Honda); 3. L. Haslam (Ducati); 4. Byrne (Honda); 5. C. Walker (Suzuki); 6. Sykes (Honda); 7. Lavilla (E, Ducati); 8. Bridewell (Suzuki); 9. Emmett (Suzuki); 10. K. Harris (Honda).
Race II: 1. J. Rea (Honda); 2. L. Haslam (Ducati); 3. Kiyonari (J, Honda); 4. Sykes (Honda); 5. Byrne (Honda); 6. C. Walker (Suzuki); 7. Camier (Honda); 8. K. Harris (Honda); 9. Emmett (Suzuki); 10. Bridewell (Suzuki).

15th July - Oulton Park
Race I: 1. Kiyonari (J, Honda); 2. Byrne (Honda); 3. C. Walker (Suzuki); 4. L. Haslam (Ducati); 5. Crutchlow (Suzuki); 6. Camier (Honda); 7. S. Smart (Kawasaki); 8. Hill (Yamaha); 9. Bridewell (Suzuki); 10. G. Martin (Honda).
Race II: 1. J. Rea (Honda); 2. K. Harris (Honda); 3. Byrne (Honda); 4. L. Haslam (Ducati); 5. Camier (Honda); 6. Sykes (Honda); 7. Rutter (Kawasaki); 8. C. Walker (Suzuki); 9. Bridewell (Suzuki); 10. Lavilla (E, Ducati).

22nd July - Mallory Park
Race I: 1. Byrne (Honda); 2. Rea (Honda); 3. L. Haslam (Ducati); 4. C. Walker (Suzuki); 5. Lavilla (E, Ducati); 6. Sykes (Honda); 7. Hill (Yamaha); 8. Camier (Honda); 9. Crutchlow (Suzuki); 10. S. Smart (Kawasaki).
Race II: 1. Kiyonari (J, Honda); 2. L. Haslam (Ducati); 3. Byrne (Honda); 4. Sykes (Honda); 5. Crutchlow (Suzuki); 6. C. Walker (Suzuki); 7. Lavilla (E, Ducati); 8. Rutter (Kawasaki); 9. Hill (Yamaha); 10. S. Smart (Kawasaki).

12th August - Croft
Race I: 1. Kiyonari (J, Honda); 2. J. Rea (Honda); 3. Sykes (Honda); 4. Crutchlow (Suzuki); 5. L. Haslam (Ducati); 6. Lavilla (E, Ducati); 7. Camier (Honda); 8. C. Walker (Suzuki); 9. Byrne (Honda); 10. Hill (Yamaha).
Race II: 1. Kiyonari (J, Honda); 2. J. Rea (Honda); 3. Sykes (Honda); 4. Lavilla (E, Ducati); 5. Camier (Honda); 6. L. Haslam (Ducati); 7. Byrne (Honda); 8. Rutter (Kawasaki); 9. Andrews (Yamaha); 10. C. Walker (Suzuki).

27th August - Cadwell Park
Race I: 1. L. Haslam (Ducati); 2. Kiyonari (J, Honda); 3. Sykes (Honda); 4. Byrne (Honda); 5. Crutchlow (Suzuki); 6. Hill (Yamaha); 7. Lavilla (E, Ducati); 8. C. Walker (Suzuki); 9. Haydon (Kawasaki); 10. S. Smart (Kawasaki).
Race II: 1. J. Rea (Honda); 2. Kiyonari (J, Honda); 3. Lavilla (E, Ducati); 4. Crutchlow (Suzuki); 5. Sykes (Honda); 6. C. Walker (Suzuki); 7. Hill (Yamaha); 8. Haydon (Kawasaki); 9. Plater (Yamaha); 10. Rutter (Kawasaki).

23rd September - Donington
Race I: 1. L. Haslam (Ducati); 2. Sykes (Honda); 3. Byrne (Honda); 4. Lavilla (E, Ducati); 5. J. Rea (Honda); 6. C. Walker (Suzuki); 7. S. Smart (Kawasaki); 8. Haydon (Kawasaki); 9. Rutter (Kawasaki); 10. Plater (Yamaha).
Race II: 1. L. Haslam (Ducati); 2. Sykes (Honda); 3. Kiyonari (J, Honda); 4. C. Walker (Suzuki); 5. Lavilla (E, Ducati); 6. Byrne (Honda); 7. J. Rea (Honda); 8. Rutter (Kawasaki); 9. Plater (Yamaha); 10. K. Harris (Honda).

14th October - Brands Hatch Indy
Race I: 1. Lavilla (E, Ducati); 2. J. Rea (Honda); 3. Kiyonari (J, Honda); 4. L. Haslam (Ducati); 5. Crutchlow (Suzuki); 6. Byrne (Honda); 7. C. Walker (Suzuki); 8. Rutter (Kawasaki); 9. Andrews (Yamaha); 10. Plater (Yamaha).
Race II: 1. Lavilla (E, Ducati); 2. J. Rea (Honda); 3. Crutchlow (Suzuki); 4. Kiyonari (Honda); 5. L. Haslam (Ducati); 6. C. Walker (Suzuki); 7. Sykes (Honda); 8. K. Harris (Honda); 9. Haydon (Kawasaki); 10. Rutter (Kawasaki).

FINAL CLASSIFICATION

1. Ryuichi Kiyonari (J)	Honda	433 points
2. Jonathan Rea	Honda	407
3. Leon Haslam	Ducati	387

4. G. Lavilla (E, Ducati), 368; 5. S. Byrne (Honda), 293; 6. R. Sykes (Honda), 279; 7. C. Walker (Suzuki), 225; 8. L. Camier (Honda), 199; 9. C. Crutchlow (Suzuki), 152; 10. T. Hill (Yamaha), 138. 36 finishers.

ITALY CHAMPIONSHIP

125 GP

22nd April - Mugello
1. Lacalendola (Aprilia); 2. Sancioni (Aprilia); 3. Ferro (Honda); 4. Massei (Aprilia); 5. Lamborghini (Aprilia); 6. F. Biaggi (Friba); 7. Musco (Honda); 8. Zenari (Honda); 9. Mosca (Aprilia); 10. Ravaioli (Aprilia).

6th May - Monza
1. Sancioni (Aprilia); 2. Lacalendola (Aprilia); 3. Savadori (Aprilia); 4. Ferro (Honda); 5. Vivarelli (Honda); 6. Conti (Honda); 7. Moretti (Honda); 8. Palumbo (Aprilia); 9. F. Biaggi (Friba); 10. Ravaioli (Aprilia).

10th June - Vallelunga
1. Lamborghini (Aprilia); 2. Palumbo (Aprilia); 3. F. Biaggi (Friba); 4. Lacalendola (Aprilia); 5. Ferro (Honda); 6. Moretti (Honda); 7. Sancioni (Aprilia); 8. Musco (Honda); 9. Massei (Aprilia); 10. Zenari (Honda).

24th June - Misano
1. Pellino (Aprilia); 2. F. Biaggi (Friba); 3. Sancioni (Aprilia); 4. Ferro (Honda); 5. Lacalendola (Aprilia); 6. Palumbo (Aprilia); 7. Conti (Honda); 8. Massei (Aprilia); 9. Stirpe (Honda); 10. Moretti (Honda).

16th September - Misano
1. Lacalendola (Aprilia); 2. Sancioni (Aprilia); 3. Moretti (Honda); 4. Ferro (Honda); 5. Stirpe (Honda); 6. Pellino (Aprilia); 7. Massei (Aprilia); 8. Zenari (Honda); 9. Ravaioli (Aprilia); 10. Ciavatta (Honda).

14th October - Mugello
1. Ferro (Honda); 2. Savadori (Aprilia); 3. Vivarelli (Honda); 4. Stirpe (Honda); 5. Conti (Honda); 6. Moretti (Honda); 7. Ravaioli (Aprilia); 8. Capuano (Aprilia); 9. Bugatti (Honda); 10. Massei (Aprilia).

FINAL CLASSIFICATION

1. Roberto Lacalendola	Aprilia	94 points
2. Gabriele Ferro	Honda	91
3. Simone Sancioni	Aprilia	90

4. F. Biaggi (Friba), 53; 5. R. Moretti (Honda), 51; 6. F. Massei (Aprilia), 43; 7. A. Palumbo (Aprilia), 38; 8. M. Ravaioli (Aprilia), 38; 9. F. Lamborghini (Aprilia), 36; 10. L. Savadori (Aprilia), 36. 31 finishers.

SUPERSPORT

22nd April - Mugello
1. Roccoli (Yamaha); 2. Vizziello (Yamaha); 3. Marrancone (Yamaha); 4. C. Migliorati (Kawasaki); 5. Cruciani (Honda); 6. Giansanti (Yamaha); 7. Brannetti (Yamaha); 8. Velini (Yamaha); 9. Corradi (Yamaha); 10. Antonello (Kawasaki).

6th May - Monza
1. Roccoli (Yamaha); 2. Vizziello (Yamaha); 3. Cruciani (Honda); 4. C. Migliorati (Kawasaki); 5. Marrancone (Yamaha); 6. Boccolini (Kawasaki); 7. Sassaro (Yamaha); 8. Cipriani (Yamaha); 9. Velini (Yamaha); 10. Corradi (Yamaha).

10th June - Vallelunga
1. Cruciani (Honda); 2. Roccoli (Yamaha); 3. Marrancone (Yamaha); 4. Zerbo (Yamaha); 5. Brannetti (Yamaha); 6. Giugovaz (Kawasaki); 7. Boccolini (Kawasaki); 8. Sassaro (Yamaha); 9. C. Migliorati (Kawasaki); 10. Giansanti (Yamaha).

24th June - Misano
1. Roccoli (Yamaha); 2. Cruciani (Honda); 3. Vizziello (Yamaha); 4. Velini (Yamaha); 5. C. Migliorati (Kawasaki); 6. Sassaro (Yamaha); 7. Corradi (Ducati); 8. Lunadei (Honda); 9. Giansanti (Yamaha); 10. Ciavattini (Honda).

16th September - Misano
1. Vizziello (Yamaha); 2. Roccoli (Yamaha); 3. Cruciani (Honda); 4. Clementi (Triumph); 5. Sassaro (Yamaha); 6. C. Migliorati (Kawasaki); 7. Lunadei (Honda); 8. Corradi (Ducati); 9. Ciavattini (Honda); 10. Giugovaz (Kawasaki).

14th October - Mugello
1. Roccoli (Yamaha); 2. Clementi (Triumph); 3. Vizziello (Yamaha); 4. Marrancone (Yamaha); 5. Corradi (Ducati); 6. Cruciani (Honda); 7. Sassaro (Yamaha); 8. Giugovaz (Kawasaki); 9. Lunadei (Honda); 10. C. Migliorati (Kawasaki).

FINAL CLASSIFICATION
1. Massimo Roccoli — Yamaha — 140 points
2. Stefano Cruciani — Honda — 98
3. Gianluca Vizziello — Yamaha — 97
4. D. Marrancone (Yamaha), 60; 5. C. Migliorati (Kawasaki), 60; 6. A. Sassaro (Yamaha), 51; 7. A. Corradi (Ducati), 41; 8. R. Lunadei (Honda), 38; 9. I. Clementi (Triumph), 35; 10. A. Velini (Yamaha), 33. 24 finishers.

SUPERSTOCK

22nd April - Mugello
1. Pirro (Yamaha); 2. Corti (Yamaha); 3. Baiocco (Yamaha); 4. Dionisi (Suzuki); 5. Prattichizzo (Suzuki); 6. Pellizzon (Ducati); 7. Iannuzzo (Kawasaki); 8. Toti (Yamaha); 9. Rozza (MV-Agusta); 10. Dell'Omo (MV-Agusta).

6th May - Monza
1. Corti (Yamaha); 2. Baiocco (Yamaha); 3. Pirro (Yamaha); 4. Toti (Yamaha); 5. Rozza (MV-Agusta); 6. Dionisi (Suzuki); 7. Iommi (Kawasaki); 8. Dell'Omo (MV-Agusta); 9. Melone (Suzuki); 10. A. Aldrovandi (Yamaha).

10th June - Vallelunga
1. Baiocco (Yamaha); 2. Pirro (Yamaha); 3. Toti (Yamaha); 4. Corti (Yamaha); 5. Dionisi (Suzuki); 6. Prattichizzo (Suzuki); 7. Pellizzon (Yamaha); 8. Goi (Suzuki); 9. Dell'Omo (MV-Agusta); 10. Salvatore (Yamaha).

24th June - Misano
1. Dionisi (Suzuki); 2. Pirro (Yamaha); 3. Toti (Yamaha); 4. Prattichizzo (Suzuki); 5. Iannuzzo (Kawasaki); 6. L. Biliotti (MV-Agusta); 7. Romanelli (Ducati); 8. Dell'Omo (MV-Agusta); 9. Verdini (Yamaha); 10. Goi (Suzuki).

16th September - Misano
1. Corti (Yamaha); 2. Pirro (Yamaha); 3. Dionisi (Suzuki); 4. Goi (Suzuki); 5. A. Aldrovandi (Yamaha); 6. Prattichizzo (Suzuki); 7. Perotti (Yamaha); 8. Verdini (Yamaha); 9. Dell'Omo (MV-Agusta); 10. Tocca (Ducati).

14th October - Mugello
1. Corti (Yamaha); 2. Dionisi (Suzuki); 3. Baiocco (Yamaha); 4. A. Aldrovandi (Yamaha); 5. Pirro (Yamaha); 6. Pellizzon (Ducati); 7. Prattichizzo (Suzuki); 8. Perotti (Yamaha); 9. Saltarelli (Suzuki); 10. Romanelli (Ducati).

FINAL CLASSIFICATION
1. Michele Pirro — Yamaha — 112 points
2. Claudio Corti — Yamaha — 108
3. Ilario Dionisi — Suzuki — 95
4. M. Baiocco (Yamaha), 77; 5. T. Toti (Yamaha), 53; 6. M. Prattichizzo (Suzuki), 53; 7. A. Aldrovandi (Yamaha), 39; 8. D. Dell'Omo (MV-Agusta), 36; 9. F. Pellizzon (Ducati), 29; 10. I. Goi (Suzuki), 27. 28 finishers.

SUPERBIKE

22nd April - Mugello
1. Borciani (Ducati); 2. Brignola (Ducati); 3. Lucchiari (Ducati); 4. Gramigni (Yamaha); 5. Pini (Yamaha); 6. Mauri (Ducati); 7. Di Maso (Suzuki); 8. Faccietti (Yamaha); 9. Di Giannicola (Suzuki); 10. Zannini (Ducati).

6th May - Monza
1. Borciani (Ducati); 2. Badovini (MV-Agusta); 3. Brignola (Ducati); 4. Sanchini (Kawasaki); 5. Lucchiari (Ducati); 6. Mauri (Ducati); 7. Gramigni (Yamaha); 8. Morelli (Ducati); 9. Di Giannicola (Suzuki); 10. Scatola (Yamaha).

10th June - Vallelunga
1. Borciani (Ducati); 2. Brignola (Ducati); 3. Badovini (MV-Agusta); 4. Conforti (Honda); 5. Lucchiari (Ducati); 6. Pini (Yamaha); 7. Caselli (Yamaha); 8. Gramigni (Yamaha); 9. Mazzali (MV-Agusta); 10. Di Maso (Suzuki).

24th June - Misano
1. Borciani (Ducati); 2. Brignola (Ducati); 3. Conforti (Honda); 4. Lucchiari (Ducati); 5. Caselli (Yamaha); 6. Gramigni (Yamaha); 7. Pini (Yamaha); 8. Mauri (Ducati); 9. Di Maso (Suzuki); 10. Battisti (Honda).

16th September - Misano
1. Brignola (Ducati); 2. Borciani (Ducati); 3. Pini (Yamaha); 4. Lucchiari (Ducati); 5. Mauri (Ducati); 6. Conforti (Honda); 7. Caselli (Yamaha); 8. Gramigni (Yamaha); 9. Di Maso (Suzuki); 10. Faccietti (Yamaha).

14th October - Mugello
1. Badovini (MV-Agusta); 2. Brignola (Ducati); 3. Scassa (MV-Agusta); 4. Borciani (Ducati); 5. Lucchiari (Ducati); 6. Conforti (Honda); 7. Mauri (Ducati); 8. Gramigni (Yamaha); 9. Caselli (Yamaha); 10. Pietri (Yamaha).

FINAL CLASSIFICATION
1. Marco Borciani — Ducati — 133 points
2. Norino Brignola — Ducati — 121
3. Mauro Lucchiari — Ducati — 75
4. A. Badovini (MV-Agusta), 61; 5. A. Gramigni (Yamaha), 56; 6. L. Conforti (Honda), 49; 7. L. Mauri (Ducati), 48; 8. L. Pini (Yamaha), 46; 9. D. Caselli (Yamaha), 38; 10. F. Di Maso (Suzuki), 32. 29 finishers.

SWITZERLAND CHAMPIONSHIP

SUPERSTOCK 600

6th - 8th April - Lédenon - France
Race I: 1. K. Foray (F, Triumph); 2. Savary (Yamaha); 3. Chèvre (Suzuki); 4. Rüegg (Yamaha); 5. Dähler (Yamaha); 6. Raschle (Kawasaki); 7. Leemann (Kawasaki); 8. Labarthe (Yamaha); 9. Bellaire (F, Yamaha); 10. Girard (Yamaha).
Race II: 1. K. Foray (F, Triumph); 2. Savary (Yamaha); 3. Chèvre (Suzuki); 4. Rüegg (Yamaha); 5. Dähler (Yamaha); 6. Raschle (Kawasaki); 7. Bellaire (F, Yamaha); 8. Leemann (Kawasaki); 9. Riboulet (Suzuki); 10. Labarthe (Yamaha).

29th April - Lausitz - Germany
1. Chèvre (Suzuki); 2. Leemann (Kawasaki); 3. Dähler (Yamaha); 4. Raschle (Kawasaki); 5. Girard (Yamaha); 6. Heuberger (Suzuki); 7. Labarthe (Yamaha); 8. Nadalet (Kawasaki); 9. Pradier (F, Yamaha); 10. Gétaz (Yamaha).

11th - 13th May - Schleiz - Germany
Race I: 1. Chèvre (Suzuki); 2. Leemann (Kawasaki); 3. Rüegg (Yamaha); 4. Dähler (Yamaha); 5. Leemann (Kawasaki); 6. Heuberger (Suzuki); 7. Labarthe (Yamaha); 8. Plüss (Kawasaki); 9. Von Gunten (Suzuki); 10. C.-A. Jaggi (Triumph).
Race II: 1. Chèvre (Suzuki); 2. Raschle (Kawasaki); 3. Dähler (Yamaha); 4. Rüegg (Yamaha); 5. Nadalet (Kawasaki); 6. Leemann (Kawasaki); 7. Heuberger (Suzuki); 8. Von Gunten (Suzuki); 9. Plüss (Kawasaki); 10. C.-A. Jaggi (Triumph).

15th - 17th June - Most - Czech Republic
Race I: 1. Reichelt (D, Kawasaki); 2. Chèvre (Suzuki); 3. Dähler (Yamaha); 4. Rüegg (Yamaha); 5. Raschle (Kawasaki); 6. Nadalet (Kawasaki); 7. Plüss (Kawasaki); 8. Von Gunten (Suzuki); 9. Labarthe (Yamaha); 10. Heuberger (Suzuki).
Race II: 1. Chèvre (Suzuki); 2. Reichelt (D, Kawasaki); 3. Leemann (Kawasaki); 4. Dähler (Yamaha); 5. Von Gunten (Suzuki); 6. Nadalet (Kawasaki); 7. Labarthe (Yamaha); 8. Heuberger (Suzuki); 9. Plüss (Kawasaki); 10. Gétaz (Yamaha).

13th - 15th July - Dijon - France
Race I: 1. Gines (Yamaha); 2. Savary (Yamaha); 3. Junod (Yamaha); 4. Chèvre (Suzuki); 5. Raschle (Kawasaki); 6. Dähler (Yamaha); 7. Rüegg (Yamaha); 8. C. Von Gunten (Suzuki); 9. Labarthe (Yamaha); 10. Pradier (F, Yamaha).
Race II: 1. Junod (Yamaha); 2. Gines (F, Yamaha); 3. Savary (Yamaha); 4. Leemann (Kawasaki); 5. Raschle (Kawasaki); 6. Chèvre (Suzuki); 7. Rüegg (Yamaha); 8. Dähler (Yamaha); 9. C. Von Gunten (Suzuki); 10. Labarthe (Yamaha).

17th - 19th August - Rijeka - Croatia
Race I: 1. Junod (Yamaha); 2. C. Von Gunten (Suzuki); 3. Plüss (Kawasaki); 4. Dähler (Yamaha); 5. Girard (Yamaha); 6. Labarthe (Yamaha); 7. Nadalet (Kawasaki); 8. Rüegg (Yamaha); 9. Gétaz (Yamaha); 10. Dafflon (Suzuki).
Race II: 1. Junod (Yamaha); 2. Leemann (Kawasaki); 3. Girard (Yamaha); 4. Plüss (Kawasaki); 5. Rüegg (Yamaha); 6. Dähler (Yamaha); 7. Nadalet (Kawasaki); 8. Labarthe (Yamaha); 9. Dafflon (Suzuki); 10. Gétaz (Yamaha).

FINAL CLASSIFICATION
1. Raphael Chèvre — Suzuki — 175 points
2. Werner Dähler — Yamaha — 137
3. Remo Leemann — Kawasaki — 112
4. R. Raschle (Kawasaki), 106; 5. C. Rüegg (Yamaha), 105; 6. G. Junod (Yamaha), 91; 7. B. Labarthe (Yamaha), 84; 8. M. Savary (Yamaha), 76; 9. C. Von Gunten (Suzuki), 73; 10. D. Plüss (Kawasaki), 69. 30 finishers.

SUPERSTOCK 1000

6th - 8th April - Lédenon - France
Race I: 1. Wildisen (Suzuki); 2. Flückiger (Kawasaki); 3. Balestra (Suzuki); 4. Künzi (MV-Agusta); 5. J. Schmid (Suzuki); 6. Sennhauser (Kawasaki); 7. Gisler (Suzuki); 8. Schubiger (Suzuki); 9. Duvoisin (Honda); 10. Demily (Suzuki).
Race II: 1. Wildisen (Suzuki); 2. Devoyon (Suzuki); 3. Balestra (Suzuki); 4. Künzi (MV-Agusta); 5. Flückiger (Kawasaki); 6. Gisler (Suzuki); 7. J. Schmid (Suzuki); 8. Demily (Suzuki); 9. Sennhauser (Kawasaki); 10. Schubiger (Suzuki).

29th April - Lausitz - Germany
1. Flückiger (Kawasaki); 2. Künzi (MV-Agusta); 3. Sennhauser (Kawasaki); 4. Balestra (Suzuki); 5. Schmid (Suzuki); 6. Lupberger (Suzuki); 7. Gisler (Suzuki); 8. Steinemann (Yamaha); 9. Beglinger (Suzuki); 10. Demily (F, Suzuki).

11th - 13th May - Schleiz - Germany
Race I: 1. Flückiger (Kawasaki); 2. Wildisen (Suzuki); 3. Künzi (MV-Agusta); 4. Schmid (Suzuki); 5. Sennhauser (Kawasaki); 6. Pollheide (D, Suzuki); 7. Demilly (F, Suzuki); 8. Müller (MV-Agusta); 9. Beglinger (Suzuki); 10. Marchat (F, Suzuki).
Race II: 1. Stamm (Suzuki); 2. Wildisen (Suzuki); 3. Künzi (MV-Agusta); 4. Sennhauser (Kawasaki); 5. Schmid (Suzuki); 6. Flückiger (Kawasaki); 7. Pollheide (D, Suzuki); 8. Müller (MV-Agusta); 9. Gisler (Suzuki); 10. Beglinger (Suzuki).

15th - 17th June - Most - Czech Republic
Race I: 1. Wildisen (Suzuki); 2. Flückiger (Kawasaki); 3. Sennhauser (Kawasaki); 4. Künzi (MV-Agusta); 5. Beglinger (Suzuki); 6. Schmid (Suzuki); 7. Steinemann (Yamaha); 8. Urbanic (CZ, Suzuki); 9. Demily (F, Suzuki); 10. Gisler (Suzuki).
Race II: 1. Wildisen (Suzuki); 2. Flückiger (Kawasaki); 3. Sennhauser (Kawasaki); 4. Künzi (MV-Agusta); 5. Marchat (F, Suzuki); 6. Steinemann (Yamaha); 7. Beglinger (Suzuki); 8. Demily (F, Suzuki); 9. Lupberger (Suzuki); 10. Gisler (Suzuki).

13th - 15th July - Dijon - France
Race I: 1. Muff (Suzuki); 2. J. Millet (F, Yamaha); 3. Flückiger (Kawasaki); 4. Saiger (A, Suzuki); 5. Sutter (Yamaha); 6. Künzi (MV-Agusta); 7. Wildisen (Suzuki); 8. Sennhauser (Kawasaki); 9. Schmid (Suzuki); 10. Balestra (Suzuki).
Race II: 1. J. Millet (F, Yamaha); 2. Muff (Suzuki); 3. Sutter (Yamaha); 4. Flückiger (Kawasaki); 5. Saiger (A, Suzuki); 6. Künzi (MV-Agusta); 7. Balestra (Suzuki); 8. Koch (Yamaha); 9. Sennhauser (Kawasaki); 10. Steinemann (Yamaha).

17th - 19th August - Rijeka - Croatia
Race I: 1. Wildisen (Suzuki); 2. Flückiger (Kawasaki); 3. Sennhauser (Kawasaki); 4. Beglinger (Suzuki); 5. Künzi (MV-Agusta); 6. Schmid (Suzuki); 7. Gisler (Suzuki); 8. Scherrer (Suzuki); 9. Marchat (F, Suzuki); 10. Lupberger (Suzuki).
Race II: 1. Wildisen (Suzuki); 2. Flückiger (Kawasaki); 3. Sennhauser (Kawasaki); 4. Beglinger (Suzuki); 5. Schmid (Suzuki); 6. Künzi (MV-Agusta); 7. Gisler (Suzuki); 8. Scherrer (Suzuki); 9. Marchat (F, Suzuki); 10. Lupberger (Suzuki).

FINAL CLASSIFICATION
1. Thomas Flückiger — Kawasaki — 200 points
2. Marc Wildisen — Suzuki — 199
3. Christian Künzi — MV-Agusta — 145
4. L. Sennhauser (Kawasaki), 136; 5. J. Schmid (Suzuki), 93; 6. M. Beglinger (Suzuki), 79; 7. K. Gisler (Suzuki), 71; 8. J. Balestra (Suzuki), 60; 9. F. Demilly (F, Suzuki), 49; 10. G. Marchat (F, Suzuki), 57. 31 finishers.

SUPERMOTARD

PRESTIGE 450 S2

6th May - Büron
Race I: 1. Götz (KTM); 2. Baumann (Suzuki); 3. Volz (D, KTM); 4. Müller (Yamaha); 5. Meusburger (A, Yamaha); 6. P. Dupasquier (KTM); 7. Züger (KTM); 8. Kammermann (Honda); 9. Näpflin (Kawasaki); 10. P. Schüpbach (Husqvarna).
Race II: 1. Götz (KTM); 2. D. Müller (Yamaha); 3. Baumann (Suzuki); 4. Volz (D, KTM); 5. Meusburger (A, Yamaha); 6. P. Dupasquier (KTM); 7. S. Scheiwiller (Yamaha); 8. Näpflin (Kawasaki); 9. P. Schüpbach (Husqvarna); 10. Höfliger (Kawasaki).

3rd June - Hoch-Ybrig
Race I: 1. P. Dupasquier (KTM); 2. Volz (D, KTM); 3. D. Müller (Yamaha); 4. Züger (KTM); 5. Näpflin (Kawasaki); 6. P. Schüpbach (Husqvarna); 7. Herger (Suzuki); 8. Reinhard (Honda); 9. Waeber (Yamaha); 10. Walker (Yamaha).
Race II: 1. P. Dupasquier (KTM); 2. Volz (D, KTM); 3. D. Müller (Yamaha); 4. Meussburger (A, Yamaha); 5. Züger (KTM); 6. P. Schüpbach (Husqvarna); 7. Herger (Suzuki); 8. Näpflin (Kawasaki); 9. Tschupp (Husqvarna); 10. Waeber (Yamaha).

24th June - St Stephan
Race I: 1. Volz (D, KTM); 2. P. Dupasquier (KTM); 3. Herger (Suzuki); 4. D. Müller (Yamaha); 5. Zurflüh (KTM); 6. Züger (KTM); 7. Meusburger (A, Yamaha); 8. Kalberer (Yamaha); 9. Marti (Kawasaki); 10.

Tellenbach (KTM).
Race II: 1. Gautschi (Aprilia); 2. Herger (Suzuki); 3. Volz (D, KTM); 4. D. Müller (Yamaha); 5. Meusburger (A, Yamaha); 6. Züger (KTM); 7. Tellenbach (KTM); 8. Kalberer (Yamaha); 9. Aggeler (Yamaha); 10. S. Scheiwiller (Yamaha).

5th August - Moutier
Race I: 1. P. Dupasquier (KTM); 2. Götz (KTM); 3. D. Müller (Yamaha); 4. Volz (D, KTM); 5. Züger (KTM); 6. Reinhard (Honda); 7. Meusburger (A, Yamaha); 8. Tellenbach (KTM); 9. Näpflin (Kawasaki); 10. Möri (Yamaha).
Race II: 1. P. Dupasquier (KTM); 2. D. Müller (Yamaha); 3. Volz (D, KTM); 4. Götz (KTM); 5. Züger (KTM); 6. Tellenbach (KTM); 7. Näpflin (Kawasaki); 8. Meusburger (A, Yamaha); 9. Baruth (D, KTM); 10. Herger (Suzuki).

23rd September - Aarberg
Race I: 1. P. Dupasquier (KTM); 2. Götz (KTM); 3. D. Müller (Yamaha); 4. Volz (D, KTM); 5. Züger (KTM); 6. Herger (Suzuki); 7. Tellenbach (KTM); 8. Meusburger (A, Yamaha); 9. P. Schüpbach (Husqvarna); 10. Marti (Kawasaki).
Race II: 1. Götz (KTM); 2. Volz (D, KTM); 3. D. Müller (Yamaha); 4. P. Dupasquier (KTM); 5. P. Schüpbach (Husqvarna); 6. Züger (KTM); 7. Tschupp (Husqvarna); 8. Marti (Kawasaki); 9. Meusburger (A, Yamaha); 10. Kalberer (Yamaha).

7th October - Frauenfeld
Race I: 1. Götz (KTM); 2. P. Dupasquier (KTM); 3. D. Müller (Yamaha); 4. Becher (D, Kawasaki); 5. Kammermann (Honda); 6. Meusburger (A, Yamaha); 7. Herger (Suzuki); 8. Reinhard (Honda); 9. Volz (D, KTM); 10. Kalberer (Yamaha).
Race II: 1. P. Dupasquier (KTM); 2. D. Müller (Yamaha); 3. Volz (D, KTM); 4. Becher (D, Kawasaki); 5. Herger (Suzuki); 6. Kammermann (Honda); 7. Meusburger (A, Yamaha); 8. Tellenbach (KTM); 9. Tschupp (Husqvarna); 10. Reinhard (Honda).

FINAL CLASSIFICATION

1. Philippe Dupasquier	KTM	242 points
2. Daniel Müller	Yamaha	240
3. Markus Volz (D)	KTM	237

4. H. Meusburger (A, Yamaha), 170; 5. M. Götz (KTM), 162; 6. S. Züger (KTM), 161; 7. R. Herger (Suzuki), 134; 8. P. Tellenbach (KTM), 104; 9. H. Näpflin (Honda), 97; 10. K. Reinhard (Honda), 88. 40 finishers.

CHALLENGER

6th May - Büron
Race I: 1. Erne (Suzuki); 2. Willimann (KTM); 3. Haag (Yamaha); 4. Burch (Yamaha); 5. Schnegg (Yamaha); 6. Spichtig (Kawasaki); 7. Nyffeler (Yamaha); 8. Studer (KTM); 9. Tanner (Suzuki); 10. Murer (Husaberg).
Race II: Schnegg (Yamaha); 2. Willimann (KTM); 3. Tanner (Suzuki); 4. Studer (KTM); 5. Moor (Suzuki); 6. Nyffeler (Yamaha); 7. Burch (Yamaha); 8. Haag (Yamaha); 9. Murer (KTM); 10. Minoggio (Honda).

3rd June - Hoch-Ybrig
Race I: 1. Oechslin (KTM); 2. Erne (Suzuki); 3. Schnegg (Yamaha); 4. Hüsler (Honda); 5. Nyffeler (Yamaha); 6. Moor (Suzuki); 7. Lechthalter (Husaberg); 8. Burch (Yamaha); 9. Willimann (KTM); 10. L. Minoggio (Honda).
Race II: 1. Schnegg (Yamaha); 2. Erne (Suzuki); 3. Oechslin (KTM); 4. Hüsler (Honda); 5. Lechthalter (Husaberg); 6. Nyffeler (Yamaha); 7. Tanner (Suzuki); 8. Moor (Suzuki); 9. Mettler (Yamaha); 10. L. Minoggio (Honda).

24th June - St Stephan
Race I: 1. L. Minoggio (Honda); 2. Lechthalter (Husaberg); 3. Erne (Suzuki); 4. Bader (Kawasaki); 5. Murer (Husaberg); 6. Sieber (Yamaha); 7. J. Minoggio (Yamaha); 8. Schnegg (Yamaha); 9. Lanz (KTM); 10. Haag (Yamaha).
Race II: 1. L. Minoggio (Honda); 2. Erne (Suzuki); 3. Schnegg (Yamaha); 4. Bader (Kawasaki); 5. Lechthalter (Husaberg); 6. Haag (Yamaha); 7. Murer (Husaberg); 8. J. Minoggio (Yamaha); 9. Lanz (KTM); 10. Willimann (KTM).

5th August - Moutier
Race I: 1. Erne (Suzuki); 2. Eberle (A,KTM); 3. Schnegg (Yamaha); 4. Lechthalter (A, Husaberg); 5. Willimann (KTM); 6. J. Minoggio (Yamaha); 7. Moor (Suzuki); 8. L. Minoggio (Honda); 9. Lanz (KTM); 10. Burch (Yamaha).
Race II: 1. Erne (Suzuki); 2. Schnegg (Yamaha); 3. Eberle (A, KTM); 4. Willimann (KTM); 5. Tanner (Suzuki); 6. L. Minoggio (Honda); 7. Moor (Suzuki); 8. Burch (Yamaha); 9. Nyffeler (Yamaha); 10. Bader (Kawasaki).

23rd September - Aarberg
Race I: 1. Schnegg (Yamaha); 2. Moor (Suzuki); 3. Peissard (Yamaha); 4. Spichtig (Kawasaki); 5. Erne (Suzuki); 6. Tanner (Suzuki); 7. J. Minoggio (Yamaha); 8. Burch (Yamaha); 9. L. Minoggio (Honda); 10. Bader (Kawasaki).
Race II: 1. Tanner (Suzuki); 2. Peissard (Yamaha); 3. Burch (Yamaha); 4. Willimann (KTM); 5. Lanz (KTM); 6. Bader (Kawasaki); 7. L. Minoggio (Honda); 8. J. Minoggio (Yamaha); 9. Murer (Husaberg); 10. Moor (Suzuki).

7th October - Frauenfeld
Race I: 1. Wehrli (KTM); 2. Erne (Suzuki); 3. Eberle (Yamaha); 4. Lanz (KTM); 5. Murer (Husaberg); 6. Spichtig (Kawasaki); 7. Sauvain (KTM); 8. J. Minoggio (Yamaha); 9. Bader (Kawasaki); 10. Burch (Yamaha).
Race II: 1. Wehrli (KTM); 2. Lanz (KTM); 3. Eberle (Yamaha); 4. Schnegg (Yamaha); 5. L. Minoggio (Honda); 6. Murer (Husaberg); 7. Erne (Suzuki); 8. Bader (Kawasaki); 9. Spichtig (Kawasaki); 10. Nyffeler (Yamaha).

FINAL CLASSIFICATION

1. Beat ErneSuzuki		220 points
2. Nicolas Schnegg	Yamaha	204
3. Laurent Minoggio	Honda	156

4. R. Willimann (KTM), 152; 5. U. Burch (Yamaha), 141; 6. D. Tanner (Suzuki), 126; 7. M. Moor (Suzuki), 124; 8. R. Lanz (KTM), 115; 9. M. Bader (Kawasaki), 114; 10. R. Nyffeler (Yamaha), 113. 34 finishers.

PROMO

6th May - Büron
Race I: 1. Gautschi (KTM); 2. A. Heierli (Husaberg); 3. Senn (Kawasaki); 4. Fuhrer (KTM); 5. Abbühl (KTM); 6. Moret (Yamaha); 7. Schilliger (KTM); 8. Föhn (Yamaha); 9. Delacombaz (Husqvarna); 10. Troxler (KTM).
Race II: 1. Delacombaz (Husqvarna); 2. Fuhrer (KTM); 3. Moret (Yamaha); 4. Schilliger (Yamaha); 5. Senn (Kawasaki); 6. Troxler (KTM); 7. A. Heierli (Husaberg); 8. Baumann (Honda); 9. Lechthaler (Yamaha); 10. Ziegler (KTM).

June - Hoch-Ybrig
Race I: 1. Moret (Yamaha); 2. Baumann (Honda); 3. Senn (Kawasaki); 4. Abbühl (KTM); 5. Troxler (KTM); 6. Delacombaz (Husqvarna); 7. Gautschi (KTM); 8. Moulin (Husqvarna); 9. Sieber (Yamaha); 10. Abt (TM).
Race II: 1. Moret (Yamaha); 2. Abbühl (KTM); 3. Senn (Kawasaki); 4. Sieber (Yamaha); 5. Delacombaz (Husqvarna); 6. Abt (TM); 7. Baumann (Honda); 8.Troxler (KTM); 9. Föhn (Yamaha); 10. Gautschi (KTM).

4th June - St Stephan
Race I: 1. Fuhrer (KTM); 2. Schärer (KTM); 3. Baumann (Honda); 4. Frei (KTM); 5. Troxler (KTM); 6. Delacombaz (Husqvarna); 7. Moret (Yamaha); 8. Altherr (KTM); 9. Weiss (KTM); 10. Senn (Kawasaki).
Race II: 1. Fuhrer (KTM); 2. Schärer (KTM); 3. Abbühl (KTM); 4. Baumann (Honda); 5. Troxler (KTM); 6. Frei (KTM); 7. Moret (Yamaha); 8. Weiss (KTM); 9. Gautschi (KTM); 10. Altherr (KTM).

5th August - Moutier
Race I: 1. Widmer (TM); 2. Schärer (KTM); 3. Abbühl (KTM); 4. Moret (Yamaha); 5. Baumann (Honda); 6. Wyer (Husqvarna); 7. Ziegler (KTM); 8. Abt (TM); 9. Troxler (KTM); 10. Föhn (Yamaha).
Race II: 1. Schärer (KTM); 2. Senn (Kawasaki); 3. Baumann (Honda); 4. Gyger (Honda); 5. Troxler (KTM); 6. Föhn (Yamaha); 7. Abbühl (KTM); 8. Gisler (Yamaha); 9. Wyer (Husqvarna); 10. Gautschi (KTM).

23rd September - Aarberg
Race I: 1. Schärer (KTM); 2. Fuhrer (KTM); 3. Senn (Kawasaki); 4. Abbühl (KTM); 5. Moret (Yamaha); 6. Troxler (KTM); 7. Gautschi (KTM); 8. A. Heierli (Husaberg); 9. Wyer (Husqvarna); 10. B. Müller (Yamaha).
Race II: 1. Abbühl (KTM); 2. Senn (Kawasaki); 3. Fuhrer (KTM); 4. Troxler (KTM); 5. Baumann (Honda); 6. Gautschi (KTM); 7. Schärer (KTM); 8. Moret (Yamaha); 9. Ziegler (KTM); 10. Koch (Husaberg).

7th October - Frauenfeld
Race I: 1. Fässler (KTM); 2. Herzog (KTM); 3. Baumann (Honda); 4. Senn (Kawasaki); 5. Delacombaz (Husqvarna); 6. Föhn (Yamaha); 7. Schärer (KTM); 8. Schmied (Yamaha); 9. Troxler (KTM); 10. Buess (Husqvarna).
Race II: 1. Fässler (KTM); 2. Herzog (KTM); 3. Abbühl (KTM); 4. Senn (Kawasaki); 5. Baumann (Honda); 6. Schmied (Yamaha); 7. Geissbühler (Gas-Gas); 8. Egger (Aprilia); 9. B. Müller (Yamaha); 10. Troxler (KTM).

FINAL CLASSIFICATION

1. Marcel Senn	Kawasaki	202 points
2. Christian Baumann	Honda	193
3. Martin Abbühl	KTM	186

4. J. Moret (Yamaha), 173; 5. R. Troxler (KTM), 171; 6. R. Schärer (KTM), 157; 7. A. Gautschi (KTM), 130; 8. O. Delacombaz (Husqvarna), 120; 9. R. Föhn (Yamaha), 107; 10. A. Heierli (Husaberg), 107. 35 finishers.

ROOKIE

6th May - Büron
Race I: 1. C. Scheiwiller (Yamaha); 2. Britschgi (Yamaha); 3. S. Birrer (Suzuki); 4. Joos (Yamaha); 5. Birchler (KTM); 6. Bürgler (Yamaha); 7. Reynaud (Husqvarna); 8. Limacher (Yamaha); 9. Waldburger (Yamaha); 10. Calabresi (Yamaha).
Race II: 1. C. Scheiwiller (Yamaha); 2. Birchler (KTM); 3. Britschgi (Yamaha); 4. S. Birrer (Suzuki); 5. Joos (Yamaha); 6. Waldburger (Yamaha); 7. M. Weibel (Yamaha); 8. Reynaud (Husqvarna); 9. Aeschbacher (KTM); 10. Calabresi (Yamaha).

3rd June - Hoch-Ybrig
Race I: 1. C. Scheiwiller (Yamaha); 2. Britschgi (Yamaha); 3. Joos (Yamaha); 4. Limacher (Yamaha); 5. Birchler (KTM); 6. Waldburger (Yamaha); 7. S. Birrer (Suzuki); 8. M. Weibel (Yamaha); 9. Costa (Suzuki); 10. Aeschbacher (KTM).
Race II: 1. C. Scheiwiller (Yamaha); 2. M. Weibel (Yamaha); 3. Limacher (Yamaha); 4. S. Birrer (Suzuki); 5. Würsch (Suzuki); 6. Birchler (KTM); 7. Calabresi (Yamaha); 8. Joos (Yamaha); 9. Waldburger (Yamaha); 10. Aeschbacher (KTM).

24th June - St Stephan
Race I: 1. C. Scheiwiller (Yamaha); 2. S. Birrer (Suzuki); 3. M. Weibel (Yamaha); 4. Rüdisüli (KTM); 5. Limacher (Yamaha); 6. Calabresi (Yamaha); 7. Waldburger (Yamaha); 8. Reynaud (Husqvarna); 9. Birchler (KTM); 10. Würsch (Suzuki).
Race II: 1. C. Scheiwiller (Yamaha); 2. S. Birrer (Suzuki); 3. Rüdisüli (KTM); 4. M. Weibel (Yamaha); 5. Birchler (KTM); 6. Waldburger (Yamaha); 7. Calabresi (Yamaha); 8. Joos (Yamaha); 9. Reynaud (Husqvarna); 10. Limacher (Yamaha).

5th August - Moutier
Race I: 1. C. Scheiwiller (Yamaha); 2. M. Weibel (Yamaha); 3. Joos (Yamaha); 4. Limacher (Yamaha); 5. S. Birrer (Suzuki); 6. Birchler (KTM); 7. Britschgi (Yamaha); 8. Rüdisüli (KTM); 9. Waldburger (Yamaha); 10. Reynaud (Husqvarna).
Race II: 1. C. Scheiwiller (Yamaha); 2. M. Weibel (Yamaha); 3. S. Birrer (Suzuki); 4. Birchler (KTM); 5. Joos (Yamaha); 6. Waldburger (Yamaha); 7. Britschgi (Yamaha); 8. Calabresi (Yamaha); 9. Rüdisüli (KTM); 10. Limacher (Yamaha).

23rd September - Aarberg
Race I: 1. C. Scheiwiller (Yamaha); 2. Joos (Yamaha); 3. Birchler (KTM); 4. Bürgler (Yamaha); 5. Britschgi (Yamaha); 6. Reynaud (Husqvarna); 7. M. Weibel (Yamaha); 8. Calabresi (Yamaha); 9. Känel (Honda); 10. S. Birrer (Suzuki).
Race II: 1. C. Scheiwiller (Yamaha); 2. M. Weibel (Yamaha); 3. Joos (Yamaha); 4. Reynaud (Husqvarna); 5. S. Birrer (Suzuki); 6. Birchler (KTM); 7. Bürgler (Yamaha); 8. Britschgi (Yamaha); 9. Känel (Honda); 10. Calabresi (Yamaha).

7th October - Frauenfeld
Race I: 1. S. Birrer (Suzuki); 2. Joos (Yamaha); 3. Reynaud (Husqvarna); 4. Britschgi (Yamaha); 5. Limacher (Yamaha); 6. Rüdisüli (KTM); 7. Waldburger (Yamaha); 8. M. Weibel (Yamaha); 9. Birchler (KTM); 10. Walder (KTM).
Race II: 1. C. Scheiwiller (Yamaha); 2. S. Birrer (Suzuki); 3. Rüdisüli (KTM); 4. Reynaud (Husqvarna); 5. Joos (Yamaha); 6. Limacher (Yamaha); 7. Britschgi (Yamaha); 8. Calabresi (Yamaha); 9. Birchler (KTM); 10. M. Weibel (Yamaha).

FINAL CLASSIFICATION

1. Cyrill Scheiwiller	Yamaha	275 points
2. Simon Birrer	Suzuki	224
3. Reto Joos	Yamaha	196

4. M. Weibel (Yamaha), 195; 5. A. Birchler (KTM), 189; 6. A. Britschgi (Yamaha), 170; 7. P. Limacher (Yamaha), 153; 8. M. Waldburger (Yamaha), 145; 9. L. Reynaud (Husqvarna), 143; 10. O. Calabresi (Yamaha), 142. 27 finishers.

YOUNGSTER 125/250

6th May - Büron
Race I: 1. Tellenbach (KTM); 2. Felder (Yamaha); 3. Fischer (Yamaha); 4. Lindegger (Yamaha); 5. Peter (Kawasaki); 6. Inderbitzin (Kawasaki); 7. Stocker (Yamaha); 8. Martignoni (Husqvarna); 9. Sidler (Yamaha); 10. Brägger (Yamaha).
Race II: 1. Tellenbach (KTM); 2. Inderbitzin (Kawasaki); 3. Ehrenzeller (KTM); 4. Lindegger (Yamaha); 5. Martignoni (Husqvarna); 6. Matti (Yamaha); 7. Stocker (Yamaha); 8. Portmann (Suzuki); 9. Brägger (Yamaha); 10. Sidler (Yamaha).

3rd June - Hoch-Ybrig
Race I: 1. Fischer (Yamaha); 2. Tellenbach (KTM); 3. Inderbitzin (Kawasaki); 4. Loretter (KTM); 5. Ehrenzeller (KTM); 6. Lindegger (Yamaha); 7. Felder (Yamaha); 8. Pitteloud (Husqvarna); 9. Peter (Kawasaki); 10. Martignoni (Husqvarna).
Race II: 1. Tellenbach (KTM); 2. Fischer (Yamaha); 3. Inderbitzin (Kawasaki); 4. Lindegger (Yamaha); 5. Pitteloud (Husqvarna); 6. Ehrenzeller (KTM); 7. Brägger (Yamaha); 8. Stocker (Yamaha); 9. Felder (Yamaha); 10. Martignoni (Husqvarna).

24th June - St Stephan

Race I: 1. Tellenbach (KTM); 2. Fischer (Yamaha); 3. Inderbitzin (Kawasaki); 4. Felder (Yamaha); 5. Martignoni (Husqvarna); 6. Lindegger (Yamaha); 7. Pitteloud (Husqvarna); 8. Amrein (Kawasaki); 9. Stocker (Yamaha); 10. Brägger (Yamaha).
Race II: 1. Fischer (Yamaha); 2. Tellenbach (KTM); 3. Inderbitzin (Kawasaki); 4. Felder (Yamaha); 5. Loretter (KTM); 6. Brägger (Yamaha); 7. Lindegger (Yamaha); 8. Pitteloud (Husqvarna); 9. Ehrenzeller (KTM); 10. Portmann (Suzuki).

5th August - Moutier

Race I: 1. Tellenbach (KTM); 2. Inderbitzin (Kawasaki); 3. Felder (Yamaha); 4. Loretter (KTM); 5. Ehrenzeller (KTM); 6. Martignoni (Husqvarna); 7. Pitteloud (Husqvarna); 8. Lindegger (Yamaha); 9. Stocker (Yamaha); 10. Peter (Kawasaki).
Race II: 1. Tellenbach (KTM); 2. Inderbitzin (Kawasaki); 3. Loretter (KTM); 4. Ehrenzeller (KTM); 5. Martignoni (Husqvarna); 6. Felder (Yamaha); 7. Pitteloud (Husqvarna); 8. Peter (Kawasaki); 9. Lindegger (Yamaha); 10. Portmann (Suzuki).

23rd September - Aarberg

Race I: 1. Tellenbach (KTM); 2. Inderbitzin (Kawasaki); 3. Ehrenzeller (KTM); 4. Brägger (Yamaha); 5. Fischer (Yamaha); 6. Sidler (Yamaha); 7. Lindegger (Yamaha); 8. Gloggner (Yamaha); 9. Martignoni (Husqvarna); 10. Gosso (Yamaha).
Race II: 1. Tellenbach (KTM); 2. Fischer (Yamaha); 3. Felder (Yamaha); 4. Brägger (Yamaha); 5. Ehrenzeller (KTM); 6. Inderbitzin (Kawasaki); 7. Peter (Kawasaki); 8. Portmann (Suzuki); 9. Lindegger (Yamaha); 10. Gloggner (Yamaha).

7th October - Frauenfeld

Race I: 1. Tellenbach (KTM); 2. Fischer (Yamaha); 3. Inderbitzin (Kawasaki); 4. K. Würterle (D, Kawasaki); 5. Felder (Yamaha); 6. Brägger (Yamaha); 7. Stocker (Yamaha); 8. Ehrenzeller (KTM); 9. Loretter (KTM); 10. Lindegger (Yamaha).
Race II: 1. Fischer (Yamaha); 2. Felder (Yamaha); 3. Lindegger (Yamaha); 4. Brägger (Yamaha); 5. Gloggner (Yamaha); 6. Tellenbach (KTM); 7. Inderbitzin (Kawasaki); 8. Sidler (Yamaha); 9. Loretter (KTM); 10. Ehrenzeller (KTM).

FINAL CLASSIFICATION

1. Fabian Tellenbach   KTM   284 points
2. Philipp Inderbitzin Kawasaki 232
3. Lukas Fischer   Yamaha   209
4. E. Felder (Yamaha), 186; 5. Y. Lindegger (Yamaha), 180; 6. R. Ehrenzeller (KTM), 165; 7. S. Brägger (Yamaha), 161; 8. J. Martignoni (Husqvarna), 130; 9. P. Stocker (Yamaha), 121; 10. D. Loretter (KTM), 103. 27 finishers.

YOUNGSTER 85

6th May - Büron

Race I: 1. Raffin (Honda); 2. Schmidt (Suzuki); 3. D. Staub (KTM); 4. Baumgartner (KTM); 5. S. Staub (Honda); 6. R. Müller (Yamaha); 7. Linssen (Suzuki); 8. Hug (Suzuki). 8 finishers.
Race II: 1. Schmidt (Suzuki); 2. Raffin (Honda); 3. Baumgartner (KTM); 4. D. Staub (KTM); 5. R. Müller (Yamaha); 6. S. Staub (Honda); 7. Hug (Suzuki); 8. Linssen (Suzuki). 8 finishers.

3rd June - Hoch-Ybrig

Race I: 1. Schmidt (Suzuki); 2. Baumgartner (KTM); 3. D. Staub (KTM); 4. R. Müller (Yamaha); 5. S. Staub (Honda); 6. Linssen (Suzuki). 6 finishers.
Race II: 1. Schmidt (Suzuki); 2. Baumgartner (KTM); 3. D. Staub (KTM); 4. R. Müller (Yamaha); 5. S. Staub (Honda); 6. Linssen (Suzuki). 6 finishers.

24th June - St Stephan

Race I: 1. Schmidt (Suzuki); 2. Baumgartner (KTM); 3. D. Staub (KTM); 4. S. Staub (Honda); 5. Geider (KTM); 6. R. Müller (Yamaha). 6 finishers.
Race II: 1. Baumgartner (KTM); 2. Schmidt (Suzuki); 3. S. Staub (Honda); 4. R. Müller (Yamaha); 5. Geider (KTM); 6. D. Staub (KTM); 6 finishers.

5th August - Moutier

Race I: 1. Schmidt (Suzuki); 2. Baumgartner (KTM); 3. R. Müller (Yamaha); 4. D. Staub (KTM); 5. S. Staub (Honda); 6. Linssen (Suzuki). 6 finishers.
Race II: 1. Schmidt (Suzuki); 2. Baumgartner (KTM); 3. R. Müller (Yamaha); 4. D. Staub (KTM); 5. S. Staub (Honda); 6. Linssen (Suzuki). 6 finishers.

23rd September - Aarberg

Race I: 1. Schmidt (Suzuki); 2. Baumgartner (KTM); 3. R. Müller (Yamaha); 4. D. Staub (KTM); 5. S. Staub (Honda); 6. Freidinger (KTM); 7. Geider (KTM); 8. Zimmermann (KTM); 9. Linssen (Suzuki). 9 finishers.
Race II: 1. Baumgartner (KTM); 2. Schmidt (Suzuki); 3. Freidinger (KTM); 4. D. Staub (KTM); 5. R. Müller (Yamaha); 6. S. Staub (Honda); 7. Zimmermann (KTM); 8. Geider (KTM); 9. Linssen (Suzuki). 9 finishers.

7th October - Frauenfeld

Race I: 1. Baumgartner (KTM); 2. Schmidt (Suzuki); 3. D. Staub (KTM); 4. J. Würterle (D, Kawasaki); 5. Geider (KTM); 6. Zimmermann (KTM); 7. R. Müller (Yamaha). 7 finishers.
Race II: 1. Schmidt (Suzuki); 2. Baumgartner (KTM); 3. J. Würterle (D, Kawasaki); 4. D. Staub (KTM); 5. R. Müller (Yamaha); 6. Geider (KTM); 7. Zimmermann (KTM); 7 finishers.

FINAL CLASSIFICATION

1. Marc-Reiner Schmidt Suzuki   288 points
2. Marcel Baumgartner   KTM   267
3. Dominic Staub   KTM   223
4. R. Müller (Yamaha), 206; 5. S. Staub (Honda), 164; 6. M. Linssen (Suzuki), 111; 7. D.-W. Geider (KTM), 90; 8. J. Raffin (Honda), 47. 8 finishers.